P9-EEU-238

HOME
FOOD

HOME FOOD

44 GREAT AMERICAN CHEFS COOK 160 RECIPES ON THEIR NIGHT OFF

DEBBIE SHORE AND
CATHERINE TOWNSEND OF
SHARE OUR STRENGTH
WITH LAURIE ROBERGE
PHOTOGRAPHS BY LINK NICOLL
FOREWORD BY CALVIN TRILLIN

CLARKSON POTTER/PUBLISHERS
NEW YORK

Pages 5–11 menu & recipe © 1995 Paul Albrecht; pages 13–21 menu & recipe © 1995 John Ash; pages 23–31 menu & recipe © 1995 Monique Barbeau; pages 33–41 menu & recipe © 1995 Lidia Bastianich; pages 43–51 menu & recipe © 1995 Rick Bayless; pages 53–59 menu & recipe © 1995 Patrick Clark; pages 61–67 menu & recipe © 1995 Noel Cunningham; pages 69–75 menu & recipe © 1995 Roberto Donna; pages 77–83 menu & recipe © 1995 Tom Douglas; pages 85–91 menu & recipe © 1995 Todd English; pages 93–101 menu & recipe © 1995 Kurt Fleischfresser; pages 103–111 menu & recipe © 1995 David and Anne Gingrass; pages 113–119 menu & recipe © 1995 Joyce Goldstein; pages 121–127 menu & recipe © 1995 Vincent Guerithault; pages 129–135 menu & recipe © 1995 Hector Guerra; pages 137–143 menu & recipe © 1995 Madeleine Kamman; pages 145–151 menu & recipe © 1995 Emeril Lagasse; pages 153–159 menu & recipe © 1995 Zarela Martínez; pages 161–169 menu & recipe © 1995 Jack McDavid; pages 171–179 menu & recipe © 1995 Mark Miller; pages 181–187 menu & recipe © 1995 Mary Sue Milliken; pages 189–199 menu & recipe © 1995 Partrick O'Connell; pages 201–211 menu & recipe © 1995 Bradley Ogden; pages 213–223 menu & recipe © 1995 Louis Osteen; pages 225–233 menu & recipe © 1995 Jean-Louis Palladin; pages 235–241 menu & recipe © 1995 Debra Ponzek; pages 243–251 menu & recipe © 1995 Alfred Portale; pages 253–261 menu & recipe © 1995 Stephan Pyles; pages 263–269 menu & recipe © 1995 Michel Richard; pages 271–277 menu & recipe © 1995 Doug Rodriguez; pages 279–285 menu & recipe © 1995 Michael Romano; pages 287–295 menu & recipe © 1995 Jimmy Schmidt; pages 297–305 menu & recipe © 1995 Nancy Silverton and Mark Peel; pages 307–313 menu & recipe © 1995 Susan Spicer; pages 315–321 menu & recipe © 1995 Allen Susser; pages 323–329 menu & recipe © 1995 Tommy Tang; pages 331–339 menu & recipe © 1995 Elizabeth Terry; pages 341–347 menu & recipe © 1995 Barbara Tropp; pages 349–355 menu & recipe © 1995 Tom Valenti; pages 357–363 menu & recipe © 1995 Alice Waters; pages 365–369 menu & recipe © 1995 Sylvia Woods; and pages 371–376 menu & recipe © 1995 Roy Yamaguchi

Photographs copyright © 1995 by Link Nicoll

Published by Clarkson N. Potter, Inc., 201 East 50th Street, New York, New York 10022. Member of the Crown Publishing Group.

Random House, Inc., New York, Toronto, London, Sydney, Auckland

Clarkson N. Potter, Potter, and colophon are trademarks of Clarkson N. Potter, Inc.

Manufactured in the United States of America

Design by MARGARET HINDERS

Library of Congress Cataloging-in-Publication Data
Shore, Debbie.
Home food: 44 great American chefs cook 160 recipes on their night off/Debbie Shore and Catherine Townsend of Share Our Strength.—1st ed.
p.   cm.
Includes bibliographical references and index.
1. Cookery. 2. Menus. 3. Cooks—United States. I. Townsend, Catherine. II. Share Our Strength. III. Title.
TX714.S548 1995   94-281737
641.5—dc20   CIP

ISBN 0-517-59778-0

10 9 8 7 6 5 4

First Edition

This book is dedicated to Bill Shore, the founder and executive director of Share Our Strength, whose good ideas, vast energy, enthusiasm, and commitment provided the foundation for and the lasting success of SOS. He has been an inspiration as a friend and as a brother.

Acknowledgments

First, we give tribute to the thousands of chefs and volunteers from around the country and Canada who have dedicated their time and talents to Share Our Strength. Because of them, SOS has become one of the nation's largest organizations dedicated to fighting hunger.

We are especially grateful to the forty-four chefs who created original menus of their favorite recipes for this book and allowed us into their homes and their lives. Thanks to their assistants and spouses for helping to coordinate every detail. To Sheila Reines and Nancy Moule Rowe, who helped test these wonderful recipes. To our photographer, Link Nicoll, for capturing the chefs at home in the manner we were hoping for. To Michael Rosen, for adding style to our words and to Calvin Trillin for expressing the perfect sentiment.

Special thanks to our agent, Philippa Brophy, for her creative vision, commitment to SOS, and friendship, and to the crew at Clarkson Potter responsible for the production of this book, especially Maggie Hinders, Howard Klein, and Kim Hertlein. We express our greatest thanks to Katie Workman, our editor, whose skill, guidance, endless patience, and love for this project made it all possible and fun at the same time.

We thank the SOS team for their for their overall support, encouragement, and assistance whenever it was needed, especially Lisa Richardson and Jason Lonstein. And, finally, to Laurie Roberge, our special assistant on this project, for collecting and organizing each chapter, adding her own personal touches, and bringing her passion for food to every page. Her dedication to this project, attention to detail, and hard work were unmatched.

DEBBIE SHORE
CATHERINE TOWNSEND

To my brother, Billy, for his unwavering love, faith, and support. His energy and passion for life never ceases to amaze me. To Catherine Townsend, my partner at SOS and coauthor, for her many wonderful attributes, especially her immeasurable patience, which she delivers with a smile. And finally, to my tabby cat, Macgiver, who kept me company during the countless hours I spent at home, though I do blame him for missed deadlines as he delighted in jumping on top of the manuscript and across the keyboard of my computer!

DEBBIE SHORE

I wish to thank my parents, my brother, Christopher, and sisters, Jennifer and Jacqueline, for their advice and encouragement, and for giving me the strength to pursue the things that are important to me. To Bradley Pine, my husband and the love of my life, for his patience, constant appreciation for my work, friendship, love, and great sense of humor. To my son, Jack, who was a beautiful gift of life during the making of this book. And to my partner and friend, Debbie Shore, for all the hard work, the thrills, the laughs, and the rewards.

CATHERINE TOWNSEND

Contents

Foreword

There was, of course, a time—not that many years ago—when distinguished chefs were assumed to be foreign gentlemen with names like Jean-Pierre, just as conductors of major symphonies were assumed to be foreign gentlemen who took it for granted that they would be addressed as maestro.

The chefs were always pictured in toques even higher than their soufflés. You could imagine them ending a dispute on the true properties of a classically prepared veal Orloff by invoking Escoffier in orotund tones, the way a Baptist preacher might clear up some routine moral dilemma by quoting a single sentence from Corinthians. I sometimes wonder whether anybody guessed in those days that when America actually had its own distinguished chefs they would be the sort of people who wore baseball caps.

Lucky for us that they were. The chefs who began to emerge in America after the shaking up of American society in the late sixties and seventies turned out to be, in comparison with Jean-Pierre, less formal, less magisterial, less respectful of received wisdom—in other words, more American.

As they developed a distinctly American cuisine—inventing here, borrowing there—they seemed to be having a good time. But no occupational group I know of has been more serious about its responsibilities to Americans who need help. When Share Our Strength began to mobilize the food industry on behalf of hunger relief, in 1984, the chefs were in the forefront. As SOS has emerged as one of the leading national organizations fighting hunger, they remain in the forefront.

So it's no surprise to see that so many chefs have contributed to this book. It's never a surprise to see their names connected to benefits raising money to fight AIDS or homelessness or hunger—including SOS's Taste of the Nation evenings, which are now held annually in dozens of American cities.

The chefs don't simply put in an appearance at such events. They tend to arrive hauling boxes of some ingredient that, they're convinced, is found in its most succulent form only in a certain country at a certain time of year. They spend hours preparing the meal. At the end of the evening, they're brought out to be introduced. Usually, their chef's whites show the effect of proximity to the saucepan. Usually, some of them acknowledge the cheers by waving their baseball caps.

—CALVIN TRILLIN

Introduction

from Debbie Shore and Catherine Townsend

What do the chefs who preside over the kitchens of America's greatest restaurants prepare on that rare night when they find themselves cooking at home? We asked more than forty of them and the menus they provided proved to be as mouthwatering as the fare in their renowned restaurants—only easier to prepare and more affordable. And once we got them talking, we discovered more than original recipes. We heard stories about their childhood and their culinary influences, joined in their treasured family rituals, and shared their passionate accounts of how meaningful their time off with family and friends is.

For the past ten years, we have served as associate directors of Share Our Strength, in close contact with the thousands of generous chefs across the United States and Canada who are at the center of our organization's efforts to raise funds for hunger relief. Connecting those who prepare food for a living with those in need of food offered itself as a natural connection, and the results have been phenomenal.

Through this decade of collaboration, SOS has been able to distribute more than $20 million, making a significant impact on the lives of millions in need. In the United States, these funds provide emergency food assistance to children and their families, but beyond that, the money raised supports the clinical efforts aimed at treating the most severe victims of malnutrition and the long-term educational and advocacy efforts designed to prevent hunger. SOS funds also support programs that increase food production and self-sufficiency in developing countries. The funds raised from this book will help provide necessary revenue for such programs.

We have gained an appreciation for each chef's tireless efforts, as well as for the wonderful food that has earned each one his or her much deserved fanfare. What's more, many have become our friends and even teachers, helping us to understand the significance of food and nutrition. These chefs give their time and talent, offer their support, suggestions, advice, recipes, and contacts, and participate in several programs, including our annual food and wine tasting benefit Taste of the Nation. They also donate their excess food to food-rescue programs and some contribute their time off to teaching the basics of nutrition, food budgeting, and cooking to young mothers on assistance.

The idea of compiling a cookbook with a selection of our most talented and dedicated chefs was one that often surfaced in the hallways at SOS. Finally, we decided the one cookbook that we were uniquely positioned to produce was one that shared a side of the chefs that is rarely visible in their restaurants, even to their most frequent patrons—the side that reveals the person beneath the toque. Who are their influences and mentors? What are their cooking habits and frustrations? Which were their favorite childhood foods? But, perhaps most important, we wanted to give readers the chance to visit their homes and to meet the families and friends with whom the chefs so lovingly share some of their most important meals.

We asked each chef to create a meal that they would prepare at home on a night off. The resulting menus consisted of a dazzling variety of recipes that range from the simple to the moderately sophisticated, incorporating foods from all over the world. Most dishes can be prepared, at least partially, in advance and some will require a little adventurous shopping. Jean-Louis Palladin will send you searching for vanilla beans and saffron threads in specialty food stores, while Paul Albrecht's instant mashed potato flakes will not take you further than your kitchen pantry or neighborhood grocery store. Susan Spicer will send you into your own garden or local green market for mint, basil, tomatoes, and peppers, while the richness of David and Anne Gingrass's Chocolate-Raspberry Mousse Cake will send you over the moon.

If you want to update your traditional Thanksgiving dinner, try Alfred Portale's Roast Wild Turkey Stuffed with Chanterelles, Sausage, and Mashed Potatoes. When searching for that perfect romantic dinner for two, consider Noel Cunningham's Roast Loin of Pork with Dried Cherries, Mushrooms, and Roasted Potatoes with Carrots and Broccoli topped off with Cappuccino Soufflés, which he prepared to woo his wife, Tammy. If you're craving soul food, try Sylvia Wood's menu of Collard Greens with Bacon, Fried Sweet Potatoes, and Southern-Style Corn Bread with Fresh Corn. And if you want to involve the kids in the cooking fun, turn to Tommy Tang's menu with its Neon Fruit dessert, featuring a squeeze bottle of puréed fruit to paint the plates. *Home Food,* above all, is a bounty of menus from which to choose, whether you are having a birthday lunch, a traditional Southern banquet, a Mexican fiesta, a family beach party, or a cocktail party with an array of hors d'oeuvres.

Although the chefs tested their own recipes, we rounded up the entire staff at SOS (on *our* day off), their families, and a few extra friends for a recipe testing party. We put on our aprons to experiment, sampling bites from each plate, swapping cooking stories, praising our culinary achievements, and sharing, too, what it means to have a day off and enjoy cooking at home.

We hope you will enjoy this collection of recipes and find, as we have, the many rewards of getting to know more about these chefs than simply their "signature" restaurant dish. Their work and the work of the many other SOS chefs has helped to bring food, nutrition, and flavor into the homes of many who otherwise would have gone without. Please savor these culinary gifts from their homes to yours.

PAUL ALBRECHT

Good food, good conversation, a warm home . . . life is grand." This is the simple philosophy of Paul Albrecht. He was practically born into the restaurant industry, as his father and grandfather were successful restaurateurs in Germany. Paul pursued his career throughout Germany and Switzerland, "but the real opportunities for my career in cooking were in the United States," says Paul. In 1968, he came to Washington, D.C., and found work as a sous-chef at the Hotel Sonesta. Two years later he moved on to become the executive chef at the Lodge of the Four Seasons in Missouri, where he prepared continental dishes with French influences. It was back in Washington that he met chef Pano Karatassos and together they embarked on a partnership that would soon heighten fine dining in Atlanta. Pano and Paul dreamed of opening their own place in the South, and when Pano made a visit to his hometown in Georgia, he knew he had found the spot.

And so in 1979, the dynamic duo opened their first restaurant, Pano's & Paul's, where Paul remains as the executive chef. To the delight of Atlantans and

MENU

Campari, Vodka, and Grapefruit Cooler

—

*Baked Georgia White Shrimp with Parsley,
Garlic, and Potato Flakes*

—

*Thyme- and Rosemary-Roasted Veal Rack
with Root Vegetables*

—

Buttery Egg Dumplings

—

*Flourless Chocolate Melt Cakes
with Raspberry Coulis*

visitors, they have opened seven other successful restaurants, including 103 West and Atlanta's Fish Market, and have permanently integrated themselves into the food scene of this bustling city.

The recipes selected here reflect both Paul's German heritage and his American lifestyle—presenting fresh and textured food to be shared in a tranquil setting. "While authentic German food is heavy, mostly controlled by the country's cold climate, new German cuisine, like some of the dishes I recommend here, is lighter." Paul rarely uses his huge formal dining room at his suburban home, preferring to re-create for guests the family-style meals he remembers from his youth. When Paul's entire family gets together, his wife, Barbara, and their four sons hang out as the food is being prepared in their wide-open kitchen, "enjoying the wonderful robust aromas, and of course, picking and tasting."

To stimulate their appetites, he offers his guests a Campari, Vodka, and Grapefruit Cooler, also a perfect beverage for a hot summer day in the South. Everyone sips this drink while nibbling the Baked Georgia White Shrimp appetizer, seasoned with fresh herbs, garlic, and lemon. The Thyme- and Rosemary-Roasted Veal Rack with Root Vegetables is served with Paul's Buttery Egg Dumplings, prepared in authentic German style. Spring vegetables such as baby carrots, asparagus, and mushrooms can be served in place of the root vegetables, to adjust the menu seasonally.

Paul remembers how difficult it was to serve veal when he first came to Atlanta fifteen years ago. "Basically, Atlanta was a steak and potatoes town, and lamb was popular, too. But these days, with everyone conscious of their diet, white meat is more desirable. I like to roast veal to get the most flavor out of it." For dessert, Paul whips up individual moist flourless chocolate cakes served warm with raspberry sauce and white chocolate shavings. Sometimes he serves homemade coconut cookies instead, accompanied by an unusual garnish, but a personal favorite: Gummi Bears. "Whether I am cooking at home or at the restaurant, my approach is never off-the-wall. It is always simple, yet elegant and classic at the same time."

Campari, Vodka, and Grapefruit Cooler

This refreshing beverage, spiked with fresh ginger, makes a nice opener to any occasion with food and friends.

1½ cups Campari

½ cup vodka

2 cups fresh grapefruit juice

2 cups club soda

2 tablespoons finely grated fresh ginger

1 lime, thinly sliced

½ cup sugar syrup, or to taste
   (see box, page 333)

Crushed ice

6 sprigs fresh mint, for garnish

Combine all the Campari, vodka, grapefruit juice, club soda, ginger, and lime in a large jug and stir. Add the sugar syrup. Pour into glasses filled with crushed ice and garnish with mint.

Serves 6

Baked Georgia White Shrimp with Parsley, Garlic, and Potato Flakes

Who would have thought instant mashed potato flakes would be incorporated into such a sophisticated dish! In this chef's delicious innovation, fresh shrimp are coated with potato flakes to add a lightly crisp texture.

Paul prefers white shrimp from the Georgia coast for their sweet taste. They also shrink less and have a nice pink color when cooked. If you cannot get ahold of these regional treats, use the freshest shrimp available; frozen shrimp will not do.

1½ pounds medium white shrimp,
   peeled and deveined

1¼ cups extra-virgin olive oil

¾ cup chopped fresh parsley

5 garlic cloves

1 teaspoon dried oregano

Salt and freshly ground pepper to taste

⅓ cup fresh lemon juice

1 cup instant potato flakes

1 lemon, cut into 6 wedges, for
   garnish

Parsley sprigs, for garnish

Preheat the oven to 375° F. Place the shrimp in a baking dish or casserole and set aside. Combine 1 cup of the olive oil with the parsley, garlic, and oregano in a food processor and process until finely chopped. Add the salt and pepper and lemon juice and process until smooth. Pour this mixture over the shrimp, toss to coat, and marinate for 10 to 15 minutes.

Pour the potato flakes onto a plate. Roll the shrimp in the potato flakes to coat, then place the shrimp on a baking sheet. Drizzle with the remaining ¼ cup olive oil and bake for 6 to 8 minutes, until the flakes are golden. Evenly divide the shrimp on individual serving plates. Garnish with a lemon wedge and parsley, and serve immediately.

SERVES 6

THYME- AND ROSEMARY-ROASTED VEAL RACK WITH ROOT VEGETABLES

Served with Paul's Buttery Egg Dumplings (recipe follows), this recipe is both elegant and "homey." He recommends a 1984 Château La Ville Haut-Brion to accompany this dish.

1 5-pound veal rack, trimmed (6 meaty bones)	**½ cup diced celery root**
	½ cup diced parsnips
Salt and freshly ground pepper to taste	**½ cup peeled pearl onions**
3 sprigs fresh thyme	**1 bay leaf**
2 sprigs fresh rosemary	**¼ cup dry white wine**
½ cup extra-virgin olive oil	**1 cup chicken stock or water**
¼ cup diced carrot	

Preheat the oven to 375°F. Sprinkle the veal with salt and pepper and rub with the fresh thyme and rosemary. Place in a roasting pan, bones facing down, and drizzle with the olive oil. Roast in the oven for 30 minutes, basting occasionally with the pan juices. Sprinkle the carrot, celery root, parsnips, and pearl onions around the roast and cook for 45 minutes longer, basting every 15 minutes. After cooking for 1 hour and 15 minutes total, add the bay leaf, wine, and stock or water to the roasting pan. Stir until all coagulated juices are dissolved. Roast for 10 more minutes in the oven. Remove the veal from the oven and let rest, covered loosely with foil, for 20 minutes before slicing. Remove bay leaf. Place the vegetables on a large serving platter. Slice the veal rack between the bones and place the chops on top of the vegetables. Surround with dumplings and serve family style.

SERVES 6

Veal Facts

Veal is the term used to describe the meat from a very young calf, usually no more than three months old. If the calf has not been weaned, it is called milk-fed veal; this meat is especially firm and pale in color, and is considered the most delicate and flavorful. Veal is most readily available in late winter and spring, and it should be firm and smooth in texture. Look for meat that is creamy white with no pronounced pinkness, and for pure white fat. Be careful not to overcook veal as it will dry out easily, affecting its delicate taste and texture. Cooking time for the veal rack is 15 to 18 minutes per pound. For a 5-pound rack, the total cooking time will be about 1 hour and 25 minutes.

BUTTERY EGG DUMPLINGS

To make this traditional German dish, you'll need a colander with large holes the size of green peas.

2 quarts water

2 cups all-purpose flour

4 large eggs

½ cup milk

Salt and freshly ground pepper to taste

Freshly grated nutmeg to taste

½ cup (1 stick) unsalted butter

In a large pot, bring 2 quarts of salted water to a boil over medium-high heat. Mix the flour, eggs, milk, salt and pepper, and nutmeg in a medium bowl with a wooden spoon until it becomes an elastic dough that shows some bubbles. Pour half the mixture into a strainer with large holes the size of green peas and push it through with a spoon into the boiling water. Let simmer for 2 to 3 minutes, stirring occasionally. In the meantime, melt the butter in a large skillet over medium heat. Lift out the dumplings with a slotted spoon and rinse with hot water. Drain. Repeat with the second half of the dough. Toss all the dumplings into the skillet with the butter and sauté for 1 minute. Season with additional salt, pepper, and nutmeg.

SERVES 6

FLOURLESS CHOCOLATE MELT CAKES WITH RASPBERRY COULIS

Best described as a cross between chocolate mousse and a warm chocolate soufflé, these individual desserts are made in small soufflé cups. Skip the cheaper everyday chocolate and splurge on the good stuff—the better the chocolate, the better the cake. The coulis can be made up to two days in advance.

15 ounces good-quality semisweet chocolate (preferably Lindt)
1 cup (2 sticks) unsalted butter
6 large eggs

18 ounces frozen raspberries, thawed
9 ounces white chocolate, coarsely chopped or shaved, for garnish

Preheat the oven to 350° F. Lightly butter and flour six 8-ounce soufflé cups. Melt the semisweet chocolate and the butter in a double boiler or a metal bowl over simmering water, stirring occasionally until fully melted. Transfer the chocolate mixture to a large bowl and set aside.

Place the eggs in a double boiler or a metal bowl over simmering water and whisk until warm to the touch. Transfer the eggs to a bowl and beat with an electric mixer until tripled in volume and cool.

Using a rubber spatula, fold half the eggs into the chocolate mixture until almost incorporated. Fold in the remaining eggs until just blended with no streaks of egg remaining. Spoon the mixture into the prepared soufflé cups. Place the soufflé cups in a roasting pan with enough hot water to come up 1 inch on the sides of the cups. Bake for 25 minutes. Let cool on a wire rack for approximately 5 minutes.

While the cakes are baking, make the raspberry coulis. Purée the raspberries in a blender or food processor and strain through a fine sieve to remove the seeds. Refrigerate, tightly covered, until ready to use.

Invert each soufflé cup onto a serving plate, pour the raspberry coulis around each cake, and garnish with the white chocolate. Serve warm.

SERVES 6

Types of Chocolate

Chocolate is made from the solid chocolate liquor and the cocoa butter that are extracted from roasted cacao beans. The liquor gives chocolate its rich, ambrosial cocoa flavor and the cocoa butter binds the chocolate components together, giving it its smooth, melt-in-your-mouth texture. The type of chocolate depends primarily on the proportions of chocolate liquor, cocoa butter, and sugar. Other ingredients, such as vanilla and lecithin (a natural fatty substance), may be added to improve flavor and texture, but they are not essential to chocolate. The following are different types of chocolate. Please note that, unless specified, one type cannot be substituted for another.

BITTER CHOCOLATE, also referred to as UNSWEETENED or BAKING CHOCOLATE, contains only chocolate liquor and cocoa butter. This is usually melted and added to sweetened batters for such things as chocolate cakes and brownies. It is too bitter to be eaten on its own.

BITTERSWEET, SEMISWEET, and DARK CHOCOLATES, favored for their pronounced chocolate flavor, contain chocolate liquor, cocoa butter, sugar, and sometimes vanilla. The amount of chocolate liquor varies in these types, bittersweet having the most.

Available in bar, block, or chip form, these chocolates are generally interchangeable, as the only real difference is taste—ranging from slightly bitter to fairly sweet. They are most often used in desserts, such as chocolate mousse, cakes, and tortes, and in sauces.

MILK CHOCOLATE contains dried milk solids and butterfat in addition to chocolate liquor, cocoa butter, and sugar. The mild, mellow chocolate is used mostly to make candies rather than dessert confections, as it does not take well to baking. Because of the milk solids this chocolate is very sensitive to heat, and therefore it should be melted very slowly over low, indirect heat to prevent it from scorching.

WHITE CHOCOLATE is milk chocolate without the chocolate liquor. With that exception, it is not really "chocolate" by American standards and cannot be labeled as such. American brands, therefore, are labeled as white confectionery bar, coating bar, or white baking bar. Check the label for cocoa butter to be sure the product is *real* white chocolate, as there are poor imitations made with inferior cocoa butter substitutes. The *real* thing is ivory, creamy, and not too sweet. Like milk chocolate, white chocolate must be heated gently when melting.

COCOA POWDER is unadulterated chocolate liquor that has been refined and pulverized to a powder. This is not the same as sweetened cocoa. It is generally used in making baked chocolate desserts and sometimes in chocolate sauces.

JOHN ASH

Garden's Harvest

John Ash's approach to food is to let the ingredients themselves be the focus of the dish. "My job is to be the stage director. The ingredients are the stars, and my most important role is to coax the most out of them." And what better ingredients to direct than the more than 1,000 varieties of fruits, vegetables, herbs, and edible flowers that are grown on the seven-acre, biodynamic organic garden at the Fetzer Valley Oaks Food and Wine Center, in Hopland, California, where John has been the culinary director since 1990.

John joined Fetzer when he was taken by Fetzer's philosophy in organic gardening and sustainable agriculture—processes by which crops are planted and harvested so they cause minimal damage to the soil and allow maximum crop output. After taking classes at La Varenne and Cordon Bleu in London in the mid-1970s and then cooking in France for two years, he became completely hooked on food. "I realized that everything I did as a painter in my college studies I could do with food. Pushing colors around on canvas was the same as playing with different ingredients. But what I liked more about food was that you could eat it and your creation went away. With a painting, it was with you forever, even if you dis-

MENU

"Fire and Ice" Melon

◆

Cucumber Yogurt Salad

◆

Beggars Purses of Basil Crepes with Garden Greens and Warm Lemon Sauce

◆

Lemon Polenta Cake with Rosemary Syrup and Fresh Berries

liked it," John says. "As you mature, you never want to imagine that you ever created something awful."

While living and working in France, he became accustomed to the European style of cooking, which involved going to the local market and selecting whatever was fresh that day for the menu. Back in the States, he found chefs just starting to embrace this approach, especially in Northern California. So in 1980 he opened his first restaurant, John Ash & Co., in Santa Rosa, where he stayed for seven successful years before moving the restaurant to the nearby Vintner's Inn.

Since coming to the wonderful garden at Fetzer, John has become much more of a vegetarian at home, although he still occasionally eats meats and fish. Along with adopting this new, almost vegetarian eating style, John now cooks more simply at home. The menu he presents here is a dinner he prepares frequently at home. In addition to Fetzer's organic garden, John maintains his own garden of ornamental plants and Meyer lemons (see box, page 19), and grows eight varieties of herbs, including tarragon, chives, basil, garlic, and thyme. "I especially love to cook with thyme because it has a wonderful aroma that persists long after you pick it," says John.

At home, John loves life's domestic routines, such as family dinners. When his kids were younger, regular mealtimes were very important to them. Now that they are busy teenagers, when they do all eat together it's special. His two children are both full vegetarians. "We've had many discussions about organic farming and how it's important for the planet and the body. I guess I planted a seed that changed their eating habits."

On a given night, John's menu at home might involve something as simple as an assortment of tomatoes drawn from the more than 100 varieties grown in the Fetzer Valley Oaks garden, splashed with different herbs from his home garden. "There are infinite possibilities for combining things to eat. The greatest gift is to have access to these wonderful gardens of such diversity. The message of eating from the bottom of the food pyramid, and its effect on both my own health and the health of the planet, has made a real impact on me."

"Fire and Ice" Melon

This recipe is a perfect example of food that excites more than one area of the palate. It blends the cool sweetness of melon with sour lime and hot chili syrup. Any ripe, firm-fleshed melon will work here. Once the chili syrup is made, this dish can be thrown together just before serving. Make sure that the nasturtium blossoms are pesticide-free.

⅓ cup sugar

¼ cup water

2 teaspoons seeded and minced serrano chili pepper, or more to taste (see box, page 176)

¼ cup fresh lime juice

1 tablespoon minced fresh mint

2 tablespoons minced red, yellow, or green bell pepper (preferably a mixture of all three)

2 large honeydew, cantaloupe, crane, or other firm-fleshed ripe melon

Fresh figs, sliced, for garnish (optional)

Nasturtium blossoms, for garnish (optional)

In a small saucepan, make a chili syrup by combining the sugar and water over medium-high heat and boiling until the sugar is dissolved. Pour into a small bowl and let cool. Stir in the chili, lime juice, mint, and bell peppers.

Cut the melons in half and remove the seeds. Cut into wedges or other interesting shapes and arrange attractively on 8 chilled plates. Drizzle about ½ cup of the chili syrup, or to taste, over all the melon and garnish with sliced figs and nasturtium blossoms, if desired. Reserve the remaining chili syrup for another use.

Serves 8

Wine Suggestions

John says both the melon and the cucumber salad go well with a chilled, fruity, lower-alcohol white wine such as Gewürztraminer or Riesling. The lemon and herbal flavors of the Beggars Purses match well with a steely, nonoaked Chardonnay or a classic grassy-style Sauvignon Blanc. If you're going the distance, a crisp, clean California sparkling wine is also a great choice.

Flavored Syrups

Spice- and herb-infused syrups are a trademark of John Ash. He uses them in a variety of ways to add a complexity to dishes and tantalize the taste buds. They can be stored indefinitely, tightly sealed in the refrigerator.

Experiment with his syrups either by integrating them in other recipes or by substituting other herbs and spices to achieve new taste sensations. Try using his chili syrup to make a tasty base for summer drinks. John likes to combine it with a mixture of fruity white wine, such as Gewürztraminer, and sparkling soda. Also try replacing or supplementing the chili peppers in the chili syrup with green herbs such as cilantro, basil, or tarragon to drizzle over the melon or any other fruit. For a twist on the rosemary syrup, which enhances the polenta cake, substitute tarragon or any woody stemmed herb such as thyme (lemon thyme is especially nice).

CUCUMBER YOGURT SALAD

In this rendition of a traditional Middle Eastern salad, John suggests using English or Armenian cucumbers because they are not so bitter and watery, and their skins are not waxed. The best choice, if you can find them, are lemon cucumbers, which many home gardeners grow.

2 large English, Armenian, or other unwaxed cucumbers (approximately 1¾ pounds), or 3 regular cucumbers

2 teaspoons coarse salt

1¼ cups plain yogurt

1 cup finely chopped red onion

1 teaspoon minced garlic

¾ teaspoon minced serrano chili pepper, or to taste (see box, page 176)

1 tablespoon chopped fresh basil

½ teaspoon toasted, crushed cumin seeds (see box, page 18)

1 tablespoon chopped fresh mint

1½ teaspoons salt, or to taste

¼ teaspoon freshly ground pepper

2 teaspoons sugar

3 tablespoons seasoned rice vinegar

¼ cup toasted pine nuts or toasted, blanched, slivered almonds (see box, page 117)

1 pint whole, small Toy Box tomatoes, or 2 cups seeded and diced cherry or Roma tomatoes

Mint sprigs, for garnish

With a vegetable peeler, remove the skin from the cucumbers in alternating strips, resulting in a striped effect. For waxed cucumbers, peel completely. Cut the cucumbers in half lengthwise and scrape out seeds with a teaspoon. Slice crosswise into ¼-inch-thick slices, sprinkle with the coarse salt, and set aside in a colander for at least 1 hour to drain. (The salt removes the water and the bitterness from the cucumber.)

Meanwhile, mix the yogurt, onion, garlic, chili, basil, cumin, mint, salt, pepper, and sugar in a large bowl. Set aside. Rinse the salt from the cucumbers and pat dry with paper towels. Toss the cucumbers with the rice vinegar in another large bowl, then stir into the onion-yogurt mixture. Cover and refrigerate at least 2 hours before serving to allow flavors to develop and marry. Just before serving, stir in the pine nuts and tomatoes. Garnish with mint sprigs.

S E R V E S 8

BEGGARS PURSES OF BASIL CREPES WITH GARDEN GREENS AND WARM LEMON SAUCE

Your guests will find it hard to cut into these adorable ribbon-tied pouches stuffed with spinach, cheese, and shiitakes. One bite, though, will tell them that this dish does much more than feed the eyes.

This recipe is especially easy to prepare if you have the crepes made in advance. Let the crepes cool completely, then layer them with sheets of waxed paper or plastic wrap to keep them from sticking together. Store them in an airtight container or wrapped in foil in the refrigerator for up to three days, or in the freezer for up to two months. The crepe recipe can be doubled if you want to freeze the extra for future use.

2 tablespoons extra-virgin olive oil

2 cups coarsely chopped red onions

2½ cups washed and diced fresh shiitake or crimini mushrooms (see box, pages 36–37)

1½ pounds fresh spinach, washed and stemmed

¼ teaspoon freshly grated nutmeg

¼ cup minced fresh basil, or 2 tablespoons dried

Salt and freshly ground pepper to taste

⅔ cup grated Monterey jack or Gruyère cheese, or a mixture

Whole chives or thin strips of leek, for tying purses

Basil Crepes (recipe follows)

Warm Lemon Sauce (recipe follows)

4 tablespoons finely diced red or yellow bell peppers, or a mixture, for garnish (optional)

Fresh herb sprigs, for garnish

Toasting Seeds

TO TOAST cumin and other seeds, such as sesame, place them in a small, dry skillet over medium heat and cook until they are lightly toasted and fragrant, shaking the pan occasionally to toast all sides. Watch that they don't burn. Let cool, then, for cumin seeds, either crush in a mortar with a pestle or roll under a rolling pin.

In a skillet, heat 1 tablespoon of oil over medium heat and sauté the onions for 2 minutes; do not let them brown. Add the mushrooms and continue cooking until the onions are soft, 4 to 5 minutes. Transfer with a slotted spoon to a medium bowl and set aside.

Add the remaining oil to the pan, raise the heat to high, and add the spinach, stirring, to wilt quickly, about 1 minute. Remove the spinach to another plate and blot dry with paper towels. Roughly chop the spinach and combine it with the onion and mushroom mixture. Stir in the nutmeg, basil, and salt and pepper. Mix in the cheese.

Bring a medium pot of water to a boil and set aside a bowl of ice water. Drop the chives or leeks into the boiling water for 2 to 4 seconds. Remove with a slotted spoon and transfer at once to the ice water. Drain and pat dry.

Place a dollop of filling in the center of each of the 16 crepes. Gather each crepe together just above the filling and tie very gently with a chive or strip of leek. Place 2 purses on each plate and surround with the Warm Lemon Sauce and a garnish of diced peppers, if desired, and herb sprigs. Purses can be served warm (heat in a preheated 300° F. oven for 7 minutes or in a microwave) or at room temperature.

SERVES 8

BASIL CREPES

1 cup water	6 tablespoons extra-virgin olive or
1 cup whole milk	vegetable oil
1½ cups all-purpose flour	¾ teaspoon salt
4 large eggs	5 tablespoons minced fresh basil

Combine the water, milk, flour, eggs, 3 tablespoons of the oil, and salt in a blender or food processor until smooth, about 15 seconds. Add the basil, pulsing just a few times to mix in. Transfer to a bowl, cover, and chill for at least 1 hour or overnight.

Lightly oil a 10-inch crepe pan or nonstick skillet as needed with the remaining 3 tablespoons of oil and place over medium heat. When hot, pour in ¼ cup of batter and tilt in all directions to just cover the bottom of the pan. Pour out any excess. Cook for approximately 1 minute, or until the center of the crepe is dry and the bottom lightly browned. Turn with a spatula and cook the other side for 30 seconds or so. Cool on a wire rack. Repeat until all the batter has been used.

MAKES APPROXIMATELY SIXTEEN 8-INCH CREPES; SERVES 8

WARM LEMON SAUCE

1½ cups rich vegetable stock
½ cup dry white wine
3 large egg yolks

5 tablespoons fresh lemon juice
Salt and ground white pepper to taste
2 tablespoons minced chives

In a small saucepan, bring the stock and wine to a boil over high heat and reduce by half, about 8 to 10 minutes. In a separate bowl, whisk together the egg yolks and lemon juice. Gradually whisk the reduced stock a little at a time into the egg mixture, being careful not to cook the egg yolks. Return the mixture to the saucepan and place over medium heat and cook, stirring constantly, until the sauce thickens slightly, about 3 minutes. Immediately strain, season to taste with salt and pepper, and stir in the chives. Keep warm over very low heat until ready to serve with the Beggars Purses.

MAKES APPROXIMATELY 1½ CUPS

Meyer Lemons

Meyer lemons are a unique oddity. They are a cross between a lemon and an orange and taste like a mild citrus fruit, with a sweet flavor and an aroma of lemon. They are grown almost exclusively in Northern California by home gardeners, where they grow better in the colder weather than any other fruit. John grows them in his backyard and cooks with them often, squeezing the fruit liberally over many foods. If you're lucky enough to live in Northern California, or know someone who could mail them to you, you should try this wonderful variation on a lemon for the Warm Lemon Sauce, the Lemon Polenta Cake (page 20), or anywhere else you might use a regular lemon!

LEMON POLENTA CAKE WITH ROSEMARY SYRUP AND FRESH BERRIES

John loves this rustic "grandma" cake for its crunchy texture. He uses stone-ground cornmeal because it is coarser than regular cornmeal, which gives the cake its crunchiness. The rosemary-infused syrup adds a nice nonfat twist to this cake, which can be served warm or at room temperature.

1 cup yellow cornmeal, preferably stone-ground

½ cup all-purpose flour

1½ teaspoons baking powder

¼ teaspoon salt

1 cup sugar

2 large eggs

2 large egg whites

2 tablespoons (¼ stick) unsalted butter, softened

¼ cup vegetable oil

½ cup plain yogurt

1½ tablespoons grated lemon zest

2 tablespoons fresh lemon juice

1 pint fresh strawberries or raspberries, washed and picked over

Rosemary Syrup (recipe follows)

Whipped cream (optional)

Rosemary sprigs, for garnish

Preheat the oven to 350° F. Line the bottom of an 8-inch round cake pan with parchment or waxed paper and lightly oil.

Sift the cornmeal, flour, baking powder, and salt together in a bowl and set aside.

With an electric mixer, beat the sugar, eggs, and egg whites in a large bowl until smooth. Beat in the butter, oil, yogurt, lemon zest, and lemon juice until creamy. Fold in the dry ingredients just until combined; do not overmix.

Pour the batter into the prepared pan and smooth the top with a spatula. Bake for 35 to 40 minutes or until a toothpick inserted in the center comes out clean. Cool for 15 minutes on a wire rack. Invert, peel off the paper, and cool completely. (The cake can be made in advance up until this point and stored, wrapped in plastic wrap, in the refrigerator for up to 5 days or frozen for 1 month.)

To serve, cut the cake into 8 wedges and place on plates. Scatter berries around the cake, drizzle a tablespoon or two of Rosemary Syrup over the berries, and place a dollop of whipped cream on the cake, if desired. Garnish with rosemary sprigs.

SERVES 8

ROSEMARY SYRUP

This is also wonderful drizzled over strawberries, which combine extremely well with the balsamic-enriched syrup.

¾ cup sugar

¾ cup dry white wine

⅓ cup water

3 tablespoons roughly chopped fresh
  rosemary

1 large bay leaf

½ teaspoon slightly crushed black
  peppercorns

3 tablespoons fine balsamic vinegar

Place all of the ingredients in a saucepan over high heat. Bring to a boil, reduce the heat to medium-low, and simmer for 10 minutes. Cool and strain. The syrup can be stored in a jar in the refrigerator for up to 1 week.

MAKES APPROXIMATELY 1¼ CUPS

Organic Farming

John explains the philosophy of organic farming by saying, "healthy soils produce healthy plants, which in turn produce healthy food." By eliminating the use of synthetic materials, chemicals, herbicides, pesticides, and growth promoters in farming, organic farming allows us to reduce the amount of chemicals we consume through our food. Also, studies are now finding that organically grown produce is higher in nutritional elements than nonorganic produce. Furthermore, chemical-free farming preserves the soil and other fragile components of the earth's natural systems, making the land richer.

The quality of organic produce is superior to that of conventional produce. You can taste the healthful difference. Sugars tend to be more concentrated and varietal flavors are more intense. This is due to the higher mineral content found in organically farmed soils. "Using organic produce gives the cook an opportunity to be part of an important change in what we are eating in America." So, urge your local markets to stock organically grown produce and give yourself and the planet a healthy boost!

MONIQUE BARBEAU

A Northwest Family Dinner

Monique loves the casual atmosphere of cooking at home. She regularly makes the two-hour drive to her family's home in Vancouver, where she prepares dinner for anyone and everyone who drops by. She approaches cooking at home in a much less formal fashion than at her acclaimed restaurant, Fullers at the Seattle Sheraton Hotel & Towers. "Of course, I miss the fact that I don't have all the spices or the staff that I have at Fullers," she jokes, "but cooking at home is much more fun, and I find deep gratification in cooking for my family, especially my mother and father, who have supported me through my career."

Monique credits her mother and grandmother—both of whom are great cooks—for piquing her interest in becoming a chef. Monique's mother taught her about healthful eating, while her grandmother tempted her with the more luxurious and indulgent tastes of butter and cream. When Monique was a young girl, in the early 1970s, her grandfather was lieutenant governor of British Columbia. Monique often watched and helped the official cooks in the com-

MENU

Spicy Caesars

~

Homemade Herb and Shallot Focaccia

~

Northwest Mushroom Soup

~

*Warm Spinach Salad with
Pancetta Vinaigrette and
Rosemary Pita Bread Croutons*

~

*Sautéed Shrimp and Roasted
Eggplant Lasagna*

~

Lemon Tart with Cornmeal Crust

mercial kitchen at Government House in Victoria. Ten years later, after finishing high school, she decided to move to New York to attend the Culinary Institute of America in Hyde Park. After graduating, she worked as a cook for five years in New York City and then spent two years in Miami to earn her bachelor's degree. Monique then decided to return to the West Coast. She was pulled back by the outdoors, the good produce markets, and the burgeoning food scene in Seattle. She saw this growing town as the perfect city in which to progress in her career, and even more important, she wanted to be close to her family, which includes a twin brother, two sisters, and her parents.

Drawing on the teachings of her mother and grandmother, Monique created a menu that is healthful and simple but recalls the smooth richness of her grandmother's creamy sauces. "I rarely use butter and cream in my cooking techniques today, but there are times when I can't resist using them in some fashion," says Monique. "Still, I have become more sensitive about using healthy ingredients, because as people are dining out more often and getting more health conscious, they expect it of me." One can enjoy the lightness and flavor of her vinaigrettes, purées, and reductions, which are components of her Warm Spinach Salad and the Sautéed Shrimp and Roasted Eggplant Lasagna, and savor a little cream and butter in the rich, full-bodied Northwest Mushroom Soup, or the downright luscious Lemon Tart.

Many of the recipes Monique prepares at home are adapted from her menu at Fullers. Her lasagna is a simpler version of one of the restaurant dishes, the spinach salad was at one time a restaurant special, and her mushroom soup was one of the required recipes she had to create and prepare during her job interview for Fullers. "I enjoy bringing home some of my favorite recipes, and sometimes I surprise myself when I prepare a better dish than before."

At twenty-nine, Monique is still growing in her career and enjoying the challenge. But no matter what, she makes sure to visit her family in Vancouver at least once a month for the ritual family dinner, which she always looks forward to preparing.

SPICY CAESARS

Monique enjoys having one super-strong cocktail to serve with the appetizers. This is her favorite, made with wasabi for a serious kick. Her brother and sisters always ask her to stir up a batch.

1½ tablespoons coarse salt

2 teaspoons lemon pepper

1 lime wedge

1½ teaspoons wasabi powder (available
   at Asian or specialty stores)

1½ tablespoons fresh lime juice

Ice cubes

1¼ cups vodka

8 5½-ounce cans Clamato juice
   (tomato and clam juice)

Tabasco sauce to taste

Worcestershire sauce to taste

3 teaspoons grated fresh horseradish

Juice of 1 lemon

Pickled sweet peppers or celery stalks,
   for garnish (optional)

Combine the salt and lemon pepper on a small plate. Rub the rim of each glass with the lime wedge and dip the rim of the glass in the salt and lemon pepper mixture. In a cup, blend together the wasabi powder with the lime juice and set aside. Pack 8 pint glasses with ice and distribute the vodka evenly among the glasses. Fill each glass with 1 can of Clamato juice and season each with Tabasco sauce, Worcestershire sauce, horseradish, wasabi and lime mixture, and lemon juice. Stir well. Garnish each glass with pickled sweet peppers or a celery stalk, if desired.

SERVES 8

Focaccia

Focaccia (Italian for "under the fire") is a thick flat bread with a chewy crust that was traditionally cooked by the Italians on the floor ("under the fire") of the wood-burning stove. Its dough is similar to that of pizza, but the addition of olive oil and herbs gives it enough flavor to be eaten on its own. This bread is irresistible when served warm with toppings. Try different toppings such as black olives and feta cheese, roasted red peppers and garlic, or anything your taste buds desire.

   Bake the focaccia ahead of time and as soon as it has cooled completely, freeze it, tightly wrapped in plastic wrap or foil. To serve it, thaw the focaccia, wrapped, at room temperature, then unwrap it and warm in a 250°F. oven.

HOMEMADE HERB AND SHALLOT FOCACCIA

Monique's twist to this popular Italian flat bread is to add shallots, the milder-flavored relative of onion and garlic, to the dough. This recipe can be doubled for a larger group or more generous portions, and baked in a 12 × 17-inch rimmed baking sheet. Serve this with the mushroom soup as a first course.

1 package (2¾ teaspoons) active dry yeast

1¾ cups warm water (not more than 110° F.)

1 tablespoon sugar

6 tablespoons extra-virgin olive oil

½ cup chopped shallots

5–5½ cups bread or all-purpose flour

1 tablespoon salt

¾ teaspoon ground white pepper

¼ cup chopped fresh herbs, such as sage, rosemary, or thyme

In a small bowl, combine the yeast, ½ cup of the warm water, and sugar. Stir until dissolved. Set aside until the mixture foams, approximately 5 minutes. Meanwhile, in a skillet, heat 1 tablespoon of the oil over medium heat. Sauté the shallots until golden brown and crisp, about 7 minutes. Strain off the excess oil, set aside, and cool. The reserved oil will have a good shallot flavor, and it can be used to brush the top of the focaccia prior to baking.

In the bowl of an electric mixer fitted with a dough hook, or in a large mixing bowl by hand with a wooden spoon, mix the flour, shallots, salt, and pepper. Slowly add the yeast mixture and the remaining 5 tablespoons of olive oil. Continue mixing and gradually add the remaining 1¼ cups of warm water until the dough is elastic and slightly sticky. Transfer the dough to a lightly floured surface and knead for 3 minutes. If mixing by hand, knead for 10 minutes on a floured surface. Shape the dough into a ball and place in a lightly greased bowl. Cover with plastic wrap or a towel and let rise in a warm place until it doubles in volume, 1 to 1½ hours.

Preheat the oven to 425° F. Lightly oil a 13 × 7-inch pan or, for a free-form focaccia, a baking sheet. Using your hands, punch down the dough and press it into the pan, making sure to press it into the corners; for a free-form shape, press the dough out to an even thickness of 1½ inches. Brush the top of the focaccia with the reserved shallot olive oil and bake for 5 minutes, until slightly golden in color. Reduce the temperature to 375° F. Brush again with olive oil. Sprinkle generously with fresh herbs and continue baking for approximately 10 to 15 minutes, until golden brown. Remove from the oven and allow to cool slightly before cutting into squares. Serve warm or at room temperature.

SERVES 8

NORTHWEST MUSHROOM SOUP

This creamy, savory soup is not too filling and makes a nice opener to the meal, accompanied by a medium-bodied Pinot Noir. The soup will hold for three to four days in the refrigerator.

2 tablespoons extra-virgin olive oil

1 cup diced celery

1¼ cups diced carrots

1 cup diced white onion

1 garlic clove, chopped

2 pounds button mushrooms, cleaned, stemmed, and finely chopped

¾ cup dry white wine

6½ cups chicken stock

1 potato, peeled and cut into eighths

1 bouquet garni containing 5 sprigs parsley, 10 crushed black peppercorns, and 1 bay leaf (see box, page 266)

½ cup heavy cream

2 teaspoons salt

1 teaspoon freshly ground pepper

2 teaspoons fresh lemon juice

GARNISH

2 tablespoons extra-virgin olive oil

1½ cups (about 8 ounces) chopped mixed fresh wild mushrooms, such as shiitake, oyster, and portobello (see box, pages 36–37)

2 tablespoons chopped shallots

2 tablespoons chopped mixed fresh herbs, such as marjoram, thyme, parsley, and chervil

In a large saucepan, heat 1 tablespoon of the oil over medium heat until it is lightly smoking. Add the celery, carrots, and onion and cook until the onion is slightly caramelized (browned) and soft, about 5 minutes. Add the garlic and half of the chopped mushrooms, and cook for 5 minutes until all the moisture from the mushrooms is released. Add the white wine to deglaze the pan, scraping up any brown bits from the bottom, and cook until there is no liquid left, 4 to 5 minutes. Add the chicken stock, potato, and bouquet garni; bring to a boil over medium-high heat, then reduce the heat to low and simmer for 15 minutes, until the potatoes are tender. Discard the bouquet garni, making sure to squeeze out all the liquid. Stir in the cream and cook for another 5 minutes. In a blender or food processor, purée the liquid and vegetables until smooth. Return to the saucepan, season with salt, pepper, and lemon juice, and bring the soup back to a simmer over low heat.

In a large skillet, heat the remaining tablespoon of oil over medium heat. Add the remaining chopped mushrooms and sauté until dry, 6 to 8 minutes, then add to the soup.

To prepare the garnish, heat the olive oil in a skillet over medium heat. Add the wild mushrooms and sauté until golden brown, about 5 minutes. Sprinkle on the shallots and herbs and cook for 1 minute longer, stirring. To serve, ladle the soup into bowls and place a heaping spoonful of the wild mushroom garnish in the center of the soup.

SERVES 8

WARM SPINACH SALAD WITH PANCETTA VINAIGRETTE AND ROSEMARY PITA BREAD CROUTONS

Savory pancetta vinaigrette warms the fresh, crisp spinach ever so slightly for an appetizing fall or wintertime salad. Be sure to toss in the rosemary croutons, as they round out the flavor and texture of the salad and are so easy to make. These croutons can be made up to three days in advance and stored in a sealed container. A light, crisp Pinot Grigio, Vernaccia, or other similar dry Italian white wine is best with this salad.

4 ounces pancetta or bacon, chopped

4 garlic cloves, minced

4 shallots, chopped

1½ tablespoons honey

½ cup fresh lemon juice

½ cup dry white wine

1 cup extra-virgin olive oil

Salt and freshly ground pepper to taste

1 pound fresh spinach, washed, dried, stemmed, and torn into bite-size pieces

Rosemary Pita Bread Croutons (recipe follows)

In a small saucepan, cook the pancetta over medium-high heat until all the fat is rendered, about 5 minutes. With a slotted spoon, remove half of the pancetta and reserve. Add the garlic and shallots and sauté until the rest of the pancetta is soft, about 5 minutes. Add the honey, lemon juice, and wine. Cook until the liquid is reduced by two-thirds, about 10 minutes. Transfer the mixture to a blender or food processor and blend or process at high speed. With the motor running, slowly add the oil. Transfer the vinaigrette to a saucepan over very low heat, then add the reserved pancetta and salt and pepper. Keep warm until ready to serve. Toss the spinach and vinaigrette in a large salad bowl. Garnish with Rosemary Pita Bread Croutons.

SERVES 8

ROSEMARY PITA BREAD CROUTONS

¼ cup extra-virgin olive oil

2 tablespoons sherry vinegar

Juice of ½ lemon

2 teaspoons chopped fresh rosemary

1 tablespoon chopped shallot

½ teaspoon salt

Freshly ground pepper to taste

4 6-inch pita breads, cut into 6 wedges
  each

In a small bowl, whisk together the oil, vinegar, lemon juice, rosemary, shallot, salt, and pepper and let stand at room temperature for 1 hour.

Preheat the oven to 450° F. Place the pita wedges in a bowl. Pour just enough vinaigrette over the pita bread to coat lightly and toss. Place the pita wedges in a single layer on an ungreased baking sheet and bake until the wedges are golden brown and crisp, about 3 minutes. Remove from the oven and drizzle the remaining vinaigrette over the crisp croutons.

MAKES APPROXIMATELY 1½ CUPS

SAUTÉED SHRIMP AND ROASTED EGGPLANT LASAGNA

The rich smoky overtones of this no-pasta lasagna are best matched with a Sauvignon Blanc or Sémillon dry white wine. Between the layers of shrimp and seasoned eggplant are layers of tomatoes, fresh herbs, and tangy goat cheese. If you can get yellow tomatoes, alternate layers of red and yellow tomatoes for a mix of vibrant color. The eggplant mixture can be made up to three days in advance and kept tightly covered in the refrigerator.

½ cup water

2 large eggplants

4 tablespoons extra-virgin olive oil

8 garlic cloves, peeled

1 red bell pepper, stemmed, seeded,
  and finely diced

1 yellow bell pepper, stemmed, seeded,
  and finely diced

2 anchovy fillets, rinsed and minced

Juice of 1 lemon

½ cup chopped mixed fresh herbs,
  such as marjoram, oregano, and basil

Salt and freshly ground pepper to taste

24 large shrimp, peeled, cleaned, and
  deveined

6 large tomatoes, cored and cut into
  ¼-inch slices

1 cup crumbled goat cheese, such as
  Montrachet

Preheat the oven to 500° F. Pour ½ cup of water into a rimmed baking sheet. Cut each egg-plant in half lengthwise and place the halves cut side down in the water. Cover the baking sheet tightly with foil and bake in the oven for 15 minutes, or until the eggplant is tender. Remove from the oven and let cool. Lower the oven temperature to 350° F.

In a skillet, combine 3 tablespoons of the olive oil and the garlic. Over medium heat, gently cook the garlic until golden brown and tender, about 5 minutes. Remove the garlic with a slotted spoon; allow the garlic to cool, then chop it finely and reserve. Sauté the peppers in the same pan with the garlic oil until tender, about 5 minutes, then set aside to cool.

Gently scoop out the roasted eggplant from its skin and roughly chop. In a skillet over medium heat, lightly sauté the eggplant until the mixture is dry, about 7 minutes. Add the garlic, peppers, and anchovies, and stir to combine. Transfer the eggplant mixture to a bowl, and mix in half of the lemon juice, half of the mixed herbs, and the salt and pepper. Set aside.

To prepare the shrimp, heat the remaining tablespoon of oil in a large skillet over medium heat. Add the shrimp and cook until they begin to turn pink, about 1 minute. Add the rest of the lemon juice and salt and pepper. Cook for 1 minute, then remove from the heat. Let cool, roughly chop, and set aside.

Arrange approximately one-third of the tomatoes in an even layer to cover the bottom of a 9 × 7-inch or 12-inch round ovenproof casserole dish. Lightly season the tomatoes with salt and pepper and about one-third of the remaining fresh herbs. Spread half of the eggplant mixture over the tomatoes and sprinkle half the shrimp mixture over the eggplant, followed by a sprinkling of half the goat cheese. Layer another third of the tomatoes and season with salt and pepper and fresh herbs. Then layer the remaining eggplant, shrimp, and goat cheese, in that order, and finish off with one last layer of tomatoes seasoned with salt and pepper and the last of the fresh herbs. Cover with foil and bake for 35 to 40 minutes, until the lasagna is hot throughout. Serve immediately.

SERVES 8

Lemon Juice

Here's a quick trick for getting the most from a lemon: Before juicing, place the uncut lemon on its side on a hard, flat surface and roll the lemon back and forth while applying pressure with the palm of the hand. This releases the juice from the pulp. Then cut the lemon in half crosswise and juice away!

Lemon Tart with Cornmeal Crust

This tempting lemon tart will satisfy any sweet craving and refresh the palate after Monique's menu of bold flavors. With the addition of cornmeal, the crisp, butter-rich crust is slightly crunchy and is a wonderful contrast to the smooth lemon filling.

If there is no time to make a crust, just pour the lemon mixture into a quiche pan or casserole dish to set. Spoon the lemon curd onto plates and top with a mint leaf and a few fresh raspberries.

1¾ cups fresh lemon juice (approximately 6 lemons) (see box, opposite)

Zest of 2 lemons, finely chopped (see box, page 269)

1½ cups sugar

7 large eggs

5 large egg yolks

¾ cup (1½ sticks) cold unsalted butter, cut into pieces

1 10-inch Cornmeal Pie Crust, baked and cooled (recipe follows)

In a heatproof mixing bowl placed over gently simmering water, whisk together the lemon juice, lemon zest, sugar, eggs, and egg yolks. Whisk vigorously until the mixture has thickened to the consistency of a Hollandaise sauce, 5 to 7 minutes. Remove from the heat and whisk in the butter until it is melted. Pour the filling into the cooled crust and let sit at room temperature for at least 1 hour, or until the filling is set, before serving.

Serves 8

Cornmeal Pie Crust

3 cups all-purpose flour

1 cup yellow cornmeal

¾ teaspoon salt

1¼ cups (2½ sticks) unsalted butter, softened

1½ cups sugar

6 large egg yolks

Preheat the oven to 350°F. In a large mixing bowl, sift together the flour, cornmeal, and salt. Set aside. In the bowl of an electric mixer, cream the butter and sugar together. Add the egg yolks, one at a time, blending well after each addition. Add the dry ingredients and mix until the dough forms a ball. Shape the dough into a disk and flatten. Place the dough in a 10-inch pie pan and gently mold the dough, using your fingers, in an even layer to line the pie pan. Even off and decoratively crimp the edges, then prick the dough in several spots with a fork. Bake for 15 to 20 minutes, until golden brown. Cool completely on a wire rack before filling.

LIDIA BASTIANICH

Authentic Italian

A true Italian meal will consist of many different, small amounts of intense flavors," says Lidia Bastianich. Lidia is co-owner and chef of the distinguished Felidia Ristorante in New York City, as well as co-owner with her son, Joseph, of Becco, which is located in New York's theater district. She is from Istria, the Adriatic peninsula that was part of Italy until World War II, then was given to Yugoslavia, and finally became part of Croatia. Lidia recollects that in Istria her grandparents produced all their own food, from wine to prosciutto. "I remember being sent out to fetch the eggs for the frittata, still warm from the goose," she says.

In 1958, when she was eleven years old, Lidia's family immigrated to the United States to settle in New York City. "When I came to the States I was absolutely mesmerized by packaged food, particularly Jell-O and Duncan Hines cake mixes. I couldn't believe how fast everything could be made, and I was having a ball preparing these foods when my mother was at work. My father wasn't too happy about it, and fortunately, this fascination passed quickly."

Lidia often found herself in restaurant or food-related jobs, so when she mar-

MENU

*Grilled Polenta with Grilled
Porcini Mushrooms*

Braised Beef in Barolo Sauce

Potato-Carrot Purée

Sautéed Spinach

Chestnut Purée

Pears and Grapes Baked in White Wine

ried Felice, who is also from Istria, they borrowed money from her parents to open Buoniva, a restaurant in Queens. "Felice worked the front of the house and I assisted the chefs in the kitchen." Lidia paid close attention to the chefs, learning basic techniques, adding some of her own touches here and there. Three years later, Lidia took over as head chef, and she recalls, "Once people started to respond to my cooking, I began to really blossom." In 1981, Lidia and Felice opened Felidia, which serves, as Lidia describes, "ninety percent culturally true, authentic Italian cuisine." She returns to Italy at least four times a year and, she says, "to revive my sense of flavor." With a strong reverence for tradition and culture, Lidia is constantly challenged to find the appropriate proportions and quantity of food that satisfies but doesn't overwhelm the American appetite and palate.

At home, Lidia prepares 100-percent authentic Italian meals, and without her restaurant kitchen crew she relies on her two assistants—her mother, who cleans and chops the vegetables, and Felice, who is in charge of the salad and selecting the wine. At least one weekend a month Lidia likes to cook at home, "I'm a real mother hen, much like my own mother, and love cooking for the family." Family and friends arrive at her home around 2 P.M. and slowly gather in the kitchen. Felice invites one of the guests to accompany him to the cellar to help select the evening's wines, and Lidia begins to serve platters of grilled polenta and toothsome porcini mushrooms. Lidia braises the beef in wine because it "adds a richness to the beef as well as having a tenderizing effect," and she serves it with a Potato-Carrot Purée, Sautéed Spinach, and, for a touch of sweetness, a Chestnut Purée that Lidia says is "as aromatic as a bouquet of roses." Pears and grapes are baked in white wine for dessert. This velvety finish will "fill your whole mouth with warmth and a sense of the earth."

After dinner Lidia serves espresso, maybe some biscotti, and a little grappa for sipping. The real fun begins when Felice brings out his accordion and encourages everyone to join in singing folk songs. Eventually, the guests make their way back into the kitchen and unwrap the platters of food that have been put away, and begin to eat all over again.

GRILLED POLENTA WITH GRILLED PORCINI MUSHROOMS

Porcini, known as cèpes to the French, are prized for their meaty texture and woodsy flavor. Paired with polenta, which is grilled just until crisp on the outside and creamy inside, the mushrooms maintain every ounce of their character. Look for these wild treasures in specialty markets in autumn; otherwise, use portobellos or a mix of wild and domestic mushrooms.

Double recipe Basic Polenta (recipe follows)

$\frac{1}{2}$ cup extra-virgin olive oil

6 garlic cloves, sliced

4 sprigs fresh rosemary, leaves crushed slightly

Salt and freshly ground pepper to taste

8 large porcini mushrooms, brushed clean, stems trimmed, and cut lengthwise into $\frac{1}{2}$-inch slices (see box, pages 36–37)

Prepare the polenta for grilling, as specified in the box on page 38. While the polenta is cooking, light the grill (see Note). Combine 4 tablespoons of the olive oil, the garlic, and the rosemary in a small bowl. Set the mixture aside at room temperature to let the flavors blend (preferably for at least 1 hour). Add the salt and pepper just before using.

When the grill is medium-hot, dip the mushroom slices in the flavored oil and set on a mesh grill. Grill for 4 minutes, turning once. Cut the set polenta into 8 pieces. Lightly brush both sides of the polenta with the remaining plain olive oil, using the rosemary sprigs for a brush, and set on the grill for about 2 minutes per side.

Evenly divide the mushroom slices into 8 portions and place on top of each polenta square. Drizzle with the remaining herbed olive oil.

SERVES 8

NOTE: If grilling is not an option, cook the polenta and mushrooms in a skillet. Do not slice the mushrooms before cooking. Heat a small amount of olive oil in a nonstick skillet over medium-high heat. Add the mushrooms and sauté for 5 minutes or until lightly browned. Thinly slice the mushrooms and drizzle with the herbed olive oil. For the polenta, follow the directions in the box (see page 38) for pan-frying.

Wild Mushrooms

Most of the thousands of wild mushrooms that grow around the globe are imported, but a handful of varieties are now being cultivated in the United States. Nowadays you'll find several varieties at specialty food shops year-round and even at some supermarkets seasonally.

Wild mushrooms are expensive, but the good news is that they can be used sparingly as they impart a lot of flavor.

Most wild mushrooms must be cooked to be enjoyed, and generally can be sautéed, grilled, broiled, or oven-roasted. Keep in mind that mushrooms have a high water content that varies by type, so you'll want to cook the mushrooms at a low enough temperature to allow them to release their natural water without stripping them of their flavor and texture by overcooking. Avoid rinsing mushrooms and do not immerse them in water; otherwise, you'll end up with mushy, spongy specimens, rather than firm and meaty mushrooms. To clean mushrooms, wipe them with a damp cloth or brush them clean.

During months when your favorite wild mushroom is out of season, try substituting dried wild mushrooms for fresh. Still not cheap, they are much less expensive and can be stored indefinitely before using. Unfortunately, they can't be substituted in all cases. Dried work fine in sauces, stocks, risotto, and other dishes in which they are cooked in other foods for a longish time, but not where the mushrooms are a main attraction, as in Lidia's Grilled Polenta with Grilled Porcini Mushrooms. To use them, simply reconstitute them in just enough very hot water to cover for about 20 minutes or until softened. Drain and add the mushrooms to the dish. The liquid may also be strained and reserved to flavor a sauce or stock.

Types of Wild Mushrooms Available in the United States

Each variety of wild fungus has its own personality, varying in taste, shape, water content, "meatiness," and, very important, toxins. Stick with the mushrooms you find at the market and avoid those you might come across in your backyard, as many mushrooms are poisonous. A good general rule to remember is, the darker the mushroom cap, the stronger the flavor. Look for mushrooms that are plump; have closed, undamaged gills; and are small to medium in size for their variety. Fresh mushrooms are very perishable, so use them within a day or two of buying.

The following edible wild varieties are among those that are available in the United States:

CHANTERELLES are small yellow and orange mushrooms with a funnel- or trumpet-shaped cap and a thin stem. They are enjoyed for their subtle nutty and sometimes fruity flavor. Imported and grown domestically, these slightly chewy mushrooms are most available during the summer and winter months.

CRIMINI mushrooms are very similar in appearance and texture to white button mushrooms. They are darker in color, however, and have an earthy and slightly spicy taste. Crimini are also domesticated, and are readily available year-round.

MORELS, like truffles, are among the most prized fungi—loved for their complex blend of smoky, nutty, and woodsy flavors. You'll find more of these dark brown honeycomb-capped mushrooms in specialty markets during the spring months, starting in April.

OYSTER mushrooms are now being cultivated in the United States and are available year-round. They are one of the few wild varieties that can be eaten raw. Uncooked they have a bold flavor with a hint of pepper; cooked, they are milder. This grayish-brown fan-shaped Asian mushroom, resembling an actual oyster, is available in specialty stores and Asian markets.

PORCINI are readily available in France and Italy during the warmer months; fresh porcini are a rarity in the States. They vary drastically in size, weighing anywhere from 1 ounce to 1 pound, and the pale cap ranges from 1 to 10 inches in diameter. You may use the more readily available, though less intensely flavored, portobello for this species. The season for porcini is autumn, but they often pop up in the spring as well.

PORTOBELLO are big, hardy mushrooms. The brown cap ranges from 4 to 10 inches round and is about 1 inch thick. When cooked, the flesh becomes juicy and almost steaklike, and is delicious baked or grilled with butter and fresh herbs. They are available in specialty markets and many supermarkets year-round.

SHIITAKES, first grown in Japan and Korea and now in several U.S. states, are available in many supermarkets year-round, but they are more affordable during the spring and fall. They are favored for their tender, meaty, and full-flavored flesh. The relatively thin, dark tan to brown cap ranges from 3 to 10 inches in diameter. Look for ones with firm, plump caps with the edges curled under. Unlike most mushrooms, shiitakes release very little water and tend to absorb the liquid in which they are being cooked.

BASIC POLENTA

Not only will you have a delicious creamy cornmeal dish at the end of this recipe, if you make this with some frequency you will have impressive biceps to boot.

4 cups water	**2 tablespoons coarse salt**
1 tablespoon unsalted butter	**1½ cups coarse yellow cornmeal**
1 bay leaf	

In a large enameled or cast-iron saucepan or other heavy pot, bring the water, butter, bay leaf, and salt to a low simmer over medium heat. Very slowly begin to sift the cornmeal into the pan through the fingers of one hand, stirring constantly with a wooden spoon or whisk.

Gradually sift all of the cornmeal into the pan, continue to stir, and reduce the heat to medium-low. Stir until the polenta is smooth and thick and pulls away from the sides of the pan as it is stirred, about 30 minutes. Discard the bay leaf. See box for serving options.

SERVES 4

Serving Polenta

Polenta may be served soft in a bowl as a side dish, similar to mashed potatoes, or topped with a stew of sorts as a main dish, much the way rice is used as a bed for gumbo. When serving polenta in a large bowl, let it rest for 10 minutes. Dip a large spoon into water and scoop the polenta onto individual dishes, dipping the spoon into the water between scoops.

Alternatively, polenta may be spread on a flat surface, cooled until firm, and cut, then grilled, baked, or pan-fried. The result is a crispy outside and a soft inside. In Italy, people often top polenta cooked this way with vegetables such as roasted peppers or grilled mushrooms, for a first course. To do so, immediately spread the hot, cooked polenta on a lightly greased baking sheet in a layer about ¼ inch thick using a rubber spatula dipped in cold water. Refrigerate until firmly set, then cut it into squares, triangles, or any other shape.

TO BAKE, place the slices on a lightly oiled baking sheet and place in a preheated 375°F. oven for 6 to 8 minutes.

TO GRILL, lightly brush each side with olive oil and place on a hot grill for about 2 minutes on each side.

TO PAN-FRY, heat a small amount of olive oil in a nonstick skillet over medium-high heat. Add the polenta slices and cook for about 2 minutes on each side.

BRAISED BEEF IN BAROLO SAUCE

Braising allows the beef to absorb the "essence of violets, blackberries, and a tinge of tar" in the Barolo wine—prized by Italians for its complexity and robust bouquet. Don't be too shocked by the hefty price of the wine. If your budget doesn't allow for this type of red wine, another full-bodied, fruity wine will work. Lidia suggests serving this dish with Barbaresco wine, for a nice contrast. Another bottle of Barolo, however, would be quite good.

½ cup extra-virgin olive oil

1½ cups minced onion

2 tablespoons chopped pancetta or bacon

Salt and freshly ground pepper to taste

1 cup shredded carrots

6 bay leaves

6 whole cloves

1 teaspoon chopped fresh rosemary

3½ pounds eye of round beef

3 tablespoons tomato paste

2 bottles Barolo wine

1 cup canned peeled Italian plum tomatoes, drained and roughly chopped

6–8 cups beef stock

In a large, deep casserole or stockpot, heat the olive oil over medium heat. Add the onions and pancetta and sauté until the onions are golden and soft, about 7 minutes. Season with salt and pepper. Add the carrots, bay leaves, cloves, and rosemary. Stir well. Remove the mixture from the pan with a slotted spoon and set aside.

Season the meat with salt and pepper and add it to the pan. Cook over medium-high heat until lightly browned on all sides, about 15 minutes in all. Return the onion and pancetta mixture to the pan, add the tomato paste, and stir.

Then add the wine and simmer over medium-low heat for 30 minutes. Add the tomatoes and 6 cups of stock and simmer, covered, skimming frequently and stirring occasionally, until the meat is tender, about 2½ hours. Add the remaining 2 cups of stock as needed to keep the meat covered. Turn the meat regularly so it does not scorch.

Remove the meat from the pot and set aside. Pass the sauce through a sieve, pressing the solids with a spoon to extract as much liquid as possible. Discard the solids, return the meat and strained sauce to the pan, and simmer until the liquid reduces to about 3½ cups, skimming any foam from the surface as it forms, 30 to 60 minutes. Transfer the meat to a cutting board and slice. Arrange the slices on a serving platter and top with the sauce.

SERVES 8

POTATO-CARROT PURÉE

This wonderful side dish has all the sweetness of carrots and the smooth, satisfying consistency of mashed potatoes. Parmigiano-Reggiano cheese and nutmeg add just the right touch.

3 large Idaho potatoes, scrubbed
2 medium carrots, peeled and trimmed
½ cup milk
1 tablespoon extra-virgin olive oil

2 tablespoons unsalted butter
¼ cup freshly grated Parmigiano-Reggiano cheese
Dash of freshly grated nutmeg
Salt to taste

In a medium saucepan, boil the potatoes and carrots with enough water to cover over medium-high heat until tender, about 15 minutes. Drain. When cool enough to handle, peel the potatoes. Pass the potatoes and carrots through a ricer, or mash until smooth by hand, and return to the saucepan. Heat the milk in a small saucepan over low heat until warm to the touch. Add the milk, oil, butter, cheese, and nutmeg to the potatoes and carrots. Whisk over low heat until smooth. Season with salt.

SERVES 8

SAUTÉED SPINACH

Italians appreciate spinach for its slightly bitter taste and often serve it as a side dish to balance the flavors of the meal, as Lidia does in this menu.

Fresh spinach is available year-round, so there is no need to use frozen (and forget canned altogether). Any fresh spinach will do as long as the leaves are crisp and bright green. The leaves should be washed in several rinsings of cold water and patted dry.

2 tablespoons extra-virgin olive oil
6 garlic cloves, smashed
2 pounds spinach, washed and stemmed

Salt to taste
Hot red pepper flakes to taste

In a large saucepan or deep skillet with a lid, heat the olive oil over medium heat. Add the garlic and sauté until golden. Add the spinach, salt, and red pepper flakes and stir. Cover and cook, tossing occasionally, until wilted, 3 to 4 minutes. Discard the garlic and transfer to a warm serving plate.

SERVES 8

Chestnut Purée

Just a dollop of chestnut purée complements the Braised Beef in Barolo Sauce. In the restaurant, Lidia decoratively pipes the purée onto individual plates with a pastry bag. For a meal at home, she serves it in a small serving dish passed at the table.

1 8-ounce can chestnut purée (available at most supermarkets and specialty stores)

2 tablespoons heavy cream

Place the chestnut purée in a small bowl and stir in the cream to lighten the mixture. Transfer to a small serving bowl.

SERVES 8

Pears and Grapes Baked in White Wine

No Italian meal is complete without fruit, which satisfies the sweet tooth without being too filling and helps to digest the meal. Here, Lidia bakes pears and grapes in a white wine and brandy syrup steeped with spices. Star anise adds a hint of sweet licorice.

While Lidia suggests red seedless grapes, this dish will work well with any grapes you prefer.

3 cups dry white wine
3 tablespoons fresh lemon juice
1 cup plus 2 tablespoons sugar
¼ cup brandy
3 whole cloves
2 cinnamon sticks

4 star anise (available at Asian and specialty markets, as well as some supermarkets)
8 pears, halved and cored, such as Bosc or Bartlett (see box, page 305)
1 pound grapes of choice, halved and seeded if necessary

Preheat the oven to 350° F. Combine the wine, lemon juice, 1 cup of the sugar, brandy, cloves, cinnamon, and star anise in a saucepan over medium-high heat and cook for about 30 minutes, until reduced by half. It will be somewhat syrupy, but not as thick as honey. Strain the wine and sugar mixture, discarding the cloves, cinnamon sticks, and star anise. Place the pears halves, cut side down, in a deep glass baking dish. Sprinkle with the remaining 2 tablespoons of sugar, pour over the wine and sugar mixture, and bake for 15 minutes. Add the grapes to the pears and bake for another 5 minutes. Serve warm.

SERVES 8

RICK BAYLESS

A Meal from Two Homelands

After studying, traveling, and eating his way through much of Mexico, Rick found a new home in the traditions of this authentic indigenous cuisine. "I was raised in an Oklahoma barbecue rib restaurant, and I knew what it meant to really satisfy your body and soul with dishes that your people had eaten for generations," he says. "Surprisingly, in Mexico I felt a similar satisfaction: new soul mates, new flavors and textures that resonated as much with me as those of my ancestors."

It's no wonder that this menu includes dishes that may, at first, seem typically American, but actually have their roots in the rustic cooking of the Mexican heartland. The Chipotle-Glazed Country Ribs may appear to have been inspired by Rick's family's restaurant, but are in fact a classic Mexican dish. Rick explains, "I'm predisposed to liking ribs in any shape or form. The Rustic Apple Pie is a take-off on an American classic, but Rick's unique version includes distinctive rustic Mexican flavorings such as raw sugar, strong molasses, and cinnamon.

Rick first pursued an undergraduate degree in Spanish language and literature and Latin American culture at the University of Oklahoma, and then went on to receive a graduate degree in linguistics at the University of Michigan. But the experience

MENU

Soup of Mexican Greens,
Tomatillo, and Tomato

—

Chipotle-Glazed Country Ribs

—

Drunken Beans with Tequila

—

Rustic Apple Pie with
Brown Sugar and Cinnamon

of working in his family's restaurant while growing up, and the various culinary jobs he held during his school years, eventually led Rick to give up his pursuit of a Ph.D. and devote himself full time to teaching cooking classes, running a catering business, and hosting *Cooking Mexican,* a PBS television show. "During that time, I wanted to cook and teach all kinds of cuisines to give me a solid base of skills," says Rick.

Finally, the demands of his profession compelled him to choose among his various culinary interests. His travels to South America and studies of the richness of Latin American culture led him to concentrate on Mexican food. He decided to make a complete grassroots exploration of the country's diverse regional cooking. For four years in the early 1980s, he and his wife, Deann, traveled from town to town, studying what the people were eating in the markets, in the local restaurants, and on the streets.

A few years after returning from Mexico, Rick and his wife decided to offer an authentic taste of Mexico in the United States, and they opened two restaurants under one roof in Chicago—the casual Frontera Grill and the dressier Topolobampo—where he pleases an endless stream of customers. However, Rick feels a special fulfillment when he cooks at home. "All day long at the restaurant, I evaluate and enjoy mouthfuls of numerous different dishes. I worry and ponder and improve, and, in the end, really love what we've been able to do. But none of that compares with the satisfaction I get from transforming a few wonderful ingredients into simple dishes to share with my friends and family," he says. "Here it's pretty much a hodgepodge from my two 'homelands,' most of the dishes showing off a rustic, full-flavored character that's probably more Mexican than anything else."

Rick frequently invites guests over for breakfast on Sundays, mornings being his favorite time of the day. Or on a Sunday evening, he'll prepare a menu like this one, piling his Chipotle-Glazed Country Ribs high on a big platter and serving the Drunken Beans in a large bowl that can be passed around the table family style, for a change of pace from the "plated" serving style at his restaurants. Says Rick, "It's the wholeness of this kind of experience that leads me back to the restaurant with a renewed spirit."

Soup of Mexican Greens, Tomatillo, and Tomato

Purslane is not widely available in supermarkets, but this tangy green makes this hearty soup really special. Ask for it at farmers' markets; plant it in your garden; or scavenge it from the wild.

1 tablespoon extra-virgin olive or
    vegetable oil

1 large white onion, diced

2 large garlic cloves, minced

Hot green chili peppers to taste
    (roughly 2 serrano chilies or 1
    jalapeño), stemmed, seeded, and
    minced (see box, page 176)

2 ripe tomatoes, cored and diced

10 ounces (about 5 medium) tomatil-
    los, husked and cut into 8 wedges
    each

1½ quarts chicken stock

¼ teaspoon dried marjoram

¼ teaspoon dried thyme

2 bay leaves

2 large boiling potatoes, peeled and
    diced

Salt to taste

2 cups packed fresh purslane, lamb's
    quarters, or Swiss chard (stemmed),
    washed, and chopped into ½-inch
    pieces (see box, page 46)

½ cup chopped fresh cilantro, for
    garnish

In a 3-quart stockpot, heat the olive oil over medium heat. Add the onion and cook, stirring regularly, until browned, about 7 minutes. Add the garlic and chili peppers and cook for 2 minutes. Stir in the tomatoes and tomatillos, and cook, stirring frequently, until the mixture is nearly dry, 10 to 15 minutes. Add the stock and the marjoram, thyme, and bay leaves, bring to a simmer over medium-low heat, and continue to cook for 30 minutes. Stir in the potatoes and simmer until tender, about 10 minutes. Discard the bay leaves. Season with salt. (You can make the soup up to this point up to 2 days in advance; let cool, refrigerate covered, then reheat the soup to continue.)

Just before serving, bring the soup to a rolling boil over medium-high heat. Add the purslane or other greens and simmer until thoroughly tender, about 6 minutes. Serve the soup in warm bowls, generously sprinkled with chopped cilantro.

Serves 6

Purslane and Swiss Chard

These greens are very different from one another, and while Rick really loves this soup with purslane, Swiss chard makes a good substitute. Its flavor, however, is much more mellow than the deliciously spicy purslane.

Purslane has tender leaves that are traditionally used in tomatillo or tomato sauces in Mexico, but they can be eaten in a variety of ways: served raw in salads or as a garnish or cooked in soups and stews. The stalk is tender and can be left attached, unlike the tough, thick stalks of Swiss chard, which should be removed and cooked separately from the leaves.

Purslane is usually imported from France or Belgium, but it is grown all over the United States and is available during the warm months in most farmers' markets. It's harder to find in winter, but in some areas, such as California, it is sold year-around.

Swiss chard is in the beet family, and its leaves can be prepared in many of the same ways as spinach and purslane. There are several varieties of Swiss chard ranging in color from light green leaves with white stalks and veins to dark green leaves with red stalks and veins, which has a more pronounced flavor. To remove the stalk, tear (do not cut) the leafy part from it. The leaves should then be torn across the veins. Be sure to wash this green thoroughly, as it can be quite sandy. Swiss chard is available mostly in the summer, but some varieties are available year-round.

Chipotle-Glazed Country Ribs

The sweet-and-spicy tang of these toothsome ribs is really delicious. When the platter is empty, Rick says he's usually already thinking about when he'll have the chance to make them again.

Rick uses pork country ribs, which are a completely different cut from the more commonly known spare ribs. The bones are fairly large and often make up almost half the weight of the ribs, so be certain to ask your butcher for the meatiest ribs available.

3½ pounds (about 12) meaty pork
    country ribs
¾ cup Chipotle-Chili Paste
    (recipe follows)
2 tablespoons cider vinegar

½ teaspoon ground cinnamon
Pinch of ground cloves
½ teaspoon salt
¼ cup water
3 tablespoons honey

Place the ribs in a large, nonreactive bowl. In a small bowl, combine the chili paste with the vinegar, cinnamon, cloves, and salt. The mixture should be the consistency of canned tomato sauce. Smear half the mixture evenly over the ribs. Reserve the remaining chili paste mixture. Cover and refrigerate for several hours, or preferably overnight.

Preheat the oven to 325°F. Transfer the ribs to a large baking dish in a single layer, spreading any remaining marinade on the ribs. Drizzle the water in the pan, cover the pan with foil, and bake for 1 hour. Remove the foil and baste the ribs with the liquid in the pan. Bake uncovered for another 30 minutes, until most of the liquid has evaporated and the ribs are tender.

Raise the oven temperature to 350°F. Add the honey to the remaining chili paste mixture, smear heavily on the ribs, and bake until they are glazed and crusty, 12 to 15 minutes. Serve hot and have lots of napkins available.

Serves 6

CHIPOTLE-CHILI PASTE

Add olive oil to this paste and it becomes a marinade for chicken or fish.

4 garlic cloves, unpeeled

2 ounces mild to medium-hot dried
  chili peppers, such as ancho, guajillo,
  or pasilla, stemmed and seeded
  (see box, opposite)

½ 7-ounce can Chilies Chipotles en
  Adobo (a generous ⅓ cup, including
  the canning liquid)

¼ teaspoon freshly ground cumin

½ teaspoon freshly ground black
  pepper

¾ teaspoon salt

¼ cup water

In a heavy, ungreased skillet set over medium heat, roast the garlic cloves, turning occasionally, until they are blackened in spots and soft, 10 to 15 minutes. Remove the garlic from the pan, cool, and slip off the papery skins.

While the garlic is roasting, heat an ungreased griddle or heavy skillet over medium heat. When hot, toast the dried chilies a few at a time by slicing them open and laying them spread open, skin side down, on the hot, flat surface. Press the chilies with a metal spatula for a few seconds until they start to crackle and blister and even send up a faint wisp of smoke. Flip them and press down to toast the other side. Transfer the toasted chilies to a large bowl and cover with boiling water. Weight the chilies down with a plate, small enough to fit in the bowl, to keep them submerged and let soak 30 minutes. Drain.

Combine the garlic, canned chipotles, cumin, pepper, salt, water, and drained chilies in a blender or food processor and purée until smooth and thick. Stop and stir up the mixture every couple of seconds, and add a few more drops of water if the mass just won't move through the blades. Be sure to add the water sparingly, as you want a thick paste, the consistency of canned tomato paste. Using a rubber spatula, work the paste through a medium-mesh strainer, repeatedly scraping it off the bottom, then smearing and pressing it through the strainer again, until you have only skins and seeds left in the strainer and all the paste has been well strained. Store in a tightly closed glass or stainless-steel container in the refrigerator for up to 1 month.

MAKES 1 CUP

Combining Dried Chilies

In addition to the smoky-hot chipotles that give this paste its name, Rick's favorite combination of dried chilies is ancho ("for its deep, rich sweetness") and guajillo ("for its uncomplicated fiery tartness"). Guajillos by themselves make a great—if rather loud and spicy—paste. Mellow-tasting anchos all by themselves seem to lack a little pizzazz, though pairing them with a little pasilla or mulato pepper fills in some missing notes.

New Mexico chilies, both hot and mild, are quite good, too. They taste like toned-down guajillos. Beware of the thin guajillo known as pulla—it is very hot. The same is true of pasillas if not paired with milder chilies. Mulatos on their own seem to be missing so much of the flavor spectrum that they are not recommended unless you add a few smoky chipotles or cascabels to add complexity.

Because each type of chili has a different ratio of flesh to skin, an exact weight is difficult to give. The flesh is where the flavor and heat are. If you have anchos for the recipe, use a little less than the 4 ounces called for because anchos are very fleshy. Guajillos, on the other hand, are probably the least fleshy of all chili peppers, so you may want to use a little more than the specified amount.

DRUNKEN BEANS WITH TEQUILA

Rick's Mexican friend Maria Dolores Torres Izabal passed this recipe onto him. He loves the way the earthy beans play against the aromatic cilantro, stinging chili, and pungent tequila. Served in small bowls alongside those "addictive" country ribs, this is, as Rick says, "truly good eating!"

½ pound (about 1¼ cups) dried pinto or other light beans, picked over

5½ cups water

2 ounces boneless fatty pork, such as shoulder, ham hock, or bacon, cut into ½-inch cubes

4 thick slices bacon, cut into ½-inch pieces

½ medium yellow onion, diced

Hot green chili peppers to taste (roughly 1 serrano chili or ½ jalapeño), stemmed, seeded, and sliced (see box, page 176)

Salt to taste

1½ tablespoons tequila

¼ cup roughly chopped fresh cilantro

Rinse the beans and place them in a 4-quart pot. Add 2 quarts water and remove any beans that float. Soak the beans for 6 to 8 hours, until the water has penetrated to the core of the beans. Or quick-soak by boiling the beans in water to cover for 2 minutes, then letting them stand in the water, covered, for 1 hour.

Drain the soaked beans, then return them to the pot. Measure the 5½ cups fresh water into the pot of beans, add the pork, and slowly bring to a boil over medium-high heat. Partly cover the beans and simmer over medium-low heat, stirring occasionally, until the beans are tender, 1 to 2 hours. Do not overcook. The water should always be at the same level as the beans, so add water as needed, or uncover and simmer until water is reduced.

Fry the bacon in a medium skillet over medium-low heat until crisp, about 10 minutes. Remove the bacon, pour off all but 2 tablespoons of the fat, and raise the heat to medium. Add the onion and chilies and sauté until the onion is a deep golden brown, about 8 minutes.

Add the onion mixture, bacon, and salt to the cooked beans. Cover and continue to simmer over medium-low heat, stirring occasionally, for 20 to 30 minutes to blend the flavors. The beans are meant to be in a broth but, if they are very soupy, uncover and raise the heat and simmer away the excess liquid. If you prefer a thicker mixture, similar to a bean soup, purée 2 cups of beans, with some liquid, in a food processor or blender and return to the pot.

Just before serving, stir in the tequila and cilantro, then additional salt, if desired. Serve in warm bowls.

SERVES 6 AS A SIDE DISH

RUSTIC APPLE PIE WITH BROWN SUGAR AND CINNAMON

Rick grew up with good American pies, but he found that adding a few traditional Mexican seasonings resulted in a tasty alternative to an American classic. The apples are first sautéed in butter, lime juice, and brown sugar to rouse the juices from the apples. Then the apples are strained and the juice is reduced to a thick, tangy sauce enhanced with cinnamon that is tossed with the apples before baking. The concentrated apple flavor embellished with a bit of molasses and the perfume of cinnamon puts this apple pie in a class by itself.

3½ pounds tart cooking apples, such as Granny Smith or Rome Beauty, peeled, cored, and sliced

¼ cup fresh lime juice

⅔ cup granulated sugar, plus a little for sprinkling on the pie

1 cup dark brown sugar

1½ teaspoons ground cinnamon

½ cup (1 stick) unsalted butter

1 tablespoon all-purpose flour

Dough for one 10-inch deep-dish double-pie crust (see page 223)

Combine the apples, lime juice, sugars, and cinnamon in a large bowl. Melt the butter in a large skillet over medium heat. Add the apple mixture and cook, stirring frequently, until the apples are barely tender, about 12 minutes. Spoon the mixture into a colander set over a bowl. Drain for several minutes. Return all the juice to the skillet and cook over medium-high heat until it has reduced to a thick sauce and begins to caramelize, about 5 minutes. Transfer the apples to a large bowl and stir the reduced sauce into the apples. Stir in the flour. Set aside and cool to room temperature.

Preheat the oven to 400°F. Roll out half the pie dough on a lightly floured surface to fit a 10-inch pan. Line the pie pan (preferably Pyrex) with the pastry, leaving a ½-inch overhang on all sides. Roll out the remaining dough on a lightly floured surface to a 12-inch circle. Quickly spoon the cooled filling into the lined pan, then brush the edges of the bottom crust with water. Place the other pastry circle on top, trim off the excess, and decoratively crimp the edges to seal. Brush the top lightly with water and sprinkle with a little granulated sugar. With the tip of a sharp knife, cut vents in the crust to allow steam to release. Bake for 15 minutes. Reduce the oven temperature to 325°F. and bake 30 minutes longer, until nicely browned and bubbling. Cool slightly on a wire rack before cutting. Serve warm.

MAKES ONE 10-INCH PIE

PATRICK CLARK

Pure Indulgence

Being a chef has its advantages and disadvantages. One advantage is having a fully equipped kitchen to cook, play, and experiment with food and flavors. The disadvantage is spending fifteen hours a day away from my wife and five children." When Patrick Clark does get to spend time at home his children, who have "a penchant for seafood," are eager to have him cook and are willing to try almost anything he serves up.

Patrick was just ten years old when he started experimenting in the kitchen. One day his mother came home and found him sautéing pork chops for dinner. "I used to make cheesecake all the time and often spent my allowance buying cream cheese." Born in Brooklyn, the son of a chef, he received his early culinary training at the New York City Technical College, which his father had also attended. When his professor took a keen interest in him and encouraged him to study in England for a semester, Patrick took his advice and attended the Bournemouth Technical College of Great Britain. In 1975, Patrick apprenticed with Michel Guérard in France, and it was under his tutelage that Patrick was profoundly inspired. "He had a respect for the raw product, cooking and plating that simply blew me away."

Upon returning to the United States, he worked his way through several fine

MENU

Sautéed Shrimp Cakes with
Roasted Red Pepper Aioli

❧

Lobster Pie

❧

Warm Bananas with Brandy Nutmeg Cream

restaurants in New York, including Cafe Luxembourg and Odeon, where his cooking was reflective of French *nouvelle cuisine*: "I was still making small portions, dainty food." But soon Patrick developed his own style of contemporary, "deceptively simple" American cuisine with French influences, and opened Metro, a popular bistro in New York. "I want people to understand my food and know what they are eating. Sauces and accompaniments should enhance, not overpower, the dish, so I took all the complicated stuff I learned and simplified it." Now the executive chef at Washington, D.C.'s Hay-Adams Hotel, across the street from the White House, Patrick caters to a "power dining" crowd.

Shrimp and lobster are on the top of his kids' "favorite foods" list, which is why he has chosen these relatively simple dishes. Preston and Ashley, his two oldest children, help in the kitchen while his wife, Lynette, usually stays out of his way. "Sometimes I forget I'm in my kitchen at home and tend to give too many orders." The shrimp cakes are a variation of crab cakes, but are less expensive and easier to prepare. A dollop of Roasted Red Pepper Aioli is served on the side or could be painted on the cakes with a squeeze bottle to spruce up the dish. Patrick is proud of Preston's acquired skill when it comes to using a knife and asks him to do most of the chopping and dicing, while Ashley is still mastering the art of adding ingredients to the bowl and stirring. And when it comes to handling the live lobster, it is Preston's job to drop it in the boiling water, which he does unflinchingly. Lobster from Maine is "the best in the world," says Patrick, and he enhances it with basic seasonings so the delicate flavor of the shellfish comes  through. "The pie part is just something fun I do for the kids." The warm bananas are a personal favorite of Patrick's and are added to a rich Brandy Nutmeg Cream just before serving. Some of the dishes on this menu are a bit on the expensive side, and obviously not for the diet-conscious, but as Patrick says, "We can all splurge once in a while, can't we?"

Sautéed Shrimp Cakes with Roasted Red Pepper Aioli

Aioli (ā-ōlē) is like a garlicky mayonnaise. The addition of sweet roasted red pepper makes the aioli an ideal accompaniment to these fresh shrimp cakes.

Although it is easier to peel and devein uncooked, rather than cooked, shrimp, Patrick prefers to poach shrimp in their shells because they are full of flavor (see Note for Patrick's tip on deveining).

2 quarts court-bouillon (see box, page 56) or water

2¼ pounds medium shrimp

12 ounces sole fillet, diced and well chilled

4½ tablespoons chopped scallions, including greens

3 tablespoons minced fresh chives

3 tablespoons chopped fresh parsley

1½ tablespoons fresh lemon juice

4 tablespoons mayonnaise

Salt and freshly ground pepper to taste

Cayenne pepper to taste

Olive oil, for pan-frying

Flour or fine bread crumbs, for dredging

1½ cups Roasted Red Pepper Aioli (recipe follows)

Bring the court-bouillon to a boil over high heat. Add the shrimp and cook just until they turn pink, about 2 to 3 minutes. Drain the shrimp and cool in the refrigerator, then remove the shells and tails and devein (see Note). Then dice the shrimp into small pieces.

Purée the sole in a food processor until smooth. Transfer to a large bowl and mix in the diced shrimp, scallions, chives, parsley, lemon juice, and mayonnaise until well blended. Season with salt and pepper and cayenne. Shape the mixture into 12 patties about 1 inch thick and 2 inches wide. (The shrimp cakes can be prepared up to this point 4 to 6 hours in advance; cover the patties with plastic wrap and refrigerate until ready to cook.)

In a large skillet over medium heat, add enough olive oil to fill the pan ½ inch deep and heat until hot. Dredge each cake in the flour or bread crumbs until well coated, shaking off any excess. Sauté the cakes for 3 minutes on each side, until golden brown and cooked through, and remove with a slotted spoon to drain on paper towels. Place 2 warm cakes on each serving plate with the aioli.

Serves 6

Note: To cleanly devein shrimp, make an incision slightly to the side of the vein to avoid crushing it, using the tip of a paring knife, then lift it out in one piece.

ROASTED RED PEPPER AIOLI

Patrick prefers to use sherry vinegar because it pairs nicely with the red pepper. However, it is generally available only at specialty markets and is relatively pricey. Red wine vinegar is a fine substitute.

The aioli makes a wonderful sandwich spread and vegetable dip. It is particularly good with steamed artichokes.

1 large egg yolk
½ cup mild extra-virgin olive oil
1½ tablespoons sherry vinegar or red wine vinegar
1 garlic clove, minced

½ tablespoon Dijon mustard
1 red bell pepper, roasted, peeled, seeded, and chopped (see box, page 186)
1 teaspoon fresh lemon juice

Put the egg yolk in a blender or food processor. With the motor running, add the oil in a thin stream, followed by the vinegar. When the mixture is emulsified like a mayonnaise, add the garlic, mustard, bell pepper, lemon juice, and salt and pepper and blend until smooth. Store, covered, in the refrigerator for up to a week.

MAKES APPROXIMATELY 2 CUPS

Court-Bouillon

Court-bouillon (koor-bwee-YAWN) is a flavored poaching liquid most often used for seafood and sometimes for chicken.

TO MAKE 2 quarts of court-bouillon, bring 2 quarts (8 cups) of water to a boil over high heat. Add 1 chopped onion, 1 chopped celery stalk, 1 chopped carrot, and 1 bouquet garni (see box, page 266) containing a few whole peppercorns, 1 sprig thyme, 1 sprig parsley, and 1 bay leaf. You may add a cup or two of dry white wine, if desired. Simmer over medium-high heat for 30 minutes. Strain the mixture into another pot, discarding the solids. Proceed with the recipe, or cool the broth to room temperature and refrigerate. The court-bouillon will last in the refrigerator for up to three days or in the freezer for one month.

On Raw Eggs

The controversy over raw eggs has everyone in a tizzy, and a definitive set of rules seems impossible to establish. Basically, any time raw eggs are used there is a risk of salmonella. However, most chefs maintain that with very fresh eggs, preferably straight from a farm, the risk is minimized. Since getting farm-fresh eggs is not feasible for most people, buy eggs the day they are to be used with an expiration date as far in advance as possible (at least ten days). Don't leave them out at room temperature, and store them in the coldest part of the refrigerator. And never use eggs that are cracked.

LOBSTER PIE

A lobster-infused custard is topped with sautéed lobster meat, corn, roasted red peppers, and herbs for an I'll-start-my-diet-tomorrow main-dish pie.

3 1½-pound live lobsters

Unsweetened pie dough for a 9-inch deep-dish pie pan, either store-bought or homemade (see page 223)

CUSTARD (SEE NOTE)

2 tablespoons extra-virgin olive oil

1 carrot, peeled and diced

1 onion, diced

1 leek, washed and diced

2 shallots, chopped

4 cups heavy cream

1 bouquet garni consisting of parsley, thyme, peppercorns, and a bay leaf (see box, page 266)

2 ripe tomatoes, cut in quarters, seeded, and drained

3 large eggs

3 large egg yolks

Salt and freshly ground pepper to taste

⅛ teaspoon cayenne pepper

TOPPING

3 tablespoons unsalted butter

¼ cup diced red onion

1½ cups fresh or frozen corn kernels, thawed

Salt and freshly ground pepper to taste

1 red bell pepper, roasted, cored, peeled, and diced (see box, page 186)

¼ cup sliced scallions, including greens

¼ cup chopped mixed fresh herbs, such as parsley, tarragon, chives, chervil

Preheat the oven to 350° F. Bring a very large pot of water to a rolling boil over high heat. Drop the lobsters head first into the water and boil for 6 minutes. Remove the lobsters with a pair of tongs and break off the claws. Return the claws to the boiling water to cook for another 2 minutes. When the lobsters have cooled, remove the tail and claw meat, cracking the shells carefully to keep the claw and tail meat intact. Keep the claw meat whole and cut the tail meat crosswise into ½-inch medallions. Reserve the lobster meat for the topping. Reserve the shells for preparing the custard.

On a lightly floured surface, roll the dough out to a 12-inch circle, about ⅛ inch thick. Line a 9-inch deep-dish pie pan with the dough and trim and decoratively crimp the edges. Prick the dough in several spots with a fork. Line the crust with foil and fill it with rice or dried beans, and place the crust in the oven for 15 to 20 minutes to partially bake. Remove the beans and foil and cool the crust on a wire rack.

To prepare the custard, crush the lobster shells into small pieces by putting the shells in a paper bag and smashing them with a hammer. Heat the oil in a large saucepan over medium heat. Add the carrot, onion, leek, and shallots and cook, stirring, for 3 to 5 minutes; do not let the vegetables brown. Add the lobster shells and stir for another 3 to 5 minutes. Add the cream and the bouquet garni, and bring to a boil over medium–high heat. Add the tomatoes, reduce the heat to medium, and simmer for about 30 minutes, stirring occasionally.

Preheat the oven to 325° F. Strain the lobster cream through a fine, sturdy sieve, crushing the shells and vegetables with the back of a spoon to extract as much flavor as possible. You should have about 3 cups of strained cream. Discard the solids and set the liquid aside to cool. In a medium bowl, lightly beat the eggs and yolks together, then whisk in the lobster cream. Season with the salt and pepper and cayenne.

Fill the partially baked pie shell two-thirds full with the lobster custard. Cover the edges of the crust with foil to prevent burning. Bake in the center of the oven for about 25 minutes, until the custard is set. It should be firm, but not split and dry looking.

In the meantime, prepare the topping. In a large skillet, melt 2 tablespoons of the butter over medium heat. Add the red onion and sauté for 2 to 3 minutes. Add the corn and stir for another 3 to 4 minutes, without allowing it to brown. Add the sliced tail meat, reserving the claw meat, and season with salt and pepper. Continue to cook the mixture until the lobster is warm and the corn is tender, 5 to 7 minutes. Toss in the pepper and scallions and recheck the seasoning. Set aside.

In another skillet, heat the remaining tablespoon of butter over medium heat (do not let the butter brown) and sauté the claw meat for 2 to 3 minutes on each side, until hot. Season with salt and pepper.

Let the pie cool for 5 minutes on a wire rack. Using a slotted spoon, distribute the lobster tail and corn mixture over the entire pie. Place the claws on top in a circle with narrow ends facing toward the center, denoting the 6 portions. Top with herbs and cut into wedges.

SERVES 6

NOTE: This recipe makes more custard than is needed for the Lobster Pie. Bake the additional custard in another 9-inch pie pan and use it as a base for sautéed vegetables, seafood, or cavier.

WARM BANANAS WITH BRANDY NUTMEG CREAM

This is a simple dessert that is really fast to make, and chances are you will have all the ingredients on hand. Use bananas that are just ripe, pure yellow with no green streaks or specks of brown.

When served over ice cream in deep bowls, as Patrick suggests, these warm bananas with cream are the ultimate comfort food—basically a very grown-up banana split. When served in individual long-stemmed wine glasses with white and dark chocolate shavings, it becomes an elegant ending to any dinner.

1 cup heavy cream
2 tablespoons (¼ stick) unsalted butter
2 tablespoons brandy
¼ teaspoon salt
¼ cup sugar

¼ teaspoon freshly grated nutmeg
6 bananas, peeled and sliced diagonally
Chocolate or vanilla ice cream
(optional)

Combine the cream, butter, brandy, salt, sugar, and nutmeg in a medium saucepan over medium-high heat and bring to a boil. Reduce the heat to medium and simmer for 5 minutes or until the mixture thickens enough to coat the back of a spoon. Add the banana slices and warm for 30 seconds. Serve in goblets or over chocolate or vanilla ice cream.

SERVES 6

NOEL CUNNINGHAM

A Romantic Dinner for Tammy

Charitable, warm, and passionate about everything, describes Noel Cunningham, owner and chef of Strings restaurant in Denver. Born and raised in Dublin, Ireland, Noel remembers winning first prize for a cake he made for a Boy Scouts' contest when he was ten years old. His first apprenticeship was at age fourteen, learning how to cook French food with his uncle, who was the chef at the Dublin airport restaurant. His search for formal training took him to the Savoy Hotel in London, where the executive chef, Louis Virot, was among his greatest influences. "The man taught me so much about cooking with excellence; but what affected me the most was probably the fact that he was a man with a big heart who really cared about his staff and knew how to show it." On his one day off from work each week, Noel attended Westminster College in London, and earned a degree in the culinary arts.

What began as a vacation to Disneyland with his twin daughters in 1976 turned into a ten-year stint in California. "Everyone looked so healthy and happy, I decided to stay." After cooking for several years at Chianti and Harry's Bar and Grill, Noel became the executive chef at the prestigious Touch Club in Los Angeles. "It was a great time to be a chef, as restaurants were redefining themselves with the birth of California cuisine."

Los Angeles was his home until 1986,

MENU

Warm Goat Cheese and Mixed Greens Salad

❧

Roast Loin of Pork with Dried Cherries, Mushrooms, and Roasted Potatoes with Carrots and Broccoli

❧

Cappuccino Soufflés

when a colleague convinced him to become a partner and chef at a new venture in Denver. "I took one look at that beautiful red brick building that is now Strings and packed my bags." Today, Strings and his two other restaurants, Ciao! Baby and 240 Union, are among Denver's most popular spots. Noel's commitment to freshness is evident in his food; all three restaurants cook with herbs straight from their very own small gardens. "Casual contemporary cuisine" is how Noel describes the food at Strings, explaining, "It is a combination of my life experiences; the craziness of the airport, the hautiness of the Savoy, and the casualness of California. Cowboys with spurs, Bono from U2, prom kids, and Shirley MacLaine—everyone goes to Strings."

An infrequent night off will find Noel with his true love, Tammy—his wife, companion, and an important influence in the success of his restaurants. "Tammy always spoils me, and my biggest treat is returning the favor with a simple but perfectly prepared meal at home with touches of romance evident in the soufflés I prepare a selection of and her favorite cheeses." Tammy sets the table while Noel prepares dinner: "We prefer not to have everything prepared in advance, so we can chat and I can have her company while chopping, peeling, or whatever—it's kind of a ritual."

The roast loin of pork is prepared almost exactly the way Noel's mom used to make it when he came home for a visit from England, although the dried cherries are Noel's own special touch. Their dogs, an Irish Setter and a Pomeranian, have their places under the table, hoping for leftovers. Noel says, "They prefer the pork without shiitake mushrooms." Warmed goat cheese spruces up a plain salad to start off this meal, and the

Cappuccino Soufflés end the dinner on a light note as they are prepared without egg yolks (although the sauce is a definite splurge). This easy but dazzling dessert is one of the dishes that Noel made when he was trying to win Tammy's affections—and obviously it worked. A lover of tea, Noel has  at least a dozen cups a day and serves his favorite with fresh Brie cheese and grapes for post-meal nibbling. "There is no need to reinvent the wheel," Noel says. "Good food and romance are best when not overdone."

WARM GOAT CHEESE AND MIXED GREENS SALAD

Goat cheese goes very nicely with lettuces of all kinds, and when warmed its creaminess and piquant flavor become even more pronounced.

4 cups mixed greens, such as arugula, endive, chicory, raddichio, and Bibb lettuce, washed, dried, and torn into bite-size pieces
Balsamic Vinaigrette (recipe follows)

½ cup shelled whole pecans, toasted (see box, page 117)
11 ounces goat cheese in log form, such as from Laura Chenel

Place the greens in a large salad or mixing bowl. Toss with enough vinaigrette to coat well and to suit your taste, reserving ¼ cup. Evenly divide the salad among 4 small plates and top with equal amounts of the pecans. Set aside.

Heat ¼ cup of the vinaigrette in a skillet over medium-low heat. Slice the goat cheese crosswise into ¼-inch-thick slices. Add the goat cheese slices to the warm skillet and heat just until warm. Using a spatula, place 2 or 3 slices of goat cheese on top of each salad and serve immediately.

SERVES 4

BALSAMIC VINAIGRETTE

1 teaspoon brown sugar
½ cup balsamic vinegar
2 tablespoons garlic oil or extra-virgin olive oil mixed with 1 finely chopped small garlic clove

½ teaspoon Dijon mustard
¼ cup walnut oil
⅔ cup extra-virgin olive oil

In a small bowl, whisk the brown sugar with the vinegar to dissolve. Whisk in the garlic, mustard, and walnut and olive oils until emulsified. Store, tightly covered, for up to 1 week in the refrigerator.

MAKES 1½ CUPS

Balsamic Vinegar

Balsamic vinegar is relatively new to most American kitchens. It is made from white Trebbiano grape juice that is aged in wooden barrels, and its distinctive sweet and somewhat fruity flavor sweetens and mellows with time—those aged for twenty or more years are even served as a *digestif* in Italy! It is used most commonly in salad dressings, sauces, and marinades for chicken and fish. It also seems to do something magical to fruit: strawberries drizzled with this vinegar taste all the more sweet and delicious.

Real balsamic vinegar comes only from the Modena region of Italy and must be aged in wooden barrels for a minimum of four years. The price of a bottle can range from quite affordable to exhorbitant, depending on age and quality.

ROAST LOIN OF PORK WITH DRIED CHERRIES, MUSHROOMS, AND ROASTED POTATOES WITH CARROTS AND BROCCOLI

Noel dresses up pork with sweet-tart cherries, woodsy shiitake mushrooms, and a port wine sauce. Simple vegetables such as broccoli, carrots, and potatoes are all you need to serve alongside.

1½ pounds boneless pork loin, trimmed

Salt and freshly ground pepper to taste

¼ cup extra-virgin olive oil

8 new potatoes, scrubbed and cut or left whole as desired (depending on size)

1 celery stalk, chopped

2 carrots, peeled and chopped

1 leek, washed well and chopped, dark green part discarded

1 onion, chopped

2 garlic cloves

½ cup port wine

1¼ cups beef or veal stock

¼ cup (½ stick) unsalted butter

½ cup cleaned and sliced domestic button mushrooms

¼ cup cleaned and sliced shiitake mushrooms

1 tablespoon dried cherries

Carrots and Broccoli (recipe follows)

Preheat the oven to 375°F. Season the pork loin with salt and pepper. In an ovenproof skillet large enough to hold the pork loin, heat the olive oil over high heat. Add the pork and the potatoes. Cook until the meat and potatoes are browned on all sides, turning to brown evenly, 3 to 5 minutes. Remove the pork and potatoes to a platter and add the celery, carrots, leek, onion, and garlic to the skillet. Put the pork and potatoes on top of the vegetable mixture, and place in the oven for about 1 hour, basting and turning the pork every 15 minutes or so until the center reaches 150° F. and the pork is opaque throughout; do not overcook. Remove the meat and potatoes from the skillet to a large serving platter, and cover loosely with foil. Set aside while you make the sauce.

Add the wine to the skillet, scraping up any browned bits from the bottom, and simmer over medium-high heat until it has reduced by half, about 4 minutes. Add the stock and simmer for another 10 minutes.

In another large skillet over medium heat, melt the butter. Add the mushrooms and dried cherries and sauté until the mushrooms are limp, 2 to 3 minutes. Then strain the wine sauce through a fine sieve into the skillet with the mushrooms. Adjust the seasoning with salt and pepper.

Just before serving, cut the pork loin into ¼-inch-thick slices. To serve, fan a few slices of pork at the bottom of each of 4 plates. Arrange equal portions of potatoes at the top of each plate, then put carrots on one side and broccoli on the other. Ladle the sauce over the meat.

SERVES 4

Goat Cheese

Goat cheese, called *chèvre* in French, is a pure white, tangy cheese made from goat's milk. Different brands vary in texture and degree of sharpness, and shapes range from logs and discs to buttons and pyramids. The most common and best-known goat cheeses are French: Montrachet, Banon, Bucheron. However, American-made varieties are becoming much more common and are being produced from coast to coast. Among the brands are Laura Chenel from Sonoma Valley, which Noel likes, and Coach Farms from upstate New York.

The types of chèvre seem infinite; they can be coated or wrapped with herbs, spices, peppercorns, leaves, or ash, and the flavor and consistency vary with age, content, and method of preparation. Texture can be soft and creamy or dry and somewhat hard and crumbly. Experiment with different kinds for different purposes and find your own favorites.

Purists beware: some cheeses may be labeled "goat cheese" but actually contain some cow's milk. Look for *pur chèvre* on the label of French brands and check the ingredients list on American varieties.

CARROTS AND BROCCOLI

½ pound carrots, peeled and sliced
1 head broccoli, quartered, stem
  trimmed

¼ cup (½ stick) unsalted butter
Salt and white pepper to taste

Bring 2 large pots of water to a boil over medium-high heat and set aside 2 large bowls of ice water. Plunge the carrots and broccoli into separate pots of boiling water. Cook the carrots for about 5 minutes and the broccoli for about 2 minutes, until crisp-tender. Drain and immediately transfer the vegetables to separate bowls of ice water to stop the cooking. When the vegetables are cool, drain and pat dry.

Melt half the butter in a large skillet over medium-high heat. Add the carrots and sauté until tender, 1 to 2 minutes. Remove the carrots and add the rest of the butter to the skillet. When the butter is melted, add the broccoli and sauté until tender, 1 to 2 minutes. Season both vegetables with salt and white pepper and transfer to a plate.

SERVES 4

CAPPUCCINO SOUFFLÉS

Soufflés have a reputation for being temperamental, but success is assured if you follow this recipe precisely, measuring accurately and substituting nothing. Noel fills the centers of these coffee and chocolate soufflés with a warm mocha sauce—for a "sublime dessert experience," as Tammy will tell you.

¼ cup (½ stick) unsalted butter, softened
½ cup plus 2 tablespoons all-purpose
  flour
2 cups milk
2 tablespoons instant espresso granules
  (instant coffee cannot be substituted)
4 tablespoons sweetened good-quality
  cocoa, such as Ghirardelli Sweet
  Ground Chocolate
1 tablespoon brown sugar

6 large egg whites, at room
  temperature
1 teaspoon granulated sugar
SAUCE
2 cups heavy cream
2 tablespoons brown sugar
1 tablespoon instant espresso granules
2 tablespoons sweetened good-quality
  cocoa, such as Ghirardelli Sweet
  Ground Chocolate
Confectioners' sugar, for dusting

Generously butter four 4-ounce soufflé cups, then coat them with granulated sugar and set aside in the refrigerator. In a small bowl, stir the butter and flour together to make a roux. In a medium saucepan, bring the milk to a boil over medium-high heat. Reduce the heat to medium and stir in the espresso, cocoa, and brown sugar. Simmer for 2 to 3 minutes. Gradually add the roux, whisking constantly for 1 to 2 minutes, just until the mixture has thickened slightly. Remove from the heat and set aside to cool. (The base can be prepared up to 1 day in advance if kept refrigerated and brought to room temperature before proceeding with the recipe.)

Preheat the oven to 375° F. Just before serving, in a mixing bowl beat the egg whites with the granulated sugar to stiff peaks; quickly, but gently, fold them into the soufflé base just until incorporated. Pour equal amounts of the mixture into the prepared soufflé molds, filling to just below the rim and making sure they are level (see box, below). Place the molds on a baking sheet in the oven. Bake for 15 minutes. The soufflés should rise 1 to 2 inches above the rims of the dishes, and will be light brown on top.

While the soufflés are baking, prepare the sauce. Combine the cream, brown sugar, espresso, and cocoa in a medium saucepan over medium heat. Simmer gently for 3 minutes, stirring occasionally, then raise the heat to medium-high and bring to a boil just before serving.

Remove the soufflés from the oven and dust the tops with the confectioners' sugar. Make a hole about the size of a quarter in the center of each soufflé. Pour about 2 tablespoons of the warm sauce into each hole and serve immediately.

SERVES *4*

Successful Soufflés

For a picture-perfect soufflé—one that rises high and straight up above the rim—follow these tips from the chef:

1. Make sure the sides and rim of the ramekin are well buttered.

2. Wipe off any bits of mixture that may fall on the inside edges of the dish.

3. After filling the ramekin with the soufflé mixture, tap the dish lightly three times to level out the mixture before putting it in the oven. Old-fashioned French chefs might gasp at this suggestion because the aerated mixture is so delicate, but Noel assures us that the result will be a perfectly even soufflé.

ROBERTO DONNA

Bollito Misto from Piedmont

Born and raised in the Piedmont region of Italy, Roberto Donna has been working in restaurants since he was nine years old, starting in a little *trattoria* situated next door to his parents' grocery store near the town of Torino. When he was thirteen, he attended cooking school; and by the time he was seventeen, the finest restaurant in Torino hired him as executive chef. For the next several years, Roberto traveled and honed his skills in kitchens across England, France, and Switzerland.

In 1980, at age nineteen, Roberto arrived in Washington, D.C., and took his first job at the prestigious Romeo and Juliet restaurant. In 1984, he was ready to create his own vision, and he opened his first restaurant, Galileo, located in downtown Washington, where he showcased his innovative and highly acclaimed Italian cuisine. In 1989, Roberto opened I Matti Trattoria in the lively ethnic neighborhood of Adams Morgan. His most recent ventures include Il Pesce and his new gourmet pizzeria, Il Radicchio. He is regarded as one of the most popular and energetic culinary personalities to ever hit Washington, D.C.

With so many diverse and bustling restaurants in Washington, D.C., it is hard to imagine Roberto having the time or the inclination to cook at home.

MENU

Bagna Cauda with Roasted Red Peppers

*Bollito Misto with Salsa Verde
and Agliata*

Panna Cotta with Grappa

But on his day off, his love for cooking and entertaining inspires him to prepare a hearty and robust meal; in this case, a winter spread for friends. "I love to eat as much as I love to cook, so Sunday I stay at home and have friends over. It is a time for fun, relaxation, and, of course, good food and wine."

To start the feast, Roberto prepares Bagna Cauda, a warm garlic and anchovy paste. "I just think of the aroma of the wonderful pepper, anchovy, and garlic paste that fills the house. We serve it with polenta, homemade breads, and vegetables for dipping—there is nothing like it." The main course, Bollito Misto, is a grand meal served buffet style with an abundance of extravagant meats, such as veal, beef, and lamb. This is accompanied by a variety of lightly cooked fresh vegetables, the thick flavorful Salsa Verde, and the garlicky Agliata sauce.

"Dessert is always a traditional part of the feast, and my favorite of all Italian desserts is the Panna Cotta. This custard-like treat is enhanced with a little grappa flavoring, and it always reminds me to offer my guests a glass of grappa after our great feast." In addition to the grappa, meals with his friends must always include good wine. "Winter days like these are perfect times for rich wines, straight from the cellar." Roberto recommends Barbera and Barbarescos, both red wines from the Piedmont region. "This menu is certainly one reason I enjoy the long, cold winter months!"

Bagna Cauda

Bagna Cauda (BAHN-yah COW-dah), a Piedmont specialty, is a warm garlic and anchovy dipping sauce. The anchovies and thinly sliced garlic are "melted" and served in a terra-cotta pot with a flame underneath to keep it warm. In Piedmont, Bagna Cauda is served with a variety of vegetables, such as roasted red peppers, roasted onions, steamed artichokes, and white truffles, that are dipped into the mixture with a fork. You can also spread the Bagna Cauda on homemade bread or even on baked or grilled polenta (see Lidia Bastianich's recipe on page 38).

BAGNA CAUDA WITH ROASTED RED PEPPERS

The wonderful aroma will draw everyone to the table, and the flavor and fun of eating from a communal dish will keep them gathered around the pot. You can serve any vegetables you like for dipping (see box, opposite). You'll need a terra-cotta pot with a heat source or a fondue set to prepare and serve the Bagna Cauda.

Roberto likes the salt-packed anchovies because "they taste more of the sea." You can find them at specialty food shops or Italian markets. This dish can be prepared with anchovies packed in oil if that's what's available.

½ cup extra-virgin olive oil
¼ cup (½ stick) butter
4 garlic cloves, very thinly sliced
7 ounces anchovies preserved in salt,
   cleaned and bones removed

6 roasted peppers (see box, page 186),
   a mixture of red, green, and yellow,
   sliced into strips
1 loaf crusty bread, sliced

Heat the olive oil and butter in a 2-quart terra-cotta or fondue pot over low heat. Add the garlic and anchovies and cook until the anchovies "melt" into a paste, about 10 minutes. Bring the pot to the table with the roasted peppers and slices of bread on the side. Keep the pot over a very small flame, such as a Sterno, in order to keep the Bagna Cauda hot while it is being enjoyed. Serve with long fondue-type forks for dipping.

SERVES 8

Anchovies

The only "true" anchovies come from southern Europe and the Mediterranean, although other countries use this name to describe the tiny fish of their region. These fish are most often sold filleted, packed in salt or salt-cured, and then canned in oil. The salt-packed tastes far better than the canned, and the meatiest ones are best. They must be rinsed well under cold water. If they haven't been filleted, scrape the skin off with a knife, then open the fish lengthwise, pry the spine off, and separate the anchovy into two boneless halves. Both canned anchovies and those packed in salt have an indefinite shelf life.

Anchovies have a wonderfully intense flavor. Most people who say they don't like them usually mean they don't go for the salty slabs lying across Caesar salads. When used well, their rich flavor can contribute indispensably to the complex flavor of many savory dishes.

BOLLITO MISTO WITH SALSA VERDE AND AGLIATA

Bollito Misto (see Note) is a traditional Italian family-style meal consisting of boiled veal, beef, lamb, pork, and vegetables. It is served with the Italian Salsa Verde, a thick, savory green sauce, and Agliata, a creamy garlic and basil sauce. Both sauces are used sparingly, as condiments.

1 calf's foot

2 pounds lean beef plate or short ribs

4 pounds boneless bottom round beef

1 pound beef shank

1½ pounds lamb shoulder

1 pound veal breast

½ pound lean pork belly or slab of bacon

1 onion

1 garlic clove

2 carrots, peeled and sliced

2 turnips, peeled and sliced

2 tomatoes, peeled (see box, page 311), seeded, and chopped

Bouquet garni consisting of 2 sprigs fresh thyme, 2 sprigs parsley, 1 bay leaf (see box, page 266)

Salt and freshly ground pepper to taste

VEGETABLE GARNISH

1 pound new potatoes, scrubbed

12 white onions

2 quarts chicken stock

1 pound 6 different vegetables in season, such as cabbage, peas, zucchini, turnips, cauliflower, cut into bite-size pieces as necessary

Salsa Verde (recipe follows)

Agliata (recipe follows)

In a medium pot, place the calf's foot and add just enough cold, salted water to cover. Bring to a gentle boil over medium heat, then reduce the heat to medium-low and maintain a low simmer for 40 minutes. Drain. Place the beef, lamb shoulder, veal breast, and calf's foot in a very large stockpot and cover with cold water. In a medium pot, cover the pork belly with cold water. Slowly bring both pots to a boil over medium-high heat. Occasionally skim the scum off the surfaces while meats are cooking. When the beef mixture has reached a boil, add the onion, garlic, carrots, turnips, tomatoes, and bouquet garni and season with salt and pepper. Reduce the heat to medium-low and simmer for about 3 hours, removing the individual cuts of meat as they become tender. The veal and the lamb will take about 1½ to 2 hours; the calf's foot will take about 2 hours; the beef will be fully cooked after about 3 hours. The pork belly should cook for 2 hours or until tender. Transfer the cooked meats to a deep bowl and cover with foil to keep warm. Strain and reserve the cooking broth from the big pot. Remove the pork belly and discard the broth.

About 1 hour before serving time, begin to prepare the vegetable garnish. Place the potatoes and onions in 2 separate saucepans with water to cover over medium-high heat and boil until tender, 25 minutes for the potatoes and 20 minutes for the onions. Drain, set aside, and keep warm. Meanwhile, in another large stockpot, bring the chicken stock to a low simmer over low heat. Add the vegetables for garnish in order of cooking times so that they are all cooked to the point of tenderness at the same time. Drain, discarding the stock.

To serve, arrange the meats on a large platter or in a shallow bowl and pour in some of the reserved meat broth. On a separate platter, arrange the vegetable garnish and the potatoes and onions. Pass the Salsa Verde and Agliata in separate bowls.

SERVES 8 TO 10

NOTE: Bollito Misto is a favorite meal in Piedmont, not only for its wonderful flavors but because it is always a feast to be served with good company. Unfortunately, in the United States the variety meats are not as widely available or as affordable as in Italy. Veal breast is very expensive and beef shank, calf's foot, and pork belly will probably be found only at a good butcher shop.

Most Americans are not accustomed to eating such cuts of meat as beef shank, calf's foot, and pork belly, but Roberto assures us "they add so much flavor to this dish you'll be missing out if you omit them." You may make adjustments to accommodate your budget and taste; of course, it won't be the *real* thing. Roberto says chicken makes a fine substitute for the pork belly, although the flavor is altogether different. For this recipe, use 1 small (4-pound) chicken, quartered. Place it in a saucepan or stockpot with enough cold, salted water to cover along with 1 onion, 1 carrot, 1 celery stalk, all sliced thickly, and 1 bay leaf; cook at a low simmer for 1 hour and 20 minutes, or until the meat is opaque throughout and the juices run clear. Remove the chicken and discard the broth and vegetables.

Digesting Garlic

Some people, Italians and non-Italians alike, have a hard time digesting garlic when it is eaten in heavy doses, as in the Bagna Cauda. To avoid this, Roberto lets us in on an Italian secret: cook the garlic in milk before adding it to the recipe.

To do so, place the peeled garlic in a saucepan and cover it with milk. Cook slowly over low heat until the milk is completely reduced and the garlic becomes a paste. Add this paste to the oil and anchovies and proceed with the recipe.

SALSA VERDE

The parsley provides the color, hence the name Salsa Verde, or Green Sauce. This piquant sauce should have a thick, but not dense or runny, consistency.

1 1-ounce piece white bread, crust
    removed

½ cup red wine vinegar

4 tablespoons chopped fresh parsley

2 anchovies preserved in salt, well
    rinsed and finely chopped

1 garlic clove, minced

1 hard-boiled egg, finely chopped

1 teaspoon drained capers

2½ cups extra-virgin olive oil

Salt and freshly ground pepper to taste

Soak the bread in the vinegar until all the liquid is absorbed and squeeze dry. Discard the excess liquid. Combine the parsley, anchovies, garlic, egg, and capers in a blender or food processor until finely chopped. Add the bread and blend until well combined. Pour in the olive oil and blend until very smooth. Adjust the seasoning with salt and pepper.

MAKES ABOUT 3 CUPS

AGLIATA

Try serving this with other meat dishes as well, especially beef.

1 small (2-ounce) bread roll, crust
    removed

6 tablespoons white wine vinegar

4 garlic cloves, chopped

4 fresh basil leaves

6 tablespoons chopped fresh Italian
    parsley

1½ cups extra-virgin olive oil, prefer-
    ably Ligurian

Salt and freshly ground pepper to taste

Soak the bread in the vinegar until it absorbs all of the liquid. Then squeeze the bread dry and discard the residual liquid. Place the bread, garlic, basil, parsley, and olive oil in a blender and process until the mixture becomes creamy. Adjust the seasoning with salt and pepper. Refrigerate until ready to use, for up to 1 day. Serve in a small bowl and pass at the table.

MAKES 2½ CUPS

Panna Cotta with Grappa

This eggless custard is a specialty of the Piedmont region of Italy. The rich, silky cream, spiked with grappa, (an Italian eau-de-vie or colorless brandy), or espresso, if you prefer, is set in a mold lined with caramel. When unmolded the caramel drizzles down the sides of the free-standing custard, forming a pool of syrup. Keep a watchful eye on the stove when cooking the sugar and water mixture as caramel burns easily. Immediately remove the pot from the stove when the caramel turns golden as it will continue to cook in the hot pan.

6 tablespoons granulated sugar

¼ cup water

1 cup milk

3 cups heavy cream

1½ cups confectioners' sugar

2 scant tablespoons unflavored gelatin

1½ ounces (3 tablespoons) grappa or 6 tablespoons espresso

Fresh berries, for garnish

Have handy a 4 × 8-inch loaf pan. In a small saucepan over low heat, combine the granulated sugar with the water. Cook, stirring occasionally, just until the sugar turns to a golden brown syrup, about 15 minutes; do not let the mixture turn dark brown. Remove from the heat and immediately pour the caramel into the loaf pan. Set aside to harden for approximately 10 minutes.

In a medium saucepan, combine ½ cup of the milk, the cream, and the confectioners' sugar. Bring to a boil over medium-low heat. Meanwhile, in a small bowl, stir the remaining ½ cup milk with the gelatin and set aside for 3 minutes, until the gelatin is completely dissolved. Remove the boiled milk mixture from the heat and gently stir in the gelatin and milk mixture, then add the grappa or espresso.

Pour the custard into the mold and refrigerate for at least 2 hours or until the mixture is very firm. Just before serving, invert the mold and cut the loaf into eight 1-inch slices. Arrange a slice on each plate, spoon any caramel sauce remaining in the mold on top of the slices, and garnish with fresh berries.

Serves 8

TOM DOUGLAS

Tom's Favorite Birthday Lunch

Tom Douglas feels lucky to live in the Pacific Northwest, which has an abundance of high-quality food products, especially fish. While growing up in Wilmington, Delaware, Tom always thought fish was something that came in a can. He left his hometown for Seattle in the mid-1970s, after dabbling in various occupations and discovering what fresh foods are all about, Tom was determined to be a chef and take advantage of the incredible ingredients that were now at his fingertips. It was a time when the city's restaurants were just beginning to wake up to the lure of local food products. Tom wanted to absorb it all, and he did so by tasting every bit of it. "I didn't bring anything with me to Seattle," says Tom, "only my appetite."

It wasn't enough just to taste; he wanted to know how every dish was made and what its components were. Tom then took the ingredients that he liked best and combined them in different ways to create new flavors and dishes. He exposed his friends to his ever-increasing repertoire of food in his home, until he brought his skill to Café Sport in 1984. There, Tom was able to help define the Northwest style, or Pacific Rim cuisine, as it is sometimes called, by drawing on the foods of Asia, Alaska, California, and Canada.

In 1989, Tom opened his own restaurant in downtown Seattle and called it Dahlia Lounge, marking it with a neon

MENU

Thai Basil and Lime Kamikaze

—

Tom's Tasty Tuna Salad with Scallion Pancakes and Fresh Cucumber Pickles

—

Spiced Angel Food Cake with Orange Crème Anglaise

sign above the front door featuring a fat chef holding a wiggling fish by the tail. The comfortable restaurant conveys the easy-going, friendly style of its chef-owner, who is most likely found in his trademark T-shirt, shorts, apron, and athletic shoes, instead of the typical chef whites.

Tom loves exploring his local markets. "At the market you can constantly discover new foods and flavors; it's a valuable experience." Along with his wife, Jackie, and their daughter, Loretta, Tom spends his day off scouting the market, picking out the freshest ingredients for the afternoon or evening menu. On workdays he just turns to the refrigerator and makes a meal from the ingredients on hand.

The creation of the meal includes the entire family. Although Loretta is not old enough to assist in the preparation, Tom and Jackie take turns playing with her while the other prepares some of the meal. "Jackie is the 'vegematic.' She loves to do the prep work before I cook. She takes the first half-hour while I play with Loretta, and when it's my turn, I arrive in the kitchen to find little bowls with perfectly chopped ingredients," says Tom. At home, their goal is to get everything prepared and served in an hour.

This menu is a special lunch that he enjoys each year on his birthday. "It's all my favorite things to eat," says Tom. "I like foods that are easy to throw together, and I don't like being in the kitchen for too long on my days off." For his Tasty Tuna Salad, Tom uses only the highest grade of tuna, which he defines as "the star of the show." Everything else is an accessory, highlighting the freshness of the fish.

Becoming a professional chef with no formal training came naturally to Tom. "Eating out in restaurants is my hobby, my love," he says. "I learn more at the table, eating and tasting the food, than studying it in books and classes." It is the discovery, the experimentation, with the end result always a new creation, that is so rewarding for Tom. But also important to him is following good taste, not the latest trends. "When I like what I taste, I bring it home and put it

on a plate." With the simple principles of good cooking as his base, Tom has always been willing to try anything.

THAI BASIL AND LIME KAMIKAZE

This pairs especially well with Asian food, such as Tom's Tasty Tuna Salad with its nuances of sake and soy sauce.

Ice cubes

4½ ounces vodka

5–6 ounces Triple Sec, or other
orange-flavored liqueur, to taste

2 limes, cut into small wedges

4 sprigs Thai basil (available at Asian
produce markets; see box, below)
or Italian basil

Pack a large (16-ounce) glass with ice. Add the vodka, Triple Sec, and lime wedges. Using a mortar, bar stick, or long teaspoon, crush the mixture in the glass until the lime breaks up, to extract the oils and juice from the limes and chill the liquid. Strain through a fine sieve and pour an equal amount in each of 4 martini glasses. Serve straight up (without ice), with a sprig of Thai basil.

SERVES 4

Thai Basil

There are 140 kinds of basil. In the United States, the most common variety of this herb is Italian basil, which has bright green leaves and a pungent scent and flavor.

Thai basil, also known as red basil because of its red stems, is not to be confused with Holy basil, which is also from Thailand. Thai basil has smaller leaves and a milder flavor and aroma than the Italian variety, which has stronger flavors of anise and cloves, explains Tom. It pairs nicely with lime or in combination with mint and cilantro, which, according to Tom, "creates a fresh-tasting flavor that explodes in your mouth." Tom also recommends using Thai basil to garnish soups.

Thai basil is best served on the side, so people can spice up their drink or dish to suit their own tastes.

TOM'S TASTY TUNA SALAD WITH SCALLION PANCAKES AND FRESH CUCUMBER PICKLES

Nothing like the flaky, deli-variety tuna salad, this is fresh, raw tuna turned into salad with a Japanese twist. Buy the freshest tuna from a trusted seafood merchant. Because sushi-grade fish is expensive, Tom prepares small portions, making just the right amount for a lunch entrée or appetizer.

Rice vinegar has a lighter, sweeter, fruitier taste than regular vinegar. You'll find it in Asian markets and many supermarkets.

1 pound cleaned and boned sushi-grade tuna, cut into ¼-inch cubes

⅓ cup chopped scallions

1 heaping cup fresh bean sprouts

⅓ cup loosely packed fresh cilantro

½ cup or more Sake Sauce (recipe follows), chilled

1½ tablespoons peanut oil

1 teaspoon Oriental sesame oil (see box, below)

Scallion Pancakes (recipe follows)

Lime wedges, for garnish

Radishes, for garnish

Fresh Cucumber Pickles (recipe follows)

Place the sliced tuna cubes in a bowl with the scallions, bean sprouts, and cilantro. Add enough Sake Sauce to coat everything well. Toss gently. Drizzle with the peanut and sesame oils and toss gently again.

To serve, place equal amounts of tuna salad on each of 4 plates and garnish with one Scallion Pancake, lime wedges, radishes, and Cucumber Pickles.

SERVES 4

Sesame Oil

There are two kinds of sesame oil. Regular sesame oil is light in color, cold pressed, and well suited for stir-frying with its high burning point of 440°F. The darker Oriental sesame oil is more strongly flavored, so this nutty-tasting extract from sesame seeds is used in salad dressings and in meat and poultry marinades. Oriental sesame oil is available in Asian markets, health and specialty food stores, and some supermarkets. It goes wonderfully with flavors such as scallions, ginger, and garlic.

SAKE SAUCE

The sauce must be chilled before dressing the tuna, so plan ahead. It can be stored, tightly sealed, in the refrigerator for up to one week.

½ cup sake (Japanese rice wine; available at Asian markets)

¼ cup soy sauce

¼ cup rice vinegar

¼ teaspoon chopped garlic

1 serrano chili pepper, seeded and chopped (see box, page 176)

½ teaspoon chopped fresh ginger

1 tablespoon sugar

Combine the sake, soy sauce, rice vinegar, garlic, chili pepper, ginger, and sugar in a small saucepan over medium-low heat and cook, stirring, until the sugar dissolves. Remove from the heat and allow to cool slightly at room temperature before refrigerating. Store, covered, in the refrigerator until well chilled.

MAKES APPROXIMATELY 1 CUP

SCALLION PANCAKES

This is a much simplified version of a traditional Asian dish.

2 teaspoons sesame seeds

1 large egg

2 teaspoons Oriental sesame oil (see box, opposite)

4 8-inch flour tortillas

2 scallions, finely chopped

2 tablespoons vegetable oil, or more as needed

In a small skillet over medium heat, toast the sesame seeds until golden, shaking the pan often. It should take less than 5 minutes; watch that they don't burn. Transfer the seeds to a small bowl or plate and set aside.

In a small bowl, lightly beat the egg with the sesame oil. Brush one side of each tortilla with the egg mixture to coat lightly (you will not use all the egg wash). Sprinkle each tortilla with the scallions and sesame seeds. Fold the tortillas in half, pressing down to seal.

Heat the vegetable oil in a 10-inch skillet over medium heat. Add 2 pancakes at a time and cook until lightly browned on both sides, about 2 minutes on each side, using more oil as needed. Transfer the pancakes to a plate and cover to keep warm until ready to serve.

SERVES 4

FRESH CUCUMBER PICKLES

Here's Tom's quick method for pickling cucumbers. They are tangy and crunchy, and make a wonderful textural contrast to the tuna.

Tom prefers to use English cucumbers because they are firmer and hold up better when sliced. Also, their seeds are smaller and there are far fewer of them. A regular cucumber may be used, but it must be peeled and seeded.

1 English cucumber, very thinly sliced, or 2 regular cucumbers, peeled, seeded, and thinly sliced

1 cup rice vinegar
¼ cup sugar
¼ teaspoon hot red pepper flakes

Place the sliced cucumber in a bowl and set aside. Combine the vinegar, sugar, and red pepper flakes in a small saucepan over medium-high heat and bring to a boil. Pour the boiling liquid over the cucumber slices, toss, and set aside for at least 30 minutes. Cover and refrigerate until well chilled. Drain the mixture just before serving.

SERVES 4

SPICED ANGEL FOOD CAKE WITH ORANGE CRÈME ANGLAISE

Unlike most birthday cakes, Tom's is neither complicated nor rich. Its simplicity allows you to enjoy the spices and textures of the spongy cake, moistened with the rich and zesty Cointreau-flavored custard sauce. Chinese five-spice powder is the secret ingredient here. It's a pungent combination of ground spices, usually consisting of cinnamon, cloves, fennel seed, star anise, and Szechuan peppercorns. This premixed seasoning is available at Oriental markets and in many supermarkets.

1 cup cake flour
¼ teaspoon salt
1 teaspoon Chinese five-spice powder
1¼ cups sugar
10 large egg whites, at room temperature

1 teaspoon cream of tartar
½ teaspoon vanilla extract
1 teaspoon almond extract
Orange Crème Anglaise to serve (recipe follows)

Preheat the oven to 350° F. In a small bowl, sift together the flour, salt, and five-spice powder twice. In another small bowl, sift the sugar. In a large bowl, with an electric mixer, beat the egg whites and cream of tartar until soft peaks form. Gradually add the sugar, vanilla extract, and almond extract, until the peaks are firm but not dry; be careful not to overbeat, as the whites will separate. Add the flour mixture and, using a rubber spatula, fold it into the egg whites until thoroughly blended. Pour the batter into an ungreased 10-inch tube pan and place on the middle oven rack. Bake for 45 minutes, or until a toothpick inserted in the middle of the cake comes out clean. Immediately invert the pan onto a cake rack or the neck of a wine bottle and let it cool and stretch in the pan. When completely cool, invert again and gently run a knife around the edge of the pan to loosen the cake. Turn the cake over onto a serving plate. Use a serrated knife to slice the cake and serve each slice in a pool of Orange Crème Anglaise.

MAKES ONE 10-INCH CAKE

ORANGE CRÈME ANGLAISE

This cream sauce is simple to make, in theory. However, it is often ruined by experienced and novice cooks alike. The key to a successful crème anglaise is gentle heat and a watchful eye to avoid boiling the milk and egg mixture. Boiling will cook the eggs and leave you with a lumpy rather than smooth cream sauce. Cooks with gas stoves will have a better chance at success as they can control the heat.

2 cups heavy cream
½ cup sugar
Zest from 1 orange

6 large egg yolks
1 tablespoon Cointreau, or more to taste

To make the crème anglaise, heat the cream, sugar, and orange zest in a medium saucepan over medium-high heat, stirring occasionally, until it almost comes to a boil. Remove the scalded liquid from the heat and set aside for 30 minutes to steep.

In a medium bowl, whisk the egg yolks. Return the cream mixture to just below a boil. Temper the eggs by pouring a small amount of the scalded cream mixture into the yolks, whisking constantly. Then add the yolk mixture to the saucepan with the remaining cream. Stir over medium heat until the mixture is thick enough to coat the back of a spoon, about 5 minutes; make sure the mixture does not come to a boil. Strain the crème anglaise through a fine sieve into a clean bowl, cover, and chill in the refrigerator. When cold, stir in the Cointreau. (The crème anglaise can be made up to 2 days in advance, and stored covered in the refrigerator.)

MAKES 2½ CUPS

TODD ENGLISH

The Best of Summer

When Todd English and his wife, Olivia, decide to have a meal at home, it is most often a last-minute decision, and consequently the meal he prepares is simple, yet always flavorful and fun. "Isabelle, our baby girl, usually sits in her high chair in the middle of the kitchen and Oliver, our young son, is adventurous and likes to help stir things—usually this means that much of what he is stirring leaves the bowl and ends up on the counter or floor. If it makes it to the floor, one of our two dogs gets in on the project."

At the age of fifteen, Todd entered L'Aubergine, a French restaurant in Atlanta, where he started off washing dishes and moved on to the prep station. He enrolled in the Culinary Institute of America, which he says was a "natural path to take," in 1981 and graduated with honors. It was in Italy, apprenticing at fine restaurants, that Todd developed his individual cooking style. "When I got to Italy, everything I learned confirmed my notion that this was the approach I needed to take. I aim for abundance and full flavors while respecting all of the ingredients." In 1986, when he was just twenty-five years old, he returned to the United States and opened the award-winning Northern Italian restaurant Michela's, in Boston,

MENU

Parmesan Pudding with Sweet Pea Sauce

*Char-Grilled Tuna and Avocado Salad
with Toasted Corn Vinaigrette*

*Honey and Brown Sugar Fig Sundae
with Crumbled Amaretto Cookies
and Vanilla Ice Cream*

where he cooked exciting, innovative fare for three years. He is currently the chef-owner of Olives, a Mediterranean-inspired bistro, and Figs, a pizzeria serving a local crowd not-so-traditional pizzas and pastas, both located just outside of Boston in Charlestown, Massachusetts.

Cooking in a restaurant kitchen certainly has its advantages, says Todd, admitting "the equipment, availability of prepared items, and a brigade of cooks make a big difference in efficiency." But this doesn't prevent him from whipping up a great meal at home, where "everyone gets involved and we make a big mess." In the winter, Todd lights the fire in his kitchen hearth

and cooks hearty, stick-to-your-ribs food. In the warmer weather, he enjoys taking road trips to local farmstands to find New England produce at its best, and inviting friends over to grill in the backyard, as he does for this meal.

"I like this menu so much because it combines tradition with my own ideas, and emphasizes simplicity with attention to freshness and wonderful ingredients." Fresh peas are chosen for the sauce for the Parmesan Pudding, which is quite rich but gives the illusion of lightness. Seasonal vegetables are selected to accompany the tuna and the high-piled greens, and the creamy avocado, sweet, yellow corn, and acidic tomato provide balance to the color and flavor of the ruby-red fish. Todd suggests a tart Italian wine, such as Pinot Bianco or a Pinot Grigio, to accompany the meal.

For Todd, cooking at home means playing with flavors and measurements. "I find myself experimenting with ingredients that I am intrigued by but that haven't yet found their niche at Olives or Figs." For dessert, Todd prepares a Honey and Brown Sugar Fig Sundae with Crumbled Amaretto Cookies and Vanilla Ice Cream. This combination of hot and cold components, smooth and crunchy textures, promises to satisfy any and all sweet cravings.

"Food tastes the best to me when cooked in the relaxed comfort of home," says Todd, "whether it is homemade *kimchee,* a stuffed pork loin, or a burned pancake that my three-year-old helped me make."

Parmesan Pudding with Sweet Pea Sauce

This pudding is actually more like a creamy custard, bound with eggs, milk, and cream, and is delight-fully undietetic. Plan ahead for this first course; it needs to be refrigerated for several hours or overnight.

1 tablespoon unsalted butter

¼ cup all-purpose flour

½ cup milk

1 cup heavy cream

1 large egg

5 large egg yolks

1 cup freshly grated Parmesan cheese

1 cup light cream

Pinch of freshly grated nutmeg

½ teaspoon salt

¼ teaspoon white pepper

SWEET PEA SAUCE

2 cups freshly shelled or frozen sweet
   peas, thawed

1 cup chicken stock

1½ cups heavy cream

Salt and freshly ground pepper to taste

Freshly shelled peas, for garnish
   (optional)

Preheat the oven to 250°F. In a large, straight-sided saucepan over low heat, make a roux: Melt the butter; then, using a whisk, slowly stir in the flour so that no lumps form. Cook the roux (see box, page 89) for approximately 10 minutes, whisking frequently. The color of the roux should not change.

While the roux is cooking, heat the milk and cream in a medium saucepan over medium-high heat until just before boiling. Slowly whisk the scalded mixture into the roux and cook, whisking constantly, for another 4 to 5 minutes over medium-low heat. Again, the color should not change. Whisk in the egg, egg yolks, and cheese and continue whisking so no lumps form. One at a time, whisk in the light cream, nutmeg, salt, and white pepper.

Grease an 8½ × 4½-inch pan or another 6-cup oven-safe mold with butter, then cut parchment paper to line the bottom and sides of the pan. Pour the mixture into the pan and place in a larger pan filled with enough hot water to reach halfway up the side of the pan. Bake the pudding in the water bath for 2 hours. Remove the pudding from the oven and let the mold cool on a wire rack for 1 hour. Refrigerate, covered with plastic wrap, for at least 6 hours.

In the meantime, make the sauce. If using fresh peas, bring a medium pot of water to a boil over high heat and set aside a bowl of ice water. Add the peas to the boiling water and cook for 1 minute. Drain and immediately transfer the peas to the ice water to stop the cooking process. Drain the peas. In a blender, place the blanched fresh or thawed peas, the chicken stock, cream, and salt and pepper and purée until smooth. Refrigerate, covered, until ready to serve.

To serve, preheat the oven to 250°F. Unmold the pudding onto a platter and remove the parchment paper. Cut the pudding into ½-inch-thick slices and place 2 overlapping slices in the center of each of 6 small plates. Put the plates in the oven for 10 to 12 minutes, until the pudding is warm to the touch. While the pudding is heating, heat the sauce in a small saucepan over medium heat until it is hot, stirring occasionally. Pour the sauce around each portion and garnish with fresh peas, if desired.

Serves 6

CHAR-GRILLED TUNA AND AVOCADO SALAD WITH TOASTED CORN VINAIGRETTE

Todd recommends using the freshest ruby-red tuna available. Most fishmongers refer to this as sushi-grade or number-one tuna. This may cost a bit more, but the flavor and quality are crucial to this dish, in which the tuna is charred on the outside and left very rare on the inside.

Zest and juice of 1 orange
1 tablespoon chopped fresh rosemary
4 tablespoons chopped fresh basil
1⅔ cups extra-virgin olive oil
1½ tablespoons chopped garlic
1 teaspoon plus 1 tablespoon minced fresh ginger
1¼ pounds sushi-grade tuna steaks, cut into 1-inch cubes
1½ cups fresh corn kernels (from 3–4 ears), or frozen kernels, thawed
1 red onion, finely chopped
4 scallions, including 1 inch of the green part, chopped

½ cup balsamic vinegar (see box, page 64)
1 tablespoon chopped fresh thyme
1 tablespoon chopped fresh cilantro
Salt and freshly ground pepper to taste
1 pound mesclun greens (see box, page 90) or mixed greens (such as bibb, romaine, radicchio, endive, arugula), washed and patted dry, torn into bite-size pieces
1½ ripe avocados
Cilantro sprigs, for garnish

In a large mixing bowl, combine the orange zest, rosemary, 2 tablespoons of the chopped basil, 1 cup of the olive oil, 1 tablespoon of the garlic, and 1 teaspoon of the ginger. Add the tuna and toss to coat well. Cover and let marinate in the refrigerator for at least 1 hour.

In the meantime, make the corn vinaigrette. In a heavy-bottomed skillet, pour enough olive oil to coat the bottom of the pan and warm the pan over medium heat. Add the corn and toast it, stirring to let kernels brown slightly on the edges, about 4 minutes. Add the red onion and scallions and let them sweat until they are translucent and limp, about 5 minutes, stirring constantly; do not let the onions brown. Add the ½ tablespoon of garlic and the remaining tablespoon of ginger, cooking for another 2 to 3 minutes. Add the balsamic vinegar and orange juice, stir, and remove from the heat. Stir in the remaining olive oil, the remaining basil, the thyme, cilantro, and salt and pepper. Leave at room temperature until cooled and ready to use.

Preheat the grill. Prepare the salad by placing an equal amount of greens in the center of each of 6 plates. Slice the avocados in half, remove the pit, and peel off the skin, keeping the flesh whole. Slice each half in half again, then slice each quarter into thirds and fan out over the top of the greens.

When the grill is medium-hot, place the tuna on the grill, using a mesh grill cover to prevent the pieces from falling through, and char on all sides, leaving the inside rare. Be sure not to overcook the tuna. Place several pieces of tuna on top of the avocado, then spoon the corn dressing over the tuna. Garnish with cilantro sprigs and serve immediately.

SERVES 6

Roux

A roux is a blend of flour and fat that is used as a thickener for sauces, soups, and other dishes. There are three different colors, or types, of roux: white, blond, and brown. A white roux, which is called for in Parmesan Pudding with Sweet Pea Sauce, is cooked for a short time over very low heat, thus preventing its color from changing. A blond roux is cooked until it turns light gold, and both the blond and white roux are used to thicken light-colored dishes such as white sauces or cream soups. A brown roux has a richer flavor and is often made with darker fats, such as meat drippings. It is cooked until it becomes deep brown and is used in more full-flavored dishes such as rich sauces and gumbos.

Mesclun

This mixture of young leaves and herbs originated in France and has worked its way into America's culinary vocabulary. It usually is a blend of various wild and cultivated baby greens, such as chicory, arugula, oak leaf lettuce, mâche, chervil, purslane, romaine, and dandelion. The flavors are delicate and blend well with balsamic dressings such as the Toasted Corn Vinaigrette Todd created. If premixed mesclun isn't available at your supermarket or green market, try buying several types of young lettuces and mixing your own.

HONEY AND BROWN SUGAR FIG SUNDAE WITH CRUMBLED AMARETTO COOKIES AND VANILLA ICE CREAM

For this sophisticated ice cream sundae, Todd flambés the figs in brandy or grappa to enhance their flavor. Amaretto cookies are available at specialty food stores and can be substituted with almond cookies.

1 cup water
½ cup light brown sugar
1 cup honey
2 cinnamon sticks
2–3 bay leaves
Pinch of fresh lemon zest
3 tablespoons unsalted butter

12 ripe Black Mission figs, cut in half or thirds
2 tablespoons brandy or grappa
½ gallon vanilla ice cream or frozen yogurt
2 cups crumbled amaretto cookies

In a saucepan, combine the water with the brown sugar, honey, cinnamon sticks, bay leaves, and lemon zest and bring to a boil over medium-high heat. Let boil for 2 to 3 minutes, then reduce the heat to low and continue to simmer.

In a separate skillet, melt the butter over high heat. Add the figs and brandy. Heat the brandy so it is warm to the touch, remove from the heat, and flambé (see box, opposite). Let the figs cook in this liquid 2 to 3 minutes, allowing the fire to burn itself out. Add the figs and any residual liquid to the honey and brown-sugar mixture and remove from the heat. Discard the bay leaves.

In 6 individual bowls, place 2 scoops of the ice cream or frozen yogurt. Spoon equal amounts of the fig mixture, including 4 fig halves, over the ice cream, then sprinkle the crushed cookies over the top. Serve immediately.

SERVES 6

The Art of Flambéing

Flaming a food in a liqueur or spirit infuses it with the flavor of the liquid while burning off the alcohol. To flame or flambé a mixture in a skillet, follow instructions carefully. First, tie back any long hair and watch for any loose clothing. Heat the alcoholic mixture until it is warm. Remove the pan from the stove and, keeping your face away from the pan, hold a long lighted match to the side of the pan so that the alcohol comes into contact with the fire. Allow the flame to burn itself out.

KURT FLEISCHFRESSER

Celebrating Fall in Oklahoma

While working in the cafeteria at Oklahoma State University during college, Kurt Fleischfresser approached a fellow who had walked into the kitchen wearing chef whites, and he discovered that the young man was a chef's apprentice working to get his culinary degree. "I had never known that you could earn a living as a chef," Kurt says. With this realization Kurt wanted to know what it took to wear this trademark white hat and jacket.

When he was only nineteen years old, Kurt went to McHenry, Illinois where he worked at Le Vichyssoise for the acclaimed French chef Bernard Crétier. It is Crétier whom Kurt most credits for shaping his career: "I have a lot of respect for Bernard," says Kurt. "He's a chef's chef. Chefs come from all over to eat his food." There, Kurt served a two-and-a-half-year traditional French apprenticeship, starting in the pantry preparing salads, pâtés, and cold dressings, and then moving on to the stove as sous-chef. "I use this same training today in my restaurants," Kurt says.

After finishing his apprenticeship and before making Oklahoma City his home,

MENU

Sun-Dried Tomato Tapenade with
Olive Bread

Pumpkin Soup with Sage-Polenta Croutons

Whole Roasted Rack of Pork with
Braised Red Onions and Apricot Chutney

Country-Style Potato Tart

Warm Fall Fruit Compote with
Rum Pound Cake

Kurt traveled the country, refining his skills. He eventually moved back to Oklahoma because he thought it was the best place to raise his family. "I love the laid-back lifestyle and the quality of life. It's such a pleasure to be able to go home every day and be in the country."

This menu is a popular meal at the Fleischfresser home, especially the Pumpkin Soup, which has been a family favorite for many years. "My wife only likes certain kinds of foods, but when I prepare this menu, she has no problem cleaning her plate," Kurt says. This menu often turns up at the family dinner table on one of Kurt's few free Sundays when he is not working at the Coach House, where he has played a starring role as executive chef for the past seven years, or overseeing the chefs at his three restaurants: the Metro Wine Bar & Bistro, Portobello, and the Ground Floor Cafe. "Because most of my friends are in the  restaurant and wine business, Sundays are the best days to get together," he says. "We make a full day of it, playing boccie ball on the lawn or fishing at the pond before we all move inside to start cooking and eating."

Kurt's ultimate goal is to be at home cooking and eating with his family more often. "Cooking at home gives me the opportunity to play around with different tastes and create new flavor combinations," Kurt says. "In fact, I'm more creative and personal than at the restaurant." But Kurt rarely takes the time to write down the precise measurements and ingredients he tosses into his creations. "I've been preparing variations of these dishes for years, so the measurements have become instinctual. For these recipes I had to concentrate especially hard to remember all the specifics to write down so they could be re-created by another cook."

This menu reflects Kurt's favorite food time of the year in Oklahoma: fall. "It's a season of great variety and bounty," he remarks. "With the first cool snap and the last pickings from our garden, we look forward to rustic and hearty foods, shared with friends and enjoyed in front of a crackling fire."

SUN-DRIED TOMATO TAPENADE WITH OLIVE BREAD

This crowd-pleasing recipe takes almost no time and can be made up to three days in advance.

4 ounces sun-dried tomatoes
1 cup water
4 tablespoons drained capers
1 tablespoon freshly ground black pepper

1 large garlic clove
¼ cup extra-virgin olive oil
1 anchovy fillet

In a small saucepan, combine the sun-dried tomatoes with the water and simmer over medium-low heat for 10 minutes. Drain. Purée the tomatoes, capers, pepper, garlic, olive oil, and anchovy in a food processor, pulsing just until combined. Transfer the purée to a porcelain container and serve at room temperature with Olive Bread.

MAKES APPROXIMATELY 1½ CUPS

OLIVE BREAD

Slathered with Sun-Dried Tomato Tapenade or another lusty spread, this bread wakes up your palate before a richly flavored meal.

Kurt suggests using Kalamata or dry-cured olives because they have so much punch. Unlike the oil-cured style, in which much of the olive's flavor is lost to the oil, dry-curing extracts the water from the fruit and retains all of the pure olive flavor. He especially likes the dry-cured variety because they reconstitute during the baking of the bread, and carry their rich flavor throughout the loaf.

1 package (2¾ teaspoons) active dry
** yeast**
2¼ cups warm water (about 110°F.)
6½ tablespoons extra-virgin olive oil
1 cup finely chopped black olives,
** preferably Kalamata or**
** dry-cured**

1 cup finely chopped green olives with
** pimientos**
1 tablespoon fresh rosemary leaves
1 tablespoon coarse salt
9 cups all-purpose flour
1 teaspoon sugar
Cornmeal, for dusting

In the bowl of an electric mixer or a large bowl, dissolve the yeast in the water until bubbly, about 5 minutes. Add the oil, olives, rosemary, and salt. Mix the flour and the sugar in another bowl and add half to the yeast mixture. Using the dough hook of an electric mixer or a wooden spoon, mix until combined. Add the rest of the flour and mix on medium speed until the dough is smooth and elastic, 8 to 10 minutes. Or turn the dough out onto a lightly floured surface and knead until smooth and elastic.

Turn the dough into a lightly oiled bowl, cover lightly, and let rise until it doubles in size, about 45 minutes. Preheat the oven to 450°F. Divide the dough into 4 balls and form into 4 oval loaves. Liberally sprinkle 2 baking sheets with cornmeal and place 2 loaves on each pan. Let these loaves rise until they double in size, about 45 minutes. Bake for 20 to 30 minutes, rotating the baking sheets if needed, until the loaves are evenly browned.

MAKES 4 SMALL LOAVES

PUMPKIN SOUP WITH SAGE-POLENTA CROUTONS

The Sage-Polenta Croutons make this soup incredibly special. However, if you don't have time to make the polenta, you can make regular croutons by sautéing bread cubes in sage, garlic, and butter until lightly browned.

¼ cup extra-virgin olive oil
1 small white onion, sliced
1 leek (white part only), washed well
   and thinly sliced
3 garlic cloves, smashed
Salt and freshly ground pepper to taste
1 2-pound pumpkin, peeled, seeded, and
   cut into 2-inch squares (about 4 cups)

1½ quarts chicken stock
½ cup heavy cream
1 cup grated Gruyère cheese
2 cups Sage-Polenta Croutons
   (recipe follows)

In a large, heavy saucepan, heat the olive oil over medium-low heat and sauté the onion, leek, and garlic until slightly brown, about 3 to 5 minutes. Season with salt and pepper. Add the pumpkin and chicken stock, and simmer until the pumpkin is tender, about 15 minutes. Purée the mixture in a blender or food processor and strain through a medium strainer. (The soup can be made in advance up to this point. Let cool and keep refrigerated until serving time. When ready to serve, bring the soup to a simmer before proceeding.)

Return the soup to the saucepan. Add the cream, simmer for 1 minute, and adjust the seasoning. Pour into shallow soup plates and top evenly with the cheese and croutons.

MAKES 8 SERVINGS

SAGE-POLENTA CROUTONS

At home Kurt uses instant polenta, which can be found at specialty food stores, for utmost convenience. If you are feeling extra ambitious, try Lidia Bastianich's polenta recipe on page 38.

1 1-pound package instant polenta, about 3½ cups

1 tablespoon chopped fresh sage, or 1 teaspoon dried

¼ cup freshly grated Parmesan cheese

Prepare the polenta according to the instructions on the package, stirring in the sage and Parmesan at the very end. Immediately after it has finished cooking, spread the polenta to a ½-inch thickness on a flat, buttered baking sheet, squaring off the sides. Let cool until firm.

Preheat the oven to 400°F. Cut the polenta into ½-inch squares and place them on a buttered baking sheet. Bake until golden brown, about 8 minutes, tossing occasionally. Place the croutons on paper towels to absorb the excess butter.

MAKES APPROXIMATELY 1½ CUPS

Wine Suggestions

"The great thing about having a party of eight or more is that you can open different varietals and vineyards at the same sitting." The chef suggests beginning this menu with a California Chardonnay—maybe offering a couple of different labels or regions. With the pork, he suggests a red Zinfandel or a Merlot; the Zinfandel should be spicy enough to stand up to the chutney in the sauce, while the Merlot is a softer and more subtle contrast to the sauce. As for dessert, "the compote would be fun to taste against just about any dessert wine. The spices and fruit would show many of the different dimensions in the wine."

WHOLE ROASTED RACK OF PORK WITH BRAISED RED ONIONS AND APRICOT CHUTNEY

This recipe requires marinating the pork overnight to allow the garlic and herb flavorings to be fully absorbed. Kurt makes a wonderful sauce with the braised onions and apricot chutney combined with the meat drippings to accompany the pork. Kurt, of course, makes chutney from scratch, but store-bought works just fine.

4 tablespoons chopped fresh rosemary

2 tablespoons fresh thyme leaves

5 tablespoons freshly ground pepper

8 garlic cloves, smashed

1 rack of pork, French cut, with back-bone trimmed and cap removed (see box, opposite)

4 small red onions

1 cup dry white wine

2 cups chicken stock

1 cup apricot chutney, store-bought (available at most supermarkets) or homemade

Rub the rosemary and thyme leaves, pepper, and garlic over the meat, place the coated pork into a container or roasting pan, and cover tightly with foil. Refrigerate overnight.

About 2 hours before dinner, preheat the oven to 375°F. Heat a very large, heavy ovenproof skillet over medium-high heat and place the pork fat-side down. Cook the meat on each side for 3 or 4 minutes to brown it evenly. Add the red onions to the pan and place in the oven. Turn the onions every 10 minutes and the rack every 20 minutes until the meat reaches an internal temperature of 150°F., about 40 minutes.

Remove the pork and onions from the pan and let rest for 10 to 15 minutes. In the mean-

Seasoning Tips

Kurt recommends using coarse salt when cooking almost everything. "It's like using a time-released salt: as you sauté or roast, it dissolves slower than finely ground salt and bastes the meat or fish while cooking."

Whether you use table or coarse salt, Kurt suggests seasoning lightly with salt and pepper after each major addition when cooking. He seasons a soup or sauce to taste each time he adds a major ingredient, resulting in a fuller flavor with less seasoning actually added in the end. "If you season only toward the end of the cooking, the dish will just taste salty."

time, drain the grease from the pan, then add the wine to deglaze the pan, scraping up any browned bits from the bottom, and cook over medium-high heat until the wine is reduced to ¼ cup, about 10 minutes. Add the chicken stock and reduce by half, 10 to 15 minutes. Add the chutney and bring to a boil. Remove from the heat. Cut the onions in half and cut the pork between the bones.

To serve, place a pork chop and some of the sauce on each plate with an onion half and a slice of the Country-Style Potato Tart.

S E R V E S   8

French-Cut Rack of Pork

It is best to have your rack of pork butchered professionally so you do not have to do this at home. Ask your butcher for a "Frenched" rack of pork and have him trim the backbone off and take the cap off. (The cap is a small piece of meat with a lot of fat around it.) When the butcher has finished the trimming process, the rack of pork should look like the classic lamb rack with eight rib bones and a shallow cut in the shape of an *X* or diamond where the fat is exposed, which allows the flavors of the marinade to be better absorbed and excess fat to drain. Letting your butcher do the work means all you have to do later is cut it into portions when cooked.

COUNTRY-STYLE POTATO TART

This rustic tart is a wonderful addition to any hearty cold-weather meal. For a delicate, multilayered crust, Kurt uses puff pastry. This tart is made free-form without a pan; however, for the less experienced cook, Kurt has thoughtfully provided instructions for baking the tart using a pan (see Note).

3 large russet potatoes, peeled and sliced ¼ inch thick

4 shallots, finely sliced, or 1 medium yellow onion, finely sliced

3 garlic cloves, finely chopped

1 teaspoon fresh thyme

1 teaspoon chopped fresh rosemary

2 tablespoons chopped fresh parsley

Salt and freshly ground pepper to taste

Cornmeal, for dusting

½ pound puff pastry dough, thawed if frozen (available, frozen, at specialty markets and some supermarkets)

1 cup heavy cream

1 cup half-and-half

Preheat the oven to 375°F. In a large bowl, toss the potato slices with the shallots, garlic, thyme, rosemary, and parsley. Season generously with salt and pepper. Generously sprinkle a baking sheet with cornmeal. On a lightly floured surface, roll out the puff pastry to a ¼-inch thickness, then place it on the baking sheet. Put the potato mixture in the center, leaving a 3-inch border on all sides. Fold the edge of the dough up around the potatoes, forming a ridge, and place the baking sheet in the oven. Pour equal amounts of cream and half-and-half onto the tart until the liquid threatens to spill over. (If there is cream or half-and-half remaining, you can add it to the tart after 10 minutes of baking.) Bake until the potatoes in the center are fork-tender and the crust is golden brown, about 1 hour. Remove the tart from the oven and let rest for 10 minutes before cutting.

SERVES 8

NOTE: If baking a free-form tart on a baking sheet is too intimidating, use the collar of a 9-inch springform pan to support the edges of the tart. Simply roll out the dough and trim to a 14-inch circle. Place the collar on the cornmeal-dusted baking sheet and lower the dough into the collar. Create a 3-inch standing border, fitting the dough within the collar. Add the potatoes and cream, and bake until the potatoes are tender, about 1 hour.

Unsalted Butter

Kurt, like most chefs, prefers unsalted butter to salted butter when cooking and baking. "Salt is a preservative that allows the butter to age more slowly, but causes the butter to change its flavor," he explains. With unsalted butter you get the pure butter taste, which is cleaner and fresher with a slightly sweeter taste than salted butter. But in order for it to stay fresh, Kurt recommends storing it in the freezer until the day you're ready to use it, and then keeping it tightly wrapped in the refrigerator.

WARM FALL FRUIT COMPOTE WITH RUM POUND CAKE

This is an easy way to turn a store-bought pound cake into a homey, seasonal dessert. You can use any mixture of fresh and dried fruits that you like; Kurt has included his favorites in this recipe. Ice cream can be substituted for the sweetened whipped cream, if you like.

1 Granny Smith apple, cored and sliced ¼ inch thick

½ small acorn squash, peeled, seeded, and sliced ¼ inch thick

1 Bosc pear, cored and sliced

1 banana, peeled and sliced

2–2½ cups mixed dried fruit, such as apricots, figs, cranberries, blueberries, currants, or golden raisins

2 cinnamon sticks

1 vanilla bean, split in half

½ cup (1 stick) unsalted butter, cut into pieces and softened

¼ cup honey

¼ cup dark rum, plus extra for drizzling

1 cup heavy cream

2–3 tablespoons brown sugar, or to taste

1 store-bought pound cake, sliced into 8 slices

Preheat the oven to 350° F. Fold a full sheet of parchment paper (16 × 24 inches) in half to a 12 × 16-inch sheet. Snip a small (about 1-inch) triangle off the corners that are not folded. Open the paper up and smear butter around the outside edge of the paper. Put the apple, squash, pear, and banana slices (and any other fresh fruit) on one half of the paper, leaving a 2-inch border. Place the dried fruit, cinnamon sticks, and vanilla bean on top. In a blender or food processor, blend the butter, honey, and ¼ cup rum; drizzle this mixture over the fruit. Fold the top sheet of paper over, sandwiching the fruit in the middle. Fold and crimp the buttered edges to seal. Put the fruit "package" on a baking sheet and bake until the paper is almost dark brown, 15 to 20 minutes.

While the fruit is baking, whip the cream with the brown sugar until soft to medium peaks form. Place cake slices on individual plates and drizzle each with rum, then top with a dollop of whipped cream.

Place the fruit package on a heatproof plate and bring to the table along with the plates of pound cake. Tear open the bag, which will release a flood of aromas, and spoon the fruit over each piece of pound cake, discarding the cinnamon sticks and vanilla bean.

SERVES 8

DAVID AND
ANNE GINGRASS

Schnitzel & Spaetzle

Anne and David Gingrass are the husband-and-wife team at Postrio, located in the heart of San Francisco. This dynamic pair formed when the two attended the Culinary Institute of America, where they became a couple almost immediately after beginning the program. For Anne, attending the CIA was a continuation of the culinary education she started years before by assisting her mother, who owned a catering business. For David, who started cooking at seventeen via part-time restaurant jobs, his father was the most compelling reason to enroll in culinary school. "My father believed heavily in going to school," says David. "Pick a focus and go to school in that area, he would say, so off I went to culinary school, which made sense to me."

After graduating in 1983, the two moved west to California and worked in various restaurants. Anne hopped back and forth between northern and southern California, working under the instruction of Wolfgang Puck at Spago, under Jeremiah Tower of Stars, and then back at Spago again. David joined Anne at Spago in 1985, and their professional relationship with Wolfgang Puck was cemented. For five years Anne was the chef while David added high notes to the menu with his signature homemade breads,

MENU

Cabbage and Bacon Soup

*Vienna Schnitzel with
Lemon Sauce and Arugula*

Spaetzle with Browned Butter

Chocolate-Raspberry Mousse Cake

sausages, and smoked salmon. They were married in 1986 and returned to San Francisco to open Postrio with Wolfgang Puck in April 1989. Anne serves as chef while David provides the building blocks, taking care of all the buying, butchering, and bread baking, as well as running the business side of the restaurant.

The two have different and established roles for themselves at home as well. "Anne does all the cooking," says David, "and I do all the dishes." They cook at home once a week on average and eat the rest of their meals out. They have an eight-year-old daughter who loves to help pick herbs, wash the salad, and bake pastries. On frequent occasions she can be found in the kitchen at Postrio, making her own tarts.

When they cook at home they invite friends to share a low-key meal. The Gingrasses prepare roasted or grilled meats, fish, or pasta, accompanied by breads and

salad, but they rarely do any complicated prep work. Occasionally, they'll prepare the schnitzel that's presented here because David loves German food. "It's one of my favorite things to eat," says David. "I grew up in Milwaukee, which has a strong German influence, so preparing it reminds me of home." The Cabbage and Bacon Soup, which his mom used to make, is surprisingly clean and light. They rarely prepare dessert because Anne and David prefer to end a meal with a glass of Calvados, or apple brandy liqueur, when it's just the two of them. But for a group of friends they prepare this cake because "it's very easy to make and the flavor is to die for." David and Anne suggest a good beer to accompany this meal, or a dry Riesling or Gewürztraminer.

In the course of their twelve-year relationship, Anne and David have learned to separate their work life from their home life. "Working together is a great opportunity for us to work as a team and appreciate each other's skills in the workplace," they say. "But we make sure to leave the bickering at the restaurant so we can relax at home."

CABBAGE AND BACON SOUP

Sweet and nutty cabbage is the star of this soup; the bacon (or ham, if you prefer) gives it a smoky accent while the potatoes, which are cooked until they begin to fall apart, thicken the soup slightly.

This soup makes a terrific first course or a rib-sticking meal on its own when larger portions are served.

3 tablespoons extra-virgin olive oil

1 cup sliced yellow onion

1 cup sliced fennel bulb, halved, then cut across the grain into ¼-inch strips

2 cups sliced savoy cabbage, cut lengthwise 1 inch thick (see box, page 106)

6 cups chicken stock

2 russet potatoes, peeled, halved lengthwise, and cut into ¼-inch half-moon slices

2 tablespoons slivered bacon or smoked ham

1 tablespoon chopped fresh Italian parsley

Salt and freshly ground pepper to taste

6 slices crusty bread, such as a baguette, brushed with olive oil and toasted

Heat the 3 tablespoons of oil in a large saucepan over medium-high heat. Add the onion and fennel and sauté until tender, about 10 minutes. Add the cabbage and continue to cook for another 5 minutes, stirring occasionally. Add the chicken stock and potatoes. Bring to a low simmer, reduce the heat, and simmer slowly until the potatoes are very soft and begin to fall apart, about 20 minutes. Remove from the heat and add the bacon or ham and parsley. Stir until well combined and season with salt and pepper. Place 1 slice of toast in each bowl and ladle in the soup.

SERVES 4 TO 6

Cabbage

Cabbage is "an incredibly versatile, wonderful vegetable," says David Gingrass, who loves cabbage for its mellow blend of sweetness and earthiness. Cabbage can be prepared raw, baked, or braised. Three kinds of cabbage are:

GREEN OR RED CABBAGE—David's least favorite—the familiar round, hard head of tightly packed smooth, pale green to white or red leaves. The leaf is heavy and has firm thick ribs that are best to remove before using. These cabbages are rich in vitamin C and also are a source of vitamin A. Stored tightly wrapped, they will keep for up to one week in the refrigerator.

NAPA OR CHINESE CELERY CABBAGE, which David describes as a "light lettuce," with thin, crisp wrinkled white leaves with pale green tips, similar in shape to romaine lettuce. It is a good source of vitamin A and potassium. It can be wrapped and refrigerated for up to three days.

SAVOY CABBAGE, David's preference, a fairly loose, round head of pale to dark green wrinkled leaves. The mellow-flavored leaves are of medium firmness, in relation to the other two varieties, and take well to cooking. Keep it wrapped tightly in the refrigerator for three to five days.

David often stir-fries savoy cabbage with freshly grated ginger and a little soy sauce until slightly golden, and then tosses it with a rice vinaigrette. Shredded napa or savoy cabbage tossed with a simple vinaigrette elevates cole slaw to a new level.

Vienna Schnitzel with Lemon Sauce and Arugula

A lemon sauce made with butter and shallots and a peppery arugula garnish turn a basic breaded and pan-seared veal cutlet into an elegant dish guaranteed to impress your guests.

VIENNA SCHNITZEL

1 pound boneless veal loin, trimmed
   and cleaned
2 teaspoons chopped fresh thyme
Salt and freshly ground pepper to taste
2 large eggs
½ cup all-purpose flour
2 cups fresh bread crumbs (dried will
   work, but not quite as well; see box,
   page 108)
½ cup extra-virgin olive oil

LEMON SAUCE

2 tablespoons (¼ stick) unsalted butter
1 shallot, minced
1 tablespoon chopped fresh parsley
1 teaspoon fresh lemon juice
Salt and freshly ground pepper to taste

About 1 cup arugula leaves, smaller
   leaves left whole, larger ones torn
   into bite-size pieces

To prepare the veal, first slice the loin across the grain into 4 equal pieces. Then butterfly each piece by cutting horizontally through the middle of each without cutting all the way through. Open each piece up (it will resemble the shape of a butterfly), and place it between 2 sheets of plastic wrap on a flat surface. Using a meat pounder or the flat side of a cleaver, pound the meat until it is uniformly ¼ inch thick. (You may prefer to ask your butcher to do this for you.) After the meat has been pounded, sprinkle even amounts of thyme and salt and pepper over both sides of each piece.

To bread the veal, you will need 3 separate wide, shallow containers such as pie pans. Crack the eggs into one of the containers and beat them well. Place the flour and bread crumbs separately in the two other containers. Season the flour with salt and pepper. Dredge each piece of veal in the flour and then dip the floured meat into the egg, turning to coat both sides. Lift the meat over the pan, allowing the excess egg to drip back into the pan. Lay the veal in the bread crumbs, allowing the crumbs to adhere. Turn over to coat the other side; you may need to press the bread crumbs lightly into the meat to coat it completely. Transfer the breaded veal cutlets to a flat pan or baking sheet.

Preheat the oven to 250° F. Heat 2 tablespoons of the olive oil in a large skillet over medium heat until hot but not smoking. Place one piece of veal at a time in the pan and cook until golden brown on the bottom, about 2 minutes. Then flip the veal and cook until the meat is opaque, another 2 to 3 minutes. Remove the veal to a baking sheet lined with paper towels to absorb excess oil and place in the oven to keep warm. Repeat with the remaining olive oil and veal cutlets. Transfer the veal pieces to 4 large individual serving plates and return to the warm oven while you make the sauce.

Heat a large skillet over high heat and add the butter. When the butter is melted and lightly browned, add the shallot and parsley, and cook, stirring, for 1 minute. Stir in the lemon juice and remove from the heat. Season with salt and pepper. Spoon the sauce evenly over the veal and sprinkle the arugula around each plate. Serve immediately with spaetzle.

SERVES 4

Homemade Bread Crumbs

David and Anne prefer breading the veal with "big, light, and fluffy" fresh bread crumbs rather than dried or toasted, which are finely ground and crunchy. While the recipe will work with either, the results are different: dried crumbs coat the veal with a thin, crisp layer and fresh crumbs give a thick and tender coating.

TO MAKE fresh bread crumbs, you can use any stale white bread, crusts removed. (Leaving the bread out overnight, unwrapped, will make it stale.) The easiest method is to grate the bread using the shredding device of a food processor. If the pieces are too uneven, sift them through a colander.

TO MAKE dried bread crumbs, first toast the bread in slices until golden brown in the oven or toaster. Then crumble the toast in a food processor or a mortar and pestle, until you get a fine, even crumb.

Store-bought crumbs are okay to use, "but who knows how long they've been on the shelf?" wonders David. He suggests a Japanese brand of packaged medium bread crumbs called Panko, which is available in Asian and specialty markets.

Spaetzle with Browned Butter

These delicate dumplings are a popular German side dish and are very simple to prepare. David and Anne season them with chives to complement the lemon and arugula of the schnitzel.

³⁄₄ **cup all-purpose flour**
Pinch of salt
¹⁄₄ **teaspoon baking powder**
2 medium eggs, lightly beaten
¹⁄₄ **cup whole milk**

¹⁄₂ **teaspoon extra-virgin olive oil**
4 tablespoons (¹⁄₂ stick) unsalted butter
1 tablespoon chopped fresh chives
Salt and freshly ground pepper to taste

In a large bowl, sift together the flour, salt, and baking powder. Stir the eggs into the dry ingredients to form a thick batter. Blend the milk into the batter in 3 equal parts, mixing until combined after each addition. When all of the milk has been incorporated, the mixture should resemble a thick cake batter. Allow the batter to sit at room temperature for 20 minutes to relax.

While the batter rests, bring a large pot of lightly salted water to a rolling boil over high heat, and set aside a large bowl of ice water. Place a colander with large holes the size of peas above the pot and pour in roughly ¹⁄₂ cup of the batter at a time. Use a rubber spatula to push the batter through the holes of the colander into the boiling water. Stir the mixture once to prevent the spaetzle from sticking together. They will rise to the surface of the water when they are done, in 2 to 3 minutes. Remove them with a slotted spoon or strainer and place them in the ice water to cool. Drain well and toss lightly in a bowl with the olive oil to prevent sticking. Repeat this process until all the batter is used. (The spaetzle can be prepared up until this stage earlier in the day, but they must be stored in a single layer in a baking pan covered with plastic and refrigerated.)

Just before serving, heat a medium skillet over medium-high heat. Add the butter, stirring until it browns lightly. Add the spaetzle and chives and cook, stirring and tossing, until heated through. Season with salt and pepper and serve hot.

Serves 4

CHOCOLATE-RASPBERRY MOUSSE CAKE

Chocolate, chocolate, and more chocolate! Layers of moist chocolate cake and a silky smooth chocolate mousse are wrapped in (you guessed it) chocolate and topped with fresh raspberries.

There will be plenty of leftovers from this three-inch-deep confection, which you may want to send home with the guests, lest you be tempted to eat more than your share. The cake will remain good for two or three days if kept wrapped in the refrigerator.

CAKE

1 pound good-quality semisweet
    chocolate, coarsely chopped

¾ cup (1½ sticks) unsalted butter, cut
    into 1-inch pieces

10 large eggs, separated and at room
    temperature

4 tablespoons sugar

2 tablespoons pastry or cake flour

MOUSSE

8 ounces good-quality semisweet
    chocolate, coarsely chopped

¼ cup water

¼ cup sugar

5 large egg yolks

1 cup heavy cream, chilled

GARNISH AND GLAZE

1 pint raspberries, washed

12 ounces good-quality semisweet
    chocolate, coarsely chopped

¼ cup (½ stick) unsalted butter,
    softened

2 tablespoons corn syrup

1 tablespoon brandy

Preheat the oven to 350°F. Cut 3 circles of parchment or waxed paper to fit inside three 9-inch cake pans and place in the pans; do not butter or flour the pans. In a double boiler or a metal bowl placed over a pan of lightly simmering water, melt the chocolate and the butter, stirring occasionally until smooth. Remove from the heat and set aside.

In a large bowl, whip the egg yolks and 2 tablespoons of the sugar with an electric mixer until the mixture is light yellow and thick. Stir in the melted chocolate, then fold in the flour until incorporated.

Whip the egg whites in a separate bowl until stiff but not dry, gradually adding the remaining 2 tablespoons sugar. Gently fold the egg whites into the chocolate and yolk mixture until fully incorporated. Divide the batter evenly among the 3 cake pans and bake for about 10 minutes, until the centers spring back when touched. Cool the cakes in their pans on a wire rack before unmolding. To unmold, run a knife around the edges of the cakes and turn them out. Peel off the parchment paper from the back and cover loosely with plastic wrap until ready to use, or wrap tightly in plastic wrap and refrigerate for up to 3 days.

Melt the chocolate for the mousse in a double boiler or a metal bowl placed over a pan of lightly simmering water, stirring occasionally until smooth. Meanwhile, combine the water and sugar in a small saucepan and bring to a boil over medium-high heat.

Transfer the melted chocolate to a large mixing bowl. Place the egg yolks in a large mixing bowl and slowly add the hot sugar-water, while whipping with an electric mixer until light yellow and thick. Fold the whipped yolks into the melted chocolate, a third at a time, until incorporated. Set aside.

Whip the cream in a chilled mixing bowl with an electric mixer until stiff peaks form. Fold the whipped cream, in thirds, into the chocolate mixture just until incorporated. Cover the mousse and chill it in the refrigerator for at least 2 hours or overnight.

When the mousse is set and the cake is cooled, assemble the cake. Divide the mousse in half and spread each portion evenly over 2 cake layers. Set one-third of the raspberries into each layer of the mousse. Then stack one mousse-layered cake over the other and top with the remaining cake layer. With a spatula, smooth over any mousse that squeezes out from between the layers. Loosely cover with plastic wrap and refrigerate.

To make the chocolate wrapping, melt the chocolate in a double boiler or a metal bowl set over lightly simmering water, stirring occasionally until smooth. Measure a piece of waxed paper 28 inches long and 3 inches high (the height of the cake) and place on the counter, shiny side up. Carefully pour half the melted chocolate on top of the waxed paper and spread it evenly to all edges with a small spatula. Let the chocolate become slightly firm but not dry, then wrap the chocolate around the cake, waxed-paper side out. Remove the waxed paper and return the cake to the refrigerator to harden the chocolate completely. The assembled cake should be refrigerated for about 2 hours before serving.

Make the glaze by adding the softened butter, corn syrup, and brandy to the remaining melted chocolate. Mix until completely blended. Pour the glaze over the top of the cake, spreading it to the edges with a spatula and allowing it to drip behind the chocolate wrap. Arrange the remaining raspberries around the perimeter of the top to decorate.

To cut the cake, place a large knife under warm running water before making each cut.

SERVES 12

JOYCE GOLDSTEIN

A Feast from the Middle East

Cooking is Joyce Goldstein's creative and artistic outlet. She was a painter before she made the transition to cooking teacher, and when asked why she made the switch, she replies, "Three children! When I had my children, there was no more time to paint quietly for five to six hours straight. While cooking, I could put the children on the floor with pots, pans, and spoons, and let them romp around, while I took the time to play around with recipes."

Joyce graduated Magna Cum Laude from Smith College in 1956 and then went on to receive her master's degree in 1959 from Yale University's School of Art and Architecture. After spending six years painting and exhibiting at the San Francisco Museum of Art, she began cooking for pleasure. "When cooking, you can be creative in a half an hour or an hour, instead of five hours when painting." It wasn't long before her "pleasure" became a profession. From her kitchen, she moved on to teach cooking, culinary history, and kitchen design for more than twenty years, mostly at the California Street Cooking School, which she founded and directed. Toward the end of her teaching

MENU

Prawns and Greens with Tarator Vinaigrette

❧

*Grilled Chicken Skewers in a
Spiced Yogurt Marinade*

❧

Rice and Noodle Pilaf

❧

Spinach with Chickpeas

❧

Spiced Carrots

❧

Middle Eastern Custard

career, she ventured into the kitchen of Chez Panisse, where she learned the restaurant business first-hand in the course of three years as a chef and manager. "I was the substitute that never left," she says. Joyce finally opened her own restaurant so she could make the most of her eclectic talents. In 1984 she launched Square One, which for more than a decade has received numerous awards for food, wine, and service.

But for Joyce nothing matches the feeling she gets when cooking at home. "Cooking at home compared to cooking in my restaurant is like night and day," says Joyce. "It's so precious and I can take the time to enjoy the cooking process. I can savor each physical task and stop to smell the garlic or the basil. It's not an exercise in beat-the-clock." She always cooks on Sundays and Mondays, and Sunday is the day her family gets together. "I wake up in the morning, enjoy my coffee and the paper, and then cook all day, in my bathrobe, while listening to the radio," she says. "I don't get dressed until late in the day, when the guests are about to come over." It's a time for her to be creative, but also a time to touch base with her family and play with her young grandchild. "The next day, we're all back in the saddle."

She selected this Middle Eastern menu because she likes the fragrant aroma of this type of food as well as its taste. "As a working chef, I like to cook food at home that is not labor-intensive," says Joyce. "The marinated chicken is easy and you can broil it in the oven, or on a nice day you can grill it outside." She begins this meal with a salad with a tarator vinaigrette. "Tarator is a traditional Middle Eastern sauce, used for dipping fried prawns or veggies, or it is poured over fish. But thinned out with olive oil, it makes a great vinaigrette." Joyce teams up the chicken with a pilaf, carrots, and spinach with chickpeas to add balance and more nourishment to the meal. She ends the meal with a Middle Eastern custard served with fresh berries or poached dried fruit. "For guests, I can't resist the candied rose petals," she says.

After cooking at a leisurely pace all day, Joyce sits down to enjoy a relaxing meal with her family or friends. "What counts are the warm feelings that come from being with people you love." And because she cooked, she doesn't have to do the dishes.

Prawns and Greens with Tarator Vinaigrette

Tarator is a classic Middle Eastern tahini-based sauce and here it becomes a great vinaigrette. It can be made hours ahead of time but may need to be thinned out with additional water, because it thickens as it stands. Prawns are the West Coast term for shrimp.

3 cups dry white wine or water, or a
    mixture of both

1½ pounds medium shrimp (prawns),
    shelled and deveined

1½ tablespoons finely minced garlic
    (4–5 cloves)

1 cup toasted walnuts (see box,
    page 117), plus ½ cup chopped, for
    garnish (optional)

4 tablespoons sesame tahini

4–5 tablespoons fresh lemon juice, or
    to taste

½ cup extra-virgin olive oil

½ cup water, or as needed to thin the
    dressing

Salt and freshly ground pepper to taste

4 cups watercress or romaine lettuce,
    or a mixture of both, washed and
    torn into bite-size pieces

1 cup fresh Italian parsley leaves

½ cup fresh mint leaves

1 cucumber (preferably English),
    peeled, seeded, and sliced or diced

¾ pound feta cheese, crumbled
    (optional)

Bring the wine or water to a simmer over medium heat in a large saucepan. Add the shrimp, adjusting the heat to maintain a light simmer, and poach until pink and opaque throughout, about 4 minutes. Drain the shrimp, discarding the poaching liquid; cover, and refrigerate until chilled.

Put the garlic, walnuts, tahini, and lemon juice in a blender or food processor. Pulse to combine. Add the olive oil and enough water to reach a liquid consistency. Season with salt and pepper. Toss the shrimp with ¼ cup of the vinaigrette.

In a large bowl, toss the watercress or romaine lettuce, parsley, mint, and cucumber with the remaining vinaigrette until evenly coated. Evenly divide the greens among 6 salad plates. Top with equal portions of the shrimp, and add the chopped walnuts and crumbled feta, if desired.

Serves 6

GRILLED CHICKEN SKEWERS IN A SPICED YOGURT MARINADE

Marinating a chicken infuses the meat with flavor, and the yogurt also acts as a tenderizer.

4 garlic cloves

1 small onion, chopped

1 tablespoon paprika

1 teaspoon ground cinnamon

1 teaspoon turmeric

½ teaspoon freshly ground cardamom

¼ teaspoon cayenne pepper

¼ cup fresh lemon juice

1 cup plain yogurt

18 boneless chicken thighs or 12 boneless breasts, cut into 1½-inch cubes

Extra-virgin olive oil as needed

Salt to taste

1 teaspoon freshly ground black pepper

Chopped fresh Italian parsley, for garnish

Lemon wedges, for garnish

Combine the garlic, onion, paprika, cinnamon, turmeric, cardamom, cayenne, lemon juice, and yogurt in a blender or food processor and process until combined. Place the chicken in a nonreactive bowl and toss with the marinade to coat well. Cover and refrigerate for 4 to 6 hours for breast meat and up to 12 hours for thighs.

Soak wooden skewers in water for 30 minutes to prevent them from burning. Preheat the broiler or grill. Thread the chicken pieces on the skewers, brush with a little olive oil, and sprinkle with salt and pepper. For thighs, cook for 4 to 5 minutes, then flip over for another 4 to 5 minutes; or cook 3 to 4 minutes per side for breast cubes, or until opaque throughout. Sprinkle with parsley and serve with lemon wedges.

SERVES 6 GENEROUSLY

RICE AND NOODLE PILAF

This is a basic noodle and rice pilaf that is common in the Middle East. The vermicelli add a textural contrast to the rice. For still more textural interest, add toasted almonds if you are not already serving the nut-based prawn salad.

6 tablespoons (¾ stick) unsalted butter
1 cup vermicelli, broken into 1-inch pieces
1½ cups basmati rice, soaked for 1 hour and drained well (see box, page 185)

3 cups chicken stock or water
2 teaspoons salt
Toasted almonds, for garnish (optional; see box, below)

In a heavy saucepan, melt the butter over medium heat. Add the vermicelli and sauté for a few minutes until lightly browned. Then add the rice and sauté for a few minutes longer. Add the stock or water and the salt. Raise the heat to medium-high and bring to a boil. Reduce the heat to medium-low, cover the pan, and simmer until all the liquid is absorbed, about 20 minutes. Serve hot, garnished with toasted almonds, if desired.

SERVES 6

Toasting Nuts

Toasting nuts or seeds is a quick and easy step that should not be skipped when called for, as it brings out their natural flavors and livens up the dish.

TO TOAST nuts or large seeds such as pumpkin, place them in a single layer on a shallow baking pan in an oven preheated to 350° F. for about 10 minutes, tossing occasionally to toast evenly. Keep a watchful eye on the oven, as baking times will vary according to the age and size of the nuts. Toast just until fragrant; overcooked nuts or seeds will taste bitter or burnt. If a recipe calls for chopped or ground nuts or seeds, always toast them first.

Smaller seeds such as cumin and sesame seeds are best toasted in a dry skillet over medium heat (see box, page 18).

Spinach with Chickpeas

The tartness of the greens serves as a nice foil for the starchy chickpeas in this Mediterranean dish.

¼ cup extra-virgin olive oil

1½ cups diced onion

1 garlic clove, minced

2 cups peeled, diced, and seeded
   tomatoes (see box, page 311)

2 pounds spinach, stemmed, washed,
   and coarsely chopped

2 cups chickpeas, cooked or canned,
   rinsed, and drained

Salt and freshly ground black pepper
   to taste

Heat the olive oil in a large skillet over medium heat. Add the onion and sauté until translucent, 8 to 10 minutes. Add the garlic and tomatoes, and cook for 2 more minutes. Add the spinach in batches, stirring often to moisten the leaves, until all are barely wilted. Stir in the chickpeas and simmer for 5 minutes, stirring often. Season generously with salt and pepper.

SERVES 6

Spiced Carrots

Here's an exciting way to serve up this sweet and tender root vegetable.

¼ cup extra-virgin olive oil

1 cup chopped onion

1–2 tablespoons grated fresh ginger

1 teaspoon ground cinnamon

1 teaspoon ground toasted cumin seeds
   (see box, page 18)

3 tablespoons sugar or honey

2 pounds carrots, trimmed, peeled,
   and sliced ¼ inch thick

3 cups chicken stock or water or as
   needed

Salt to taste

3 tablespoons chopped fresh dill or
   cilantro

Warm the olive oil in a large saucepan over medium heat. Add the onion and cook until tender and translucent, 8 to 10 minutes. Add the ginger, cinnamon, cumin, and sugar or honey and cook for another 2 minutes. Add the carrots and enough stock or water to just barely cover the carrots. Simmer, covered, stirring occasionally, until the carrots are tender and the liquid is reduced, 15 to 20 minutes. Season with the salt and sprinkle with the herbs.

SERVES 6

MIDDLE EASTERN CUSTARD

This recipe is a cross between a classic baked French custard or Spanish flan and a Middle Eastern pudding. The fragrance of the spices mingled with the scent of rosewater or almonds will transport your guests eastward. Serve with berries or sliced peaches or apricots, or top with candied rose petals (see box, below).

2 cups half-and-half or light cream
½ cup honey
¼ teaspoon ground cardamom
¼ teaspoon ground cinnamon
2 large eggs
2 large egg yolks

½ teaspoon vanilla extract
1–2 teaspoons rosewater or almond
   extract, or to taste
½ cup toasted almonds or pistachios,
   coarsely chopped (optional; see box,
   page 117)

Preheat the oven to 300°F. In a small saucepan over medium heat, combine the half-and-half or light cream with the honey, cardamom, and cinnamon and bring to just below a boil to scald. In a medium bowl, whisk the eggs and egg yolks lightly and gradually pour in the cream, whisking constantly. Stir in the vanilla and rosewater or almond extract. Strain the mixture through a fine sieve into a pitcher, then pour into 6 custard cups or individual ramekins. Place the cups in a roasting pan and pour in hot water to reach halfway up the sides of the cups. Cover the pan with foil and bake for 50 to 60 minutes, or until the custard does not ripple when lightly tapped. Allow the custards to cool to room temperature before serving. (If you do not serve within 3 or 4 hours, cover the custard cups tightly with plastic wrap and refrigerate for up to 1 day. Bring the custards to room temperature before serving.) Garnish with toasted almonds or pistachios, if desired, or serve with fruit.

SERVES 6

Candied Rose Petals

These are surprisingly easy to make. Gently rinse and pat dry whole fresh rose petals (make sure the flowers are pesticide-free). Using a small pastry brush, brush the petals with lightly beaten egg white and immediately dip both sides in sugar placed in a shallow dish. Place the sugar-coated rose petals on a wire rack, in a single layer, to dry. Just before serving, arrange a few atop each custard. These edible rose petals should be made the day of serving.

VINCENT GUERITHAULT

French with a Southwestern Twist

In 1976 Vincent Guerithault decided to move "temporarily" to the United States from France to work as sous-chef for Jean Banchet at Le Français in Wheeling, Illinois. "I was supposed to stay only for six months," he says, "but instead I worked there for four years, and never moved back to France."

From then on, the United States was Vincent's home, and after finishing his term at Le Français, he moved to Scottsdale, Arizona, to improve the French cuisine at the Mexican-French restaurant Oaxaca. Vincent's innovations were strong enough to stand alone; and eventually the French portion of the restaurant did so, evolving into Vincent's French Cuisine, a separate establishment.

Not long after, in 1986, Vincent opened Vincent Guerithault on Camelback, and it became one of the most popular places to eat in the Southwest. He began to use many Southwestern flavors in his cooking, including cactus, jicama, cilantro, and chilies, and he created new dishes such as his notorious "duck tamale," which incorporates classic duck confit into a Southwestern tamale made with corn masa, complemented with a cilantro beurre blanc. "When I came to Arizona, I started experimenting with the

MENU

Blue Corn Blinis with Caviar

⌣

*Roasted Rack of Lamb with
Roasted Jalapeños and Garlic*

⌣

Herbed Gratin Dauphinois

⌣

*Peaches and Strawberries
Poached in Heavy Syrup*

local ingredients, and found them to be interestingly different, and giving me something a little more fun and new to do," says Vincent.

Vincent has spent most of his life mastering the art of French cuisine. At the age of sixteen, he began his career at L'Oustau de Baumanière in the town of Les Baux in Provence. Three years later, Vincent continued his apprenticeship at Maxim's in Paris, and he then used his mandatory one-year tour in the French navy to further develop his cooking skills. He became a chef at Fauchon, one of Paris's most famous gourmet shops, before accepting an opportunity to work with Banchet in the United States.

The menu that the chef presents here is pure Vincent. He begins with Blue Corn Blinis with Caviar: "I chose my first course because I love caviar, and while it's not something I indulge in often, if I'm entertaining at home I like to make it special for my guests." The blinis work equally well with smoked salmon.

When Vincent was growing up in France, rack of lamb was always part of holiday meals and other celebrations, and it brings back warm memories of his family gathered at the table. Because the weather is so beautiful in Arizona, Vincent and his wife and children spend a great deal of time outdoors, so he suggests grilling the lamb over an open flame to just brown the exterior, as an alternative to sautéing, before cooking the meat in the oven. "I'm a fan of chilies and the jalapeño chili is a good one to season the lamb because most people like it," he says.

To complement the meal, he's chosen Herbed Gratin Dauphinois, a classic French side dish of scalloped potatoes that he's always been fond of, and for dessert he tops vanilla ice cream with his favorite fruits, peaches and strawberries, poached in a sugar syrup. "It's nice to end the meal with something sweet but not too rich or heavy," says Vincent.

Now that he has made Arizona his home, Vincent focuses most of his energies on his family and his restaurant, but he makes time every summer to travel back to France to rest, enjoy his homeland, and rekindle his creative vigor.

BLUE CORN BLINIS WITH CAVIAR

Blue cornmeal, cilantro, corn, peppers, and chili powder give these Russian pancakes a Southwestern twist, which will give your guests something to talk about.

1 cup blue cornmeal (available at specialty stores), or yellow or white cornmeal (see box, page 125)

½ cup all-purpose flour

3 large eggs

½ cup milk

¾ cup heavy cream

⅔ cup fresh corn kernels (1–2 ears), or frozen corn kernels, thawed

1 red or yellow bell pepper, cored, seeded, and chopped (preferably a mixture of both)

½ green bell pepper, cored, seeded, and chopped

2 tablespoons chopped scallion

2 tablespoons chopped fresh cilantro

1 teaspoon salt

½ teaspoon sugar

½ teaspoon chimayo chili powder (available at specialty markets; cayenne pepper can be substituted)

2 tablespoons unsalted butter

Caviar (see box, page 343) or thinly sliced smoked salmon, for topping

Crème Fraîche (see box, page 237) or sour cream, for topping (optional)

Combine the cornmeal and flour in a mixing bowl. Add the eggs and mix until well combined into a thick paste. Add the milk and mix well. Add the heavy cream and mix well. Fold in the corn, peppers, scallion, cilantro, salt, sugar, and chili powder until well blended. In a nonstick or lightly oiled pan or griddle, melt the butter over medium heat. Ladle the batter in ¼-cup spoonfuls onto the griddle and cook the blini for approximately 2 minutes on each side, until golden brown. Each blini should be 4 to 6 inches in diameter. To serve, place 2 blinis on each of 12 serving plates and top each blini with a small dollop of caviar or a slice of smoked salmon, attractively folded. Add a dollop of Crème Fraîche or sour cream on top, if desired.

SERVES 12

ROASTED RACK OF LAMB WITH ROASTED JALAPEÑOS AND GARLIC

Garlic and lamb are a classic combination and the jalapeños give this dish a contemporary regional kick. Vincent roasts the jalapeños and garlic to soften their flavors; they blend perfectly with the lamb.

This recipe calls for one jalapeño and one head of garlic per person. Roasting allows the garlic to become soft, mellow, and sweet, taming the bite and pungency of the uncooked bulb, and the jalapeños lose their searing heat. You will probably have to explain this to your guests before they try a bite of either.

12 fresh jalapeño peppers (see box, page 176)

Extra-virgin olive oil as needed

12 garlic heads

1 sprig fresh thyme

1 sprig fresh rosemary

12 1-pound trimmed racks of lamb, containing 6–8 chops each (see box, page 126)

3 tablespoons chimayo chili powder or cayenne pepper

Salt and freshly ground pepper to taste

1 cup water

¼ cup chicken glaze (order from your favorite restaurant) or strong, reduced chicken stock

Preheat the oven to 350°F. Blister the jalapeño peppers by brushing them with a little oil and cooking them in a very hot, lightly oiled skillet over medium-high heat until they are black on all sides. Set aside to cool. When cool enough to handle, peel off the skins.

Cut off the top part of each garlic head, leaving them intact, held together by the root, and place them in a large roasting pan along with the thyme and rosemary. Bake for 40 to 45 minutes.

In the meantime, prepare the lamb. When the jalapeños are cool enough to handle, split each pepper in half lengthwise and remove the seeds. Make 2 slits in each rack of lamb between the bones and slide half a pepper into each slit. Brush the lamb with olive oil, then dust lightly with the chili powder and sprinkle with the salt and pepper. In a large, dry skillet over medium-high heat, sauté the lamb racks on all sides to a golden color, about 2 minutes, doing this in batches if necessary (for a nice alternative, you may also grill the lamb on each side).

After the garlic has baked for 35 minutes, add the lamb to the roasting pan and cook for another 8 minutes, or until desired doneness. Remove the lamb and the garlic heads and set aside. Transfer the roasting pan to the stovetop. Add the water and chicken glaze and bring to a boil over medium-high heat, scraping up any browned bits from the pan. Slice the lamb and serve with 1 head of garlic per person. Top each serving with 1 tablespoon of the sauce.

SERVES 12

Cornmeal

Cornmeal—dried ground corn kernels—was developed as a foodstuff by Native Americans, and so it has been a staple in North American and Latin American diets for centuries. Americans have incorporated this protein- and carbohydrate-rich starch in a myriad of recipes, using it as a thickener for soups, a base for puddings, and, most often, a flour for doughs and pastries.

Vincent notes that there really is no difference between the blue and the more familiar yellow or white cornmeal except for color, which is determined by the type of corn that is ground. For the blinis, you can substitute yellow or white cornmeal, but the blinis won't be as "visually intriguing." Cornmeal also ranges in texture from fine to coarse, depending on the grinding process. The stone-ground (a.k.a. water-ground) method produces a coarser, more nutritious meal because it leaves some of the hull and germ of the kernel. Cornmeal produced this old-fashioned way should be stored, tightly sealed, in the refrigerator for no more than four months. Unless it is labeled stone- or water-ground, chances are it is fine cornmeal, processed the modern way, with steel grinders, and it can be stored indefinitely in a cool, dry place.

Lamb Facts

Lamb is categorized according to the diet (milk- or pasture-fed) and age of the animal. Baby lamb is the youngest and is milk-fed; spring lamb is milk- and pasture-fed; and regular lamb, which is the oldest but no more than a year old (as it would be a lamb no longer, but a sheep), is generally pasture-fed. The flavor, color, and texture of the meat, ranging from very mild to strong, pale pink to red, and tender to somewhat tough, depends on the type of lamb. The younger the lamb, the more delicate the flavor, the more tender the meat, and the paler the color. As to which type of lamb is the best, it depends on personal preference. To be sure you are getting the type of lamb you want, check its color when uncooked as the best guide. For this recipe, Vincent prefers racks of baby lamb.

Rack of lamb is composed of 6 to 8 chops. For this recipe, ask your butcher to cut the racks into 1-pound portions after trimming the fat. Lamb racks are covered with a thick layer of fat that must be removed before cooking, as it imparts a strong, usually unpleasant taste to the meat.

HERBED GRATIN DAUPHINOIS

You can't go wrong with this classic French side dish that goes with almost anything. Thinly sliced potatoes are layered with cream and cheese and baked until a crusty, golden gratin forms on top.

12 baking potatoes

3 garlic cloves, crushed

3 cups heavy cream

1 tablespoon salt

1 tablespoon ground white pepper

1 tablespoon fresh thyme leaves

1–1½ cups grated Gruyère cheese (optional)

Preheat the oven to 375°F. Peel and slice the potatoes very thinly. Heavily butter the bottom and sides of a 9 × 13 × 2-inch baking pan. Rub the bottom of the pan with the crushed garlic, then discard. Layer the potatoes evenly in the pan. Season the cream with salt, pepper, and thyme and pour over the potatoes. Bake for 40 to 50 minutes, until golden brown on top and tender throughout. If desired, sprinkle the cheese on top of the baked potatoes and brown under a broiler for about 2 minutes.

SERVES 12

PEACHES AND STRAWBERRIES POACHED IN HEAVY SYRUP

Served warm, this dessert makes a wonderful topping for a rich vanilla ice cream. If you prefer a nonfat dessert, serve the fruit in the sugar syrup, chilled, with fresh raspberries.

2 cups water
2 cups sugar
6 yellow peaches, halved and pitted, skins left on

2 pints strawberries, washed and hulled

Combine the water and sugar in a large saucepan over medium-high heat and bring to a boil. Cook for 5 minutes, stirring constantly. Add the peaches, reduce the heat to medium, and simmer in the syrup for 10 minutes. Then add the strawberries and cook for another 5 minutes, or until the peaches are translucent. Serve 1 peach half and a spoonful of strawberries to each person.

SERVES 12

HECTOR GUERRA

Simply Salvadoran

From dishwasher to line cook to master chef, Hector Guerra's story is special and inspiring. During the late seventies and early eighties, thousands of immigrants from El Salvador came to the United States to escape civil war in their country. In 1979, Hector Guerra was one of many who began a new life in Washington, D.C. He was sixteen years old and arrived with little education. He landed a job washing dishes at the famous French restaurant Le Pavillon. When Hector was asked to help on the salad line, chef-owner Yannick Cam recognized the young man's talent. "Yannick taught me so much, worked with me and groomed me. He would take my hands into his own and show me how to cut, dice, and chop." Under the tutelage of Cam, Hector mastered the art of both cooking and presentation. He stayed there for twelve years before joining the kitchen staff at Roberto Donna's restaurant, Galileo, where he started to develop his own style and reputation.

During Hector's time as chef-owner of the former El Patio Restaurant in Washington, D.C., he had the opportunity to prepare meals for several political leaders and other dignitaries, including the president of El Salvador. This opened the door to his becoming the executive chef at Fonda Del Sol in San Salvador. It is one of El Salvador's finest

MENU

Red Pepper Chiles Rellenos

———

Stuffed Avocados with Portobello Mushrooms

———

*Baked Salmon with Spinach in a
Light Tomato Sauce*

———

*Empanadas Rellenos con Leche
(Half-moon Pastries with Sweet Milk Filling)*

restaurants featuring native cuisine. He returned to Washington, D.C. in 1994 to open Arucola, Roberto Donna's newest Italian bistro.

Hector is well versed in both French and Italian cuisine, but his preference at home with his family is cooking traditional Salvadoran and other Latin American food. Hector adores cooking at home for two reasons: Cathy Madeleyne, age ten, and Aenia Yvette, age five. "My girls love it when I cook, which I do on weekends. Most Salvadoran families are so large that many pairs of hands are needed in the kitchen, and while my family isn't so big, we all pitch in. I have even more fun cooking at home than I do at the restaurant because my girls like to help, they ask a lot of questions, and they are open to trying anything I prepare."

Family birthdays are usually celebrated with a brunch or dinner buffet prepared by Hector, who is the oldest of nine children. In addition, Hector also enjoys impressing his friends with simple, enticing dishes like the ones he prepares for this menu.

Dinner starts off with Red Pepper Chiles Rellenos stuffed with ham or bacon and cheese. Cilantro, one of Hector's favorite herbs, is used liberally in both the Stuffed Avocados with Portobello Mushrooms and the baked salmon, adding a "fresh, clean fla-vor" to the dishes. The salmon is served with tomatoes and spinach and, like the stuffed avocado, must be prepared and served immediately. The sweetness of the empanadas complements the vibrant flavors of the savory dishes; Empanadas Rellenos con Leche is a traditional dessert in El Salva-dor that "always delights my guests," Hector says. "I wait for that smile to come on their face when they bite into the middle and get the sweet milk filling." The empanadas can be prepared several days in advance.

Hector suggests opening a bottle of red wine with the chiles rellenos and moves on to a Chilean white wine when he serves the stuffed avocado and the salmon. Hector's delicious Latin-style meal is a great example of how pampering your family and guests does not take anything more than a bit of care and some very accessible ingredients.

Red Pepper Chiles Rellenos

These are not the usual egg-coated, deep-fried chiles rellenos. Hector's rendition uses roasted red bell peppers instead of the hot green Anaheim peppers, and he gives them a stuffing of smoky ham and a mild, melted cheese. This is chiles rellenos, Italian style. Red peppers are more expensive, but for an occasional treat, it is worth it.

The pork lends enough flavor so that no seasonings are needed. You can use any type of ham depending on your taste and budget. To make this dish even more "Italian," use prosciutto and mozzarella cheese.

4 red bell peppers, roasted (see box, page 186)

4 thin slices ham, pancetta, or prosciutto

4 1-ounce chunks Monterey jack cheese

Preheat the oven to 450° F. Immediately place the peppers in a plastic or paper bag to steam. When cool enough to handle, peel the skins from the peppers, keeping the peppers intact. Carefully remove the stems and scoop out the seeds.

Wrap one slice of the ham around each chunk of cheese and stuff each bundle carefully into a pepper. Bake the peppers on a baking sheet for 10 to 15 minutes or until the cheese has melted. Serve immediately.

SERVES 4

VARIATION: For a vegetarian dish, leave out the ham and add one or two of your favorite herbs, such as basil and oregano.

STUFFED AVOCADOS WITH PORTOBELLO MUSHROOMS

Avocados are abundant in Latin America and are served in a variety of ways, including as a dessert with sweetened sour cream. This particular dish is not native to El Salvador; it was created by Hector in the United States. His love for this creamy, buttery fruit that he grew up with inspired him to create the dish.

2 ripe avocados
¾ cup sour cream
1 tablespoon unsalted butter
2 tablespoons extra-virgin olive or vegetable oil
1 garlic clove, minced

2 large portobello mushrooms, cleaned and cut into 1-inch cubes (use all of the mushroom; see box, pages 36–37)
1 tomato, cored and diced
1 tablespoon chopped fresh cilantro
Salt and freshly ground pepper to taste

Cut the avocados in half lengthwise. Remove the pits by imbedding a knife in the pit, twisting it back and forth, and lifting the pit out. Peel the skin from each half, leaving the halves intact. Place 1 tablespoon of sour cream in each avocado half. Transfer the avocados to a small plate and set aside.

Add the butter and oil to a large skillet and heat over medium heat. When the butter has melted, add the garlic, then toss in the mushrooms and sauté for 2 minutes. Add the tomato, cilantro, and a dash of salt and pepper. Sauté for 30 seconds or until the tomato is heated. Stuff one-fourth of the mushroom mixture into each avocado half. In a small saucepan, stir the remaining sour cream over low heat until it becomes liquid and just warm to the touch; do not let the sour cream get hot because it will separate. Drizzle 2 tablespoons of melted sour cream over each stuffed avocado. Serve immediately.

SERVES 4

Avocados

Hector prefers California Haas avocados, which have an almost black, lumpy skin, a yellowish-green flesh, a buttery taste, and a creamy texture. Avocados ripen after they've been picked and are perfect if they yield to gentle pressure. To hasten the ripening process, you can put them in a brown paper bag for a day. A cut avocado will darken from exposure to the air; this can be prevented by rubbing a cut lemon on the exposed surface of the flesh, and also by cutting them as close to serving time as possible.

BAKED SALMON WITH SPINACH IN A LIGHT TOMATO SAUCE

Hector cooks the salmon with simple ingredients: chunks of tomato, garlic, and cilantro. The key here is to use very fresh salmon.

4 tablespoons extra-virgin olive or vegetable oil
¼ cup chopped onion
1 15-ounce can peeled tomatoes, chopped and drained
2 cups chicken stock or water
4 7-ounce fresh salmon fillets

2 garlic cloves, crushed
12 ounces fresh spinach, washed and stemmed
½ cup chopped fresh tomatoes, for garnish
2 tablespoons chopped fresh cilantro, for garnish

Preheat the oven to 450°F. In a large, deep skillet, heat 1 tablespoon of the oil over medium-high heat and add the onion and tomatoes. Sauté lightly for about 1 minute, then stir in the stock or water. Place the salmon in a baking dish large enough to hold the fillets in a single layer and pour the sauce over. Bake for 10 minutes for medium-rare, or until desired doneness is reached.

In the meantime, heat the remaining 3 tablespoons of oil in a large skillet. Add the garlic and sauté lightly; do not brown. Add the spinach and sauté quickly until it wilts, about 1 minute. Divide the spinach evenly onto 4 serving plates, place one fillet on top of each, and pour the sauce evenly over the fillets. Garnish with the chopped tomatoes and cilantro.

SERVES 4

EMPANADAS RELLENOS CON LECHE (HALF-MOON PASTRIES WITH SWEET MILK FILLING)

This dessert is very popular throughout Latin America. Mashed plantain is used as a dough, shaped into empanadas (meaning "half-moons") to encase a sweet milk filling, and deep-fried. Hector serves this special dessert with elegant accompaniments, such as strawberry sauce and kiwifruit.

4 ripe plantains, unpeeled (see box, opposite)

SAUCE

2 pints fresh strawberries, washed and hulled

1 cup water

½ cup sugar

2 cups milk

½ cup cornstarch

1½ cups sugar

2 teaspoons vanilla extract

Dash of ground cinnamon

Vegetable or peanut oil, for deep-frying

1 kiwifruit, sliced, for garnish

In a large saucepan, boil the plantains in water to cover for 30 minutes over medium-high heat. Drain, peel, and mash the plantains. Refrigerate, covered, while preparing the rest.

Place the strawberries, water, and sugar in a heavy saucepan and bring to a boil over medium-high heat. Purée the mixture in a blender or food processor and strain through a fine sieve to remove the seeds. Refrigerate, covered, until ready to use.

Bring the milk to a boil in a large saucepan over medium-high heat. Lower the heat to medium-low and gradually whisk in the cornstarch, ½ cup of the sugar, and the vanilla. Whisk constantly until the mixture becomes very thick, 6 to 8 minutes. Stir in the cinnamon and set aside to cool.

Heat the oil in a deep-fryer or a large, heavy saucepan to 350°F. To test if the oil is hot enough, drop a small piece of the plantain dough in the oil. If the oil bubbles and the dough begins to cook immediately, the oil is ready. Pour the remaining cup of sugar on a large plate and set aside. Form the plantain dough into 4 equal balls (moisten hands with vegetable oil to prevent sticking) and flatten into pancakes about ⅛ to ¼ inch thick and 3 to 4 inches in diameter. Place one-fourth of the filling on half of each pancake, leaving the edges uncovered, and fold over to form half-moons. Press and crimp the edges to seal well.

Deep-fry the empanadas until golden brown, turning when the undersides are browned, about 2 or 3 minutes in all. Remove with a slotted spoon and transfer to the plate with the sugar. Roll the empanadas in the sugar to coat on all sides. Arrange the kiwifruit and banana on 4 serving plates. Transfer an empanada to each plate and serve warm with strawberry sauce.

SERVES 4

Plantains

The plantain, available year-round at most supermarkets, is a variety of the banana that is popular in Latin American, Caribbean, and some African diets. It resembles the banana in shape and color but is bigger, firmer, and has a tougher peel. With less sugar and more starch, the plantain tastes more like a squash than a banana. While plantains can be eaten unripe or ripe, they must be cooked before eating. Unripe plantains are green, firm, starchy, and not sweet; it's an acquired taste not favored by many. Allow them two weeks to fully ripen. When medium-ripe, they are yellow with black speckles and mildly sweet and tender; and, when very ripe, they are black, sweet, and even more tender.

Choose plantains with unblemished skins and fresh stem ends and store at room temperature until desired ripeness. Once ripe, they may be refrigerated for three to five days, but they are best if eaten right away. Generally, plantains are peeled before cooking. To remove the tough peel, slice off one end, slit the skin from top to bottom lengthwise, and unfurl sideways.

This "cooking banana" can be baked, braised, sautéed, fried, or boiled, as in Hector's Empanada Rellenos con Leche. Cooking time will vary according to maturity: the riper the plantain, the less time is needed. A plantain cooked just right will be tender but still hold its shape. As a general guideline, a medium-ripe plantain, without the skin, will take approximately 40 minutes in a 375°F. oven or about 30 minutes when poached.

Cooked plantains are used in stews or as a side dish and are wonderful when paired with ginger, chili pepper, red peppers, or sour cream. Try them the next time you are serving brunch or tropical fare.

MADELEINE KAMMAN

Striped Pajamas and Other Childhood Favorites

Cooking at home is such an old habit for Madeleine Kamman that it has become second nature. "When someone yells, 'when's dinner?', it's on the table in twenty minutes," she says. "I learned to prepare meals quickly when I was a university student and I was forced to perfect the skill when I worked long hours as the reservation office director for an airline in Paris."

Madeleine's earliest exposure to this efficient style of cooking was through her hard-working mother while she was growing up in France. Throughout her high school years her afternoons were spent shopping, peeling vegetables for dinner, and making mayonnaise from scratch. Her childhood vacations were spent in her aunt's Michelin-starred restaurant in the Loire Valley, where one of her jobs was to prepare dinner for the staff.

The menu Madeleine presents here is in part a reflection of the foods she ate at home as a child. "The soup reminds me of when I was a little girl on a trip with my parents, when we stopped at a farm while passing through Bresse, one of the corn-meal-producing regions of France. "I remember a lady sitting there making stuff with zucchini and cornmeal," she says.

The Chicken Legs in Striped Pajamas with Anise Carrots was so named because pancetta reminds Madeleine of the nightgown her mother made her from striped

MENU

Gaudes and Chives

*Chicken Legs in Striped Pajamas
with Anise Carrots*

Pear and Romaine Salad

Baked Figs with Crème Fraîche

pajamas during World War II, when sewing material was scarce. Madeleine loves pears and feels they are a perfect complement to the slight sweetness in the romaine lettuce. "Wherever I can put pears, I put," she says. For the dessert, Madeleine is lucky enough to simply pick the figs from the trees at Beringer, or gather any of the fallen fruit from the ground. "Noboby wants them, so I take them and bake them!"

As director of Beringer Vineyard's School of American Chefs, in California's Napa Valley, Madeleine has more than thirty-three years' experience in the food industry. She is a renowned teacher of chefs, the author of several prestigious cookbooks, and a tireless culinary scholar. "Chefs come to my school to benefit from another perspective and I enjoy infusing them with renewed enthusiasm."

In 1960, she moved to the United States after marrying an American and immediately became involved in teaching her native cuisine. "I started teaching my neighbors how to cook quickly, efficiently, and as deliciously as possible." In 1969, she and her family moved to Boston, where Madeleine opened Modern Gourmet, a professional

school for chefs, and later a restaurant, Chez la Mère Madeleine, with the help of her students from 1973 to 1980, before returning to France to open another cooking school. She continued teaching both in the United States and abroad, and in 1987, she began working at Beringer. "After  bristling in the frigid winters of New England became too much to bear, we retreated toward the vineyards of the Napa Valley, where I continue teaching and sharing my long-accumulated knowledge with the young chefs of America." It was there that she met her assistant, Debra Murphy, whom she has worked with over the past seven years, and who is a regular guest at Madeleine's house for a home-cooked meal.

Decades of cooking and teaching have only reinforced Madeleine's appreciation for fine food without fanfare: "I hope you will like this ultra-simple Mama's food; it has served me in my professional cooking career, and with it, I have raised two wonderful young sons and close to six hundred professional chefs. Nothing grandiose, as you will see—simply something good for a peaceful family dinner during a California sunset."

Gaudes and Chives

Gaudes is a thick cornmeal soup from the region of the Jura mountains of France, and was a major food staple up until a couple of decades ago. It is often topped with milk, cream, or even wine; in this recipe, milk is used to thin out the soup. Do not omit the garlic from this soup, or as Madeleine says, "it will not taste civilized."

6 tablespoons (¾ stick) unsalted butter, softened

¼ cup chopped fresh chives

2 small garlic cloves, finely chopped

2 tablespoons chopped fresh Italian parsley

½ cup finely ground yellow cornmeal

2 tablespoons corn oil

2 yellow onions, finely chopped

1 small zucchini, finely chopped

3 cups chicken stock

1 cup cold milk, or more if needed

Salt and freshly ground pepper to taste

With an electric mixer, cream the butter, chives, garlic, and parsley in a mixing bowl. Transfer the butter mixture to a small container, cover, and refrigerate for at least 1 hour.

Preheat the oven to 325°F. Spread the cornmeal on a small jelly-roll pan and toast in the oven until it turns beige, checking the color at regular intervals; make sure it does not become too dark. Remove from the oven, transfer the cornmeal to a small bowl, and cool completely.

Heat the oil in a medium stockpot over medium-high heat. Add the onions and zucchini and cook until all the moisture has evaporated. Add the chicken stock and bring to a boil. Whisk the milk into the cornmeal and add to the boiling stock. Whisk until the mixture returns to a boil, add the salt and pepper, and reduce the heat to medium-low. Continue to simmer the soup until it has thickened, whisking occasionally, about 30 minutes. If a thinner soup is preferred, add a little more milk.

Just before serving, whisk in the herb butter and correct the seasoning. Serve in bowls.

Serves 6

Wine Suggestions

The chef recommends a glass of good French Beaujolais, a fruity American Zinfandel, or an Italian Grignolino to drink with the Chicken Legs in Striped Pajamas. Among each of these wine types, you'll be able to find reasonably priced wines.

CHICKEN LEGS IN STRIPED PAJAMAS WITH ANISE CARROTS

In this simple recipe, pancetta—a long-aged Italian cured pork brisket—replaces the chicken skin to keep the meat moist and add flavor. The sweet, subtle licorice flavor of anise is a great match with carrots. Madeleine says, "these carrots are overcooked by American standards to what the French call the 'melting' stage; they melt in the mouth!"

Like many chefs, Madeleine does not like to give cooking times, as every stove and oven is different, and even in the same kitchen a dish can turn out differently each time, depending on a multitude of factors. In her recipes, as in all recipes, it is important to look at, touch, smell, taste, and feel the food; and regard given times as suggested guidelines, not as concrete rules.

12 chicken thighs

12 very thin slices (½ pound) pancetta (see Note)

2 tablespoons unsalted butter or oil of your choice

1–1½ cups chicken stock

1 pound baby carrots

1 tablespoon anise seeds

Salt and freshly ground pepper to taste

Chopped fresh parsley, for garnish

Remove the skin from the chicken thighs and wrap a piece of pancetta around each thigh, pressing the end to seal.

In a large skillet, heat the butter or oil over medium-high heat, add the chicken, and cook until lightly golden on both sides. It may be necessary to do this in batches to avoid overcrowding. Pour off any fat left in the pan and add ½ cup of chicken stock to the chicken. Cover the pan with the lid left slightly askew and cook until the stock has reduced to a glaze. The cooking time will depend on the thickness of the stock and the heaviness of the skillet. Add remaining stock as needed for the desired consistency, turn the chicken over, and cook until the chicken is opaque and the juices run clear, 15 to 20 minutes, depending on the size of the thighs.

Meanwhile, put the carrots and anise seeds in a large skillet and barely cover with cold water. Place over high heat and bring to a rapid boil. Add salt and pepper and continue to boil rapidly, uncovered, until all the water has evaporated, shaking the pan regularly. Toss the carrots into the chicken pot, turn the mixture into a large serving dish, and top with parsley.

SERVES 6

NOTE: Madeleine says that you can use bacon instead of pancetta, if you prefer. She explains, "the pancetta will be better for the fall, and the bacon better for the winter, because of its lovely smoky flavor."

Homemade Meat Stock

Homemade stock cannot be beat. It has a delicate flavor that will not be found in canned stocks, which are usually loaded with salt and lacking in real meat flavor. It requires some advance planning and a butcher with leftover bones to sell. However, for the Chicken Legs in Striped Pajamas you can use any stock of your choice, from canned stock to your best chicken or veal stock. "Anything will go well," Madeleine says. The different kinds of stocks, combined with different kinds of pancetta or bacon, will lend different nuances to this dish. Mix and match to find your favorite combo.

To make homemade stock, follow a favorite beef, veal, or lamb stock recipe, or use the guidelines below. An alternative is to inquire at a favorite restaurant about purchasing some stock.

Keys to a successful stock—one that is clear, fat free, and flavorful—are:

1. Roast the bones until they are completely browned in a 400° F. oven.

2. Add the bones to the stockpot and fill with just enough cold water to cover the bones (never start a stockpot with warm or hot water).

3. Slowly simmer the stock for four to five hours, skimming the fat and "scum" as necessary; do not boil the stock.

4. Use a fine sieve to strain.

5. Allow the stock to cool and then remove the fat from the top before using. Store leftover stock in the freezer for six to eight weeks.

PEAR AND ROMAINE SALAD

Romaine lettuce is crunchy and slightly bitter, making it a perfect foil to sweet, tender pears. Discard the outermost leaves of the lettuce head, but keep the innermost small, pale green leaves; they are the best part. After rinsing the lettuce leaves, Madeleine wraps them in a towel to absorb excess moisture that might wilt the leaves, and refrigerates them until ready to use. Removing the rib or tearing the leaves long before serving time also causes wilting.

Madeleine likes this salad best when it is dressed with pistachio oil. However, the more accessible hazelnut or walnut oils are also delicious.

DRESSING

2 tablespoons corn oil

2 tablespoon pistachio, hazelnut, or walnut oil (available at specialty markets)

1 tablespoon balsamic vinegar

Salt and freshly ground pepper to taste

SALAD

3 Bosc pears, washed, cored, and cut into ¼-inch slices

2 medium heads romaine lettuce, washed and dried, ribs removed, torn into bite-size pieces

In a small bowl whisk together the oils and vinegar. Season with salt and pepper. In a salad bowl, toss the pear slices with one-third of the dressing and set aside to marinate for 15 minutes. Toss in the lettuce and add more dressing to taste.

SERVES 6

Pan Preferences

Madeleine recommends using a thick-bottomed *sauteuse,* or sauté pan, for Chicken Legs in Striped Pajamas. These pans have heavy bases and are usually made of stainless steel lined with copper, which conducts heat well. A regular skillet, frying pan, or electric frying pan can be used, but she points out that more stock may be necessary as it will evaporate more quickly.

BAKED FIGS WITH CRÈME FRAÎCHE

Figs are delicious any-which-way, but what makes this dessert even more special is baking them in the "wonderfully unctuous" California Angelica wine, made from the Mission Grape—if you are lucky enough to have access to a bottle. It is a specialty wine that originated in the Los Angeles area. Madeleine prefers the Angelica made by Heitz Cellar in St. Helena, California. If you cannot find true Angelica, use cream sherry or port instead.

12 large fresh figs, preferably Black Mission
6 tablespoons sugar

½ cup California Angelica or port
6 tablespoons Crème Fraîche, well chilled (see box, page 237)

Preheat the oven to 350° F. With a sharp knife, cut the figs lengthwise into several thin slices without cutting through the stem, so they do not separate into individual slices. Spread open the figs into fans. Grease a large baking dish with butter or oil, arrange the fanned figs in it, and sprinkle them with the sugar. Pour the wine over the figs and bake until they have softened and their juices have mixed with the wine, 10 to 15 minutes.

Remove the figs from the baking pan with a slotted spoon, placing 2 figs on each serving plate. Transfer the liquid to a saucepan over high heat and reduce to 6 tablespoons. Spoon 1 tablespoon of juice over each portion and top with 1 tablespoon of chilled Crème Fraîche.

SERVES 6

EMERIL LAGASSE

Creole Inspirations

Not many couples can boast "his and her" kitchens, but Emeril Lagasse loves to cook at home so much that he has built a separate kitchen in addition to the one his wife uses. "The new kitchen is equipped to prepare anything I like and lets me experiment at home and develop recipes for the restaurant." His fascination with cooking can be traced to his childhood in the small town of Fall River, Massachusetts, where relatives and friends had substantial fruit and vegetable gardens. He remembers people picking grapes in his backyard to make wine. It was in this environment that he began to formulate his attitude toward food, which is that "ideally, it is best to grow your own; if you want it, you grow it, respect it, and eat it." Emeril acknowledges that not everyone is in a position to grow his or her own food, but he reminds us that today top-quality foods are much more readily available.

Passing up a scholarship in music—Emeril's other passion, which he continues to develop—he chose to pursue a culinary career and attended Johnson and Wales College, earning an honorary doctorate degree in the culinary arts. After completing a study of classic cuisine in France, he returned to the United States. Combining the extraordinary and diverse flavors of Cajun, Creole, French, and Spanish food, Emeril

MENU

Creole-Cooked Artichokes

❧

Seared Medallions of Beef Tenderloin with Fire-Roasted Corn Sauce and Mashed Potatoes with Roasted Garlic

❧

Chocolate Ganache Cake with Strawberries

quickly gained fame as the king of New Orleans cuisine at the legendary Commander's Palace restaurant, where he was head chef for nearly eight years. In 1990, in the fashionable warehouse district of New Orleans, he opened Emeril's, where he is committed to using the freshest, highest-quality ingredients in his eclectic Creole-based cuisine. NOLA, Emeril's latest restaurant, opened in the French Quarter in 1992 and features casual food with an emphasis on whimsically reinvented New Orleans cuisine.

In his spacious New Orleans home Emeril thinks nothing of inviting as many as twenty friends for dinner, although this menu is suited to a more intimate gathering of four guests. "Food is an expression of fun with family and friends. Some of his best friends are his co-workers and colleagues, and he often invites them over for a leisurely Sunday feast. "The guests show up in the late afternoon and the evening winds down between nine and ten o'clock. The guys take over in the kitchen, the women chill, and my three dogs—Krug, Fino, and Crystal—keep me company while I'm cooking. During the week Emeril is constantly on the run and eats light, but by the end of the week he is in the mood for something heavier and richer. In the winter he cooks peasant style, preferring rustic foods such as roasts and gumbos; when the temperature heats up, he turns to grilled meats, vegetables, and seafoods.

Emeril starts off with Creole-Cooked Artichokes—very, very New Orleans. "I usually boil them as suggested here or steam them; they are so easy to flavor." With this course Emeril recommends Ceretto, an Italian white wine often served with artichokes in Italy. Frequently asked the secret of good New Orleans cooking, Emeril's answer is simply "the secret is in the seasoning." Emeril creates his own mixture of herbs and spices that can easily be made at home and kept on hand to spice up any dish. He uses a generous amount here to enhance the Seared Medallions of Beef Tenderloin and suggests pouring a Languedoc, a Rhône wine. Emeril finishes this hearty meal bursting with well-balanced Creole flavors with the sweet depth of

a Chocolate Ganache Cake with Strawberries and breaks open a Domaine Chandon Blanc de Noir to end the meal on a celebratory note.

CREOLE-COOKED ARTICHOKES

These spicy artichokes are served cold with an herb dressing for dipping the leaves. Both the artichokes and the dressing are made in advance for easy "night of" preparation. Delicious on their own, these artichokes can also be placed on a bed of lettuce, drizzled with the vinaigrette, and eaten as a salad.

2 lemons, cut in half

1 tablespoon salt

4 bay leaves

8 black peppercorns

2 tablespoons Creole Spice Mixture (see box, page 150)

4 large artichokes, trimmed (see box, page 209)

¼ cup extra-virgin olive oil

Herb Dressing (recipe follows)

In a large stockpot over high heat, bring about 2 quarts of water to a boil with the lemons, salt, bay leaves, peppercorns, and Creole Spice Mixture. Add the artichokes and return to a boil. Reduce the heat to a simmer and allow to cook, covered, for 40 to 45 minutes. The base of the artichoke should be easily pierced with the tip of a knife when done.

Remove the artichokes and cool in a colander under cold, running water. Drain the artichokes by turning them upside down in the colander. Toss lightly in the olive oil and refrigerate in an airtight container until ready to serve with the dressing for dipping.

SERVES 4

HERB DRESSING

2 tablespoons balsamic vinegar

½ cup extra-virgin olive oil

2 tablespoons chopped mixed fresh herbs, or 1 tablespoon dried (such as tarragon, basil, and chives)

1 teaspoon minced garlic

Salt and freshly ground pepper to taste

In a jar with a tight-fitting lid, combine all the ingredients and shake well to combine. Let stand at room temperature for at least 15 minutes to allow the flavors to blend. Adjust the seasoning with salt and pepper.

MAKES ABOUT ½ CUP

SEARED MEDALLIONS OF BEEF TENDERLOIN WITH FIRE-ROASTED CORN SAUCE AND MASHED POTATOES WITH ROASTED GARLIC

Emeril tops the seasoned beef with a complexly flavored but simply made roasted corn sauce.

12 2-ounce beef tenderloin medallions

2 tablespoons Southwestern Spice Mixture (see box, page 150)

1 tablespoon extra-virgin olive oil

2 cups Mashed Potatoes with Roasted Garlic (recipe follows)

1 cup Fire-Roasted Corn Sauce (recipe follows)

2 scallions, finely chopped

Season the beef with the Southwestern Spice Mixture and set aside for at least 20 minutes.

Heat the oil in a large skillet over medium-high heat, add the beef, and turn once after 1 or 2 minutes. Cook for an additional 1 to 2 minutes for rare, or until desired doneness is reached.

Divide the mashed potatoes evenly on 4 dinner plates. Briefly drain the medallions on paper towels to remove the excess grease. Place 3 medallions on each plate, next to the potatoes. Spoon the sauce over the beef and sprinkle the scallions over the mashed potatoes. Serve immediately.

SERVES 4

FIRE-ROASTED CORN SAUCE

1 cup fresh corn kernels (about 2 ears), or frozen kernels, thawed

½ teaspoon salt

Pinch of freshly ground pepper

¼ cup chopped scallions

¼ cup chopped onion

1 tablespoon minced garlic

1 tablespoon molasses

2 cups strong, dark veal or beef stock

1 tablespoon chopped fresh cilantro

Heat a medium saucepan over high heat until very hot. Add the corn, salt, and pepper, and cook, shaking the pan occasionally, until the corn is charred evenly, 3 to 5 minutes. Add the scallions, onion, and garlic and continue cooking for 1 minute. Add the molasses and toss the ingredients to coat evenly. Add the stock and bring to a boil. Reduce the heat to medium-low and simmer for 15 to 20 minutes. Just before serving, stir in the cilantro.

MAKES 1¼ CUPS

MASHED POTATOES WITH ROASTED GARLIC

The ultimate in comfort food for garlic lovers!

3 cups water

2 cups peeled and diced baking potatoes, preferably Idaho

2 teaspoons salt

½–¾ cup heavy cream, as desired

6 roasted and peeled garlic cloves
   (see box, below)

½ teaspoon ground white pepper

2 tablespoons (¼ stick) unsalted butter,
   softened

In a medium saucepan over high heat, bring about 3 cups of water, the potatoes, and ½ teaspoon salt to a boil. Reduce the heat to medium-low and simmer until the potatoes are tender, 8 to 10 minutes. Remove the pan from the heat and drain the potatoes in a colander.

Return the potatoes to the pan over medium heat. Add the cream, roasted garlic, white pepper, and remaining salt. Mash vigorously with a potato masher until fairly smooth. Fold in the butter until blended and serve immediately.

SERVES 4 GENEROUSLY

Roasting Garlic

Roasting mellows the flavor of garlic and softens it to a wonderful, spreadable paste. Spread on crusty French bread, roasted garlic makes a delicious hors d'oeuvre.

To ROAST a whole garlic head, Emeril cuts the garlic in half crosswise, drizzles ¼ teaspoon of extra-virgin olive oil over the top of each half, and seasons each with salt and pepper to taste. Then he wraps the garlic halves in foil cut side up, and bakes in a 350°F. oven for 20 to 30 minutes, until the garlic cloves are soft. To remove the garlic, he pushes the cloves out of their skins.

To ROAST individual garlic cloves, cut the tips off one end of each clove and toss with a little extra-virgin olive oil, salt, and pepper. Then wrap a couple of cloves together in foil and bake at 350°F. for about 15 minutes or until soft. Push the roasted clove out of its skin.

Emeril's Secret Seasonings

Emeril has found the perfect blends of herbs and spices and has created his own Creole seasonings, which you can easily make at home. Store them indefinitely in airtight containers, and keep them on hand for an easy way to spice up any dish.

SOUTHWESTERN SPICE MIXTURE. In a small bowl, thoroughly combine 2 tablespoons chili powder, 2 tablespoons paprika, 1 tablespoon ground coriander, 1 tablespoon garlic powder, 1 tablespoon salt, 2 teaspoons ground cumin, 1 teaspoon cayenne pepper, 1 teaspoon crushed red pepper flakes, 1 teaspoon freshly ground black pepper, and 1 teaspoon dried oregano. Makes about ½ cup.

CREOLE SPICE MIXTURE. In a small bowl, thoroughly combine 2½ tablespoons paprika, 1½ tablespoons salt, 2 tablespoons garlic powder, 1 tablespoon freshly ground black pepper, 1 tablespoon onion powder, 1 tablespoon cayenne pepper, 1 tablespoon dried oregano, 1 tablespoon dried thyme, and ½ tablespoon dried basil. Makes about ⅔ cup.

CHOCOLATE GANACHE CAKE WITH STRAWBERRIES

This dessert is decadent. A small piece is more than enough to satisfy, as it is so rich. Emeril serves this dense, flourless chocolate cake with strawberries and whipped cream.

8 ounces semisweet chocolate, coarsely chopped
½ cup (1 stick) unsalted butter, softened
5 large eggs, separated and at room temperature
¾ cup sugar
2 teaspoons vanilla extract
1 teaspoon Chambord or other raspberry-flavored liqueur

½ teaspoon salt

GANACHE ICING
8 ounces good-quality semisweet chocolate, chopped
½ cup heavy cream

Whipped cream
1 pint fresh strawberries, washed and hulled

Preheat the oven to 350° F. Grease a 9-inch springform pan with butter and dust with flour, tapping out any excess.

In a metal bowl over a pot of simmering water, melt the chocolate with the butter. Stir occasionally until smooth and creamy. Remove the bowl from the heat and set aside.

In a large bowl of an electric mixer, beat the egg yolks with the sugar, vanilla, and liqueur until thick, about 3 minutes. In another large bowl, whip the egg whites with the salt until stiff but not dry, about 2 minutes. Fold the chocolate into the yolk mixture, adding it slowly to keep the eggs from cooking, as the chocolate will still be warm. Gently fold in the egg whites just until combined.

Pour the batter into the prepared pan and bake in the center of the oven until spongy when pressed lightly in the center, about 40 minutes. Remove the cake from the oven and cool on a rack for 10 minutes, then remove the sides of the pan and cool completely.

In the meantime, prepare the ganache icing. In a metal bowl set over a pot of simmering water, melt the chocolate with the cream, stirring constantly until smooth. Do not allow the mixture to boil. Remove from the heat and spread over the cooled cake. Let the icing cool and harden a little.

To make cutting the cake easy, warm the knife by running it under hot water and wipe dry. Repeat this procedure after each cut. Cut the cake into small wedges. Top each slice with a dollop of whipped cream and some strawberries.

SERVES *8*

N O T E : Chocolate ganache is a chocolate icing made by melting chocolate with cream. It has a multitude of uses—as a glaze, whipped for a frosting or filling, or even poured over ice cream. Ganache can be flavored with a variety of additions, such as extracts or liqueurs.

Melting Chocolate

There are several ways to melt chocolate, and you can use whichever one is most convenient at the time. Place the chocolate either in the top of a double boiler set over low simmering water or in a metal bowl fitted over a saucepan filled with an inch of water (do not let the water touch the bowl) and stir until melted. Or microwave the chocolate in a glass bowl on medium power, in thirty-second intervals, stirring in between, until the chocolate is completely melted. If the chocolate is being melted with butter, liqueur, or some other liquid, you can put the saucepan directly over very low heat, stirring constantly so that it does not burn.

ZARELA MARTÍNEZ

Memories of Mexico

Family influences and memories of home are the soul of this traditional Sunday Mexican meal. The menu consists of the food Zarela Martínez ate growing up on a Mexican ranch and today prepares for her own children on Sunday evenings. "This menu takes me back to the kitchen, where the scent of burning wood would cling to the clothes, and if I close my eyes, the comforting smell comes back to me."

Born in Sonora, Mexico, into a family of cattle ranchers, Zarela went to El Paso, Texas, as a young girl to attend boarding school. During the holidays, she went back to Mexico where her mother, Aida, also an accomplished home cook and author of her own cookbook, prepared dinner for a house full of guests, including a bunch of children. "Mom would keep the kids entertained by giving us cooking lessons. Flour tortillas are the first thing I remember learning how to make."

In the early stages of her career, Zarela took cooking classes around the country before deciding that the best way to learn was to sample and replicate as much restaurant cooking as possible. Together, she and her mother duplicated almost everything they tried. In New Orleans, she found her best teacher when she walked into K-Paul's Kitchen. There she met Paul Prudhomme, who invited her into his own kitchen and offered to teach her Cajun cooking if she

MENU

Frijoles Maneados
(Stirred, Refried, and Baked Beans)

━

Pollo Almendrado
(Chicken in Almond Sauce)

━

Sopa Seca
(Dry Soup)

would agree to teach him Mexican. She and Paul became fast friends. "He introduced me to everyone, he taught me how to deal with the press, he grounded me," she recalls.

Zarela moved to New York City and sparked her career when she went to work at Cafe Marimba, known as the city's first restaurant to serve regional Mexican cuisine. She started out designing the menu and later became the executive chef. But she really hit her stride in 1987, when she opened her own restaurant, Zarela, where loyal diners and food writers eagerly followed. Like her home, Zarela's restaurant is decorated with fun knick-knacks picked up in Mexico during her frequent visits. While Zarela's cooking reflects all regions of Mexico, she is inspired the most by food of the southern part of the country, especially Oaxaca. "The city is so multicultural, which is reflected in the cuisine—lots of sauces, chilies, fruits, smoky and sweet flavors," she says.

This hearty fare is not at all difficult to make, though it does require some time to prepare. Frijoles Maneados (creamy refried and baked beans) is a dish from northern Mexico and a childhood favorite of Zarela's. The beans are cooked slowly and carefully with chili pepper (or *chile,* Zarela's preferred Spanish spelling) and other seasonings and are prepared in three separate stages, but the result is well worth the wait. Zarela remembers, "As children, my sisters and I fought for the delicious crust that forms on the beans; to me, it is like biting into a chocolate truffle."

Nut-based sauces are common in Mexican cooking, so Zarela shares a popular chicken dish, Pollo Almendrado, that is served with an easy-to-prepare almond sauce. This dish can be prepared six hours in advance; the chicken left slightly undercooked

so that it does not dry out, and it is then reheated in the oven before serving. The Sopa Seca (dry soup) is prepared in traditional Mexican fashion, and it resembles a pilaf but is made with small pastas. It should be prepared just before serving.

To finish this meal with something sweet, Zarela recommends simply serving ice cream topped with *cajeta,* a Mexican caramel sauce that can be found in specialty stores. Zarela's sophisticated cooking has earned her a reputation as a premier chef, but she never strays too far from her Mexican roots.

Frijoles Maneados
(Stirred, Refried, and Baked Beans)

The low-fat milk and the browned onion that flavors the fat here provide the richness in this simple bean dish from northern Mexico. The trick to obtaining the creamy texture is to simmer the puréed beans for an hour, stirring often, and then bake until a crust forms on top. White cheddar cheese and fried red chilies, such as anchos or pasillas, are a nice topping.

The beans can be prepared up to the baking stage one day in advance and baked just before serving. This recipe makes the perfect amount for this menu. However, if you're cooking for a bigger crowd, this recipe doubles nicely.

½ **pound yellow or small white beans (pinto beans may be substituted), picked over**

1 **scallion, including the green**

½ **teaspoon salt, plus more to taste**

1 **cup low-fat milk**

2 **tablespoons lard (see box, page 158)**

1 **small onion, cut in eighths**

2 **tablespoons corn or vegetable oil**

1 **ancho or New Mexico dried red chili pepper, cored, seeded, and thinly sliced (see box, page 176)**

½ **cup shredded white cheddar cheese (optional)**

Rinse the beans under cold running water and place in a large, heavy pot or Dutch oven. Add the scallion and cold water to cover the beans by at least 2 inches, about 5 cups. Bring to a boil over high heat and then lower the heat to maintain a low simmer. Cook, partly covered, for 20 to 25 minutes, until the beans are about half done (they will be somewhat chalky and dense inside). Check the water level, adding more boiling water if the beans seem to be getting dry; there should always be at least 1 inch of water covering the beans.

Continue to cook until the beans are tender, occasionally checking the water level and adding a little more boiling water if necessary. Cooking time will vary greatly depending on the age and condition of the beans. It will take as little as 45 minutes if the beans are fairly fresh, or more than 1½ hours for old, very dry beans. Season with salt toward the end of the cooking time. Discard the scallion and let the beans cool.

Strain the beans, reserving the remaining cooking liquid. Purée the beans in the food processor or blender, adding some of the cooking liquid and ½ cup of the milk. You might have to do this in batches.

Heat the lard over medium-high heat in a large, heavy saucepan or Dutch oven. Add the onion and cook, stirring often, until browned, about 8 minutes. Remove the onion with a slotted spoon and discard. Add the bean purée and the remaining ½ cup of milk to the hot lard, stirring well to combine. Cook on low heat, covered, for 1 hour, stirring often.

While the beans cook, preheat the oven to 325° F. Heat the oil in a small frying pan over medium-high heat and fry the sliced pepper until crisp but not browned, 30 to 45 seconds. Watch it carefully because a burned pepper makes the whole dish turn bitter. Remove with a slotted spoon and drain on absorbent paper towels.

Place the beans in a 1-quart baking dish and bake uncovered for 45 minutes, or until a crust forms on the top. Top with the fried pepper and cheddar cheese, if desired.

SERVES 4 GENEROUSLY

POLLO ALMENDRADO
(CHICKEN IN ALMOND SAUCE)

To enliven this dish, Zarela adds olives to the sauce for tanginess, golden raisins for sweetness, and a variety of spices that explode in the mouth. This sauce also works well with roasted pork, duck, or lamb.

For a different twist, make this sauce with peanuts and vary the spices as you wish.

1 3½-pound chicken, cut into quarters

Salt and freshly ground black pepper
　to taste

3 tablespoons vegetable oil

1 2-inch piece true Ceylon cinnamon
　(see box, opposite)

1 teaspoon coriander seeds

4 garlic cloves, chopped

1 large onion, thinly sliced

4 ancho peppers, stemmed and seeded,
　cut into strips (see box, page 176)

1 large, ripe red tomato, peeled (see
　box, page 311), cored, and sliced

1 French roll (4 or 5 inches), sliced,
　toasted, and crumbled

½ cup golden raisins

¾ cup sliced pitted green olives

1 cup blanched whole or slivered
　almonds

½ cup white wine vinegar

1 cup dry sherry

2 cups chicken stock or water

Toasted almonds, for garnish
　(optional)

Rinse the chicken pieces with cold water and pat dry with paper towels. Sprinkle with salt and pepper. Heat the oil over high heat in a Dutch oven or large saucepan until hot. Cook the chicken pieces until golden on all sides, about 4 minutes in all. Remove the chicken from the pan and set aside. Let the oil cool.

Remove all but 2 tablespoons of the oil. Stir to scrape up any browned chicken bits clinging to the bottom and return the pan to medium-high heat. When the oil is hot, add the cinnamon, coriander seeds, garlic, onion, and ancho peppers. Stir for 1 minute. Add the tomato, bread crumbs, raisins, green olives, and almonds and cook, stirring frequently, for 2 minutes more.

Return the chicken to the pan. Add the vinegar, sherry, and 1 cup of the chicken stock. Let the sauce come to a boil and simmer, covered, until the chicken is cooked through, 25 to 30 minutes.

Remove the chicken with a slotted spoon to a serving dish and keep warm. Transfer the sauce to a blender or food processor and process until it becomes a slightly coarse liquid, adding the remaining 1 cup chicken stock as needed. Process until smooth, about the consistency of heavy cream. Return the sauce to the saucepan and bring it to a boil over high heat. Pour the sauce over the chicken and serve immediately, garnished with toasted almonds, if desired.

SERVES *4*

Ceylon Cinnamon

Ceylon cinnamon (called *canela* in Mexico) is true cinnamon, from the *Cinnamomum zeylanicum* tree. The cinnamon that is used in the United States actually comes from the cassia tree (*Cinnamon cassia*), and it has a stronger, harsher flavor and a hard bark. The bark of Ceylon cinnamon is softer and thinner, with concentric layers that splinter easily when you break off a piece. The color is medium tan, not the reddish brown that you usually see. The pungent aftertones that American cooks associate with cinnamon do not belong to *canela*. The latter blends subtly with complementary seasonings and will not drown out other flavors. It is available through mail order and at Mexican markets. A regular cinnamon stick could be used, but it must be discarded before puréeing the ingredients for the almond sauce.

Lard

Zarela often uses lard in place of butter or vegetable oil because it imparts much more flavor to dishes. She claims that lard is one of the most misunderstood fats. Home-rendered lard contains oleic acid, which helps break down cholesterol. However, since lard does contain saturated fat, use canola oil instead if you're concerned about cholesterol.

TO MAKE lard at home, buy unsalted pork fat, which is available in thin sheets or slabs, from your butcher. Dice it into ½-inch squares. Heat a small amount of oil in a heavy-bottomed Dutch oven or saucepan and add the pork fat. Cook over low heat until the fat is rendered. Discard the pieces that remain. Store the lard in a tightly covered container in the refrigerator for up to two weeks or freeze for up to two months.

SOPA SECA
(DRY SOUP)

Roasted tomato and jalapeño pepper give this Mexican "pasta pilaf" a wonderful rustic flare. Zarela likes to top it off with pico de gallo, *a fresh tomato salsa, and freshly grated Parmesan cheese, which gives the pasta a nice lift.*

1 large tomato, roasted and peeled
   (see box, opposite)

1 small onion, coarsely chopped

1 large garlic clove

6 sprigs fresh cilantro

1 large jalapeño pepper, roasted (see
   box, opposite), peeled, and stemmed

¼ cup vegetable oil

7 ounces very small pasta, such as
   melon seeds, alphabet, or tiny circles

2 cups chicken stock, or water

Freshly grated Parmesan cheese

Pico de gallo (optional)

Place the tomato, onion, garlic, cilantro, and jalapeño pepper in a blender or food processor and process until almost smooth, about 1 minute. Reserve.

Heat the oil in a saucepan or Dutch oven over medium-high heat. Cook the pasta, stirring constantly, until golden, 2 to 3 minutes. Drain off all but 2 tablespoons of the oil if the pasta did not absorb most of the oil. Add the puréed tomato mixture and cook, stirring often, for 2 minutes. Reduce the heat to medium-low, add the chicken stock, and bring to a simmer. Cover the saucepan and cook for 20 minutes or until the liquid is absorbed. Serve with grated cheese and *pico de gallo*, if desired.

SERVES 4

Skillet-Roasting Tomatoes and Peppers

TO ROAST tomatoes or jalapeño peppers, blacken the vegetables on all sides in a heavy ungreased skillet or griddle over high heat. They should be well blistered. Remove the tomatoes or peppers from the pan and when cool enough to handle, remove the blackened skins, working over a bowl to catch any juice. Tomatoes and jalapeños can also be blackened under a broiler, turning them several times, but the flavor will not be as intense as skillet- or griddle-blackened tomatoes or peppers.

JACK McDAVID

A Down-Home Cocktail Party

Don't let the overalls, the baseball cap, and the accent fool you; Jack McDavid knows how to fire up a great meal—or in this case an electic selection of hors d'oeuvres—with style. "I have so much respect for homemade meals because my mom cooked three meals a day, seven days a week, every week of the year." Jack was born the youngest of five children and raised in the countryside in Clinchport, Virginia, and he remembers all the hard work that went into a home meal. "Picking strawberries, cleaning fish, or snapping green peas involved hours of labor. Procuring food for the winter was a major event when I was growing up." He also remembers coming home after a late night out and "diving into some of Granny's meatloaf."

But Jack's interest in cooking didn't surface until he began working in restaurants to help put himself through the University of Virginia, where he studied accounting. He started out handling the books for a small soup and sandwich shop and somehow found his way into the kitchen. After gaining some cooking experience, Jack decided to leave school and "get serious" about food. "Good food makes people happy—for some people, it can turn a lousy day into a great one. It's a good feeling to cook for people when they're having a bad day and watch their expressions change."

MENU

Thousand-Layer Eggplant

—

*Granny's Meatloaf with
Green Apple Ketchup*

—

*Fried Chicken Mushrooms with
Buttermilk Dressing*

—

*Pears and Gruyère
Cheese in a Blanket*

In 1980, Jack's sister convinced him to move to Washington, D.C., where he was introduced to French cooking first at the Marriott Hotel and then under Jean-Pierre Goyenvalle of the renowned Lion d'Or. Three years later he decided to move on and went to work for Georges Perrier of Le Bec-Fin in Philadelphia.

In 1987, Jack opened the Down Home Diner, his first restaurant, located inside the farmers' market at Redding Terminal in Philadelphia. Two years later, he opened Jack's Firehouse, serving mid-Atlantic "haute country" cuisine. His latest venture, the Down Home Grill, featuring casual dining, opened in 1993. The land is fertile in Pennsylvania, and Jack takes advantage of every inch, hunting far and wide for the best produce available. Everything in the restaurants is "McDavid made," from the mayonnaise and ketchup to the watermelon pickles and biscuits.

Jack says he rarely has full-fledged dinners at home, but he does enjoy inviting friends over for a few drinks and some of his favorite finger foods. He starts out with his Thousand-Layer Eggplant consisting of mushrooms, onion, spinach, cheeses, ham, several types of peppers, and, of course, lots of eggplant. "This one is a real tongue teaser," Jack says, because the many layers (Jack makes up to 100!) "dissolve into so many distinctive flavors in your mouth." Next, Jack serves Granny's Meatloaf, which his mother's mother used to make. The meatloaf is served with Jack's Green Apple Ketchup, one of at least fifty different

ketchups that he enjoys creating. The Fried Chicken Mushrooms, accompanied by a rich and creamy buttermilk dressing, "create a lot of excitement," Jack claims. Jack likes to offer rye whiskey or bourbon with this dish. The final nibble is Pears and Gruyère Cheese in a Blanket. Jack recommends using sweet Seckel pears, which he says are firm, smooth, and hold their juices well when baked. A well-made microbrewery beer, such as Yuengling, "can walk a long way with Seckel pears and local aged Gruyère cheese," according to Jack. A dessert wine such as Madeira or liqueur such as Grand Marnier also goes well with pears and cheese. Jack's sentiments are: "Simple, bold, unique, and beautiful foods, friends, and spirits come close to heaven on earth."

THOUSAND-LAYER EGGPLANT

You don't need quite as many layers as Jack stacks up, although the more the better. Not only will the dish be more visually enticing, the harmony of flavors will be more pronounced. The trick is to have layers of single vegetables sliced as thin and even as possible (between $\frac{1}{16}$ and $\frac{1}{8}$ inch).

Oyster mushrooms, Bruder Basil cheese, and Italian prosciutto are not cheap, but they are worth every penny, making this dish really lively. You can make substitutions that fit your wallet, but therein lies the difference between a good and a great Thousand-Layer Eggplant.

Here, Jack serves three-bite pieces wrapped in fresh spinach for hors d'oeuvres. A simpler variation is to serve each piece on a cracker. This also makes a nice main dish when cut into slices or a hearty sandwich served on crusty French bread.

1 red bell pepper

1 yellow or green bell pepper

1 long Italian red pepper (or another red bell pepper)

2 large eggplants, very thinly sliced lengthwise (discard outer slices with peel)

1½ pounds fresh wild mushrooms, preferably oyster mushrooms, cleaned (see box, pages 36–37)

1 large yellow summer squash, very thinly sliced lengthwise

1 large zucchini, very thinly sliced lengthwise

6 tablespoons extra-virgin olive oil

1 small onion, very thinly sliced

¼ pound spinach, washed and stemmed

¼ pound very thinly sliced ham, preferably salt-cured country ham or Italian prosciutto

¼ pound Monterey jack cheese, grated

¼ pound Bruder Basil cheese (a naturally smoked cheese available at specialty shops), very thinly sliced

45 whole spinach leaves (about ¾ pound), washed and stemmed (optional)

Light the grill (see box, page 164, for indoor alternative). Brush the peppers, eggplant slices, mushrooms, and squash and zucchini slices lightly with 4 tablespoons of the olive oil. Over high heat, grill the peppers until they are charred on all sides, then place in a paper bag to steam. When they have cooled, remove the peels, seeds, and stems and cut into small, thin strips. Then grill the eggplant, mushrooms, and squash and zucchini on both sides until tender. Grill each vegetable in separate batches and be sure to tend to the grill as the vegetables will cook very quickly because they are so thin. Cooking times will depend on the heat of your grill. (A mesh grill cover will prevent the loss of any mushrooms or thinly sliced squash or zucchini to the fire.) Set the vegetables aside until you are ready to assemble the casserole.

Preheat the oven to 275°F. In a medium skillet over medium heat, heat the remaining 2 tablespoons of olive oil. Add the onion and cook until slightly brown, about 15 to 20 minutes. Set aside.

Rinse, but do not dry, the ¼ pound of spinach and place in a skillet over medium heat. Cook until it is just lightly wilted, about 2 minutes. Line a 9 × 5 × 3-inch loaf pan or casserole dish (or any deep pan about the same size) with half the wilted spinach. Then begin layering as follows: the eggplant, ham, grated jack cheese, mixed peppers, eggplant, mushrooms, Bruder Basil cheese, ham, eggplant, mixed peppers, onion, eggplant, squash, zucchini, grated cheese, and eggplant. Repeat this pattern until all the vegetables are used up or until the casserole is full. Keep in mind there will be more layers of eggplant than anything else. Use the remaining wilted spinach for the top layer and bake until warmed through, about 15 minutes per inch deep (or 45 minutes for a 3-inch-deep casserole).

Allow the casserole to cool completely if cutting into hors d'oeuvre-size pieces, at least 2 hours. If you are serving larger portions, it will need to cool for at least 15 minutes. (The casserole can be made the day before up to this point; keep it covered in the refrigerator until ready to serve.)

To serve as an hors d'oeuvre, preheat the oven to 250°F. When the casserole is cooled, slice the layers into 45 one-inch square pieces. Using a narrow spatula, remove the pieces from the dish. Wrap each in one spinach leaf and place seam-side down on a baking sheet, if desired. Put in the warm oven for 15 minutes or so until warm through.

MAKES 45 HORS D'OEUVRES OR 6 MAIN-DISH SERVINGS

Indoor Alternative to Grilling Vegetables

Grilled vegetables taste of summer no matter what time of year you eat them. If the winter months or city living prevent you from grilling, the stove and broiler will get the job done, though you'll sacrifice the smoky flavor.

Preheat your broiler and roast the peppers following the instructions in the box on page 186. Lightly brush the eggplant, mushrooms, squash, and zucchini with olive oil. Heat a large nonstick skillet and cook each vegetable on both sides in the dry skillet until tender.

Granny's Meatloaf with Green Apple Ketchup

Sliced apples carry bite-size pieces of meatloaf, "glued" on with Jack's very own Green Apple Ketchup. Jack suggests using free-range or organic beef because they have more flavor than ordinary meat.

3 pounds ground chuck beef

2 large eggs

½ cup diced onion

¼ cup diced green bell pepper

1 teaspoon salt

⅔ teaspoon cracked black peppercorns

⅔ cup bottled ketchup

½ cup brown mustard

Pinch of fresh thyme

6 to 8 green apples

Green Apple Ketchup (recipe follows)

Preheat the oven to 375°F. In a large bowl, mix the beef and eggs using your hands. Blend in the onion and green pepper. In a small bowl, combine the salt, black peppercorns, ketchup, mustard, and thyme and mix into the ground beef mixture. Mix until well combined and shape into a rectangle. Transfer to a 9 × 5 × 3-inch loaf pan, shaping to fit the dish. Bake for 1 hour. Allow the meatloaf to sit for 30 minutes before cutting.

In the meantime, core the apples and slice into thin wedges. Dot each wedge with a teaspoon or so of Green Apple Ketchup. When cool, cut the meatloaf into 1-inch cubes and place a cube on top of each apple wedge. Serve slightly warm or at room temperature.

MAKES ABOUT 100 HORS D'OEUVRES OR 6 TO 8 MAIN-DISH SERVINGS

Green Apple Ketchup

In addition to Granny's Meatloaf, this ketchup pairs well with game and chicken.

1 tablespoon vegetable oil or unsalted butter

½ cup diced onion

¼ teaspoon minced garlic

½ cup diced celery

4 cups peeled, cored, and diced Granny Smith apples

¼ teaspoon salt

Pinch of fresh thyme

¼ teaspoon cracked black peppercorns

½ teaspoon dry mustard

½ tablespoon pickling spice

1 cinnamon stick

In a large saucepan over medium heat, heat the oil or butter. Add the onion, garlic, and celery and cook until translucent, 7 to 8 minutes. Add the apples, salt, thyme, peppercorns, mustard, pickling spice, and cinnamon stick and stir until combined. Simmer slowly for 30 minutes, until the apples are soft and mushy. Remove the cinnamon stick and push the mixture through a fine sieve using a ladle, and discard any solids. Return the ketchup to the saucepan and simmer until it is reduced to the consistency of a slightly thickened applesauce.

MAKES ABOUT 3 CUPS

FRIED CHICKEN MUSHROOMS WITH BUTTERMILK DRESSING

Imagine a mushroom that tastes like chicken! Well, it actually exists and is appropriately called a chicken mushroom. It is a wild mushroom that grows in many parts of the country and is beginning to be cultivated. Keep your eye out for them in specialty food stores.

If you cannot find chicken muchrooms, portobellos (see box, pages 36–37) will also take well to this recipe, but the taste will be altogether different.

2 pounds fried chicken mushrooms or portobellos, cleaned, stemmed, and cut into 1-inch-square pieces
Pinch of salt
Pinch of freshly ground pepper

¼ cup all-purpose flour
¼ cup cornstarch
¼ cup peanut oil
Buttermilk Dressing (recipe follows)

In a mixing bowl, toss the mushrooms in a small amount of salt and pepper and let stand for 30 minutes. Mix the flour and cornstarch in a large bowl, using your fingers to eliminate any lumps. Toss the mushrooms in the flour mixture. Heat the peanut oil in a large skillet over medium-high heat. Add the mushrooms, cooking them in batches if necessary, and pan-fry until crisp on each side, about 5 minutes per side. (If you are preparing the portobellos, cook over high heat for 2 minutes per side until crispy outside.) Remove the mushrooms from the heat. When cool enough to touch, place the mushroom pieces on short skewers and drizzle Buttermilk Dressing over the mushrooms or place the mushrooms on a platter and serve with the Buttermilk Dressing on the side for dipping.

MAKES ABOUT 35 PIECES

Buttermilk Dressing

1 cup buttermilk

1 tablespoon sour cream

1 teaspoon sherry vinegar

1 tablespoon peanut oil

¼ teaspoon salt

¼ teaspoon pepper

¼ teaspoon finely chopped fresh sage

1 teaspoon finely chopped fresh thyme

1 teaspoon finely chopped fresh rosemary

½ teaspoon finely chopped fresh parsley

¼ teaspoon minced garlic

Place all the ingredients in a sealed container with a tight lid and shake vigorously.

Makes about 1 cup

PEARS AND GRUYÈRE CHEESE IN A BLANKET

Here's Jack's sweet and savory version of pigs in a blanket. Seckel pears, which originated in Philadelphia, are Jack's favorite, but they must be perfectly ripe. Jack's advice is to "listen" to the fruit. "Fruit talks to you," he says. "If the stem wiggles and if it smells of fragrant pear when you put your nose to the stem end, the pear is telling you it's ripe [see box, page 305]. And when you bite into the pear, it will talk back to you with pure pear essence comparable to a pear liqueur."

2 recipes Herb Pie Dough (recipe
   follows) or 4 ready-made
   unsweetened pie crusts
8 ripe Seckel pears, peeled, cored, and
   diced into ½-inch pieces

3 pounds aged Gruyère cheese, grated
2 tablespoons chopped fresh chervil
   (optional; curly parsley can be
   substituted)
2 tablespoons minced fresh sage

Preheat the oven to 400°F. Roll each disk of dough on a floured surface into a rectangular shape at least 12 inches long and 6 inches wide. The dough will be thin, about 1/16 inch. Distribute one-fourth of the pears, cheese, chervil, and sage along one long edge. Gently roll in a jelly-roll fashion into a long cylinder. Repeat with the other 3 doughs. Place each roll seam-side down on an ungreased baking sheet. Bake until brown, about 20 minutes. Remove from the oven and allow to cool for 5 minutes before cutting into ¾-inch pieces. Serve warm.

MAKES 64 PIECES

Herb Pie Dough

This is your basic pie dough, with herbs added for savory pies. For fruit pies, just eliminate the sage.

4 cups all-purpose flour

2 teaspoons salt

1 teaspoon sugar

1 teaspoon minced fresh sage

1½ cups lard, unsalted butter, or solid vegetable shortening

1 large egg, beaten

2 teaspoons cider vinegar

½ cup cold water

In a large bowl, combine the flour, salt, sugar, and sage. Using a pastry cutter or a fork, cut the lard or butter into the dry ingredients until a coarse meal forms. In a small bowl, beat the egg, vinegar, and water together. Add the liquid to the flour mixture, stirring with a fork just until the mixture comes together. Shape into a flat disc, wrap in plastic wrap, and refrigerate for at least 30 minutes.

MAKES TWO 9-INCH PIE CRUSTS

MARK MILLER

Some Like it Hot!

"Cooking is self-discovery," says Mark Miller, "it is not about rules." Though he owns a collection of more than four thousand cookbooks, including several that he has authored, Mark reminds the home cook that "cookbooks are meant to be used as guides, not step-by-step manuals. The key is to balance the ingredients and learn to taste. People should learn to improvise; it makes your cooking different from someone else's."

The distinctive quality of Mark's food has always been his unique combinations of flavors from different food traditions. He was exposed early in his life to Indian, Italian, and Mexican food, so it's no wonder that at home he goes through ethnic culinary phases such as Middle Eastern, Indian, Moroccan, and Asian. At home, Mark prefers to prepare meals all in one pot accompanied by various chutneys and salsas. He creates new flavors by using the variety of spices he keeps on hand.

His fascination with the "diverse ethnicities of the Americas" led Mark to pursue a degree in anthropology at the University of California, Berkeley, in the early 1970s. "It was at that time when my interests expanded far beyond academics and I began my lifelong affair with food," says Mark. He bought his

MENU

Yellow Gazpacho with
Fresh Crab and Lemon Oil

———

Bacon-Wrapped Loin of Rabbit
with Poblano Pesto and Green Chili
and Apple Chutney

———

Baked Peaches with
Cinnamon and Vanilla Natillas

first cookbook and began spending most of his time learning to use unusual and interesting ingredients in new ways. He made his first move toward a career in the restaurant business when he published his food newsletter, "The Market Basket," distributed to Bay area food lovers.

In 1976, he began working full time with Alice Waters at Chez Panisse in Berkeley. Three years later Mark left to open his own restaurant, Fourth Street Grill, in Berkeley. "I featured spicy, rustic food—my first step toward Modern Western Cuisine," Mark says. He later opened the Santa Fe Bar and Grill, where he concentrated on an exclusively Southwestern menu with a contemporary flair, as he further developed the use of Southwestern ingredients and cooking techniques.

In the mid-1980s, he sold both restaurants and moved to Santa Fe, New Mexico, to perfect his Modern Southwestern Cuisine. In 1987, Mark opened the now renowned Coyote Cafe. Red Sage, the crown jewel of his restaurants, opened in Washington, D.C., in 1992, highlighting his Modern Western Cuisine. "I believe that Modern Western Cuisine creates a bridge between the old and the new, re-creating the adventurous spirit of the West." Mark says the Red Sage cuisine and exuberant design "reflect, to some degree, my personal history, interest in anthropology, and wide travels." In December 1993, he opened his second Coyote Cafe at the MGM Grand hotel in Las Vegas.

Mark wishes he had more time to cook at home. "At home I get the opportunity to really relish the food and to eat the entire meal," he says. "The restaurant is a different atmosphere. I don't enjoy the food as much because I have to get fifty plates out in fifty seconds, and I don't have time to taste the dish I've just prepared."

Mark's passion for food and cooking is infectious. "My hope is that the success I have had with introducing new cuisines influences other culinary professionals and restaurants to take advantage of the rich, diverse heritage of the American palate and reformulate a new uniquely American tradition." And he feels the same applies for home cooks. "Cooking is not about the brain," he says, "it's your hands and your tongue, your senses. You'll discover a world of flavors and, it is hoped, a new part of yourself along the way."

Yellow Gazpacho with Fresh Crab and Lemon Oil

This soup is a wonderful playground for aromatic spices and herbs. Red tomatoes may be used in place of yellow when they are not available, but the taste will not be quite the same, as yellow tomatoes are less acidic than red.

Kernels from 1 large ear sweet corn
  (about ¾ cup)
8 large ripe yellow tomatoes
1 medium red onion
1 English or hothouse cucumber,
  peeled, or 2 regular cucumbers,
  peeled and seeded
2 garlic cloves, chopped
2 poblano peppers, roasted (see box,
  page 186), peeled, and seeded

4 tablespoons chopped cilantro leaves,
  plus additional sprigs for garnish
Salt to taste
3 or 4 serrano peppers, roasted
  (see box, page 186), peeled, and
  finely chopped
1 tablespoon sugar
½ pound cooked backfin crab meat,
  picked over for shell
Lemon oil (optional; see box, page 174)

Bring a saucepan of water to a boil over medium-high heat, add the corn, and simmer over medium heat for 3 minutes. Drain immediately and refrigerate the corn, covered, until serving time.

Coarsely chop 6 of the tomatoes, three-fourths of the onion, and three-fourths of the cucumber (reserving 2 unblemished tomatoes and the remaining onion and cucumber for garnish) and place in a blender or food processor. Add the garlic, poblano peppers, and cilantro to the blender. Purée, adding ice water to thin if necessary. Season with salt. Place in the refrigerator, covered, until well chilled, at least 2 hours.

In the meantime, prepare the salsa garnish. Seed and finely dice the remaining tomatoes and push through a coarse strainer. Finely chop the reserved onion and cucumber and toss in a bowl with the diced tomatoes, serrano peppers, and sugar and salt. Cover and chill.

Just before serving, adjust the seasoning with salt if necessary. Evenly divide the soup among 6 shallow soup plates. Place a heaping tablespoon or so of crab meat in the center, top with a dollop of the salsa garnish, and sprinkle with the corn. Drizzle with lemon oil, if desired, and garnish with cilantro sprigs.

Serves 6

Lemon Oil

Lemon oil is fairly pricey to purchase, but it is so easy to make your own. Just keep in mind that it takes a week for the flavors to develop.

TO MAKE Mark's lemon oil, place 1 cup of either grape seed oil or vegetable oil and the zest of 2 lemons in a jar with a tight-fitting lid. Seal and store in a cool, dark place for one week, shaking the jar every two days to blend the flavors. The oil will keep for a good three weeks, tightly covered, in a cool, dark place. Use the extra in salad dressings or marinades.

BACON-WRAPPED LOIN OF RABBIT WITH POBLANO PESTO AND GREEN CHILI AND APPLE CHUTNEY

This satisfying dish can be prepared the day before, up to the point of cooking, and the pesto and chutney can be made up to one week in advance. Dried mushrooms will produce a much more intensely flavored dish.

30 thin slices (½ pound) smoked bacon, preferably applewood-smoked

Poblano Pesto (recipe follows)

12 boneless rabbit loins (about 2½ pounds total)

Bones from 1 rabbit or chicken (ask your butcher)

1 pound (about 4) white onions, diced

1½ cups diced carrots

1½ cups diced celery

1 cup dry white wine

1 quart rabbit or chicken stock

4 ounces fresh or dried mushrooms (see box, pages 36–37)

Salt to taste

Green Chili and Apple Chutney (recipe follows)

Place 5 slices of bacon, side by side and overlapping lengthwise, on a sheet of waxed paper and spread 1 tablespoon of pesto on top. Place 2 rabbit loins on top, side by side perpendicular to the bacon, and roll up jelly-roll fashion, starting with the short end. Repeat the process until you have 6 bacon-wrapped rabbit rolls. Transfer to a baking pan in a single layer, placed seam-side down, cover with plastic wrap or foil, and refrigerate for at least 2 hours.

Preheat the oven to 325°F. Place the bones in a roasting pan and bake until they begin to brown, about 15 minutes. Add the diced onions, carrots, and celery and continue to roast until the vegetables are browned, 20 to 30 minutes. Transfer the bones and vegetables to a large stockpot. Add the wine to the roasting pan over medium heat, scraping up any browned bits from the bottom of the pan, and add the wine with the stock to the stockpot; add enough water to cover the bones by 2 inches. Add the mushrooms and simmer slowly over medium heat for 4 hours. Strain the juice, discarding the solids, and simmer over medium-high heat until reduced to 2 cups. Season with salt and set aside.

Turn the oven up to 425°F. Put the rabbit in the oven and reduce the temperature to 350°F. Cook for about 20 minutes, or until the internal temperature is 130°F. It should be firm to the touch. Remove from the oven and let the rabbit rest for 10 minutes before slicing.

To serve, slice each roll crosswise into 3 pinwheels and place 3 slices on each of 6 plates. Pour the sauce around each serving and pass the Green Chili and Apple Chutney on the side.

Serves 6

POBLANO PESTO

This pesto can be used just as you would any other pesto: toss it into pasta, spread it on sandwiches, or use it as a pizza topping in place of tomato sauce. Pumpkin seeds are also known as pepitas.

2 cups peanut oil

4 large poblano peppers (see box, pages 176)

1 cup loosely packed fresh cilantro leaves

¼ cup diced red pepper roasted, (see box, page 186) peeled, and seeded

2 tablespoons extra-virgin olive oil

1 tablespoon fresh lime juice

¼ teaspoon salt

1 cup toasted pumpkin seeds, (see box, page 117)

Heat the oil in a medium skillet over medium-high heat. Add the poblano peppers and cook for 1 minute or less, just enough to blister them quickly on all sides; do not allow them to blacken. Using a pair of tongs, transfer them to a bowl and cover with a damp cloth or plastic wrap. Set aside for 20 minutes to steam. Remove the skins, stems, and seeds and place the peppers in a food processor along with the cilantro. Process until a rough paste forms. Add the roasted red pepper, olive oil, lime juice, salt, and pumpkin seeds and process until smooth.

Makes 3 cups

Types of Chili Peppers

Chili peppers are a very popular ingredient in Southwestern cuisine as well as many other cuisines. They are available in specialty markets and many supermarkets, and certainly in Mexican markets.

Fresh Chili Peppers

When buying fresh chili peppers, look for those that are firm with taut, unblemished skin. A word of caution: The heat of these peppers is mostly stored in the seeds and veins. To make them milder, you can remove the seeds and roast the peppers. Do not touch your eyes or mouth, as the oils left behind on your hands can burn.

SERRANO PEPPERS pack *a lot* of heat into their small, thin, bright-green bodies. Available in Mexican and some specialty markets.

JALAPEÑO PEPPERS are very popular in this country, used most frequently in Cajun, Mexican, and Southwestern cuisines. This dark green chili pepper is hot, but not intolerably so, and measures 2 to 3 inches long and 1 inch wide.

POBLANO PEPPERS are dark green to black and about 6 inches long, starting out wide at the stem end and tapering off to a rounded point. The darker the poblano, the more developed its flavor. Poblanos are often roasted to reduce the heat intensity, as they are very hot.

ANAHEIM PEPPERS, also known as New Mexico chili peppers, are mild, long, thin, and pale green with a mild heat level.

Dried Chili Peppers

Dried chilies have another level of intrigue to them, similar to roasted chili peppers. They are milder and sweeter than fresh. Select only those that are still pliable and unbroken and keep them tightly sealed in a cool, dry place. Before using, wipe them with a damp cloth.

ANCHO PEPPERS can range from mild to medium-hot, although in fresh form (poblanos) they are very hot. These deep, dark red chili peppers, which taste sweet and fruity, are often toasted, soaked, and puréed to add to sauces and other dishes.

PASILLA PEPPERS, very long and black, resemble anchos (dried poblanos). These medium-hot chilies are often toasted and ground into a powder, which is then added to sauces.

CHIPOTLE PEPPERS are jalapeños that have been dried and smoked. These mild chilies are dark red and lend layers of sweet, smoky, spicy, and fruity flavors to stews and sauces.

GREEN CHILI AND APPLE CHUTNEY

This sweet, spicy, and smoky chutney will keep, covered, for up to one week in the refrigerator.

1 tablespoon peanut oil

¼ cup chopped onion

2 teaspoons dried oregano

4 Anaheim or poblano peppers, roasted (see box, page 186), peeled, and diced

2 tablespoons sugar

¼ cup cider vinegar

1½ cups apple cider

3 Granny Smith apples, peeled, cored, and diced

Salt to taste

In a medium skillet, heat the peanut oil over medium-high heat. Add the onion and cook until translucent, about 5 minutes. Add the oregano and stir in the peppers and sugar. Add the vinegar and cider, scraping up any bits on the bottom of the pan. Simmer the mixture until it is reduced by half, about 10 minutes, then stir in the apples. Cook the mixture for another 3 to 4 minutes until it has thickened slightly and the liquid is almost gone. Transfer the chutney to a dish and season with salt. Set aside to cool to room temperature, then refrigerate, tightly covered.

MAKES ABOUT 2 CUPS

BAKED PEACHES WITH CINNAMON AND VANILLA NATILLAS

This mellow, refreshing dessert of warm, juicy peaches and chilled crème anglaise is a welcome treat after a chili-infused meal. The natillas—*crisp and chewy meringue cookies—are great for scooping up the sauce.*

PEACHES

3 tablespoons granulated sugar

3 tablespoons brown sugar

1½ teaspoons ground cinnamon

¼ teaspoon freshly grated nutmeg

6 ripe peaches, peeled, halved, and pitted

1½ tablespoons unsalted butter, cut into several small pieces

NATILLAS

6 large egg whites, at room temperature

⅓ cup plus 1 tablespoon granulated sugar

Pinch of cream of tartar

Vanilla Crème Anglaise (recipe follows)

¼ cup slivered almonds, toasted, for garnish (see box, page 117)

¾ tablespoon ground cinnamon, for garnish

Preheat the oven to 325° F. In a small bowl, combine the sugars, cinnamon, and nutmeg. Place the peaches in a casserole dish cut side down, and sprinkle with the sugar and spice mixture, then dot with the butter. Bake for 6 to 8 minutes, until the sugar caramelizes.

While the peaches are baking, make the *natillas*. Bring a large pot of water to a simmer over medium-high heat. Place the egg whites, sugar, and cream of tartar in a large mixing bowl and whip to stiff, but not dry, peaks. Using a tablespoon, drop 6 equally large dollops of the meringue into the simmering water and poach for 3 minutes. Turn the *natillas* over with a slotted spoon and cook for another 3 minutes, until firm. Remove with a slotted spoon and drain the *natillas* on paper towels.

To serve, coat each of 6 dinner plates with about ¼ cup of the Vanilla Crème Anglaise. Next place 2 baked peach halves in the center of each plate, cut side down. Sprinkle the slivered almonds and a pinch of cinnamon on top and around the peaches and place one *natilla* on top of each.

SERVES 6

VANILLA CRÈME ANGLAISE

Purchasing vanilla beans for this recipe is worth the expense, because they lend a pure, rich vanilla fragrance that cannot be compared to vanilla extract. This rich custard sauce is wonderful for dressing up cakes or fresh fruit.

¼ vanilla bean, split lengthwise
2 cups whole milk

2 large egg yolks
¼ cup sugar

Scrape the seeds from the vanilla bean and combine the seeds and pod with the milk in a medium saucepan over medium heat. Scald the milk by bringing it to just below a boil. In a medium bowl, whisk the egg yolks and sugar until incorporated. Once the milk comes almost to a boil, remove it from the heat and slowly pour about ¼ cup of the milk into the yolk mixture, whisking constantly. Then whisk this mixture back into the saucepan with the remaining milk and cook over low heat, stirring constantly, until the sauce coats the back of the spoon, about 5 minutes; do not boil. Strain the mixture through a fine sieve into a medium bowl placed inside a larger bowl filled with ice. Set aside to cool. Cover and refrigerate until chilled. This can be made up to 2 days in advance.

MAKES ABOUT 2 CUPS

Vanilla

Vanilla is among the most popular flavors on earth. Its aroma can be intoxicating and its flavor, divine on its own, enhances the taste of almost anything. In chocolate recipes, vanilla rounds out the flavor, making the chocolate taste even more chocolaty, and in fruit dishes, such as apple pie, vanilla adds just the right boost.

Vanilla was discovered in Mexico centuries ago. It was the Aztecs who thought to combine chocolate with vanilla, using it to refine the potent cocoa elixir *xocolatl*—the world's first chocolate beverage. Today, most vanilla comes from Madagascar or Tahiti, the latter type being more fragrant. It is available in bean form (seed pod) or liquid extract, both of which can be expensive, as the production of vanilla beans is labor-intensive. While there are several good-quality vanilla extracts around, they simply cannot match the flavor of the actual vanilla bean. However, for cakes, brownies, and several other recipes it is much more practical to use extract.

The vanilla bean can be used whole or split to flavor sauces or custards, or stored in sugar to infuse the sugar with its perfume. The whole bean can then be used again, after being rinsed, if necessary. The tiny seeds inside with their concentrated flavor can be added directly to foods and eaten. Vanilla beans can be stored, tightly wrapped, in a well-sealed container for up to six months.

If using vanilla extract, it is best to add it to cooked mixtures such as batters, custards, or sauces after they have cooled slightly to get the most flavor. When buying vanilla extracts, avoid those from Mexico, as they may contain toxins, and those not labeled "pure vanilla."

MARY SUE MILLIKEN

Middle East Meets West

For health, nutrition, and environmental reasons, I've been concentrating on meals that are composed of considerably less meat in favor of abundant grains and vegetables," says Mary Sue Milliken, co-chef and co-owner of the Border Grill in Santa Monica, California. "This menu fills those needs while still being wonderfully satisfying."

For Mary Sue, cooking at home has become a regular and important occasion, especially since she has a young son, Declan, who needs to eat by 6:30 P.M. every evening. When she must stay at the restaurant during the dinner rush, her husband and best friend, Josh, is home to do the cooking. "My home cooking is sometimes influenced by Josh," says Mary Sue. "He adores eating and is a fine cook himself." She gives him credit for introducing her to a very simple version of the crispy basmati rice presented here years ago. She's been developing the technique for it ever since, and has incorporated many tips for perfect rice that she learned from various Persian friends and books.

Her partner, Susan Feniger, is the inspiration behind the salad. "No meal with Susan is complete without olives and peppers in some form or another." And Mary Sue should know. The two met back in 1977, while working under the innovative and demanding direction of

MENU

Golden Crispy-Bottomed Basmati Rice Pot with Lamb and Spinach, Topped with Yogurt and Fresh Herbs

—

Marinated Pepper Salad

—

Honey-Glazed Walnut Cake with Fresh Strawberries

Jovan Treboyevic, former proprietor and operator of the distinquished Le Perroquet, in Chicago. Mary Sue became the first woman chef ever to work in Treboyevic's kitchen. Susan was the second. From Le Perroquet, the two went their separate ways, but they met up again in Paris in 1980 and promised to one day work together in the States.

One year later, Mary Sue joined Susan at City Cafe, in Los Angeles, and the two have worked together ever since. It was there that this team became known for smoking their own meats and other foods, and producing vinegars and pâtés, and incredible pastries. In 1985, the two reopened City Cafe as Border Grill, and two months later opened City Restaurant, also in Los Angeles. They introduced an eclectic menu that featured many of the same dishes from the original City Cafe and a number of new additions based on Milliken's travels to Thailand and Feniger's explorations in India. In March 1990, after extensive travels to Mexico, the two opened a second Border Grill in Santa Monica and showcased their unique versions of Mexican dishes. Mary Sue and Susan have since sold the original Border Grill and City Restaurant. They now put their energies into Border Grill in Santa Monica, while planning the opening of a new restaurant.

Being a chef gives Mary Sue the opportunity to be creative. "I go to the 'walk-in' refrigerator and see what foods are in abundance and then I imagine a dish," she says. "I even dream about what to cook." But although she's creative, she describes cooking in the restaurant to be much more of a science than cooking at home. "The dish goes through so many stages and tests before you can serve it. At home, cooking is much more fun because I don't have to think about such things," says Mary Sue.

At home, Declan helps her chop with his own small blunt knife and even stirs what's cooking in the pot on the stove. Mary Sue delights in having a party with a few close friends who can spend a slow-paced afternoon chatting and visiting, and help out by washing greens and peeling garlic. "They seem to love the fact that they can get their hands dirty without taking any responsibility for the food and be assured (well, usually) that the food will be good."

Mary Sue closes this menu with a delicious cake that is best served fresh.

GOLDEN CRISPY-BOTTOMED BASMATI RICE POT WITH LAMB AND SPINACH, TOPPED WITH YOGURT AND FRESH HERBS

This is Mary Sue's version of a traditional Persian one-pot dish. The mixture of ground lamb, spinach, and spices is layered atop the basmati rice and cooked on the stovetop until the rice forms a beautifully crisp, golden crust. The whole thing is then inverted onto a platter and cut into free-standing wedges. Herbed yogurt is served on the side.

3 cups basmati rice (see box, page 185)

2 tablespoons plus 1 teaspoon sea salt

4 tablespoons extra-virgin olive oil

1 large onion, finely diced

1 pound lean ground lamb

4–5 garlic cloves, minced

½ teaspoon freshly ground black pepper

1 teaspoon Hungarian paprika

½ pound spinach leaves, washed, dried, stemmed, and roughly chopped

2 tablespoons (¼ stick) unsalted butter

2 cups plain yogurt (see box, page 184)

¼ cup chopped fresh basil

¼ cup chopped fresh mint

Wash the rice in several rinsings of warm water until the water runs clear. Soak the rice for 6 to 8 hours or overnight in cold water to cover with 1 tablespoon of the sea salt. Alternatively, to save time, soak the rice in lukewarm water with the salt for 30 to 45 minutes.

Heat a large, heavy-bottomed skillet over medium heat. Add 2 tablespoons of the olive oil and the onion and cook until the onion becomes translucent, about 10 minutes. Add the ground lamb, garlic, 1 teaspoon of the sea salt, pepper, and paprika. Continue cooking, stirring often, until the meat is well browned, about 5 minutes. Drain off any excess fat. Add the spinach and cook for another 3 to 5 minutes, stirring often, until the spinach is wilted and the liquid is almost all evaporated. Set aside until the rice is ready.

Bring 2½ quarts of water to a boil with the remaining 1 tablespoon of sea salt in a large saucepan over medium-high heat. Drain the rice from the soaking liquid and add it to the boiling water. Return to a boil and cook for 10 to 12 minutes, uncovered, stirring occasionally. Test a grain of rice for doneness; it should be cooked entirely except for a small part in the center. Strain the rice in a colander and rinse with warm water; drain well.

Melt the butter with the remaining 2 tablespoons of olive oil in a large, well-seasoned or nonstick coated stockpot with a tight-fitting lid over medium heat. Add about 2 tablespoons water and sprinkle the cooked rice evenly onto the bottom of the pot a spoonful at a time until

Yogurt

While yogurt has become a very popular food in our diet-conscious culture, Middle Easterners as well as Indians and Asians have been making and enjoying it for thousands of years.

Yogurt is made by introducing live bacteria (usually from another batch of cultured yogurt) into milk (usually cow's milk). This is either done at room temperature for 24 to 36 hours, or at a higher temperature (110° F.) for less time. The milk ferments and congeals into a tart and creamy custard, which then must be refrigerated.

Yogurt is a great source of protein, iron, calcium, and B vitamins. In addition, the active cultures in yogurt help the body break down and thus absorb the nutrients in the yogurt and make it easy to digest. Furthermore, cultured dairy products fight harmful intestinal bacteria. Look for the words "contains live active cultures" on the label to make sure the product is real yogurt, as there are a few yogurtlike products that do not contain these live bacteria. Also, look for low- or nonfat yogurt, as yogurt made with whole milk is relatively high in fat and calories. Try the yogurt in soups and dips, or on baked potatoes in place of sour cream. It can be used in cooking, but it must be treated carefully so that the dish does not curdle or separate.

two-thirds of the rice has been distributed. Spread the lamb and spinach mixture evenly over the rice. Cover the lamb with the remaining rice, mounding it slightly in the center. Use the handle of a wooden spoon to poke about 5 deep holes in the rice from the surface of rice to the bottom of the pot to allow steam to escape. Cover the pot with a thick cotton dish towel and place the lid on tightly. Lower the heat to medium-low and cook for 35 to 40 minutes.

Meanwhile, mix the yogurt with the basil and mint in a small serving bowl. Set aside until serving time. Fill the sink 1 or 2 inches deep with cold water. Remove the cover from the rice and have a large, round platter ready. Place the pot in the sink for 1 minute, watching that no water enters the pot. Remove the pot and dry off the bottom, then invert the rice cake onto the platter; it should unmold itself in one piece and be golden brown. Bring the platter to the table and serve family style. Cut individual wedges from the rice cake, similar to cutting a pie, and serve it with the herbed yogurt.

SERVES 6

MARINATED PEPPER SALAD

Red, green, and yellow bell peppers are charred and peeled to give them that smoky flavor and melt-in-your-mouth texture; then they are tossed with julienne red onions and marinated in a vinaigrette.

4–6 bell peppers (mixture of red, green, and yellow), roasted (see box, page 186)

1 small red onion, thinly sliced

½ cup extra-virgin olive oil

3–4 tablespoons red wine vinegar

3 tablespoons chopped fresh oregano

1 teaspoon salt

½ teaspoon freshly ground black pepper

Lettuce leaves to line 6 serving plates

Kalamata olives, for garnish (optional)

Pepperoncini, for garnish (optional)

Peel the peppers and split them in half lengthwise to remove the seeds and stem. Cut them into julienne strips about ¼ inch wide and 3 inches long.

In a medium bowl, toss the peppers, onion, olive oil, vinegar, oregano, salt, and pepper. Allow the salad to marinate for at least 1 hour at room temperature. Line 6 salad plates with lettuce leaves and divide the marinated peppers evenly among the plates. Garnish each salad with the olives and pepperoncini, if desired.

SERVES 6

Basmati Rice

Centuries-old basmati rice is a long-grain rice with a delicate texture. Its name literally means "queen of fragrance"; its nutty taste and aroma make it one of the most flavorful and fragrant of all rices. Harvested at the base of the Himalayas, this rice has been a staple in Indian and Middle Eastern cooking for thousands of years.

TO COOK plain basmati rice, rinse the grains in several changes of cold water until the water runs clear. Then combine 1 part rice to 1½ parts lightly salted water in a saucepan and cook, covered, over medium heat for 15 to 20 minutes, or until tender and all the water has been absorbed. Fluff with a fork and serve.

Roasting Peppers

The technique for roasting chili peppers and bell peppers is the same, but that is not the only similarity between the two. Bell peppers are a very mild variety of chili pepper. Blame the confusion on Christopher Columbus, who mislabeled bell peppers, believing they were a variety of peppercorn. The latter is a spice (see box, page 249), while chili peppers and bell peppers are a fruit.

Roasted peppers have a very different flavor and texture from fresh—so different that you might not connect the two. When the outer skin is charred, the inner flesh softens and develops a sweet, smoky flavor, adding another level of complexity to the pepper. You can use the broiler, grill, oven, skillet, or an open flame. The broiler and oven methods are among the easiest:

BROILER ROASTING. Place the peppers under a preheated broiler, turning occasionally, until the skins are blackened on all sides, 5 to 10 minutes. Steam and peel as described.

OVEN ROASTING. Preheat the oven to 450° F. Roast the peppers for 20 to 30 minutes, until the skin blackens on all sides. Steam and peel as described.

TO PEEL. Immediately after roasting, place the peppers in a paper bag and seal, or in a bowl tightly covered with plastic wrap, to steam for 20 minutes or until cool enough to handle. Peel off the skin using your hands. Split the peppers in half lengthwise with a knife, and remove the stem and seeds. Do not rinse the peppers, as this will wash off some of the flavorful juices.

TO STORE. Roasted peppers can be stored, tightly covered, in the refrigerator for up to three days.

NOTE: For larger peppers, you may want to slice them in half, remove the seeds and stem before roasting, and place them cut side down in the broiler or oven.

HONEY-GLAZED WALNUT CAKE WITH FRESH STRAWBERRIES

This is one of the easiest cakes you'll ever make, and it is so delicious—perfect for one of those last-minute get-togethers. Finely ground walnuts make a dense cake that becomes incredibly moist and intensely sweet when soaked in a honey and orange juice mixture. Be sure that your walnuts are fresh and have a smooth, buttery flavor.

1 cup shelled walnuts

¼ cup all-purpose flour

2 teaspoons baking powder

½ teaspoon salt

1 teaspoon ground cinnamon

¾ cup light brown sugar

5 large eggs

½ cup honey

½ cup fresh orange juice

1 teaspoon vanilla extract

½–1 pint fresh strawberries, washed and hulled

Preheat the oven to 350°F. Butter and flour a 9-inch round cake pan. Place the walnuts, flour, baking powder, salt, and cinnamon in a food processor and blend until finely chopped. Add the brown sugar and eggs and process until smooth. Pour the batter into the cake pan and bake for 30 to 35 minutes, or until a toothpick inserted in the center comes out clean. Remove to a rack and cool in the pan for 5 minutes. Turn the cake out of the pan and cool completely on a rack.

Combine the honey, orange juice, and vanilla in a small saucepan over medium-high heat and bring to a boil. Poke the cooled cake all over with a toothpick and brush liberally with the glaze. Slice the cake and serve fresh berries on the side. Wrap the leftovers tightly in plastic wrap and store in the refrigerator for a day or two.

SERVES 6 TO 8

PATRICK O'CONNELL

Springtime in Virginia

The one night I'm off, my first choice is to go to a Chinese restaurant, have a couple of beers, and eat with chopsticks," says Patrick O'Connell. "But cooking at home is very therapeutic, and the results are often more spontaneous."

As the executive chef and co-owner of the Inn at Little Washington, located in a small country village one hour south of Washington, D.C., Patrick lives in a house adjacent to the inn, called Rose Cottage. When he's not cooking in his own home,

Patrick occasionally invades the restaurant's kitchen when the place is closed for business—"A rare pleasure, because it's usually packed elbow-to-elbow with staff members," he says. During these times, he prepares what he calls "Mama food," such as spaghetti, mashed potatoes, fried chicken, and chili. "Then I can sing, holler, and curse without an audience."

A native of Washington, D.C., Patrick began his restaurant career at the age of fifteen, working in a neighborhood restaurant after school. While studying speech and drama at Catholic University of America, he paid for his education by

MENU

Chilled Local Peach and
Virginia Riesling Soup

Soft-Shell Crab Sauté with
Hazelnuts, Cilantro, and Lime

Garden Asparagus Salad with
White Wine and Raspberry Vinaigrettes

Barbecued Boneless Rack of Lamb
in a Pecan Crust

Shoestring Sweet Potatoes

Coeur à la Crème

working as a waiter. After graduating and spending a year traveling in Europe, he began to find the "living theater," as he calls it, of the restaurant business more compelling than a career as an actor.

Along with a partner, Reinhardt Lynch, Patrick began a catering business in central Virginia in 1972. Six years later, their small business became The Inn at Little Washington. Although Patrick may have left the theater, he has not lost his deep-felt appreciation for the drama: "Running a restaurant allows you to be the producer, the director, the set designer, the orchestra leader, and a lead player in a wonderfully fractured nightly performance where the world of complete illusion in the dining room is brilliantly juxtaposed with the blood-and-guts reality of the kitchen," says Patrick. "The fact that it can never be captured or replicated simply adds spice to the intensity of the moment."

His early catering experience had an influence on his philosophy about cooking at home. "You don't really need the fanciest, high-tech equipment to be a great home cook," says Patrick. "Before opening the restaurant we catered parties on a fourteen-dollar used electric stove, and an electric frying pan bought at a yard sale for a dollar fifty."

For Patrick, opening a restaurant was not a planned event but, rather, the course he feels his life was destined to take. While I was actually predestined to become an actor, food and working with food provided a necessary, basic grounding and connection with the tangible, real world that has contributed to my remaining partly sane. I would have made a hell of an insane actor, though, but probably not been around this long."

Patrick selected this menu because it is not regularly prepared at the restaurant, and it involves a variety of foods that he loves and can easily find in his region, such as peaches, raspberries, soft-shell crabs, and asparagus. "Living in the heart of peach country, one is always looking for something different to do with the bushels and bushels that find their way to the back door during a good harvest." Like any good actor, Patrick knows how to improvise and rise to the occasion, and the dishes he presents in his menu will make you very glad he turned in the stage for a skillet.

CHILLED LOCAL PEACH AND VIRGINIA RIESLING SOUP

"This peach soup lends itself to being made well in advance and can be sipped from a cup or demitasse for a first course, or offered as a cocktail in warm weather," suggests Patrick. He adds 1½ cups of heavy cream for richness; however, you can cut this amount in half with little consequence.

2 bottles Virginia Riesling or any other Riesling

8 whole cloves

1 cinnamon stick

¼ cup brown sugar

2 bay leaves

12 medium peaches, peeled and pitted

1 orange, sliced

1 lemon, sliced

1½ cups heavy cream

Splash of lemon juice

¼ cup slivered almonds, toasted (optional; see box, page 117)

Combine the wine, cloves, cinnamon stick, brown sugar, and bay leaves in a large saucepan over medium-high heat and bring to a rapid boil. Add the peaches, reduce the heat to medium, and simmer for 20 to 25 minutes. Add the orange and lemon and cook for an additional 5 minutes.

Remove and discard the orange and lemon slices, cloves, cinnamon stick, and bay leaves from the mixture, and purée the liquid in a food processor or blender until smooth. Strain the mixture into a clean bowl and chill. Stir in the cream and season with lemon juice just before serving. Sprinkle each serving with the almonds, if desired.

SERVES 4 GENEROUSLY

SOFT-SHELL CRAB SAUTÉ WITH HAZELNUTS, CILANTRO, AND LIME

Soft-shell crabs are indigenous to Patrick's part of the country. For his specialty, he serves them on top of "tender-to-the-bite" green beans with a tangy mustard-mayonnaise.

¼ cup mayonnaise

Juice from 1 lemon

1 tablespoon Dijon mustard

½ tablespoon dry mustard

Salt and freshly ground pepper to taste

1 cup green beans, trimmed

Flour seasoned with salt and pepper, for dredging

4 soft-shell crabs, cleaned (see box, page 217)

½ cup (1 stick) unsalted butter

2 tablespoons browned butter (see box, below)

1 tomato, peeled (see box, page 311), seeded, and diced

⅓ cup hazelnuts, toasted (see box, page 117), chopped

1 tablespoon chopped fresh cilantro

Juice from 1 lime

2 tablespoons White Wine Vinaigrette (see page 195)

Lime wedges, for garnish

Cilantro leaves, for garnish

1 tablespoon chopped fresh chives

To make the sauce, mix the mayonnaise, lemon juice, Dijon mustard, and dry mustard in a small bowl until smooth. Season with salt and pepper. Set aside until serving time.

Bring a medium pot of water to a boil over high heat and set aside a bowl of ice water. Plunge the green beans into the boiling water for about 30 to 45 seconds until tender, then drain and immediately plunge into the ice water to stop the cooking process. Drain, pat dry, and set aside in a small bowl.

Browned Butter

Browned butter adds a nice, toasty flavor to foods. A little goes a long way, which is why Patrick calls for only 2 tablespoons of it in the Soft-Shell Crab Sauté. To make browned butter, heat salted butter in a skillet over medium-high heat and cook until the milk solids begin to brown and the butter becomes golden brown. *Do not* let the butter burn. Browned butter can be stored covered in the refrigerator for two to three days.

Preheat the oven to 400° F. Place the seasoned flour on a large plate and dredge the crabs, shaking off the excess flour. In a large skillet over medium-high heat, melt half of the unsalted butter. Cook two crabs at a time shell side down for approximately 2 minutes, until the shell begins to blister. Then flip the crabs over using a spatula; use caution at this stage, as the blistered shells can pop, releasing hot butter. Drain any liquid from the pan, add 1 tablespoon of the browned butter, and cook for another 30 seconds. Add half the diced tomato, half of the hazelnuts, and ½ tablespoon of the chopped cilantro. Transfer the mixture and the cooked crabs to a large baking dish.

Melt the remaining ¼ cup butter in the skillet, and cook the 2 remaining crabs in the same fashion, adding the rest of the browned butter, tomatoes, hazelnuts, and cilantro. Add the second batch of cooked crabs to the baking dish and bake them all for 2 minutes or until done. To check for doneness, fold back the shell and see that the flesh is opaque, not translucent. Remove the crabs from the oven and drizzle with the lime juice.

Add the vinaigrette to the green beans and toss. Divide into 4 equal portions and arrange them in the center of 4 serving plates. Place one crab on top of each plate of beans and garnish the plates with the tomato and hazelnut mixture, lime wedges, and cilantro leaves. Squirt the plates with the mustard-mayonnaise sauce (or dollop a tablespoon on the plates if you do not have a squeeze bottle) and sprinkle with the chives.

Serves 4

GARDEN ASPARAGUS SALAD WITH WHITE WINE AND RASPBERRY VINAIGRETTES

"I find asparagus to be wonderfully healthful—in fact, in ancient times it was regarded as a medicine—and I never get tired of eating it during the spring," says Patrick. In this recipe he serves the asparagus cold, tossed in vinaigrette with a variety of garnishes, his favorite way. "The harmonious simplicity of this salad has pleased and intrigued me for many, many years," he explains. "It even lends itself to becoming a main course at lunch with the addition of strips of poached chicken breast."

The initial step of frying the asparagus peels may seem a bit of a chore, but it really does not take that long and the fried peels lend a terrific crunch to the salad.

24 large asparagus spears, washed well, white coarse ends removed

Vegetable oil, for deep-frying

Salt to taste

White Wine Vinaigrette to taste (recipe follows)

Raspberry Vinaigrette to taste (recipe follows)

Cracked black pepper to taste

1 tablespoon drained capers

2 tablespoons coarsely chopped fresh parsley

2 tablespoons toasted pistachios (see box, page 117)

2 hard-boiled eggs, chopped

¼ cup diced beets, boiled until tender

Peel the entire asparagus stalk, leaving the tip intact. Heat the vegetable oil in a deep-fryer or a heavy, deep saucepan to 350° F. and deep-fry the peels until golden brown, about 1 minute. Remove with a slotted spoon, drain on paper towels, and salt lightly. Reserve for garnish.

To steam the asparagus, pour 2 to 3 inches of water in a saucepan with a steamer basket and bring to a boil over medium-high heat. Fill a large bowl with ice water and set aside. Lay the asparagus in the steamer basket, covered tightly, and steam for about 4 minutes, until tender. Immediately remove the asparagus and plunge it into the ice water to stop any further cooking. Drain and dry well; place on a large serving platter.

Drizzle the asparagus with the White Wine Vinaigrette and toss gently to coat. Place 6 asparagus on each of 4 plates. Place a dollop of the Raspberry Vinaigrette on top of each, season with a few grinds of cracked black pepper, and sprinkle with the fried asparagus peels, capers, parsley, pistachios, chopped egg, and diced beets.

SERVES 4

WHITE WINE VINAIGRETTE

This dressing is very versatile. It can be used for leaf salads or tossed with vegetables such as green beans and asparagus, as Patrick does in this menu. The vinaigrette will last for up to three weeks in the refrigerator.

1 cup vegetable oil
½ cup extra-virgin olive oil
½ cup white wine vinegar
¾ teaspoon salt
¼ teaspoon ground white pepper

1 tablespoon Dijon mustard
1 teaspoon chopped drained capers
1 teaspoon chopped fresh chives
1 teaspoon finely chopped fresh parsley

In a small bowl, combine the vegetable and olive oils. In another mixing bowl, whisk together the vinegar, salt, and white pepper. Then whisk the mustard into the vinegar mixture. Gradually pour in the oil mixture while whisking vigorously until the dressing is well blended and somewhat thick. Add the capers, chives, and parsley and mix well. Cover and store in the refrigerator.

MAKES APPROXIMATELY 2 CUPS

RASPBERRY VINAIGRETTE

Made with fresh raspberries and cream, this vinaigrette is best the day it is made, but it will last for two to three days in the refrigerator. Be sure to bring the cream to room temperature before adding the vinegar, otherwise it will curdle.

¼ cup heavy cream, at room
temperature
1 pint fresh raspberries
2 tablespoons raspberry vinegar
(available at specialty stores and
some supermarkets)

6 tablespoons extra-virgin olive oil
Salt and freshly ground pepper to taste
(optional)

Pour the cream into a small bowl. Wash the raspberries well, drain, and discard any that are bruised. Purée the raspberries in a food processor or blender and strain through a fine sieve to remove all the seeds. Whisk the purée into the cream until well blended. Combine the vinegar and oil in a cup or another small bowl, and then slowly add this mixture to the raspberries and cream, whisking, until the vinaigrette is thick and creamy. Add salt and pepper, if desired. Cover tightly and chill until serving time.

MAKES APPROXIMATELY 2 CUPS

BARBECUED BONELESS RACK OF LAMB IN A PECAN CRUST.

"This marinated rack of lamb is wonderful barbecued on a charcoal grill with the fat dripping into the flames and charring the skin," says Patrick. Serve a Cabernet from the Napa Valley with this dish; the chef's recommendation is a 1989 Dunn Howell Mountain.

Ask your butcher to remove the bones from the rack of lamb, but do bring home the bones to make lamb stock. Beef stock is a good substitute, but if you take the time to make stock from the lamb bones, you will be rewarded with an impeccable sauce that melds perfectly with the meat. The meat should be marinated overnight.

LAMB

2 boneless trimmed racks of lamb, about 3 pounds total

Barbecue Sauce (recipe follows)

CABERNET SAUVIGNON SAUCE

6 tablespoons (¾ stick) unsalted butter

⅓ cup domestic button mushrooms, stems included

1 carrot, peeled and diced

1 celery stalk, diced

½ small yellow or white onion, diced

1 teaspoon minced shallot

1 teaspoon minced garlic

⅓ cup chopped fresh parsley

2 teaspoons chopped fresh rosemary

2 teaspoons chopped fresh tarragon

2 bay leaves, crushed

2 cups Cabernet Sauvignon

2 tablespoons tomato paste

1 tomato

1 quart lamb or beef stock

2 tablespoons all-purpose flour

Salt and freshly ground pepper to taste

Pinch of sugar

PECAN CRUST

½ cup (1 stick) unsalted butter

1 tablespoon minced garlic

1 tablespoon minced fresh rosemary

1 cup coarsely ground toasted bread crumbs

1 cup toasted pecans (see box, page 117), coarsely ground

Salt and freshly ground pepper to taste

Divide each rack of lamb in half crosswise and brush the meat with ¼ cup of the barbecue sauce. Cover and marinate overnight in the refrigerator.

Prepare the sauce. Melt 4 tablespoons of butter in a large saucepan over medium heat and add the mushrooms, carrot, celery, onion, shallot, garlic, parsley, rosemary, tarragon, and bay leaves. Sauté for 2 minutes and add the wine, tomato paste, tomato, and stock. Raise the heat to high and cook until the liquid is reduced by half, about 20 minutes.

While the sauce is reducing, make a brown roux (see box, page 89) by melting the remaining 2 tablespoons of butter in a small saucepan over medium heat. Stir in the flour and continue stirring for 2 minutes, or until the flour is cooked and a nutty aroma is released. Once the sauce is reduced, add the roux and stir until the sauce has thickened. Add ¼ cup of the barbecue sauce. Simmer over medium heat for 15 minutes, then strain the sauce through a fine sieve, pressing with the back of a spoon to extract all the liquid from the solids. Discard the solids. Season the sauce with salt, black pepper, and sugar. (The sauce can be made up to 1 day in advance and kept covered in the refrigerator. Reheat to serve.)

To make the crust, melt the butter in a large skillet over medium heat. Add the garlic and rosemary and cook, stirring, for 1 minute. Add the bread crumbs and pecans and stir constantly. Cook for 5 to 7 minutes, until the mixture is lightly browned and crunchy. Add salt and pepper. Set aside, covered, until ready to use. (For best results, this should be made the day you intend to use it.)

About an hour before serving time, preheat a grill to hot (unless you wish to sear the meat on the stovetop) and the oven to 400° F. Grill the meat until seared on all sides, 5 minutes per side, or heat a large, heavy-bottomed oiled skillet over medium-high heat and sear on all sides, about 8 minutes in all. Transfer the lamb to a baking dish and bake for 12 minutes, or until desired doneness is reached. Remove from the oven and allow the meat to rest for 20 minutes before slicing. Place the pecan–bread crumb mixture on a large plate. Brush the meat with some of the remaining barbecue sauce and roll each half-rack in the pecan crust. Slice each half-rack crosswise into 3 medallions and arrange 3 pieces on each of 4 plates. Spoon the sauce over the meat and serve with Shoestring Sweet Potatoes.

Serves 4

BARBECUE SAUCE

This sauce can be used to make barbecued chicken and pork in addition to lamb. It is an easy sauce that can be thrown together before grilling. The recipe can be multiplied.

¼ cup ketchup

¼ cup chopped onion

2 tablespoons Worcestershire sauce

2 tablespoons white wine vinegar

½ teaspoon dry mustard

¼ teaspoon Tabasco sauce

Blend all the ingredients together in a mixing bowl. Let stand for 30 minutes to let the flavors combine. Refrigerate until ready to use. The sauce can be held for two to three weeks in the refrigerator, tightly covered.

MAKES APPROXIMATELY ³/₄ CUP

SHOESTRING SWEET POTATOES

Vegetable oil, for deep-frying

2 sweet potatoes, peeled

Heat the vegetable oil to 300°F. in a large, heavy-bottomed saucepan or deep-fryer. Slice the potatoes into long, thin julienne strips about ⅛ inch thick and wide and 3 inches long. Fry until crispy and slightly browned, 3 to 4 minutes. Remove with a slotted spoon, drain on paper towels, and season with salt.

SERVES 4

Coeur à la Crème

"Coeur à la Crème is an ancient French country concoction that is both earthy and elegant, rustic and dressy—appropriate for any occasion," says Patrick. "It's a wonderful complement to whatever summer berries are in season. It can be made in less than five minutes and never fails to knock 'em out—even more so than an elaborate cake that took two days to execute."

A perforated heart-shaped ceramic mold or a wicker basket lined with cheesecloth will be needed to drain the liquid from the mixture overnight, resulting in a firm yet silky "heart of cream." These molds are available at Williams-Sonoma and other kitchen supply stores, especially around Valentine's Day.

1 pound mascarpone cheese (an Italian double- or triple-cream cheese made from cow's milk, available at specialty shops)

1½ cups plus ⅓ cup heavy cream

2 tablespoons Chambord or other raspberry liquor

2 tablespoons fresh lemon juice

1 cup sifted confectioners' sugar

1 cup raspberry sauce (see page 10) or other fruit purée

Raspberries, for garnish

Line four 8-ounce *coeur à la crème* molds with 2 layers of damp, but not soaking wet, cheesecloth. Set aside.

In the large mixing bowl of an electric mixer, mix the mascarpone cheese, ⅓ cup of the cream, Chambord, and lemon juice until smooth and slightly runny. In another large mixing bowl, whip the remaining 1½ cups cream and the confectioners' sugar to medium-stiff peaks. Fold the whipped cream into the cheese mixture until well combined.

Evenly divide the cream cheese mixture among the molds and cover the tops with plastic wrap. Refrigerate for 4 to 6 hours or until set.

To serve, unmold each *coeur à la crème* onto a small plate and peel off the cheesecloth. Decorate each plate with the raspberry sauce and some berries.

Serves 4

BRADLEY OGDEN

An Indian-Summer Cookout

Elegant yet uncomplicated, Bradley Ogden's Indian-Summer Cookout is one of his favorite menus to eat al fresco with his family. "Jody and I, along with our three teenage boys, always plan a family feast with friends in late September. The Napa harvests are just about to come in, the San Francisco weather is at its golden best, and summer fruits and vegetables are at their peak." The flavors in this menu meld well and rely on farm-fresh, perfectly ripe ingredients that are prepared in a straightforward fashion. "I like to keep my menus simple, using the freshest ingredients available and putting them together in such a way that the flavors, colors, and textures combine to bring out the best in each other."

This type of cooking is influenced by his upbringing and early exposure to fresh American foods. "Coming from the Midwest," says Bradley, "I grew up with freshly caught trout, free-range chickens, and hand-picked fruits and vegetables. As my culinary training exposed me to new techniques and ingredients, I never lost my appreciation for those basic fresh tastes."

After graduating with honors in 1977 from the prestigious Culinary Institute of America at Hyde Park, New York,

MENU

*Grilled Oysters with
Horseradish Barbecue Sauce*

—

*Grilled Flatbreads with Figs, Balsamic
Roasted Onions, Goat Cheese,
and Fresh Herb Salad*

—

*Grilled Sea Bass with Orzo, Garden Tomato,
and Baby Artichoke Salad*

—

Blueberry–Nectarine Pie

Bradley worked for the acclaimed American Restaurant in Kansas City before moving in 1983 to San Francisco. After six years as the executive chef at the Campton Place Hotel, Bradley ventured out alone for the first time in 1989 and opened the Lark Creek Inn in Larkspur, California. His influential cooking earned him national acclaim and several awards, and he opened another restaurant in San Francisco three years later, called One Market Restaurant.

Although this forty-one-year-old native of Traverse City, Michigan, may be busy with his two restaurants, assorted television appearances, and travels around the world, he does make time for a healthful dinner at home with his family and friends. "I usually go to our local farmers' market down the street and pick out items for dinner, which always end up being a menu for the barbecue," says Bradley. Grilling is one of his favorite cooking methods, especially in hot weather.

He also tries to involve his guests and family in the creation of the meal. "It's part of the party to have everyone help prep the food," says Bradley. His children help shuck the corn, snap the green beans, or set the table—tasks that are not unfamiliar to his kids, especially the two who work occasionally at the Lark Creek Inn. "It's fun for everyone, particularly if we're making food with a festive tone." Bradley suggests a crisp California Chardonnay or Sauvignon Blanc or just old-fashioned iced tea to accompany the meal.

GRILLED OYSTERS WITH HORSERADISH BARBECUE SAUCE

Bradley proclaims, "the oyster is an ultimate indulgence food. When you add the familiarity of home-made barbecue sauce, you combine luxury and comfort."

4 pounds rock salt, available at most supermarkets (see Note)
36 fresh oysters, in the shell

Horseradish Barbecue Sauce (recipe follows)
12 lemon wedges

Light the grill. Spread the rock salt in a ½-inch layer on 6 plates. Wash the oysters under cool, running water. Open all the oysters (see box, page 204). After you have removed the lid (flat shell), nestle the oysters in their cup shells in the rock salt, placing 6 on each plate. This will keep the liquid in the oysters. Place 1 tablespoon of barbecue sauce on each oyster.

When the grill is medium-hot, carefully place the oysters, shell side down, on the grill. Cook them for about 6 minutes, until the oyster meat bubbles and curls around the edges. Serve the oysters on the plates of rock salt with the lemon wedges.

SERVES 6

N O T E : Rock salt is also available in home improvement stores and hardware stores, especially during the winter months in snow- and ice-bound areas. Be sure to buy it without chemical additives.

Grilling Tips

For grilling fish it is best to maintain a medium to low flame. Bradley suggests starting the grill about one hour beforehand. To test for the correct heat level, place your hand five inches from the rack. If you cannot hold it for more than six or seven seconds, the fire is too hot—in which case you can let it cool down a bit longer or raise the rack. If you can hold it for more than nine or ten seconds, the grill is not hot enough—in which case you can add more wood chips to the coals.

Wood chips create smoke, which gives extra flavor to foods cooked on the grill. Bradley recommends sprinkling dry wood chips over the smoldering coals for recipes such as the Grilled Sea Bass, but if you desire extra smokiness, soak the chips in water before adding them to the coals.

HORSERADISH BARBECUE SAUCE

Don't let the lengthy ingredients list keep you from making this simple sauce. The smoky chipotle pepper adds spice to its rich flavor. Feel free to double or triple this recipe, and freeze the extra for future use.

¾ cup commercial chili sauce

⅓ cup molasses

3 tablespoons soy sauce

1 tablespoon dark brown sugar

1 teaspoon Dijon mustard

1 garlic clove, crushed

3 tablespoons fresh lemon juice

⅓ cup chicken stock

¼ cup water

1 teaspoon Tabasco sauce

1 teaspoon coarse salt

2 teaspoons Worcestershire sauce

¼ teaspoon hot red pepper flakes

½ Anaheim pepper, seeded and cut into 1-inch pieces (see box, page 176)

¼ green bell pepper, seeded and cut into 1-inch pieces

½ canned chipotle pepper in adobo sauce (available at Latin or specialty markets)

¼ cup minced fresh chives

½ cup grated, peeled fresh horseradish

Oysters

Note that oysters have one flat shell and one shell that is shaped like a cup. When storing oysters, always position them cup side down so the oyster opens, you will not lose any juice. To open an oyster, rest it cup side down on a steady work surface and gently pry the flat shell from the cup shell using an oyster knife and a towel to firmly hold the oyster. An alternative is to grill the oysters briefly, cup side down, until they open slightly.

Oysters are always purchased live, and should be opened as close to eating as possible. To determine if oysters are fresh, ask to have one opened before buying them from a reputable fishmonger. The shells should be tightly closed (or should snap shut when tapped), but upon opening they should release a teaspoon or two of liquid. The meat should be firm and the liquid should be clean, not milky. They should smell fresh, like the sea. If possible, taste the oyster before you buy them—there is no better method than tasting! Store the oysters covered with a damp towel in the coldest spot of the refrigerator for no more than three days. The sooner they're eaten, the better!

Oysters are a great source of protein, vitamins, and minerals, and have a very low fat content. They are excellent in all manners of preparation—poached, broiled, grilled, fried, and, of course, raw with a squeeze of lemon or one of any number of sauces.

Combine all the ingredients except the chives and horseradish in a large, heavy-bottomed saucepan and bring to a boil over high heat. Reduce the heat to low and simmer for 15 to 20 minutes. Remove from the heat and put the sauce through a fine strainer, using a wooden spoon to push as much of the sauce through as possible. Discard the solids. Stir in the chives and horseradish. If you are not using the sauce immediately, store tightly covered in the refrigerator for up to 4 days and reheat over low heat before serving.

MAKES 2 CUPS

GRILLED FLATBREADS WITH FIGS, BALSAMIC ROASTED ONIONS, GOAT CHEESE, AND FRESH HERB SALAD

If all these figs are beyond your budget, Bradley says one pint of figs will suffice, or substitute peaches or nectarines for some of the figs. The roasted onions can be made a day ahead and refrigerated, covered, in a nonreactive dish. To save time use a premade pizza bread dough.

4 medium red onions

About 1½ cups balsamic vinegar

½ cup plus 6 tablespoons extra-virgin olive oil

Salt and freshly ground pepper to taste

Flatbread Dough, at room temperature (recipe follows), or 1 pound prepared pizza bread dough

Bread flour, for dusting

8 ounces soft goat cheese, such as Montrachet or Laura Chenel, crumbled

2 pints fresh Kadota and/or Black Mission figs, quartered

FRESH HERB SALAD

⅓ cup balsamic vinegar

⅓ cup extra-virgin olive oil

1 garlic clove, minced

1 tablespoon fresh lemon juice

Coarse salt and freshly ground pepper to taste

¾ cup fresh Italian parsley leaves, washed and dried

½ cup torn fresh chives

½ cup torn fresh basil leaves, washed and dried

Preheat the oven to 375°F. Peel the onions, leaving the roots intact. Cut the onions in half lengthwise through the root and slice again lengthwise into ½-inch wedges. In a casserole dish, place the onions in a single "cozy" layer. Drizzle enough of the balsamic vinegar over the onions to come one-third of the way up the onions. Drizzle ½ cup of the olive oil over the onions and sprinkle evenly with salt and pepper. Roast for about 15 minutes, until the onions are fork-tender and slightly crispy and browned. Remove from the oven and let cool. Drain off the liquid and use again for roasting more onions or in the vinaigrette instead of the balsamic vinegar and oil.

Preheat a covered grill to medium-low heat. Lightly dust the risen dough balls with flour and shape into six 6-inch discs no thinner than ⅓ inch. Drizzle each disc with 1 tablespoon of olive oil and season with salt and pepper. Place the discs on the grill. After about 1 minute, or when you are able to manipulate them, turn the discs a quarter turn so that they do not burn but will toast nicely. After about 3 minutes the discs will begin to puff; turn them over and distribute the roasted onions, goat cheese, and figs evenly over the breads. Close the lid of the grill and cook for another 2 minutes. If the topping is not warm before the bread cooks through, pop the flatbread into a warm oven for a few minutes.

While the bread is cooking, combine the balsamic vinegar and oil (or liquid from the onions) with the garlic, lemon juice, and salt and pepper in a mixing bowl. Add the parsley, chives, and basil and toss to combine. Divide this mixture among the cooked breads, sprinkling on top. Slice each bread into 4 pieces and serve immediately.

SERVES 6

VARIATION: BAKED FLATBREADS The flatbreads can also be baked in the oven, but the wonderful grilled flavor will be sacrificed. Preheat the oven to 400° F. Lightly brush a baking sheet with olive oil, and place the discs of dough on it. Do not crowd the breads; bake in 2 batches if the pan is not big enough. Bake for 6 minutes, then add the onions, figs, and cheese. Bake for another 6 minutes or until the flatbreads are crispy and golden brown.

Flame Douser

Lemon juice is great for dousing flare-ups on the grill, which occur when fat drips onto the coals. It is a good idea to have 3 cups of water mixed with ¼ cup lemon juice in a heat-resistant pan and a small ladle handy to pour the lemon water on the flames.

FLATBREAD DOUGH

Bradley does not recommend substituting all-purpose flour for bread flour, because it does not contain as much gluten, the ingredient that allows the dough to become more elastic so that it can stretch and rise better. If you are kneading this bread by hand, try to find a friend to share the work, or take comfort in knowing you are working off the bread before you even eat it.

3½ cups bread flour, or more as
    needed

1 teaspoon fresh cake yeast, crumbled
    into little pieces, or 1 package (2¾
    teaspoons) active dry yeast

2 teaspoons coarse salt

4 teaspoons extra-virgin olive oil

⅓ cup diced onion

1 cup plus 2 tablespoons cold water

If using an electric mixer with a dough hook, place the flour in the mixing bowl. Add the yeast, salt, oil, onion, and water and mix until the dough is smooth but not sticky; add additional flour if needed. Knead for 10 minutes to develop the gluten, until the dough is smooth and elastic. Remove the dough from the bowl.

If making the dough by hand, place the ingredients in a large bowl and mix with a wooden spoon until the mixture becomes smooth, but not sticky, adding more flour if needed. Place the dough on a floured surface and knead by hand for 15 minutes, until the dough has become smooth and elastic.

Divide the dough into 6 balls of equal size. Place them on an oiled baking sheet in a single layer, and brush with oil. Allow the dough to rise either 4 to 6 hours in the refrigerator or 1 hour in a warm place. (If the dough is refrigerated, allow it to warm to room temperature before shaping.)

MAKES 6 BALLS OF DOUGH

GRILLED SEA BASS WITH ORZO, GARDEN TOMATO, AND BABY ARTICHOKE SALAD

"Texturally, this is a 'fun' dish because you have the crisp crust of the grilled fish mingling with the juicy tomatoes, tender baby artichokes, and al dente *orzo," Bradley says. Cod, halibut, or salmon may be substituted for the bass and the chef suggests serving the fish with a homemade mayonnaise. For more flavor, he grills the sea bass over oak chips.*

For a truly stress-free dinner, grill the dish before dinner and serve it at room temperature. Grilling the fish is a quick process, so be sure to have all the ingredients and tools at hand before starting. Bradley suggests grilling one fillet at a time.

2 tablespoons (¼ stick) unsalted butter, softened

Zest and juice of ½ lemon

Salt and freshly ground pepper to taste

2 sea bass fillets (1½–2 pounds each), skin attached

About ½ cup extra-virgin olive oil

Lemon wedges, for garnish

Orzo, Garden Tomato, and Baby Artichoke Salad (recipe follows)

Prepare the grill. Blend the butter with the lemon zest and lemon juice in a small bowl. Season with a little salt and pepper, then set aside. On a large plate, brush both sides of the fish lightly with the olive oil, then season both sides liberally with salt and pepper.

When the coals are ready, lightly coat the rack with olive oil, using a brush. Place the fish flesh side down on the rack. Every 2 or 3 minutes, rotate the fish, using a spatula placed at either end, for a total cooking time of 8 or 9 minutes. Rotating the fish helps it develop an even golden brown crispness rather than burning grill marks into the flesh. Gently turn the fish over and cook for another 4 to 6 minutes, again rotating every 2 or 3 minutes depending on how hot the grill is and how well done you like your fish. The flesh should be opaque and should flake.

Gently transfer the fish to a platter and rub liberally with the lemon butter. Place the second piece of fish on the grill and cook in the same fashion. Present the fish on a platter with lemon wedges and serve warm or at room temperature with the Orzo, Garden Tomato, and Baby Artichoke Salad.

SERVES 6

Orzo, Garden Tomato, and Baby Artichoke Salad

This salad makes the most of summer flavors—sweet tomatoes, tender baby artichokes, and sharp arugula. It makes a perfect summer meal when matched with the Grilled Sea Bass.

The tomatoes must be juicy, ripe, and sweet. If baby artichokes are not available, use four large ones instead. The salad may be prepared up to one day in advance.

¾ pound orzo

2–4 teaspoons salt, plus more to taste

1 cup extra-virgin olive oil, plus more to taste

Salt and freshly ground black pepper to taste

1 lemon, zested and halved

10 baby artichokes or 4 regular artichokes, trimmed (see box, below)

4 garlic cloves, minced

1 red onion, cut in half lengthwise and thinly sliced

3 large ripe tomatoes, cored and cut into ¼-inch-thick wedges

1 pint cherry tomatoes, cut in half, or 2 regular tomatoes, cut in wedges

1 bunch (¼ pound) arugula, washed and trimmed

¾ cup dry white wine

¼ cup fresh lemon juice, plus more to taste

½ cup chopped fresh basil

Artichoke Hints

Before cooking both baby and regular artichokes, they should be trimmed. For either type, the process is virtually the same. Remove the tough dark green and discolored outer leaves. Using a sharp knife, cut the stem close to the base so it stands level. Chop off about 1 inch for regular artichokes and ½ inch for baby artichokes of the top center leaves. Then, using scissors, clip the remaining thorny tips. To keep the artichoke from turning brown, rub the artichoke all over with half of a lemon immediately after cutting, even if it is being used right away. Squeeze the other lemon half in a pot of cold water and store the artichoke in the water until ready to use.

When buying artichokes, choose those that are firm and have stiff, tightly-packed leaves. Stay away from artichokes with open leaves and black tips, which indicate the artichoke is over-ripe. Store uncooked artichokes with their stalks submerged in water; they will keep for a few days. Cooked artichokes will keep for twenty-four hours, tightly wrapped, in the refrigerator.

Bring a large pot of water to a boil over medium-high heat. Add the orzo and 1 to 2 teaspoons of the salt, and cook until tender, 7 to 10 minutes. Drain the orzo and transfer to a large bowl. Toss with ½ cup of the olive oil, then add salt and pepper and the lemon zest. Set aside.

Bring another large pot of water to a boil with 1 to 2 teaspoons of salt over medium-high heat. Rub the artichokes with a lemon half and add them to the boiling water. Bring the mixture back to a simmer and cook for 6 to 10 minutes, until the base can be pierced with the tip of a paring knife and is tender. Remove the artichokes with a slotted spoon and set aside to cool. Cut each in half lengthwise and remove the choke, with a teaspoon or paring knife. (If using large artichokes, steam them for 15 to 20 minutes, until the base is tender. Cut each artichoke in half, remove the choke, then cut each half into 6 wedges.)

In a large skillet, heat the remaining olive oil over medium heat. Add the garlic, onion, and artichokes, and cook until the artichokes are lightly browned. Add the tomatoes, cherry tomatoes, and arugula, and cook for another 1 to 2 minutes, until the arugula begins to wilt. Add the wine and lemon juice and simmer for another 1 to 2 minutes. Transfer to the orzo and toss. Fold in the basil and adjust the seasonings. Serve warm or at room temperature.

SERVES 6

BLUEBERRY–NECTARINE PIE

Use a favorite double-crust pie recipe or use the recipe for Basic Pie Dough on page 223. Store-bought pie dough also works fine.

Dough for double-crust 9-inch pie

6 cups ripe nectarine wedges (about 3 large nectarines)

1 pint fresh blueberries, washed and dried, picked over, stems removed

Zest and juice of 1 lemon

4 teaspoons cornstarch

1 cup sugar

1 teaspoon ground cinnamon

½ teaspoon freshly grated nutmeg

2 tablespoons (¼ stick) unsalted butter

1 large egg, lightly beaten with 1 tablespoon milk

Ice cream or whipped cream, to serve (optional)

Preheat the oven to 350° F. Roll out half the pie dough on a lightly floured surface to an 11-inch circle about ⅛ inch thick. Line a 9-inch pan with the dough, leaving a ½-inch overhang on all sides. Set aside.

Combine the nectarines and blueberries in a large bowl. Add the lemon zest and juice and toss gently. Set aside. Combine the cornstarch, sugar, cinnamon, and nutmeg in a small bowl. Rub together with your fingers to remove any lumps, then sprinkle this mixture over the fruit and toss gently until well combined. Transfer the fruit mixture to the pie shell. Cut the butter into small pieces and dot the pie with the butter.

Roll out the remaining dough on a lightly floured surface to an 11-inch circle. Brush the edges of the bottom crust with the egg wash. Place the top crust on top of the pie and fold and decoratively crimp the edges. Brush the top with the egg wash and make a few small slits to let steam escape. Bake for approximately 1 hour, until the crust is golden brown. Cool the pie on a wire rack, and serve plain, with ice cream or with freshly whipped cream.

S E R V E S 6

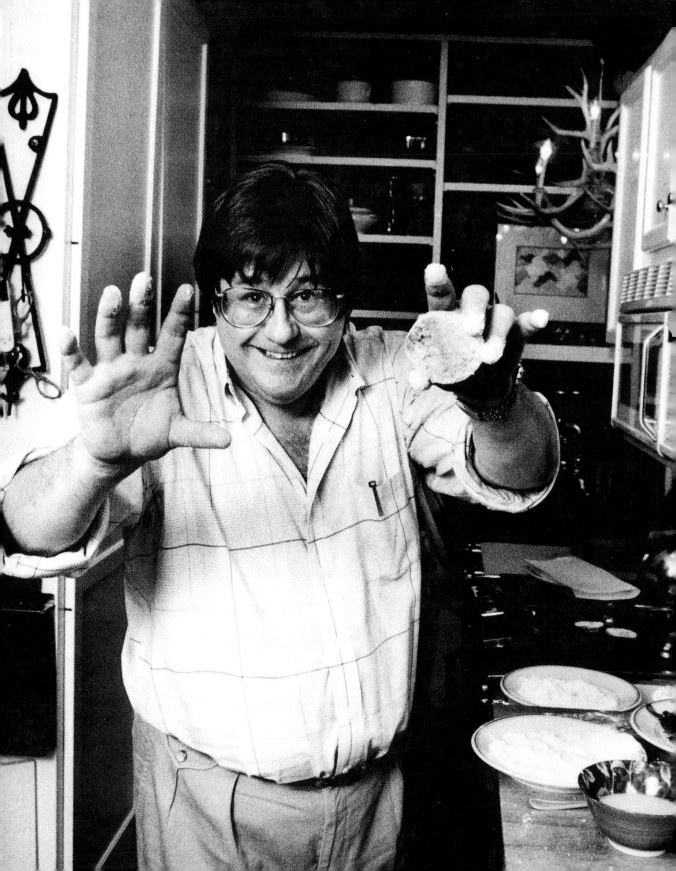

LOUIS OSTEEN

Low-Country Cooking

L ouis Osteen has come a long way from making popcorn, hot dogs, hamburgers, and French fries at his parents' drive-in theater in Anderson, South
Carolina. Today, he is the chef-creator of Louis's Charleston Grill in Charleston, South Carolina, specializing in Low-Country Southern regional cuisine. "The
food is straightforward, not very fussy, and has lots of personality and flavor," says Louis.

Many of the recipes chosen for this menu are versions of dishes Louis truly enjoyed as
a young boy. "My mother was a wonderful cook, as were my aunts and both grand-
mothers," Louis recalls. He was raised on a farm, where his mother prepared three family meals every day, fresh and from scratch. "I remember great big family gatherings for
holidays at my maternal grandmother's
colonial farmhouse, and the fun I had
poking around her kitchen."

In 1963, Louis moved to Atlanta and
opened several movie theaters, continuing
his family tradition. But several years later
he decided he needed a career change and
looked to his two hobbies: photography
and cooking. A friend helped with his
decision when he introduced Louis to a
French family who owned Le Versailles,
one of Atlanta's finest restaurants at the

MENU

Wadmawlaw Sweets Onion Tart

➤

Pan-Fried Soft-Shell Crabs

➤

Fried Green Tomatoes

➤

Stewed Rabbit Smothered with Onions

➤

Southern Biscuits

➤

Buttermilk Tart with Raspberries

time. "I couldn't have had a better introduction to a professional kitchen," Louis says. "They had a real commitment to quality ingredients and service."

In 1980, Louis opened Pawley's Island Inn with his wife, Marlene, whom he had met on Christmas Eve five years earlier. "Pawley's was my second try at ownership and it worked much better. I had more experience and the magic ingredient: Marlene at the front door." In 1989, the Osteens picked September 21 as the date they planned to open Louis's Charleston Grill—the very day that Hurricane Hugo hit Charleston. They opened a month later to immediate praise.

Marlene remembers some of the sacrifices she and Louis made when starting out in the restaurant business. "We couldn't always be at home to prepare meals for our three girls. Most of the meals were either eaten at the restaurant or sent home from the restaurant. So when we did cook at home, the meal was eagerly anticipated. They have developed a sophisticated sense of taste and a love for food," Marlene says. "Our big claim is that we have the only kids in the world who call home for recipes, not money."

When out-of-town guests are visiting the Osteens, they are often treated to a home-cooked meal. Marlene is likely to help Louis in the kitchen, which opens into their

dining room, where the guests snack on olives and a selection of the host's favorite nuts, pecans, walnuts, and macadamias. An onion tart, filled with locally grown Wadmawlaw Sweets starts off the meal. Soft-shell crabs, creamy and rich, "taste like the very essence of crab," Louis says, and are  served over crisply sautéed green tomatoes, prepared just the way his grandmother made them. Stewed rabbit is very Southern and makes a much more delicate stew than most other meats. It is made with beer for moistness and smothered in still more onions. For dessert, Louis turns to an old childhood favorite, a deliciously rich butter-milk tart topped with fresh berries. Both the onion and the buttermilk tart shells can be made the day before, and the rest is fairly quick to bring together the day of the dinner. This meal will transport even the staunchest Northerner to the Osteens' neck of the woods.

WADMAWLAW SWEETS ONION TART

Wadmawlaw Sweets onions, from the South Carolina island of Wadmawlaw, are similar in taste to Vidalia, Maui, and Walla Walla onions, and any of them can be substituted here. These Southern treasures are in season for only four to six weeks in the spring and should be used right away.

This tart is wonderful warm and fresh from the oven or at room temperature.

Unsweetened Basic Pie Dough for one 10-inch pie crust (see page 223)

½ **cup plus 3 tablespoons unsalted butter or rendered lard**

12 **cups thinly sliced Wadmawlaw Sweets or other sweet onion (about 10 large onions)**

Salt and freshly ground pepper

1 **tablespoon fresh thyme**

⅓ **cup heavy cream**

2 **large egg yolks**

Preheat the oven to 375°F. Roll the dough out on a lightly floured surface to a 12-inch circle about ⅛ inch thick. Place the dough in a 10-inch tart shell or pie pan and trim and decoratively crimp the edges. Cover the dough with foil and weight it down with rice or beans. Bake the tart shell for 15 minutes, until partially baked. Carefully remove the beans or rice and the foil and let cool on a wire rack. Reduce the oven temperature to 350°F.

In a large, heavy skillet, melt the butter over medium heat. Add the onions and salt and pepper. Stir often, until the onions "melt" and turn brown, 15 to 20 minutes. Stir in the thyme. Remove from the heat and transfer the onions to a mixing bowl. Let cool slightly.

In a small bowl, mix the cream and egg yolks until well blended. Pour the mixture into the onions, stirring until well coated. Pour the onion mixture into the cooled tart shell and bake for 20 to 30 minutes, until the tart is well browned. Remove from the oven and let cool slightly on a wire rack before serving.

SERVES 6 TO 8 GENEROUSLY

Wine Suggestions

A Riesling and the Wadmawlaw Sweets Onion Tart make a great opening match. A dry, crisp Sauvignon Blanc cleanses the palate between bites of the pan-fried crab and tomatoes. And the succulent rabbit and onions go well with a full-bodied Pinot Noir or Burgundy.

PAN-FRIED SOFT-SHELL CRABS WITH FRIED GREEN TOMATOES

Louis fries both the crabs and the green tomatoes with a coating of cornmeal. He makes a double batch of the cornmeal coating, and he dredges and fries the tomatoes before the crabs. He removes the oil and wipes the pan clean after frying the tomatoes and starts the crabs with fresh oil.

Be sure to buy the crabs from a reputable source and keep them refrigerated until cooking time.

3 cups buttermilk

2 tablespoons Tabasco sauce

6 soft-shell crabs, cleaned (have the
   fishmonger do this, or see
   box, opposite)

1 cup yellow cornmeal

1 cup all-purpose flour

½ teaspoon baking soda

1 teaspoon salt

1 teaspoon freshly ground pepper

1½ cups vegetable oil

1 tablespoon red wine vinegar

3 tablespoons fresh lemon juice

3 tablespoons water

1 cup (2 sticks) unsalted butter, cut
   into 12 pieces

4 tablespoons chopped fresh parsley or
   chervil

Fried Green Tomatoes (recipe follows)

Combine the buttermilk and Tabasco sauce in a dish deep enough to hold the crabs in a single layer. Add the crabs, turning them to coat, and set aside in the refrigerator for about 1 hour to marinate.

Combine the cornmeal, flour, baking soda, salt, and pepper in a shallow plate. Remove the crabs from the buttermilk with a slotted spoon, carefully dredge them in the cornmeal mixture, and place in a single layer on a baking sheet. Refrigerate for 30 minutes to allow the coating to dry.

Heat the oil in a heavy frying pan, such as an uncoated cast-iron pan, to about 350° F. When it is hot but not smoking (see Note), carefully place the crabs into the hot oil, bottom side down, without overcrowding. If necessary, adjust the heat to make sure the oil temperature hovers around 350° F. After 2 or 3 minutes, when golden brown on the bottom, flip the crabs and brown the top sides and cook for another 2 or 3 minutes, until nicely browned on both sides. Remove the crabs with a slotted spoon to a baking sheet, and put the baking sheet in a preheated 200° F. oven for no more than 10 minutes while making the sauce. Repeat until all the crabs are cooked.

Carefully pour all the fat from the skillet, leaving behind any small browned bits. In a small bowl, combine the vinegar and lemon juice with 3 tablespoons of water. Add this liquid to the skillet over medium heat and simmer for 30 seconds, scraping up the browned crumbs. Add the butter and whip with a whisk until incorporated into a sauce. Stir in the parsley or chervil.

To serve, place one crab atop 2 fried green tomato slices on each of 6 plates and pass the sauce on the side.

S E R V E S   6

N O T E : When cooking with very hot oil, use a thermometer to make sure the temperature does not get any hotter than it should be. And beware, hot oil is a fire hazard; be careful that it does not splash onto something flammable outside of the pan, as it could easily start a fire.

Soft-Shell Crabs

The term *soft-shell crab* does not refer to a species of crab but rather to a growth stage. Crabs shed their hard shell when they outgrow it. Crabbers have only a few days to catch crabs in their soft-shell state before the new, larger shell hardens. While crabs molt year-round, spring is the commercial season for soft-shell crabs. Soft-shell blue crabs, which are wonderfully sweet, are a specialty of Southern coastal waters. Soft-shell crabs can be baked, sautéed, deep-fried, or grilled. And yes, the shells are edible. However, the eyes, lungs, and "apron" (flap on the underside of the crab) are not edible. You can ask your fishmonger to dress and clean the crab, but it is also easy enough to do it yourself. Here's how: The eyes come off with a pinch from your thumb and finger. To remove the lungs, lift the shell from both the left and right pointed sides and pull out the saclike organs from both sides. On the underside of the crab, below the soft shell, is the apron; lift it and pull it off. Your crab is now dressed.

FRIED GREEN TOMATOES

Here's a recipe for unripened tomatoes. If green tomatoes are not available, use very firm red ones.

In the South, the traditional fat for frying tomatoes, as well as a host of other things, is rendered bacon fat. The fat is saved each morning from the breakfast bacon, after also frying the eggs and hash browns in it. To simplify things, vegetable oil is called for in this recipe, but use bacon fat if at all possible.

3 cups buttermilk

2 tablespoons Tabasco sauce

4 green tomatoes, cut into ½-inch-thick slices

1 cup yellow cornmeal

1 cup all-purpose flour

½ teaspoon baking soda

1 teaspoon salt

1 teaspoon freshly ground pepper

1½ cups vegetable oil

Combine the buttermilk and Tabasco sauce in a dish large enough to hold the tomatoes in 2 layers. Arrange the tomato slices so they are slightly overlapping in no more than 2 layers. Set aside at room temperature for about 1 hour to marinate.

Thoroughly combine the cornmeal, flour, baking soda, salt, and pepper in a shallow plate. Remove the tomatoes from the buttermilk with a slotted spoon, carefully dredge them in the cornmeal mixture, and place in a single layer on a baking sheet. Refrigerate for 30 minutes to allow the coating to dry.

Heat the oil in a heavy frying pan, such as an uncoated cast-iron pan, to about 350° F. When the oil is hot but not smoking, carefully place the tomato slices into the hot oil without overcrowding. If necessary, adjust the heat to make sure the oil temperature hovers around 350° F. After 2 minutes, or when golden brown on the bottom, turn the slices and brown the other sides. When they are nicely browned on both sides, remove the fried tomatoes with a slotted spoon to a plate lined with paper towels to drain. Serve warm. The tomatoes can be held on a baking sheet in a 200° F. oven. Repeat until all the tomatoes are fried.

SERVES 6

Biscuit and Pie Dough Tips

Many people find making pastry dough a daunting task, whether it be for pies or biscuits. The techniques are fairly simple, but expertise requires practice. A manageable and tasty dough is almost guaranteed if these basic guidelines are followed:

- Chill the fat (butter, shortening, or lard) well to start. Work quickly to prevent the fat from melting as you work the fat into the flour, when rolling out the dough, and when crimping the edges of a pie crust; otherwise, your pie crust will not be flaky and your biscuit will not rise. It helps to work in a cool environment.

- Do not overwork the dough. Overworking can produce a texture that is undesirably tough. Cutting the chilled butter or shortening into small pieces will cut down on the amount of "work." When adding liquid to the coarse meal of fat and flour, mix just until incorporated.

- Measure the ingredients precisely, especially the flour. Too much flour can make for a tough crust or biscuit. To measure the flour, scoop flour from its container into the measuring cup that is the same size as or smaller than the amount needed, so it is heaping. Using a flat utensil such as the dull side of a knife, level the cup.

- Use the specific flour called for in the recipe. Flours are often distinguished by the amount of gluten (protein) they contain. Flours with less gluten, such as a soft wheat flour, pastry flour, and cake flour, produce a tender crumb and are usually best for cakes, biscuits, and pie crusts. Flours with a high gluten content, such as bread flour, work well with yeast batters and are used in breads, focaccia, and pizza dough for a nice, chewy texture. The amount of gluten in all-purpose flour is between that of cake flour and bread flour. Usually all-purpose flour can be substituted for bread flour without much consequence, but never substitute cake flour for bread flour or vice versa.

- Use the correct temperature for baking. Always be sure the oven is at the correct temperature when you bake your dough, and watch the biscuits or crust carefully.

STEWED RABBIT SMOTHERED WITH ONIONS

The rabbit is stewed in a marinade of dark beer, herbs, and garlic, which produces a tender, richly flavored meat. Use any dark beer of choice, or Amstel Light, which Louis uses.

For a variation, grill the rabbit just until browned on the outside before baking, instead of sautéing. For an altogether different recipe, but one that is easier and less expensive, substitute chicken legs and thighs.

3 3-pound rabbits, each cut into 8 pieces

5 cups thinly sliced onions

¾ cup peeled and thinly sliced carrots

3 garlic cloves, smashed, plus 1½ tablespoons minced garlic

4 sprigs fresh thyme

2 small sprigs fresh rosemary

3 tablespoons lightly crushed black peppercorns

3 12-ounce bottles dark beer

3 tablespoons sugar

6 tablespoons (¾ stick) unsalted butter

6 tablespoons peanut oil

4¼ cups chicken stock

Salt and freshly ground pepper to taste

4½ tablespoons all-purpose flour

1 bouquet garni consisting of 3 bay leaves, 9 parsley stems, and 4 sprigs fresh thyme (see box, page 266)

Place the rabbit in a large glass or ceramic dish. Add ¾ cup of the onions and the carrots. In a large bowl combine the garlic, thyme, rosemary, peppercorns, beer, and sugar and pour the mixture over the rabbit, turning the pieces to coat. Cover the dish and refrigerate for 1 to 2 hours. Remove the rabbit pieces from the marinade and pat dry with paper towels. Strain the marinade into a large saucepan and discard the solids. Set aside.

Heat the butter and oil in a large, heavy skillet over medium-high heat until the fat is very hot. Cook the rabbit pieces in batches just until they are browned on both sides, 7 to 8 minutes. Adjust the heat to maintain a high temperature so the rabbit browns properly. Remove the browned pieces to a plate using a pair of tongs. Set aside while you cook the rest. Once all the rabbit pieces are browned, add the remaining 4¼ cups onions to the skillet over medium heat and sauté until they begin to brown, 7 to 8 minutes. Turn the onions into a strainer and let the oil drain off.

Preheat the oven to 350° F. Add the chicken stock to the reserved marinade and bring to a boil in a saucepan over high heat. Meanwhile, season the rabbit with salt and pepper and arrange them in a baking dish just large enough to hold them in a single layer. Sprinkle the flour over the rabbit. Distribute the cooked onions evenly over the rabbit. Pour the boiling liquid over the rabbit, sprinkle the minced garlic on top, and tuck the bouquet garni into the mixture. Cover the dish loosely with waxed paper and bake for about 20 minutes, or until the rabbit juices run clear when pricked with a fork and the meat comes away from the bone with ease. Adjust the seasoning of the sauce with salt and pepper. Discard the bouquet garni.

Transfer the rabbit pieces to a large serving platter using a pair of tongs, smother the rabbit with the onions, and pour some of the sauce on top.

S E R V E S   6

SOUTHERN BISCUITS

In the South, flour made from soft wheat is preferred, such as the popular White Lily self-rising flour, which Louis always uses for his biscuits. The result is a tender biscuit that is crispy and browned on the outside. If White Lily brand is not available, use another self-rising flour.

More important, Louis offers us his tips on how to eat the biscuits: "Decide how many biscuits you want to eat. When they are served, take that many. Then, instead of using a knife, use your fingers to separate the top from the bottom. Butter lavishly, replace the tops and enjoy!"

1 cup (2 sticks) unsalted butter, chilled
3 cups White Lily self-rising or other
  soft self-rising flour (see Note)

1 cup plus 2 tablespoons buttermilk

Cut 10 tablespoons (1¼ sticks) of the butter into 16 pieces and place in a mixing bowl with the flour. Work the butter into the flour with a pastry cutter, fork, or your fingertips to a coarse meal the size of a small pea. Work quickly, especially if you are using your fingertips, so the butter does not become warm. Pour all of the buttermilk into the mixture and, using a plastic spatula, fold in until the mixture becomes cohesive. Do not overmix; you should only need to fold several times.

Turn the dough out onto a lightly floured surface. Quickly and gently knead the dough 6 to 10 times, making sure it does not stick to the bottom, until just blended. Using a rolling pin, roll the dough out to a ½-inch thickness. With a lightly floured cookie cutter or glass, cut the dough into 2½-inch rounds. Collect the scraps into a ball one time and roll out again to cut more biscuits, making sure the surface is well floured and no small pieces of dough are left on the surface. Place the biscuit rounds on an ungreased baking sheet and bake for about 15 minutes, until the tops and bottoms are crispy and browned. While the biscuits are baking, melt the remaining 6 tablespoons of butter. Set aside. Remove the biscuits from the oven and brush the tops with the melted butter. Serve immediately.

MAKES ABOUT 1 DOZEN

N O T E : If self-rising flour is hard to find, substitute 1 cup of all-purpose flour, 2 cups of cake flour, 4½ teaspoons baking powder, 1½ teaspoons baking soda, and ⅜ teaspoon salt.

BUTTERMILK TART WITH RASPBERRIES

"Next to mother's milk comes buttermilk," says Louis about the importance of buttermilk to Southerners. In the South, it is found in everything from biscuits to ice cream and is even offered as a beverage.

With this Southern staple, Louis has created a simple yet elegant raspberry-studded tart. Sweet, juicy blackberries are wonderful in this dessert, too. The smooth and creamy filling is neither too sweet nor too tart. Louis suggests sharing the leftovers with the neighbors.

Basic Pie Dough for one 12-inch tart
  (recipe follows)
2½ cups sugar
2 tablespoons all-purpose flour
3 large eggs
5 tablespoons unsalted butter, melted
  and cooled

1½ cups buttermilk
1 teaspoon vanilla extract
1 teaspoon red wine vinegar
1½ pints fresh berries, such as
  raspberries or blackberries
1 cup apricot preserves
2 tablespoons brandy or water

Preheat the oven to 350°F. Roll out the pie dough to a 14-inch circle on a lightly floured surface. Line a 12-inch tart pan with a removable bottom with the dough, folding over the extra and pressing against the sides. Refrigerate the pan for 30 minutes. Prick the dough with a fork in several spots. Line the tart pan with parchment paper or aluminum foil and fill with rice or dried beans. Bake the tart for 15 minutes, remove the rice or beans and paper, and bake for another 10 minutes or so until lightly golden. Cool completely on a wire rack. Raise the oven temperature to 375°F.

To make the filling, mix the sugar and flour in a large bowl. In another large bowl, stir the eggs, melted butter, buttermilk, vanilla, and vinegar together until well combined. With a wooden spoon, stir the dry ingredients into the liquid mixture until well blended; try not to incorporate air into the mixture. Pour the filling into the baked tart shell, tap the tart pan lightly on the counter a few times, and place in the oven. Bake until the filling is lightly browned and the tart is set in the middle (if the filling ripples when moved slightly, it is not set) about 45 minutes. Let the tart cool completely on a wire rack.

To decorate, arrange the berries on top of the tart in concentric circles, beginning at the outside edge and continuing until the whole tart is covered. In a small saucepan, bring the apricot preserves and brandy or water to a boil over medium-high heat, whisking occasionally until the mixture is a smooth liquid. Remove from the heat and strain. Using a small pastry brush, brush the berries with the strained preserves. Allow the glaze to set for 10 minutes before cutting. (This tart can be made a day in advance and kept refrigerated.)

MAKES ONE 12-INCH TART

BASIC PIE DOUGH

This recipe makes enough dough for two 10-inch pie crusts. Each half of the recipe can be rolled out to fit almost any size pie or tart pan, including a 9- or 10-inch regular or deep-dish pie pan or a 12-inch tart pan. The trick is to roll the dough to about ⅛-inch thickness and large enough to fit into the pan, covering the sides, without stretching the dough. For an unsweetened dough, just omit the sugar.

Shape excess dough into a flat disc, wrap in plastic wrap or waxed paper, and store in the freezer for up to one month.

2⅔ cups all-purpose flour
½ teaspoon salt
2 teaspoons sugar (omit for unsweetened dough)

1 cup (2 sticks) unsalted butter, chilled and cut into small pieces
⅓ cup plus 1 tablespoon ice water

In a large mixing bowl, combine the flour, salt, and sugar. Using a fork, pastry cutter, or your fingertips, work the butter into the flour mixture until the mixture resembles coarse meal, with pieces about the size of peas. Make a well in the center of the mixture, add the water, and toss the mixture into the well, mixing until the dough starts to come together. Gather the dough into a mass and fold over until the dough just holds together. Divide the dough into 2 halves, shape each half into a ball, and flatten into a disc. Wrap each disc in plastic wrap or waxed paper and refrigerate for at least 1 hour before rolling out.

MAKES TWO 10-INCH PIE CRUSTS

JEAN-LOUIS PALLADIN

Elegance at Home

I came to this country eager to create a cuisine that would take advantage of the finest ingredients. With the help of farmers, growers, and fishermen from Oregon to Maine, I have been able to gather an incredible variety of fine-quality native American foods to combine with my gastronomic knowledge from Gascony."

Jean-Louis Palladin was born and raised in the Gascony town of Condom, France, by parents of Spanish and Italian heritage. As a young boy, he dreamed of becoming a surgeon, but he knew there was not enough money to send him to medical school. He left school at age twelve because he was unhappy as a student, and he immediately entered the kitchen, becoming an apprentice at Le Franco Italien, a restaurant near his home. He was exposed there to classical Italian cooking methods. Doing everything from dicing vegetables to chopping wood for the restaurant's fireplace, where much of the food was prepared, Jean-Louis found his true calling. "For some reason I was happy only when I was in the restaurant. It was the only place I wanted to be."

Already skilled at an early age in Italian, Spanish, and southern French technique, Jean-Louis felt it essential to master classical French cooking to complete his training, and he worked his way through restaurants in France to gain the experience he needed. In the course of his culinary career, he has

MENU

Corn Soup with Petit Vegetables

Salad of Seaweed and Lobster with Ginger Emulsion

Loin of Lamb with Grits

Apple Turnovers with Date Sauce

returned to Le Franco Italien on and off for a
total of twenty-one years in between other
restaurant stints, eventually becoming its
head chef.

In 1968, Jean-Louis opened La Table des
Cordeliers, where at age twenty-eight he
received two Michelin stars, the youngest
chef ever in France to be awarded such an honor. In 1979, a former U.S. ambassador to
Hungary discovered the young star and enticed him to open a restaurant bearing his
name—Jean-Louis at the Watergate Hotel in Washington, D.C. Today, Jean-Louis is considered one of the nation's most celebrated culinary geniuses, exuding charm, infectious
energy, and a unique ability to marry the most unlikely food combinations with flair.

With the exception of the Super Bowl, at which time Jean-Louis covers his pool table
and puts together a glorious spread for friends, he and his wife, Régine, enjoy a formal
atmosphere when entertaining. White tablecloths and candlelight set the stage for dinner
at the Palladin home, which is secluded in the woods just minutes outside Washington.

Jean-Louis delivers the meal to his dining room table in true Jean-Louis style—
everything is properly plated, beginning with a creamy corn soup filled with fresh diced
vegetables. "Corn was one of the first flavors I discovered when I came here from France,
and I fell in love with it." This menu is typical for Jean-Louis because it highlights
American products. The seaweed he uses in the salad with sesame oil, lobster, and ginger
comes from Maine and was introduced to him by his fish supplier. "There was an explo-
sion in my mouth the first time I tasted it." The loin of lamb made with consommé and
a variety of spices is served with grits and prepared in Jean-Louis's fireplace, which
reminds him of both his childhood home and the Italian restaurant where he spent so
many years. Instead of the traditional cinnamon flavoring, Jean-Louis incorporates an
unusual spice mixture in the apple turnover and accompanies it with a date sauce.

"I like this menu because it seems fancy and complicated when you see it, but it is,
in fact, very simple," Jean-Louis promises. "With a menu like this, you can impress
your friends without having to cook anything too complex." While Jean-Louis's idea
of simple may be more involved than your own, the results are decidedly worthwhile.

CORN SOUP WITH PETIT VEGETABLES

The creaminess of this soup is enhanced by the puréed sweet corn. Frozen corn kernels could be used in a pinch, but fresh kernels from the cob provide a taste well worth the effort. Jean-Louis's style is to ladle the soup from an oven-hot tureen at the table, where the soup plates are lined with crisp, chilled diced zucchini, carrots, turnips, and celery. The vegetables stay crunchy when the hot soup is poured over them. The petit vegetables can be prepared several hours in advance.

1 small zucchini

¼ cup plus 2 tablespoons coarse salt

⅓ cup peeled and finely diced carrots

⅓ cup peeled and finely diced turnips

⅓ cup peeled and finely diced celery

5 7-inch-long ears of yellow corn, shucked, or 3 cups frozen yellow corn kernels, cooked according to package directions and drained

2½ cups heavy cream

Fine sea salt to taste

Freshly ground black pepper to taste

Small dill sprigs, for garnish

Cut the skin from the zucchini in ⅛-inch-thick slices (keeping one-eighth of the flesh), then cut the slices into tiny dice. Set aside. (Save the core of the zucchini for another use.)

Have 2 large bowls of ice water nearby to cool the vegetables and the corn after being cooked. In a large saucepan over high heat, bring 3 quarts of water and ¼ cup coarse salt to a rolling boil and add the carrots, turnips, and celery to cook for 5 minutes. Then add the diced zucchini and cook for 1 more minute. Immediately drain the vegetables in a strainer, then lower the strainer into the ice water to cool. Drain the vegetables, pat dry, and store in a covered bowl in the refrigerator. (This may be done several hours in advance.)

Bring 3 quarts of water and the remaining 2 tablespoons of coarse salt to a rapid boil in a large saucepan over high heat. If using fresh corn, add the ears and cook just until tender, about 3 minutes. Drain and add the corn to the other bowl of ice water to cool. Drain again. Cut the kernels from the cobs. Set aside 2 tablespoons of kernels, covered, for a garnish. Purée the rest of the cooked corn in a food processor until smooth. Then transfer the purée to a 4-quart saucepan, stir in the cream, and bring to a boil over medium-high heat, stirring occasionally. Remove the soup from the heat and strain, using the bottom of a sturdy ladle to force as much through the strainer as possible. Discard any solids. Return the soup to the saucepan and season with sea salt and pepper. Set aside.

Preheat the oven to 350° F. and heat a 1-quart oven-safe soup tureen for about 10 minutes.

Spread equal portions of the chilled vegetable mixture and the reserved corn kernels in the bottom of each of 4 soup bowls and garnish with dill sprigs. Pour the soup into the hot tureen and bring to the table. Ladle the soup into the garnished bowls at the table.

SERVES 4

SALAD OF SEAWEED AND LOBSTER WITH GINGER EMULSION

This dish is easy to prepare, but Jean-Louis insists the seaweed needs to macerate in balsamic vinegar and sesame oil for one full week, so plan ahead. The salad is an exotic yet natural accompaniment to lobster.

Mixtures of seaweed are available at specialty food stores and Asian markets.

1 pound seaweed, including 4 or 5 different types, washed

9 tablespoons salt

3 teaspoons freshly ground black pepper

2 jalapeño peppers, stemmed and chopped (see box, page 176)

⅓ cup plus ¼ cup balsamic vinegar (see box, page 64), plus additional for dipping (optional)

1 cup Oriental sesame oil

5 ounces fresh ginger (about one 6-inch root), peeled

½ cup extra-virgin olive oil

¼ cup beef or chicken consommé or stock

4 1-pound lobsters

To make the seaweed salad, cut the seaweed into fine julienne strips (about 2 inches long and ⅛ inch wide) and place in a large bowl. In a small bowl whisk together 3 tablespoons of the salt, 1 teaspoon of the pepper, the jalapeños, ⅓ cup of the balsamic vinegar, and the sesame oil. Add the dressing to the seaweed and toss. Cover the bowl and set aside to macerate for about 1 week at room temperature.

Prepare the ginger emulsion on the day of the dinner. Bring enough water to cover the piece of ginger to a boil in a small saucepan over high heat. Add the ginger, reduce the heat to a gentle simmer, and poach the ginger until it is tender enough that you can easily pierce the root with a dull knife, about 20 minutes. Remove the ginger with a slotted spoon and place in a blender or food processor with the remaining 6 tablespoons salt, 2 teaspoons pepper, and ¼ cup balsamic vinegar, the olive oil, and the consommé or stock. Process until smooth and pour through a fine strainer, discarding any solids. Set aside.

Steam the lobster for about 15 minutes, until done (see box, page 233). To steam the lobsters, put a small amount of water—about 1 cup per lobster, in a stockpot with a tight-fitting lid large enough to fit all 4 lobsters. Bring the water to a boil over high heat, add the lobsters, and cover the pot to steam. The lobsters will be thoroughly cooked after 15 minutes. Remove the lobsters with a pair of tongs to a tray and let cool slightly. (You may want to save the cooking liquid to make your own lobster stock for another use.) Remove the meat from the lobster, cracking the shell carefully to keep the claws and tail meat intact. Cut the tail meat crosswise into medallions. Cover to keep warm until serving time.

To serve, drain the seaweed salad and evenly divide it among 4 serving plates. Place one lobster claw on top and the medallions from one tail around each salad. Pour the ginger emulsion around the salad. Fill small custard cups with extra balsamic vinegar to dip the lobster in, or drizzle the vinegar on the lobster meat, if desired.

SERVES 4

LOIN OF LAMB WITH GRITS

Jean-Louis suggests a homemade lamb consommé because it will give the grits a richer flavor. A strong beef stock can be substituted. Seeds from cardamom pods are preferable to ground cardamom, because this spice loses its flavor soon after being ground. And do not skimp on the saffron . . . yes, it is expensive, but less would be selling this lavish dish short.

GRITS
**8 cups lamb consommé or stock or
   beef stock**
1 bunch fresh thyme, chopped
1 tablespoon cumin seeds
**1 tablespoon whole cardamom seeds
   (about 4–5 pods)**
1 tablespoon curry powder
1 garlic clove

1 tablespoon turmeric
1 tablespoon saffron threads
1½ cups grits (not quick-cooking)
LAMB
**4 4-ounce loins milk-fed lamb,
   trimmed (see box, page 126)**
Salt and freshly ground pepper to taste
**½ cup duck fat (good-quality extra-
   virgin olive oil can be substituted)**

To prepare the grits, combine the consommé or stock with the thyme, cumin, cardamom, curry powder, garlic, turmeric, and saffron in a large saucepan over low heat and simmer until reduced by one-third, about 1 hour. Strain the spiced broth and return all but 1 quart to the saucepan. Set aside. Place the reserved 1 quart of broth in another saucepan and bring to a boil over medium-high heat. Add the grits, reduce the heat to low, and simmer for about 45 minutes, uncovered, until the liquid is absorbed and the grits are soft.

About 20 minutes after the grits begin cooking, season the lamb loins with salt and pepper and place them on a baking sheet with sides. In a small saucepan, melt the duck fat or heat the olive oil over low heat and ladle it over the lamb to coat all sides. In a large skillet heated over medium-high heat, sear the lamb until golden brown, about 2 minutes per side. Reduce the heat to medium and cook the lamb until medium-rare, 12 to 15 minutes depending on the thickness, or to desired doneness. Meanwhile, reheat the remaining spiced broth over medium-low heat.

To serve, spoon the hot grits into a large serving bowl. Cut the lamb into slices and arrange around the grits. Pour the broth around the grits and serve at the table. The broth will thin the grits to the desired consistency.

SERVES 4

APPLE TURNOVERS WITH DATE SAUCE

This is not a traditional apple turnover, but who would expect the expected from Jean-Louis? A very thin wrapping of phyllo dough encases an intensely flavored mixture of apples, almond paste, currants, Calvados, and exotic spices, which then is served with a date sauce infused with vanilla for an intense dessert experience. Vanilla extract cannot match the flavor of real vanilla beans and should not be substituted, if at all possible.

This is not a spur-of-the-moment dessert. The components of this recipe will take a couple of hours to prepare, but the filling and the sauce can be made one day in advance and the steps are not difficult.

FILLING

½ cup sliced blanched almonds

4 tablespoons (½ stick) unsalted butter, softened

2 tablespoons sugar

1 large egg

1 tablespoon all-purpose flour

1 cup pure apple juice

¼ cup dried currants

2 tablespoons Calvados or other apple brandy

½ cup peeled and finely diced tart apples, such as Granny Smith

2 tablespoons honey

1 teaspoon *ras al-hanout* or *garam masala* (see Note)

DATE SAUCE

½ cup heavy cream

3 pitted dates, cut in half

2 2-inch pieces vanilla bean

¼ cup pure apple juice

PASTRY

2 or 3 sheets frozen phyllo dough, 15 x 12 inches, thawed according to package instructions

4 tablespoons unsalted butter, melted

2 tablespoons sugar

GARNISH

2 tablespoons dried currants, soaked in ¼ cup Calvados for 1 hour before serving and drained (optional)

2 tablespoons slivered blanched almonds (optional)

In a food processor, grind ¼ cup of the sliced almonds by pulsing until they become a fine powder (do not process too much or almond butter will be the result). Set aside. Combine 2 tablespoons of the butter with the sugar and egg in a medium bowl and beat until the mixture is light and creamy, about 1 minute. Mix in the ground almonds and flour until well blended. Refrigerate the almond paste.

In a small saucepan over high heat, cook the 1 cup apple juice until it has reduced to ¼ cup, 5 to 10 minutes. Remove the juice from the heat, add the currants and brandy, and let sit for 15 minutes.

In a large nonstick skillet, melt the remaining 2 tablespoons of butter over high heat, add the remaining sliced almonds, and sauté for 30 seconds. Then add the apples, apple juice–currant mixture, honey, and *ras al-hanout* or *garam masala*. Reduce the heat to medium and continue cooking for about 3 more minutes, stirring occasionally. Strain the mixture over a bowl and reserve the strained cooking liquid for the sauce. Refrigerate the apple mixture until cool, about 15 minutes. Mix the cooled apples into the almond paste until well combined and refrigerate this filling until ready to use.

Combine the cream and dates for the sauce in a small, heavy saucepan. Cut the vanilla bean pieces in half lengthwise, scrape the seeds out with a small spoon, and add them along with the bean to the cream and dates. Bring the mixture to a boil over medium–high heat. Reduce the heat and gently simmer until the cream is reduced to about 2 tablespoons, 10 to 15 minutes. Let cool, then remove the vanilla beans (rinse and save them for another use).

Purée the cream-date mixture in a blender or food processor with the ¼ cup apple juice and the reserved strained cooking liquid until smooth. Strain the purée through a *chinois,* or fine sieve, using the bottom of a sturdy ladle to force as much through as possible; it should yield about ½ cup. Discard any solids. Set aside until serving time. Refrigerate the sauce if it is made more than 1 hour before serving and return to room temperature before serving.

Preheat the oven to 400°F. Place 1 sheet of phyllo dough on a piece of parchment or waxed paper that is slightly larger than the dough. Cover the remaining dough with a slightly damp dishtowel so it does not dry out. Use a pastry brush to brush 2 tablespoons of the melted butter on the pastry sheet. Then sprinkle 1 tablespoon of sugar evenly on top. Cut four 6-inch squares of dough from the sheet, discarding the scraps.

Mound one-fourth of the filling in the center of each square of dough. Fold over each corner of the dough, one corner at a time, so that all 4 meet in the center. If the dough square rips, discard it and cut out a replacement square from the extra sheet of phyllo, butter and sugar it, and reassemble the turnover. Place the turnovers on a heavy baking sheet lined with aluminum foil and bake uncovered for 15 minutes.

In the meantime, place another sheet of phyllo dough on parchment or waxed paper, brush the top with the remaining butter, sprinkle the top evenly with the sugar, and cut four 6-inch squares from the dough. When the turnovers have baked 15 minutes, remove the pan from the oven, leaving the oven on. You will need to work quickly, with one turnover at a time. Carefully transfer each baked turnover to the center of one of the prepared dough squares and fold the corners of dough over the turnover to meet in the center (as was done earlier), pressing the dough very gently into place. Once all 4 turnovers are covered with the second dough square, carefully return them to the baking sheet and continue baking, uncovered, until the crust is golden brown and cooked through, about 10 more minutes. Check the doneness by piercing completely through the crust layer with the tip of a pointed knife to see if the filling is tender throughout. Remove the turnovers from the oven and immediately transfer to serving plates. Let cool about 5 minutes, then spoon about 2 tablespoons of the date sauce on each plate and garnish, if desired, with a sprinkle of currants and slivered almonds. Serve immediately.

SERVES 4

N O T E : *Ras al-hanout* is a North African powdered spice mixture of cloves, cinnamon, and black pepper. Moroccans use it most often to flavor savory dishes. Jean-Louis integrates it into his Apple Turnover to intrigue the palate, making this dessert memorable. *Ras al-hanout* is available in North African markets and some specialty markets. If you cannot find it, look for *garam masala,* an Indian spice mixture of a variety of roasted spices, also including cloves, cinnamon, and black pepper.

Preparing Lobster

Jean-Louis prefers steaming to boiling lobsters because the lobster retains more of its flavor. The choice, however, is up to you. Keep in mind that if the lobsters are steamed (see Note) instead of boiled, they must be killed beforehand.

TO BOIL LOBSTERS, bring a large stockpot of water to a rolling boil over high heat. Plunge the live lobsters head-first into the water. Return to a light boil and cook for 4 minutes. The lobsters are done when the shells are bright red and the meat is opaque white. Remove the lobsters to a tray and let cool slightly.

To extract the meat from the lobster, hold the lobster over a bowl to catch the juices and twist off the claws, legs, and tail. Using a nutcracker or specially designed lobster cracker, crack the claw and tail shells, being careful not to crush the meat, and pull the meat out in one piece. Make a small incision along the top of the tail meat to remove and discard the intestinal vein. To remove the leg meat, twist the shells at the joint and use a lobster pick or toothpick to get at the meat. When making your own stock, add the lobster juices and the crushed shells to the reserved cooking liquid and reduce over medium-low heat.

The tail of the lobster will curl when cooked. When presentation is of concern, Jean-Louis first kills the lobster, then removes the tail by twisting it off before cooking. He inserts a skewer lengthwise to hold the shape, then cooks the tail. An uncurled tail is easier to cut into medallions.

NOTE: To kill a lobster that must be steamed or cut up before hand, hold the lobster by the midsection with one hand against a flat, steady surface. With your other hand, take a large, sharp knife and firmly press the knife down through the line in the center of its head. The lobster is now dead, even though reflexive nerves may continue to cause the lobster to twitch. Proceed with your recipe.

DEBRA PONZEK

A Cozy Dinner

Nobody would know I cook for a living if they had dinner at my house." Debra Ponzek, formerly of Montrachet in New York City, is referring to the easy-going and comfortable attitude with which she throws a dinner party. "I'm not worried about the plate or how the vegetables are arranged, and I often combine things on the plate so the juices run together. Of course, I want the meal to be great, but I'm just not as fussy as I was at the restaurant."

Debra was born and raised in the countryside of Morristown, New Jersey. Her interest in cooking was sparked at the age of ten by her mother, who took classical French cooking lessons and tested all her acquired knowledge at home. However, as Debra says, "Women didn't talk about becoming chefs, so moving into a professional cooking career never really occurred to me at the time." Debra attended Boston University, where she chose to study engineering. After two years she decided it wasn't for her and, at the recommendation of a friend, pursued a degree at the Culinary Institute of America. "Engineering, like cooking, is one of those things that you have to be into one hundred percent, and my heart wasn't really in it. I was raised to believe that your career should be something you really loved to do, and for me that was cooking." Upon graduation in 1984, Debra worked at a few restaurants in New Jersey,

MENU

*Pumpkin and Yam Soup with
Spiced Crème Fraîche*

➤

*Salmon with Lentils and
Red Wine Sauce*

➤

Apple Clafoutis

and then heard that Montrachet was looking for a chef. She went to check it out, had dinner, and asked to work in the kitchen for a few days.

The trial period proved to be a big hit for both the novice young chef and the restaurant. Debra was hired as sous-chef in 1986, and just ten months later, at the age of twenty-five, she was promoted to chef. Currently living in Fairfield, Connecticut, Debra is working on a cookbook, and plans for opening her own gourmet store are underway. In describing her style Debra says, "My food is modern French, not typically classic, but based in French technique favoring bold seasonings and lots of fresh herbs in my dishes." Her style is reflected in this uncomplicated autumn menu she prepares for a few friends. "I like this simple menu because it welcomes fall with apples, pumpkins, sweet potatoes, and spices. The smells from all the dishes are so warm and inviting." The Pumpkin and Yam Soup has many of the same seasonings as pumpkin pie, such as cinnamon and nutmeg, and a lot of body and flavor. She serves a salmon with lentils drizzled with red wine sauce for the main course, and most of the components of this dish can be made ahead of time. Debra winds up the meal with an Apple Clafoutis, a light, creamy custardlike dessert. This French classic, usually made with cherries, can also be made with figs, pears, or other fruits.

The setting for dinner at Debra's home in Connecticut is cozy. "I usually put out soft cheeses like a well-ripened Brie or Camembert, crackers, French bread, and maybe some Champagne." She likes to break out her collection of antique plates and unusual glassware "which don't always match," she says, and lights lots of candles to substitute for the fireplace she wishes she had. With the exception of the salmon fillets, everything for this dinner can be made at least one day ahead. "I don't like to panic over each course when my friends come over for dinner, which is why I gear entertaining at home toward advance preparation. "I'm lucky that I cook professionally because I've learned a lot of tricks to guarantee a successful dinner party at home."

PUMPKIN AND YAM SOUP WITH SPICED CRÈME FRAÎCHE

This soup can be a nice opener to a multicourse dinner, or a satisfying meal on its own with some hearty bread. The recipe doubles easily, and the leftovers are extremely welcome the next day.

¾ pound yams, peeled and cut into 1½-inch cubes (see box, page 369)

¾ pound pumpkin, peeled and cut into 1½-inch cubes

3 cups chicken stock

¾ cup Crème Fraîche (see box, below) or heavy cream

⅛ teaspoon ground cinnamon

⅛ teaspoon freshly grated nutmeg

Salt and freshly ground pepper to taste

SPICED CRÈME FRAÎCHE

¼ cup Crème Fraîche (see box, below)

Pinch of ground cloves

Pinch of ground ginger

Pinch of ground cinnamon

In a large saucepan or Dutch oven, combine the yams, pumpkin, and chicken stock and bring to a boil over high heat. Cover and simmer over medium-high heat for 45 minutes.

Meanwhile, prepare the Spiced Crème Fraîche. Whip the crème fraîche in a small bowl with the cloves, ginger, and cinnamon until it forms stiff peaks. Refrigerate until ready to serve.

When the yams and pumpkin are tender, transfer the mixture, including the cooking liquid, to a food processor or blender and purée until smooth. Do this in two batches if necessary. Strain through a fine sieve. Return the soup to the saucepan and mix in the ¾ cup Crème Fraîche and the cinnamon, nutmeg, and salt and pepper and heat through. Serve immediately in bowls with a dollop of the whipped Spiced Crème Fraîche.

MAKES 4 SERVINGS

Crème Fraîche

These days crème fraîche is available at most supermarkets. However, it is much cheaper, and very easy, to make at home—it takes just a couple of days to set. Combine 1½ cups heavy cream with 1 tablespoon buttermilk in a large bowl. Let stand, covered, at room temperature for 12 to 24 hours, until it is slightly thickened. Then refrigerate for 24 more hours to thicken further. It will keep for ten days, tightly covered, in the refrigerator and will continue to thicken.

SALMON WITH LENTILS AND RED WINE SAUCE

The cooked lentils may be refrigerated up to four days, tightly covered in the refrigerator, and the Red Wine Sauce will keep in the refrigerator tightly covered for up to ten days, which makes this rich dish an ideal candidate for a plan-ahead dinner. Debra suggests that you ask your fishmonger for extra bones, and to cut them into 2 to 3-inch pieces for the sauce.

LENTILS

1 cup green lentils

6 cups water

2 teaspoons extra-virgin olive oil

3 thick slices bacon, cut into small dice
   (about ½ cup)

3 cloves garlic, minced

2 large shallots, minced

1 ¾ cups heavy cream

½ tablespoon minced fresh thyme
   leaves

1 teaspoon minced fresh marjoram
   leaves

Salt and freshly ground pepper to taste

RED WINE SAUCE

1 tablepoon unsalted butter

5 large shallots, roughly chopped

2 cloves garlic, thinly sliced

1 cup thinly sliced leeks, green part
   only, washed

½ cup diced celery

2 sprigs thyme

1 pound salmon or other fish bones,
   cut into 2- to 3-inch pieces

3 cups chicken stock

2 ½ cups full-bodied red wine, such as
   Rhone

Salt and freshly ground pepper to taste

SALMON

4 fillets of salmon, with or without
   skin, 5 to 6 ounces each

Salt and freshly ground pepper to taste

4 tablespoons extra-virgin olive oil

1 teaspoon unsalted butter

To prepare the lentils, combine the lentils and the water in a large saucepan and bring to a boil over medium-high heat. Lower the heat and simmer until the lentils begin to become tender, about 10 minutes. Remove from the heat and drain.

In a medium saucepan over medium heat, heat the olive oil until hot, but not smoking. Add the bacon and stir for 1 minute. Add the garlic and shallots and continue to stir until the mixture is softened but not colored, about 3 minutes. Add the cream, raise the heat to medium high and bring the mixture to a boil for 1 to 2 minutes, until slightly thickened. Add the lentils, thyme, and marjoram, and return to a boil. Lower the heat to medium and simmer, uncovered, until the lentils are cooked through and tender, about 10 minutes.

To prepare the Red Wine Sauce, melt the butter in a large saucepan over medium-low heat, then add the shallots, garlic, leeks, celery, and thyme and sauté for 2 minutes. Place the fish bones on top in an even layer, cover the pan and reduce the heat to medium. Cook until the bones become opaque, 5 to 6 minutes. Raise the heat to high, add the stock and wine, and bring to a boil. Reduce the heat and simmer until 1 ½ cups of liquid remain, about 30 minutes. Strain the liquid through a strainer, pushing down on the solids to extract all the liquid.

Pour the strained liquid into a clean medium-size saucepan and reduce over medium-high heat until slightly syrupy, 10 to 12 minutes. Strain through a fine strainer or a cheesecloth. Taste the liquid and add pepper if necessary, or adjust seasonings as needed.

Preheat the oven to 400° F. Season the salmon fillets with salt and pepper. In a large oven-proof skillet heat the oil over high heat until it is smoking and sear the fillets on one side. Transfer the pan to the oven and bake until the fish is medium rare, 3 to 4 minutes. Place the pan over high heat and add the butter. Flip the fillets to sear the other side, 30 to 45 seconds.

To serve, place ½ cup of the lentil mixture in the center of each of 4 warmed plates. Cover each serving of lentils with a salmon fillet and drizzle about 4 tablespoons of the Red Wine Sauce over and around the salmon. Serve immediately.

SERVES 4

Lentils

Lentils have been around since approximately 7000 B.C., and have made their way around the globe from central Asia, to the Middle East to Europe, and finally into many American kitchens. Aside from their earthy flavor, lentils are a great source of protein, iron, vitamin B, and phosphorous, and contain very little fat, making them and other beans a very important part of vegetarian diets. Full flavors such as pork, duck, goat cheese, and vinegar (especially balsamic) highlight the hearty flavor of lentils.

There are several varieties of lentils grown throughout the world, and among the best are the French Green Puy lentils from Velay. Debra, and many other cooks, prefer them for their rich flavor and because they hold their shape well, not becoming mushy when cooked. Lentils are available in many colors, although the brown ones tend to lose their shape and lack the flavor of many of the other imported kinds.

Lentils, named for their lens shape, are always sold dry and should be stored in an air-tight container at room temperature. They will keep for up to six months. Lentils should be rinsed before cooking and picked over to remove any small stones; however, they do not require presoaking as their small, thin form allows for quick cooking.

APPLE CLAFOUTIS

A clafoutis is a dense, puddinglike French dessert consisting of fruit baked in a batter or custard. In Debra's recipe, a creamy cinnamon-spiked custard is baked with apples in a buttery, multilayered puff-pastry crust. It is both elegant and homey and makes a nice alternative to apple pie.

¾ **pound puff pastry, thawed, if frozen**

3 **tart apples, such as Granny Smith, peeled**

1 **teaspoon fresh lemon juice**

2 **teaspoons ground cinnamon**

⅓ **cup plus 1 teaspoon sugar**

1½ **cups heavy cream**

3 **large eggs**

1 **teaspoon vanilla extract**

Preheat the oven to 350° F. Roll out the pastry on a floured board to a 12- or 13-inch circle of ¼ to ⅛ inch thickness. Fit the pastry into a 10-inch tart pan, cover with aluminum foil, and weight down with dry beans or rice. Bake the pastry until it is golden brown and dry, about 20 minutes. Meanwhile, core and thinly slice the apples and toss with the lemon juice, 1 teaspoon of the cinnamon, and 1 teaspoon of the sugar. Set aside.

When the pastry is done, remove the beans and foil, and allow to cool. Whisk together the cream, eggs, vanilla, the remaining cinnamon, and ⅓ cup sugar in a bowl. Fill the pan evenly with the sliced apples and pour the cream mixture over the apples. Bake for 25 to 35 minutes, until the filling is set in the center. Serve warm or at room temperature.

SERVES 6

Debra's Wine Suggestions—French All the Way

FOR THE FIRST COURSE: St-Aubin "Les Combes" 1991, Domaine Marc Colin, is a white wine made from the Chardonnay grape in a village located near the more famous wine-producing town of Chassagne Montrachet. "It is a great value since it exhibits characteristics similar to those of the wine from its more famous neighbor," claims Debra. "It has plenty of ripe fruit that provides body and flavor to complement the richness of the soup."

FOR THE SECOND COURSE: A red burgundy such as Nuits-St-Georges "Clos des Corvées" 1989, Louis Jadot, is a great match for salmon, especially when served with a red wine sauce. "It is a sturdy wine with plenty of flavor to stand up to the heartiness of this dish."

FOR THE THIRD COURSE: Montlouis Moelleux 1989, Domaine Deletang, from the village of Montlouis, near Vouvray, is a late-harvest wine with enough sweetness for desserts, "especially from the exceptional 1989 vintage," says Debra. "Being made from the Chenin Blanc grape, it displays flavors and aromas of apple and pear with honey overtones."

ALFRED PORTALE

A Contemporary Thanksgiving

With his highly successful restaurant in New York City, Gotham Bar and Grill, making enormous demands on his time and culinary efforts, Alfred Portale relinquishes most of the daily food preparation to his wife, Helen, a professionally trained and experienced cook in her own right. Thanksgiving, however, is one of the big exceptions and Alfred closes the restaurant so that his staff can enjoy the holiday. He and his wife, with their two young daughters, Olympia and Victoria, gather as many friends and relatives as they can and spend the day in full holiday mode, cooking, eating, and talking. Alfred tells us, "One of my favorite things about holidays like Thanksgiving is the food traditions that we, as a family, have preserved. This menu is no exception."

Alfred grew up in Buffalo, New York, and his path to culinary stardom was not a straight line. He first directed his creative talents to designing jewelry. Later—drawing on many of the same skills used in jewelry making, such as precision, imagination, and vision—he redirected his artistic drive to pursue a career in cooking. Intrigued with the notion that one could go to school to become a chef, he attended the Culinary Institute of America and graduated in 1981 at

MENU

*Pear and Sweet Gorgonzola Salad
with Walnut Vinaigrette*

❦

*Roast Wild Turkey Stuffed with
Chanterelles, Sausage, and Mashed Potatoes*

❦

Winter Squash Purée

❦

Pumpkin Crème Brûlée

the top of his class. His casual attitude soon turned into a serious passion, which led him overseas and into the kitchens of French culinary greats Michel Guérard, Jean and Pierre Troisgros, and Jacques Maximin.

While patrons enjoy Alfred's complex and singular approach to the food in his restaurant, friends and family are just as impressed with the comfortable atmosphere and vibrantly flavored meals he creates at home. On this special day, guests arrive around 2:30 P.M., and each receives a specific assignment in the kitchen. Alfred explains, "I like my guests to participate in preparing the meal because it removes the formality. I don't like to be stuck in the kitchen alone, unable to enjoy my company." Working together in the kitchen for a couple of hours, guests enjoy a glass of wine or Champagne, a little *fois gras,* and classical music in the background. Meanwhile, a Thanksgiving meal to remember is taking shape.

The wild turkey recipe has been in Helen's family for generations, but Alfred updates the dish with ingredients that were not readily available years ago, such as nutty-flavored chanterelles instead of domestic mushrooms. Juniper berries are used to season the turkey and the gravy, giving everything a distinctive intense flavor. Alfred's parents' traditional Thanksgiving dinner always included mashed potatoes, while Helen's family always prepared acorn squash purée. Alfred settles the dispute by serving both: mashed potatoes in the stuffing and squash on the side. This fall menu includes a fresh Pear and Sweet Gorgonzola Salad with walnuts, a classic combination. When paired with the bitter greens, the brilliant colors and textures guarantee that "each mouthful is different and exciting."

Guests settle down to eat early, around 4:00 or 4:30, and while the adults enjoy a leisurely meal, the kids are usually finished in five minutes! Once again blending the traditional with the modern, Alfred serves Pumpkin Crème Brûlée instead of pumpkin pie for dessert. Another Portale custom is to serve unshelled nuts and roasted chestnuts after dessert. "These and a nice glass of Madeira give everyone a perfect excuse to stay around the table sharing the same family stories we always retell every year at this time."

PEAR AND SWEET GORGONZOLA SALAD WITH WALNUT VINAIGRETTE

For this salad, Alfred prefers the sweet Gorgonzola (also known as Gorgonzola dolce*) to the regular, aged Gorgonzola because it rounds out the other flavors better. The aged cheese, he says, is "out of balance" with other ingredients and is too pungent and salty to begin the meal.*

WALNUT VINAIGRETTE

¼ cup plus 2 tablespoons red wine vinegar, plus more if needed

1½ teaspoons Dijon mustard

Salt to taste

½ cup extra-virgin olive oil

½ cup plus 2 tablespoons walnut oil

White pepper to taste

SALAD

1 head Belgian endive, larger leaves cut into bite-size pieces, smaller leaves left whole

1 small head radicchio, outer leaves washed and dried, and torn into bite-size pieces

1 head frisée lettuce, leaves washed and dried and torn into bite-size pieces

1 bunch watercress, washed and dried, tough stems discarded

2 tablespoons chopped fresh chives

4 ripe Anjou pears, cored and sliced into ¼-inch wedges

6 ounces sweet, unsalted Gorgonzola cheese, crumbled (available at specialty cheese shops)

24 walnut halves, lightly toasted (see box, page 117)

In a small bowl, whisk together the vinegar, mustard, and salt. Whisk in the olive and walnut oils in a steady stream, preferably using a sauce whisk (see box, page 355). Adjust the seasoning with additional vinegar, if necessary, and salt and pepper.

In a large bowl, toss the endive, radicchio, frisée, watercress, and chives. Drizzle in the vinaigrette and toss again to coat.

Evenly divide the greens in the center of each of 6 salad plates. Decoratively arrange equal portions of the pear slices, cheese, and walnuts in a circle around the greens.

SERVES 6

ROAST WILD TURKEY STUFFED WITH CHANTERELLES, SAUSAGE, AND MASHED POTATOES

Alfred prefers wild turkey for its more pronounced, gamey flavor. It is lower in fat and slightly drier than a domestic turkey. If you cannot procure a wild turkey, look for an organic free-range bird.

The earthy flavor of the mushrooms in this potato-based stuffing blends nicely with the gaminess of the turkey, and full-flavored sausage makes for a nice contrast. Any sausage will work here, from hot and spicy to sweet and mild—it is simply a matter of preference. Because everyone loves Thanksgiving leftovers, Alfred carves up a turkey large enough to feed ten to twelve for this menu.

2½ pounds new potatoes, scrubbed and quartered

1 pound sausage meat of your choice, casing removed

1 cup (2 sticks) unsalted butter

¼ cup whole milk

1 cup thinly sliced shallots

3 garlic cloves, minced

1½ pounds chanterelles or other wild mushrooms (see box, pages 36–37), cleaned and sliced

Salt to taste

White pepper to taste

½ cup chopped fresh Italian parsley

¼ cup minced fresh chives

1 teaspoon chopped fresh thyme

1 10–12-pound wild turkey, giblets reserved (neck and liver)

2 tablespoons extra-virgin olive oil

1 tablespoon freshly ground juniper berries (see box, page 250), or more to taste (optional)

8 cups (2 quarts) rich turkey or chicken stock

1 tablespoon cornstarch (if thickening is necessary)

In a large saucepan, cover the potatoes with cold water and boil over high heat until tender, about 15 minutes. Meanwhile, cook the sausage meat in a skillet over medium-high heat until it is completely browned, stirring constantly. Set the cooked meat aside in a large bowl.

Drain the potatoes and toss in a hot skillet over medium heat for about 1 minute to dry them; do not let them brown. (Drier mashed potatoes will absorb more liquid, hence more flavor, from the mushrooms and turkey.) Return the potatoes to the saucepan with 4 table-spoons of butter and the milk, and mash with a potato masher until smooth, or press the potatoes through a ricer into a mixing bowl and beat in the butter and milk. Set aside.

In a large skillet, melt 3 tablespoons of the butter over medium heat. Add the shallots and garlic and sauté, without browning, for about 6 minutes. Transfer the mixture to the bowl with the sausage. Melt 1 tablespoon of butter in the same skillet over medium heat, add the mushrooms, and sauté until lightly browned, about 5 minutes. Season with salt and white pepper and toss into the sausage and shallot mixture. Add the mashed potatoes, and stir just to blend, being careful not to overmix. Add the parsley, chives, and thyme and adjust the seasoning with salt and white pepper. Allow the potato mixture to cool to room temperature. (The stuffing can be prepared up to 4 hours in advance and left at room temperature; do not refrigerate the stuffing as the mashed potatoes will not maintain their nice texture.)

Preheat the oven to 450° F. Just before roasting, loosely stuff the turkey neck and breast cavities with the cooled potato stuffing. (Extra stuffing may be cooked, loosely covered, in a baking dish and basted with cooking juices.) Sew or skewer the turkey closed. Rub the turkey all over with 4 tablespoons butter, the olive oil, salt, white pepper, and ground juniper, if desired. Put the turkey on a rack in a roasting pan and place in the oven. Immediately reduce the temperature to 325° F. and add 3 cups of stock to the roasting pan. Baste the turkey about every 15 minutes.

Roast the turkey for approximately 15 to 20 minutes per pound, about 2½ to 3½ hours for a 10- to 12-pound turkey. When the turkey is done the juices should run clear when the thigh is pricked with a fork and the meat is opaque. The internal temperature of the breast meat should be 170° F. Remove the turkey from the oven, cover loosely with aluminum foil, and let

Turkey Tips from Alfred

1. Figure 1 pound per person for birds up to 12 pounds and ¾ pound per person for birds over 12 pounds. This will leave you with ample leftovers.

2. Turkey should be cooked at a fairly low temperature (about 325° F.) for 15 to 20 minutes per pound for a stuffed bird; figure 1 hour less for an unstuffed bird, or 12 to 15 minutes per pound. The low temperature lets the dark meat cook thoroughly, without allowing the breast meat to dry out.

3. Always use a fresh turkey, never a frozen one. Frozen turkeys tend to be dry and tasteless. Never buy a self-basting turkey; they are injected with water and cheap vegetable oils.

4. Hens tend to be more tender than toms, though more expensive. Hens usually weigh between 12 and 18 pounds, while toms can get much larger.

5. Always rinse the bird with cold water, inside and out, and pat dry before cooking.

6. Save the wish bone!

Stuff It!

1. The basic ingredient of stuffing must be a starch: bread, rice, or potatoes. The other ingredients can vary widely; it is the starch that binds the flavors and textures together.

2. Use ¾ cup of stuffing for each pound of turkey. Stuff the bird loosely, about three-fourths full, because the stuffing will swell during the roasting. If the stuffing is packed too tightly it will become quite solid when cooked.

3. Vegetables for the stuffing should be cooked before stuffing, otherwise they will not be tender enough.

4. Never use raw meat in a stuffing; always cook meat additions first.

5. Never stuff the bird in advance; only stuff the turkey just before baking. This substantially reduces the risk of bacterial growth.

it rest for about 20 minutes before carving. Remove the stuffing and place in a serving bowl.

While the turkey is roasting, in a large saucepan cook the giblets and neck in the remaining 5 cups of stock at a low simmer for 1½ hours. Remove the giblets and neck from the stock with a slotted spoon, finely chop the meat, and set aside. When the turkey is done cooking, add the drippings from the roasting pan to the stock and return the liquid to a simmer over medium–low heat. Cook until the sauce is somewhat reduced and lightly thickened. If necessary, use the cornstarch to thicken the sauce: combine 2 tablespoons or so of the stock with the cornstarch in a small bowl until the cornstarch has dissolved and no lumps remain, then whisk this mixture into the sauce. Just before serving, season the sauce with salt, white pepper, and ground juniper, if desired. Add the reserved giblet and neck meat and swirl in the remaining 4 tablespoons butter. Carve the turkey and arrange on a serving platter. Transfer the gravy to a gravy boat and pass at the table.

SERVES 8 TO 12

WINTER SQUASH PURÉE

This thick and creamy vegetable purée can be sweetened a bit with maple syrup or brown sugar, if you like.

1–2 tablespoons vegetable oil **½ cup heavy cream**
3 acorn squash, cut in half and seeded **Salt and white pepper to taste**
½ cup (1 stick) unsalted butter **Maple syrup or brown sugar (optional)**

Preheat the oven to 375° F. Lightly oil a roasting pan with the vegetable oil and place the squash halves cut side down on the pan. Bake until the flesh is tender, about 40 minutes. Scoop the flesh into a large bowl and blend in the butter and cream with an electric mixer until incorporated, and the mixture is smooth. Season with the salt and white pepper. Sweeten, if desired, with the maple syrup or brown sugar.

SERVES 6

Where's the Black Pepper?

Black pepper, used to season both savory and sometimes sweet dishes around the world, is arguably the most popular spice. The black peppercorn is the unripened berry of the pepper plant. Oddly enough, it is nowhere to be found in Alfred's menu. Instead, he uses white pepper to season his salad, stuffing, and turkey. He explains that it is milder than the piquant black peppercorn and a better match for fowl and fish.

Actually, white pepper also comes from the berry of the pepper plant. The difference between the white and black peppercorn is in the processing of the berries. For white pepper, the berry is ripened and its skin is removed before it is dried. Also, from this same pepper plant comes the green peppercorn, which is the berry in its ripened, undried form, usually preserved in a brine. It is the least pungent of the three varieties.

Black and white pepper are available whole and ground. However, the dried peppercorn loses its flavor quickly once it is cracked and therefore is best when freshly ground.

Juniper Berries

Juniper berries are the blue-black berries of the juniper tree, used in cooking and in making gin and other spirits. They have a sharp flavor, and when raw they are too bitter to eat. Once the berries are dried, they can be used whole, crushed, or ground. Their pungent flavor goes particularly well with birds and game, although these berries can be used to season other meats, marinades, and sauces.

Look for dried juniper in the spice section of specialty food stores and buy it whole, as its perfume quickly fades once it is ground. Use a pepper mill or mortar and pestle to grind the juniper berries at home.

PUMPKIN CRÈME BRÛLÉE

Here is a nice autumn twist to the traditional French custard that lies below a thin sheet of caramel "ice": pumpkin purée is added to the cream-based custard for a quintessential Thanksgiving flavor. This can be made a day in advance.

1½ cups heavy cream

½ cup milk

½ cup plus 6 teaspoons sugar

Scant ¼ teaspoon ground cinnamon

Scant ¼ teaspoon ground ginger

⅛ teaspoon freshly grated nutmeg

⅛ teaspoon ground allspice

½ vanilla bean, split in half lengthwise

6 large egg yolks

½ cup canned pumpkin purée

Preheat the oven to 300° F. In a large, heavy-bottomed saucepan, combine the cream, milk, ¼ cup of the sugar, cinnamon, ginger, nutmeg, and allspice. Scrape the seeds from the vanilla bean and add the seeds and the bean to the saucepan. Stir over medium heat until the sugar is dissolved, then bring just to a simmer. Remove from the heat. In a medium bowl, whisk together the yolks and ¼ cup of the sugar. Remove the bean from the cream mixture and whisk a small amount (not more than ¼ cup) of the mixture into the egg yolks to temper them so they do not scramble. Slowly add all of the cream to the yolks, whisking constantly, until the mixture is smooth and pale yellow. Place the pumpkin purée in a large bowl and gradually whisk in the cream mixture until completely incorporated and smooth.

Strain the custard through a very fine sieve into a chilled pitcher. Pour the mixture into six 4-ounce molds. Set the molds in the oven in a baking pan containing enough hot water to come 1 inch up the sides of the molds. Bake for 20 to 30 minutes or until set. To test for doneness, lightly tap the sides of the custard dish; if the mixture "makes waves," then it is not done. Cool slightly on a wire rack, cover with plastic wrap, and refrigerate for at least 2 hours or overnight.

Preheat the broiler just before serving (see Note). Evenly sprinkle one teaspoon of granulated sugar on top of each custard. Broil until the sugar caramelizes, anywhere from 1 to 4 minutes, depending on the heat of the broiler. Watch carefully so the sugar does not burn; it should be a golden brown. Serve in the individual molds on dessert plates.

SERVES 6

NOTE: It is best to use a propane torch to caramelize the sugared tops of the crème brûlée. The results will be superior to that of a home broiler because you can control the heat. The torch can quickly and evenly brown the sugar without warming the custard or burning the sugar.

Beverage Suggestions

Alfred suggests a cool glass of still or sparkling water with the salad, explaining, "Everyone tries too hard to match wines with salads, but I find the acidity of vinaigrettes formidable enough to prefer water." If you would like to serve wine with the salad, however, he suggests Savennières, a dry Chenin Blanc from France's Loire region, which has a "restrained fruit and a gripping acidity" to complement the Anjou pears.

With the turkey, Alfred likes to serve a light-bodied red such as Chinon 1989 or 1990, preferably the Joquet vintage, or a full-bodied white such as a white Burgundy from Côte d'Or, particularly the vintages of Village Meursault or Saint-Autin.

Alfred suggests dessert wines from the Portuguese island of Madeira. There is a range of Madeira dessert wines differing by grape type and degree of sweetness: Sercial is the lightest and driest, often served as an aperitif; Verdelho, Bual, and Malvasia are medium-sweet; and Malmsey is the sweetest and generally is served as a *digestif*. Alfred says, "For this dessert, my vote goes out to Blandy's five-year 'Special Reserve' Bual."

STEPHAN PYLES

A Texan Spread

rowing up in his parents' Truck Stop Cafe, Stephan Pyles experienced first-hand the elements of the true down-home dining experience. "I saw people being cared for," says Stephan. "To me, food, or the experience of eating, is very much a part of nurturing and hospitality and not necessity."

Cooking is a way of life that is comfortable and pleasurable for Stephan. Compared to the restaurant, at home he's relaxed and not worried about mistakes—definitely a tension-free environment. "The menu I selected is influenced by a lot of Texas cooking," says Stephan, "but it also has a few Southern touches, which I miss from growing up." Stephan refers to most of his cooking as "range" cooking or traditional cowboy cooking, represented here by the Cowboy Beans and the Chili-Cured Beef. The sweet potatoes are the Southern influence, as are the pound cake and spoonbread—foods he grew up with and adapted for this meal. "Some days, the Cowboy Beans, a little rice, and the cornbread are enough for a nourishing and satisfying dinner," says Stephan. "Also, a big bowl of the chowder is a filling and comforting meal in itself."

Stephan's culinary education began at the early age of eight, helping his parents after

MENU

Texas Seafood Chowder with Jicama and Chipotle Chili Aioli

Chili-Cured Beef Fillet

Cowboy Beans

Jalapeño Spoonbread

Sweet Potato–Pecan Pound Cake with Cajeta Ice Cream

school in their cafe in West Texas. He took a break to go to college, earning a degree in music at East Texas State University in 1974, but still managed to cook in his spare time for himself and his friends. But it was a trip to France after graduation that truly affirmed his passion for cooking. "What I

witnessed in France changed how I felt about food forever," says Stephan. "There was a local market at every turn where everything was fresh, from the breads to the pastries to the produce."

In France, the chef's stove is referred to as his piano, with the chef "composing" each new dish. Ironically, that was the instrument Stephan studied in college. "I traded in my one piano for another piano," says Stephan. So after returning from France in 1974, he began working in various small restaurants in Dallas, reading as many cookbooks as possible, and practicing his technique, all with the determination to become a chef. In 1980, he signed on as chef's assistant at the Great Chefs of France Cooking School at the Robert Mondavi Winery in Napa Valley, California. He worked closely with such French masters as Michel Guérard, brothers Jean and Pierre Troisgros, and Georges Blanc, and then returned to France in 1981 to study pastry with Gaston Lenôtre.

In 1983, Stephan opened Routh Street Cafe in Dallas. It celebrated nine years of success and three offspring: Baby Routh Cafe in Dallas and Goodfellows and Tejas in Minneapolis. Stephan sold his partnership in 1993, and in the summer of the following year he opened Star Canyon in Dallas, highlighting his "new Texas cuisine."

Although his family's Truck Stop Cafe was sold years ago, Stephan still makes time to enjoy some home-style cooking with his immediate family about once a month, while entertaining his friends at home as often as possible. "I put my friends to work chopping and helping to prepare the meal," says Stephan. "It sets the tone if everyone has a job, and creates a communal experience." And Stephan receives great joy and satisfaction when he sees them smile after tasting a dish. "I enjoy pleasing people and giving them a dining experience they couldn't have gotten elsewhere."

Texas Seafood Chowder with Jicama and Chipotle Chili Aioli

With crawfish and oysters from the Gulf Coast plus bourbon and hots chilies, this hearty chowder would satisfy any full-blooded Texan. Stephan suggests using any combination of fish or shellfish that is available, but he prefers to use only fresh corn, not frozen or canned.

He also recommends a wine with a hint of fruit to complement the spicy flavor of the chili, preferably a dry Gewürztraminer or Riesling.

1 tablespoon unsalted butter

2 ounces salt pork or bacon, diced into medium-size pieces

½ green bell pepper, seeded and diced

1 red or yellow bell pepper, cored, seeded, and diced (or ½ of each)

1 serrano pepper, seeds and ribs removed and diced (see box, page 176)

½ cup chopped onion

½ cup chopped celery

¼ cup bourbon

1 cup dry white wine

4 cups fish or chicken stock

1 small sweet potato, peeled and cut into ½-inch cubes

Kernels from 1 small ear of corn

12 live crawfish (optional)

2 ripe medium tomatoes, peeled, seeded, and chopped (see box, page 311)

6 ounces lump crab meat, picked over thoroughly

2 dozen oysters, preferably Gulf Coast, shucked

2 teaspoons salt

2 teaspoons fresh lime juice

2 tablespoons chopped fresh cilantro

½ cup cubed jicama (see box, page 258)

8 large French bread croutons (see box, page 256)

Chipotle Chili Aioli (recipe follows)

1 lime, cut into 10–12 wedges, for

Melt the butter in a large skillet over high heat. Add the salt pork or bacon and sauté for 1 minute. Add the peppers, onion, and celery. Cook for another 3 minutes, stirring frequently. Pour in the bourbon, scraping up any bits from the bottom to deglaze the pan. Add the wine and simmer until the liquid is reduced by one-third, 3 to 5 minutes.

Add the stock and bring to a boil. Add the sweet potato and cook for 4 minutes. Add the corn and reduce the heat to medium and simmer for 3 minutes. Add the crawfish, if using, and tomatoes. Cover the pot and simmer for an additional 1½ minutes. Add the crab meat and oysters and simmer, covered, for 1 minute longer.

Season the soup with salt and stir in the lime juice, cilantro, and jicama. Divide the chowder among 8 soup bowls. Spread each crouton with aioli and float one in each bowl. Garnish each serving with a lime wedge.

SERVES 8

CHIPOTLE CHILI AIOLI

Stephan gives a Southwestern twist to this French garlic-mayonnaise sauce. It also makes a great sandwich spread or dipping sauce for shrimp or vegetables.

2 large egg yolks

1 tablespoon red wine vinegar

½ cup corn oil

¼ cup extra-virgin olive oil

1 teaspoon Chipotle Chili Purée
   (recipe follows)

¼ teaspoon paprika

¼ teaspoon pure chili powder

⅛ teaspoon cayenne pepper

½ teaspoon salt

½ shallot, minced

1 small garlic clove, minced

1 teaspoon fresh lime juice

In a mixing bowl, whisk together the egg yolks and vinegar. Combine the corn and olive oils in a small bowl. Slowly drizzle the oils into the yolks while whisking, until the mixture is emulsified (see box, page 355). Add the chili purée, paprika, chili powder, cayenne, salt, shallot, garlic, and lime juice. Whisk just long enough to combine thoroughly. The aioli can be stored, tightly covered, in the refrigerator for at least a week.

MAKES ABOUT 1 CUP

Large French Croutons

These croutons are different from traditional salad croutons; they are cut large to top with a spread for appetizers or to float in soups.

TO MAKE, use a serrated knife and cut a French baguette on the diagonal into pieces approximately 3 inches long and ¼ inch thick. Brush lightly with extra-virgin olive oil and toast on a sheet pan in a preheated 350° F. oven until golden brown, about 3 minutes per side. Remove from the oven and cool. Wait until cool before topping with aioli or another spread. The croutons will keep for two to three weeks if stored in a tightly sealed container.

Chipotle Chili Purée

10 chipotle peppers (see box, page 259)

Preheat the oven to 400°F. Place the peppers on a baking sheet and toast for 1 minute. Then place them unpeeled in a bowl with just enough warm water to cover, and let stand for about 30 minutes until softened. Drain the peppers, reserving the soaking liquid, and remove and discard their stems and seeds. Purée the peppers in a blender with just enough soaking liquid to make a thick, smooth paste, about 2 minutes. Store the purée in a tightly sealed container. It will keep for 1 week in the refrigerator, and 3 months in the freezer.

MAKES 3 TABLESPOONS

Chili-Cured Beef Fillet

Stephan chose this recipe because he wanted to showcase beef, a "typical Texan commodity." He particularly enjoys the chili-curing process because it adds spice to the beef itself. Make sure to use kosher salt.

½ cup coriander seeds

4 tablespoons black peppercorns

4 tablespoons pure chili powder

4 shallots, minced

8 garlic cloves, minced

1½ cups kosher salt

¾ cup brown sugar

2 2-pound center-cut beef tenderloins, trimmed of all fat

5 tablespoons vegetable oil

Place the coriander and peppercorns in the bowl of a food processor and process until coarsely ground. Add the chili powder, shallots, garlic, salt, and brown sugar and process until a thick paste is formed. Transfer the mixture to a large glass bowl and add the beef fillets. Thoroughly coat the beef and let it cure for 3 to 5 hours in the refrigerator, turning occasionally.

Preheat the oven to 400°F. Remove the beef from the marinade and scrape clean. Heat the vegetable oil in a large skillet over medium-high heat until lightly smoking. Add the beef to the skillet and sear on all sides, about 5 minutes in all. Transfer to a baking dish and cook in the oven for 20 minutes for medium-rare, or until desired doneness is reached. When the beef is done, remove from the oven and let rest for about 5 minutes before serving.

To serve, slice the beef and bring it to the table to serve family style with the Jalapeño Spoonbread and Cowboy Beans.

SERVES 8

Jicama

Jicama is a crisp-textured, almost turnip-shaped root vegetable or tuber (a tuber is an edible swollen underground stem such as a potato) indigenous to Mexico, hence its nickname, "Mexican potato." It has thick brown skin, a white crisp flesh, and a slightly sweet and very clean flavor, similar to that of water chestnuts. Stephan describes it as a cross between an apple and a turnip in flavor, and he likes it in sauces and relishes and cooked as a vegetable. He prefers it, however, served raw in a marinade of lime juice, cilantro, and chili powder. Jicama should be peeled just before using it so it does not discolor. It is becoming more common in American cooking, and, therefore, is more readily available.

COWBOY BEANS

These beans are hearty enough to take center stage with a slab of cornbread and some rice.

3 cups pinto beans, picked over, soaked overnight, and drained

2 quarts chicken stock or water

1 ham hock, or 4 slices bacon, diced

1 onion, diced

3 garlic cloves, minced

2 large tomatoes, peeled, seeded, and diced (see box, page 311)

¼ cup tomato-base barbecue sauce of your choice

1 bottle (12 ounces) dark beer

3 tablespoons pure chili powder

2 teaspoons ground cumin

4 jalapeño peppers, thinly sliced

2 tablespoons chopped fresh cilantro

Salt to taste

Place the soaked beans in a large saucepan over medium-high heat with the stock or water, ham hock or half of the bacon, onion, and garlic. Bring to a boil over high heat, then reduce the heat to medium and stir in tomatoes, barbecue sauce, beer, the remaining bacon, chili powder, cumin, and jalapeños. Let simmer partly covered for about 2 hours, until tender, adding more stock or water if necessary to keep the beans covered with water at all times. When the beans are tender, strain off and discard the liquid. Stir in the cilantro and season with salt. (The beans can be made a day or two in advance; simply reheat them on the stovetop.)

SERVES 8 GENEROUSLY

Jalapeño Spoonbread

Spoonbread is a cross between a pudding and a soufflé, so moist and soft it is eaten with a spoon. It is believed to have originated from the Native American porridge called suppone. *Stephan adds poblano chilies and jalapeños to give the spoonbread a special Texan flavor. In Texas, jalapeños are the "chili of choice."*

¾ cup milk

¾ cup chicken stock

½ cup yellow cornmeal

1½ teaspoons salt

¼ teaspoon ground white pepper

2 tablespoons (¼ stick) unsalted butter

2 teaspoons chopped roasted garlic (see box, page 149)

Kernels from 1 large ear of corn (about ¾ cup)

1 large poblano pepper, roasted (see box, page 186), peeled, seeded, and diced

6 tablespoons diced green or red bell pepper (preferably 3 tablespoons of each)

2 jalapeño peppers, seeded and minced (see box, page 176)

½ cup heavy cream

3 large eggs, separated

Preheat the oven to 325°F. Lightly oil a 1- to 1½-quart baking dish or soufflé mold. Combine the milk and chicken stock in a large saucepan over high heat and bring to a boil. Let it boil for 30 seconds, then reduce the heat to medium. Drizzle in the cornmeal and whisk until smooth. Remove from the heat and add the salt, pepper, and butter. Mix thoroughly until the butter has melted and transfer to a large mixing bowl. Stir in the garlic, corn, poblano pepper, bell pepper, jalapeños, and cream. Let the mixture cool slightly.

Whisk the egg yolks into the cooled mixture. In a small bowl, beat the egg whites to soft

Chipotle Chilies

Chipotle chili peppers are fully ripened jalapeños that have been smoked and dried. Stephan tells us, "Chipotles are my favorite chilies because they provide a 'layering' of flavors that is so important in Texan and Southwestern food. The palate senses not only a lingering, pointed spiciness but also an earthy smokiness that has subtle overtones of tobacco and even bitter chocolate." Stephan enjoys using the Chipotle Chili Purée in dressings for salads, such as his Southwestern Caesar salad, or in recipes that use tomatoes, such as roasted tomato salsa, soups, or sauces.

peaks and gently fold them into the cornmeal mixture. Pour the mixture into the baking dish. Place the dish inside a roasting pan and pour very hot water to reach 1 inch up the sides of the dish. Bake for about 45 minutes, or until a knife inserted in the center comes out clean. If the spoonbread is browning too quickly, cover it with foil. Serve immediately.

SERVES 8

SWEET POTATO–PECAN POUND CAKE WITH CAJETA ICE CREAM

Stephan serves this cake with Cajeta Ice Cream, but you can also use store-bought vanilla ice cream and drizzle over some store-bought cajeta *(Mexican caramel sauce), which is available at Mexican markets.*

½ cup diced, peeled sweet potatoes

1½ cups cake flour

½ teaspoon baking soda

½ teaspoon salt

½ teaspoon ground cinnamon

½ teaspoon freshly grated nutmeg

½ cup (1 stick) unsalted butter, softened

1 cup plus 6 tablespoons sugar

½ cup sour cream

3 large eggs, lightly beaten

½ cup pecans, toasted (see box, page 117) and chopped

1 teaspoon vanilla extract

Cajeta Ice Cream (optional; recipe follows) or vanilla ice cream

½ cup *Cajeta*

Preheat the oven to 300°F. In a medium saucepan filled with cold water, add the sweet potatoes and bring to a boil over medium-high heat. Simmer until the potatoes are soft, about 10 minutes. Drain, and mash or purée until smooth. Set aside to cool.

Lightly oil a 9 × 4-inch loaf pan. In a mixing bowl, sift together the flour, baking soda, salt, cinnamon, and nutmeg and set aside.

In another bowl, cream together the butter, sugar, and sour cream until smooth. Then add the eggs, sweet potato purée, and pecans, and stir all at once until incorporated. Add the vanilla. Fold in the dry ingredients, mixing just until incorporated. Do not overmix.

Pour the mixture into the prepared loaf pan and bake for 40 to 50 minutes, until a toothpick inserted in the middle comes out clean. Remove from the oven and cool on a rack for 10 minutes, then remove the cake from the pan and cool completely.

To serve, place each slice of cake on a plate and top with ice cream and a drizzle of *cajeta*.

SERVES 8 GENEROUSLY

CAJETA ICE CREAM

Cajeta *(ka-hay-ta) is a Mexican caramel sauce made with goat's milk. According to Stephan, goat's milk gives the sauce a "distinctive, earthy flavor."*

1 cup *cajeta* (available in specialty stores
   and Mexican or Spanish markets)
2 cups heavy cream
2 cups whole milk

1 teaspoon vanilla extract
8 large egg yolks
1 cup sour cream or Crème Fraîche
   (see box, page 237)

Have ready a large bowl filled with ice and a smaller bowl to chill the custard. In a large, heavy-bottomed saucepan over medium heat, combine the *cajeta,* cream, milk, and vanilla. Bring to a boil, remove from the heat, and set aside, covered.

Whisk the eggs yolks in a mixing bowl for 2 minutes. Slowly strain the cream mixture into the egg yolks, stirring with a spatula. Pour the mixture back into the saucepan and cook over low heat, stirring constantly with a wooden spoon, until the custard thickens just enough to coat the back of a spoon, 4 to 5 minutes. Immediately remove from the heat and strain the custard into the small bowl and nest it in the larger bowl filled with ice. Whisk in the sour cream or Crème Fraîche and stir occasionally until the custard has completely cooled.

Place the custard in an ice cream machine and freeze according to the manufacturer's instructions.

MAKES ABOUT 1 1/2 QUARTS

MICHEL RICHARD

A Sunday Family Supper

Simply put, Michel Richard loves food. It has been a part of his life since he was a young boy, and his love of food is what inspired him to make it his profession. When Michel was nine years old, growing up in France in a one-parent household with his four brothers and sisters, he often helped his mother prepare the meals. On Thursdays, Michel was in charge of going to the market with two dollars to buy the meat for dinner and he almost always prepared sautéed steaks and French fries. At home today, he still cooks dishes from his native country, incorporating such ubiquitous staples as tomatoes, onions, vinaigrettes, potatoes, apples, and his favorite dessert, chocolate cake.

Michel's journey to his ultimate profession began when he went to a friend's family restaurant. "The experience of seeing the chef in his white hat, making a flambé dish, impressed me so much that I took an apprenticeship at a local pastry shop almost immediately." Six years later he moved to Paris, and by the age of twenty-five he had become the top pastry chef at Gaston Lenôtre's famous pastry shop. In 1974, he arrived in Manhattan to open Mr. Lenôtre's first French pastry shop in the United States. Then in 1977, Michel decided to move west to open his own pastry shop in Los Angeles, which eventually led to the opening of Citrus, his first Southern California restaurant, in 1987. "I was tired of being a baker," says Michel. "I wanted to cook and create my own

MENU

Salad of Skate Wings with Ginger Dressing

❧

Chicken Osso Buco–Style with Penne

❧

Frozen Porcupine Cheesecake

dishes, to handle a variety of foods, not just chocolate, and be closer to the customers."

At a time when it would seem that Michel is never at home because of the time demands of his expanding restaurant business (Citrus in Los Angeles; the three off-spring of Citrus, all called Citronelle, in Santa Barbara, Washington, D.C., and Baltimore; the Broadway Deli in Santa Monica; and Michel's, in Philadelphia), in fact he makes it a priority to be home every Sunday with his wife and their four children for a family dinner. "This is a time when I don't have to try to impress as I have to do in the restaurant," says Michel. "But more important, it is an act of love to cook for my family—cooking is caring, cooking is respect, cooking is love. My only wish is to cook more at home and spend more time with my family."

On these Sundays, "everyone gets involved, especially the children. The kids sit on the counter while I cook, except when I'm chopping onions, and they love to stick their fingers in and taste the chocolate cake batter while I'm making dessert." Michel and his family take their time while eating, as well. "We'll begin at one o'clock in the afternoon and sit at the table eating and talking, for over three hours!" says Michel. "Then we'll watch *60 Minutes* and afterward eat the leftovers from lunch for dinner!"

Michel likes this menu because it includes recipes that remind him of his early years in France and incorporates ingredients from the cuisines of other countries, a trait for which he is well known. The skate wings are a childhood favorite, and he's added an Asian influence with the seaweed salad and ginger dressing. The Chicken Osso Buco–Style is a quicker version of the traditional  Italian dish, which uses veal shanks, and the Porcupine Cheesecake reminds Michel of the *vacherin*—a pastry made with meringue, ice cream, and whipped cream—he used to eat during his teen years when he was an apprentice at a pastry shop in France.

Whether it's at home or at one of his restaurants, Michel still finds time in every day to roll up his sleeves and cook. "By seven P.M. at the restaurant, I'm at the stove," he says. "Cooking in the evening is my 'dessert' for the day—like a big chocolate cake is the perfect ending to a great meal."

Salad of Skate Wings with Ginger Dressing

Skate is a large, flat, scaleless fish with pectoral fins called wings. The flesh is rich, meaty, and firm and its flavor is sometimes compared with that of the scallop. Here, the fish is sautéed and placed atop a ginger-dressed salad. Ask a fishmonger to fillet each wing. If seaweed is difficult to find, use a mixture of baby lettuce or iceberg lettuce, julienned thinly.

2 1-pound skate wings, each cut into 2 fillets and rinsed well
Salt and freshly ground pepper to taste
1 tablespoon extra-virgin olive oil
4 cups torn frisée lettuce, washed and dried

1 cup pre-mixed seaweed salad (available at Asian markets)
1 cup diced tomato
Ginger Dressing to taste (recipe follows)

Season the skate fillets with salt and pepper. Heat the olive oil in a nonstick skillet over medium heat. Add the skate wings and sauté for about 2 minutes on each side, until lightly browned and the meat is flaky.

In a medium bowl, toss the frisée, seaweed, and tomato together. Gently toss the salad with enough dressing to coat the greens. Mound about 1 cup of salad on each of 4 plates. Arrange one skate fillet on top of each salad. Serve immediately.

Serves 4

Ginger Dressing

This can be prepared ahead, covered, and set aside at room temperature for about two hours, or refrigerated until one hour before serving.

3 tablespoons mayonnaise
3 tablespoons white wine vinegar
1 tablespoon fresh orange juice
3 tablespoons extra-virgin olive oil

1 2-inch piece fresh ginger, peeled and finely grated
Salt and freshly ground pepper to taste

Mix the mayonnaise with the vinegar and orange juice in a small bowl. Whisk in the olive oil in a slow, steady stream. Add the ginger and season with salt and pepper.

Makes about ½ cup

Bouquet Garni

A bouquet garni is a bundle of spices and/or herbs that is used to flavor stocks, sauces, or stews without allowing the spices to escape into the liquid. It is removed before serving. The bouquet is made by either tying the spices together or wrapping them in cheesecloth or muslin tied with string. Cheesecloth is available at kitchen supply shops and in most grocery stores. A bouquet garni may include bay leaves, parsley, peppercorns, sprigs of thyme or rosemary, and even lemon or orange zest. The classic combination in much French cooking is parsley, thyme, and bay leaf.

For Michel's Chicken Osso Buco–Style, simply tie the thyme and bay leaf together with a piece of string and skip the cheesecloth.

CHICKEN OSSO BUCO–STYLE WITH PENNE

Osso buco *literally means "bone with the hole," which describes the marrow-filled veal shank. Michel Richard substitutes chicken drumsticks for veal in this classic preparation.*

8 chicken drumsticks

4 teaspoons all-purpose flour

2 tablespoons extra-virgin olive oil, plus additional for pasta

1 carrot, peeled and diced

1 onion, diced

1 celery stalk, diced

8 garlic cloves, chopped

1 cup dry white wine, preferably Chardonnay

2 cups tomato sauce

4 cups chicken stock

Zest and juice of 1 orange (or preferably ½ orange and ½ lemon), plus more if needed

Salt and freshly ground pepper to taste

1 bouquet garni with 1 thyme sprig and 1 bay leaf (see box, above)

1½ to 2 cups penne

1 tomato, diced, for garnish

Chopped fresh parsley, for garnish

Preheat the oven to 325° F. Sprinkle the drumsticks with the flour to coat lightly. Heat the olive oil in a large, ovenproof saucepan over medium heat. Add the drumsticks and sauté until golden brown, about 2 minutes on each side. Transfer the chicken to a plate with tongs and keep warm.

Add the carrot, onion, celery, and garlic to the saucepan and sauté over medium heat until lightly brown, about 3 minutes. Add the wine and scrape any bits from the bottom of the pan. Return the chicken to the pan. Add the tomato sauce, chicken stock, and orange zest and juice. Season with salt and pepper. Drop the bouquet garni into the pan. Cook in the oven for 20 to 30 minutes, covered, until the chicken is cooked through. When done, the chicken should be opaque and the juices should run clear when the meat is pricked with a fork.

While the chicken is cooking, bring a large pot of water to a boil. Add the pasta and cook until al dente. Drain, toss with enough olive oil to coat lightly, and keep warm until ready to serve.

Remove the chicken and the bouquet garni from the saucepan, stir the sauce, and adjust the seasoning with salt and pepper. If desired, cook the sauce a bit more over medium heat until reduced to a thicker consistency.

To serve, place 1 cup of the penne on each of 4 plates. Place 2 drumsticks on top and ladle over some of the sauce. Garnish with diced tomato and chopped fresh parsley.

SERVES 4

FROZEN PORCUPINE CHEESECAKE

This dazzling frozen dessert is actually quite easy to make. Cheesecake ice cream, topped with chantilly cream and garnished with chocolate-covered biscuit sticks arranged like porcupine spines, sits in a pool of fresh raspberry coulis, looking dangerously delicious.

This is a variation of Michel's renowned Cheesecake Ice Cream Vacherin, but the vacherin, which is a hard meringue, is replaced here with the store-bought biscuit sticks to simplify the recipe for the home cook. If you are going all out, make your own meringue sticks, as the texture contrasts wonderfully with the ice cream.

An ice cream maker and a day's forethought are needed to make this incredible ice cream. Obviously, lacking either, store-bought ice cream would be just fine.

CHEESECAKE ICE CREAM

¼ cup fresh lemon juice

¾ cup sugar

1 8-ounce package cream cheese, softened

2 cups milk, chilled

RASPBERRY COULIS

1 cup fresh raspberries, washed

¼ cup sugar

CHANTILLY CREAM

2 cups heavy cream, chilled

2 tablespoons sugar

1 teaspoon vanilla extract

Pocky sticks (a Japanese brand of chocolate-coated biscuit sticks) or LU-brand Mikado cookies

Using an electric mixer, blend the lemon juice, ¾ cup of the sugar, cream cheese, and milk in a large bowl until smooth, stopping from time to time to scrape down the sides of the bowl. Process this mixture in an ice cream maker according to the manufacturer's instructions. Transfer the ice cream to a tightly covered container and freeze for several hours to "mellow" the flavors before serving.

Purée the raspberries with the sugar in a food processor or blender. Strain through a fine sieve to remove the seeds, cover, and refrigerate until ready to use. (This can be made several hours in advance.)

Shortly before serving, whip the cream in a bowl with the sugar and the vanilla, to stiff peaks.

To serve, scoop out 2 or 3 mounded tablespoons of the cheesecake ice cream and arrange in each of 4 cold soup plates. Using a spatula, cover the ice cream entirely with the whipped cream to form a porcupine shape. Spoon some raspberry coulis around each porcupine and drizzle a little on top. Then insert a few biscuit sticks to resemble spines, and serve.

SERVES 4

Zesting Citrus Fruit

The colored, outermost skin of citrus fruit, known as the zest, contains oils that lend a pungent flavor and aroma to foods. Zest is used as a flavoring in both sweet and savory dishes. The white pith that lies directly beneath the thin skin is undesirably bitter and should not be used.

There are a few methods for removing citrus zest. The easiest for large quantities is to rub the rind back and forth against the finest side of a cheese grater until you have removed just the colored skin; stop as soon as you have uncovered the white pith and move to a new spot. The only difficulty with this method is that some of the zest catches in the prongs and requires a bit of effort to remove. Michel offers a solution: press a piece of good-quality plastic wrap over the sharp side of the grater beforehand. The zest remains on top of the plastic, so when it is lifted from the grater, all of the zest can be swept off the plastic, also leaving the grater easy to clean.

For small quantities of zest, a citrus zester comes in handy. It is a small, inexpensive utensil with five rough scraping prongs that lift the zest from the fruit, leaving the pith behind. However, the zest will come off in long thin strips, which may need to be chopped, depending on the recipe.

Likewise, using a vegetable peeler, you can remove the zest in large pieces, which you can then chop finely. When using this method, make sure to apply only light pressure to the peeler so you do not pick up any of the pith along with the zest.

DOUG RODRIGUEZ

A Champagne Brunch

Known as the "Latin from Manhattan," Doug was born the younger of two children to Cuban parents, and raised on Latin American food in New York City. Longing to be closer to their relatives and warmer weather, the family moved to Miami when Doug was in his early teens. Stretching the truth about his age by a few years in order to earn money to buy his family Christmas presents, he secured his first job in a Miami Beach kitchen at the age of fourteen. After high school he attended Johnson and Wales College, earning a degree in culinary arts. Afterward, he returned to South Florida, where he became the chef at Yuca in Coral Gables, setting the restaurant scene on fire with his innovative *nuevo Latino* cuisine. It was here, in 1991, that he met his wife, Patricia, who worked in the kitchen making desserts. She recounts the story: "Two months or so after we met, he asked to talk to me over dinner. I assumed it was business, but he showed up with flowers. He won me over with his kindness, sense of humor, and persistence; we were married in a year."

Doug and Patricia returned to New York in 1994 to begin a new venture. As chef-owner of Patria, Doug has created a very special and personal ambience featuring Latin music and low lights. In his warm and artsy restaurant, Doug specializes in new takes on the

MENU

Man Gini

➤

Spanish Potato and Onion Tortilla with Smoked Salmon and Salmon Roe Sauce

➤

Gram's Banana Bread

traditional foods of Central and South America and the Caribbean.

The excitement and vast opportunities that life in New York offers prompted Doug's return, but he truly misses his family, most of whom are still in Miami. "Now that I have moved back, I'm planning a feast for the whole family when they come to visit. My family (like most Latinos) are always ready and willing to have gatherings or parties—we don't wait for the holidays to roll around." These events always include conversations in Spanish and music by Tito Puente, Doug's favorite Cuban musician, playing loudly in the background.

One of Doug's favorite meals is brunch, and the menu he puts together here is quick and easy to throw together, perfect for whipping up after sleeping in on a Sunday. Starting off with a Man Gini, Doug re-creates the traditional Bellini by replacing the peach nectar with fresh mango purée. Frozen or refrigerated mango will do, but as with all ingredients, fresh is best. The Spanish Potato and Onion Tortilla calls for twelve large eggs (1½ per person), which can be replaced with egg substitute for those watching their cholesterol or fat intake. Doug recently lost a considerable amount of weight, but once in a while he indulges in the real thing. "If I'm going to go off my diet, I do it for the foods I love best." You will not find this dish on his restaurant menu, but it was a standard meal that Doug enjoyed often while growing up. Now he adds the Salmon Roe Sauce for a special brunch for friends and family.

Gram's Banana Bread is an old favorite that Doug loves to include in a midday menu. As the name suggests, the recipe came from his grandmother. He also suggests preparing a fruit salad with lots of fresh sliced pineapple for a bit of sweetness to accompany the meal or to be served afterward. Doug says, "the best part about this menu is that, with the possible exception of the fresh mango, all of the ingredients for this traditional Latin brunch can be found at the corner grocery store."

MAN GINI

Doug came up with this Spanish-sounding name for this sparkling wine and mango cocktail. Try it at your next brunch, instead of mimosas, for a taste of the tropics. When buying fresh mangoes, give them a squeeze to test for ripeness: the mango should be firm but give a little under pressure, and it should smell fragrant. The mango juice will keep for one day in the refrigerator.

3 very ripe mangoes, peeled, pitted, and cut into pieces
About 1 cup ice water

1 bottle Champagne or other sparkling wine (see box, below)

Purée the mangoes in a food processor or blender until they become liquid. Add ice water a little at a time, up to 1 cup, until the mixture is somewhat thin in consistency. Pour a little mango juice in each glass, then add a little Champagne or sparkling wine. You can decide the proportions based on your taste.

SERVES 6 TO 8

Champagne—The Most Festive Beverage

Who says Champagne is for celebrations only? Perhaps we should reserve the very best bubbly for special occasions, but there are plenty of good, affordable sparkling wines that can make any meal special. While sparkling wines are produced all over the world, including the United States, Italy, and Spain, only that of the Champagne region of France is true Champagne. Italian sparkling wine is called Asti Spumante; the Spanish call theirs Cava; and most American brands are labeled as sparkling wine, though some California vinters ignore the tradition and call their wine "champagne." Among each of these varieties, you will find a wide range in price and quality.

At Patria, Doug usually makes the Man Gini with Cava instead of French Champagne. He recommends Reserva Heredad Segura Viudas and Royal Cuvée Gloria Ferrer, both of which are very good, affordable, and available at many wine shops.

SPANISH POTATO AND ONION TORTILLA WITH SMOKED SALMON AND SALMON ROE SAUCE

This tortilla is not to be mistaken for the flat flour or corn pancake used in Mexican cooking to make burritos and fajitas. This is the Spanish version, inherited by the Cubans, of a crustless quiche or omelet, very similar to the Italian frittata. This simple dish is great for brunch or a light dinner.

3 tablespoons extra-virgin olive oil

2 medium potatoes, peeled and diced

1 large onion, diced

12 large eggs

½ cup milk

Salt and freshly ground pepper to taste

½ pound thinly sliced smoked salmon

Salmon Roe Sauce (recipe follows)

Heat 2 tablespoons of the olive oil in a skillet over medium-high heat. Add the potatoes and onion and sauté until tender, about 10 minutes. Remove from the heat and set aside. In a large bowl, beat the eggs and the milk well. In the large nonstick skillet heat the remaining tablespoon of olive oil over medium heat. Add the egg mixture, and when it starts to cook on the bottom, add the potato and onion mixture. Season with salt and pepper. Run a spatula along the sides of the pan, lifting up the eggs to let the uncooked egg run underneath to cook. When the tortilla is cooked, except for the very top, remove from the heat and slide onto a plate. Flip the tortilla back into the pan, runny side down, and cook for an additional 2 to 3 minutes. Slide onto a large serving platter and garnish with the sliced smoked salmon. Serve warm with the Salmon Roe Sauce.

SERVES 8

SALMON ROE SAUCE

1 cup mayonnaise

½ cup sour cream

2 teaspoons fresh lime juice

1 teaspoon horseradish

2 tablespoons grated onion

3 tablespoons chopped fresh parsley

4 tablespoons chopped fresh chives

½ cup salmon roe (see box, below)

In a medium bowl, blend the mayonnaise, sour cream, lime juice, horseradish, onion, parsley, and chives with a spoon. When it is well blended, add the roe and stir gently. Chill slightly and serve.

MAKES APPROXIMATELY 2 CUPS

Salmon Roe

Roe is the culinary term for fish eggs. Caviar is sturgeon roe that has been salted (see box, page 343), although other salted fish eggs can be labeled as caviar if the name of the fish precedes the word *caviar*. Like caviar, fish roe ranges in price and quality depending on the fish. It is best when bought fresh but is also available frozen or canned, and it can be eaten raw, as in the Salmon Roe Sauce, or cooked. Fresh roe, available in the spring, should be moist and firm and without a fishy odor.

For Doug's Spanish Potato and Onion Tortilla, the choicest roe is not necessary, and besides, the best—such as shad, herring, carp, or mackerel roe—deserves to be eaten in the simplest fashion. Salmon roe is praiseworthy, but not too expensive, and its bright red-orange color enlivens this dish. For this sauce, Doug uses roe from a jar, which you will find at specialty food stores and in some supermarkets. For a cheaper, more readily available substitute, there is red mullet roe or lump fish caviar, which also come in jars and can be purchased at most supermarkets.

Spanish Tortilla Variations

For a variation, replace the potatoes and onion in the tortilla with the following, using whatever amounts you like, and serve with a compatible salsa:

CHORIZO, a spicy Spanish pork sausage. Add it once the eggs have started to cook.

HAM AND ROASTED RED AND GREEN PEPPERS. Any ham you like will work. Finely dice the ham and sauté in a dry skillet until slightly browned on the edges. To roast the peppers, follow the instructions in the box on page 186. Add the ham and peppers once the eggs have started to cook.

BROCCOLI AND MANCHEGO CHEESE. Cut the broccoli into small pieces and steam until tender, then add to the egg mixture along with the grated cheese. Manchego, available at Latin and specialty markets, is a rich but mellow semi-firm Spanish cheese. Add the broccoli and cheese once the eggs have started to cook.

MUSHROOMS AND ONIONS TOPPED WITH CRISPY CRUMBLED BACON AND DICED TOMATOES. Crimini or button mushrooms work best here. Lightly sauté the sliced mushrooms and onions before adding to the egg mixture as they start to cook. For a tasty garnish, cut your favorite bacon into small pieces and fry until crispy. Sprinkle the bacon pieces and diced, seeded tomatoes on top of the cooked tortilla.

Gram's Banana Bread

Doug says, "My 'Gram' would let the bananas get totally black before making the bread—it makes the bread very moist and sweet." This is a fairly wet bread; if you like your bread a little drier, reduce the amount of banana to 1 cup. Doug prefers to use margarine for this recipe, but butter can be substituted. Add nuts if you wish, but "Gram left them out for me," says Doug.

⅓ cup unsalted margarine or butter,
  softened

⅔ cup sugar

2 large eggs

1½ cups mashed ripe banana

1½ cups all-purpose flour

2 teaspoons baking powder

¼ teaspoon baking soda

Pinch of salt

Preheat the oven to 375°F. Grease and flour a 9 × 5 × 3-inch loaf pan. Using an electric mixer, cream the margarine or butter and sugar in a large bowl. Add the eggs and mix until well incorporated. Mix in the banana with a wooden spoon. In a medium bowl, sift the flour, baking powder, baking soda, and salt together. Mix the dry ingredients into the banana mixture with a wooden spoon until well blended and pour into the prepared loaf pan. Bake for 20 minutes, then reduce the temperature to 350°F. and bake for another 30 to 40 minutes, until a toothpick inserted in the middle of the loaf comes out clean. Cool the pan on a wire rack.

Serves 8

MICHAEL ROMANO

A Vegetarian Risotto Dinner

I t is hard to say which came first for Michael Romano: his love for food or his passion for wine. But his knowledge of both makes for an explosive combination at the Union Square Cafe, where he has been the chef since 1988.

Growing up in a large extended Italian family in Manhattan, Michael was exposed to the authentic dishes of his mother, his grandmother, and his aunts—lasagne of all kinds, pastas, sauces, pizza, and fish. He recalls one Christmas at their home when his grandmother prepared twenty to twenty-five different fish dishes for a single meal. His desire to cook began shortly after he started college at Fordham University, where he studied liberal arts. He rented an apartment with a couple of friends, and since they all shared an avid fascination for food and wine, they were soon throwing the best dinner parties in town.

"I don't eat the way I used to when I was in college. Now, I thoroughly enjoy one or two courses instead of gorging myself the way I did when we had those crazy dinner parties. I do yoga every day and I eat very little meat, fish, or poultry." Today, relaxed in his kitchen at home, Michael prefers to limit his entertaining to four or six guests, although he says "just two is the best, especially in front of the fire in the winter. "

MENU

*Spinach, Fennel, and Portobello
Mushroom Salad*

*Gazpacho Risotto with Tomato,
Cucumber, and Pepper*

*Summer Berry Almond Tart with
Lemon Mascarpone Cream*

Michael's first cooking experience was at Serendipity restaurant in New York. "I was promoted from frozen-drink man to evening line cook and I had precious little idea what I was doing—I just knew I loved to cook." It was there that he was introduced to the illustrious James Beard, from

whom he sought advice in planning his culinary career. At Beard's recommendation Michael attended New York City Technical College, where he studied French cooking. In 1975, Michael went to France, where he received an apprenticeship at the renowned Bristol Hotel in Paris. In 1976, he studied under Michel Guérard, whom he considers the originator of *nouvelle cuisine*. "Guérard's style was strong yet had delicacy and beauty, and most of all he cooked tastefully. Even though I'm not cooking French at this time, I try and keep a certain lightness to my dishes, an approach which I learned from him."

In selecting this menu, Michael turned to some of his favorite recipes. He begins with a salad filled with spinach, fennel, and portobello mushrooms. "There is a wonderful earthiness to all the elements of this salad, which is why they blend together so well. The fennel adds a higher note of earthiness, while the hint of balsamic vinegar brings out the individual flavors." For the main course, Michael prepares risotto, more commonly known and served in the States as a side dish or first course. This not so traditional risotto made with tomato, cucumber, a little white wine, diced jalepeños, and topped with fresh cilantro is sure to please gazpacho lovers and vegetarians alike. "Cooking at home usually dictates that my menu offer something inviting and cozy," Michael notes. The dessert Michael prepares, a summer almond tart, polka-dotted with fresh berries and topped with sweet lemon mascarpone cream, meets the highest expectations.

SPINACH, FENNEL, AND PORTOBELLO MUSHROOM SALAD

For this simple meal opener, it is important to use only the best ingredients: real Parmesan cheese—Parmigiano-Reggiano—and the best balsamic vinegar will make all the difference.

Look for spinach leaves that are young and tender—flat-leaf California spinach is ideal. Toss aside any tough, curly spinach leaves with thick stems. For an elusive flavor the fennel is shaved paper-thin because larger pieces will overwhelm the salad with their pungent anise taste.

1 8-ounce piece Parmigiano-Reggiano cheese

1 small clove garlic, minced

2 tablespoons good quality balsamic vinegar (see box, page 64)

Kosher salt to taste

Freshly ground pepper to taste

¾ cup extra-virgin olive oil

4 medium portobello mushrooms, stems removed and caps wiped clean (see box, pages 36–37)

1 medium bulb fresh fennel, green top removed

¾ pound young, tender spinach leaves, washed and stemmed

Preheat the oven to 375°F. Using a cheese slicer, shave at least 12 very thin slices from the Parmigiano-Reggiano. Carefully place the shards on a plate, cover with plastic wrap, and set aside at room temperature. Finely grate the remaining cheese.

In a glass or stainless steel bowl, combine the minced garlic, balsamic vinegar, salt, and pepper. Slowly whisk in the olive oil until the sauce thickens slightly. When all the oil has been incorporated, whisk in the grated cheese. Lay the mushrooms on a baking sheet and brush them with 3 tablespoons of the oil and vinegar dressing. Roast the mushrooms in the oven for 20 to 30 minutes, or until tender.

While the mushrooms are cooking, prepare the fennel. Using a mandolin, or cheese slicer, slice the entire bulb of fennel into paper-thin slices. Arrange the slices around the rims of four chilled salad plates, or a large salad platter. Drizzle half the remaining dressing over the fennel.

Place the spinach in a large bowl, and toss with the remaining dressing until lightly coated. Arrange the spinach leaves in the center of each of the four plates, or the salad platter.

While the mushrooms are still warm, slice them very thinly on a sharp bias and arrange the slices over the spinach. Top the mushrooms with the reserved Parmigiano-Reggiano shards and serve immediately.

SERVES *4*

Parmesan Cheese

Named after Italy's city of Parma, where this hard, sharp cheese originated, parmesan is now made in a number of areas in and out of Italy, including the United States. The Italian variety comes in large wheels wrapped in an orange rind with its name Parmigiano-Reggiano stenciled in the side. It is superior in flavor and texture to all others due to the long aging process—two to four years. The flavor becomes more complex and the texture more grainy with aging. Domestic renditions are usually aged for only fourteen months.

Whether domestic or imported, there is no substitute for fresh parmesan. Always buy fresh parmesan in block form, store well-wrapped in the refrigerator, and grate just before using. Store-bought grated parmesan can't compare.

GAZPACHO RISOTTO WITH TOMATO, CUCUMBER, AND PEPPERS

This satisfying all-in-one dish becomes especially easy to prepare once the tomato and cucumber juices are made, which can be done the night before. Refrigerate them in a tightly sealed container until ready to use. Check out your local health food store for ready made, freshly juiced vegetable juice.

3–4 ripe medium tomatoes (2 pounds), cored and coarsely chopped

6 medium cucumbers, peeled, seeded, and coarsely chopped

¼ cup extra-virgin olive oil

1¾ cups Arborio rice (available at specialty food stores; see box, opposite)

½ teaspoon minced garlic

½ cup dry white wine

½ cup diced and seeded tomato

½ cup cup diced red onion

¼ cup diced jalepeño, seeded, if desired, for less heat

½ cup diced red bell pepper

2–3 tablespoons unsalted butter

1 teaspoon kosher salt

⅛ teaspoon freshly ground black pepper

2 tablespoons coarsely chopped fresh cilantro leaves

Purée the tomatoes in a food processor or blender until liquid. Strain through a fine sieve and reserve the juice (approximately 3 cups). Process the cucumbers in a blender, food processor, or vegetable juicer until smooth. Strain the pulp through a fine sieve, using a spatula to extract all of the juice (approximately 3 cups).

In a large saucepan, combine the tomato and cucumber juices over medium-high heat and bring to a simmer. Remove from the heat. In a 3-quart skillet, heat the olive oil over medium heat. Add the rice and garlic and stir together, using a wooden spoon until the rice is well coated with oil. Add the white wine and bring to a boil, stirring constantly, until all of the wine is absorbed by the rice.

Ladle ½ cup of the hot juice mixture into the saucepan and stir until it is absorbed. Continue with the rest of the juice, adding ½ cup at a time and letting each addition be absorbed completely into the rice before adding more liquid. The constant stirring allows the rice to release its starch into the cooking liquid, resulting in the characteristic risotto creaminess. When ¾ of the juice has been used, about 15 to 20 minutes, stir in the diced vegetables. Continue ladling and stirring, about 8 to 10 additional minutes. The grains of rice should be *al dente* (tender, with a bit of firmness). Swirl in the butter and season to taste with the salt and the pepper. Spoon into four shallow bowls, sprinkle each serving with the cilantro, and serve immediately.

SERVES 4

Risotto

Many of us who have appreciated a perfectly cooked risotto—one with a splendidly creamy texture and each rice kernel cooked *al dente*—are under the impression that it cannot be replicated by an amateur. Actually, the technique for preparing risotto is pretty easy; however, it does require undivided attention and is somewhat particular.

Risotto is made with a short-grain, high-starch rice, usually Italian Arborio. The rice is first sautéed in a little bit of fat and onion or other seasoning, then hot liquid, usually a stock, is added in small amounts and stirred until it is absorbed by the rice before adding more. Constant stirring helps the rice kernels release their starch, resulting in the creamy texture. The process must not be rushed or interrupted, and the stirring must be almost constant. Other ingredients can also be added, during different parts of the cooking process, depending on how long they need to cook.

Summer Berry Almond Tart with Lemon Mascarpone Cream

This dessert is remarkably simple to make and suits both elegant and casual occasions. The almond batter serves as a crust and filling to the berries, which are cooked just long enough to release their juices. For an elegant presentation, Michael bakes the dessert in individual tartlet pans. You can also use a 12-inch tart pan, but there will be about a cup of extra batter, which you can pour into muffin tins and bake.

15 ounces sliced, blanched almonds (see box, opposite)

1¼ cups sugar

¾ cup all-purpose flour

¼ teaspoon salt

5 large eggs

½ cup plus 2 teaspoons milk

10 tablespoons (1¼ sticks) unsalted butter, melted

2 tablespoons almond extract

1½–2 pints raspberries, blueberries, and/or blackberries

Lemon Mascarpone Cream (recipe follows) or Crème Fraîche (see box, page 237)

Preheat the oven to 350° F. Butter a removeable bottom 12-inch tart pan or ten 4-inch tartlet pans and dust with sugar, knocking out the excess. Set aside.

In a blender or food processor, process the almonds and sugar until finely ground. Transfer to a medium mixing bowl and blend in the flour and salt until well combined. In a small bowl, whisk together the eggs and milk. Stir in the melted butter and almond extract. Stir the egg mixture into almond-flour mixture until well blended and pour into the prepared pan(s) until three-fourths full.

Drop the berries over the surface of the batter, approximately ¼ inch apart. Bake for 15 to 20 minutes or until the tart is golden and lightly firm to the touch. Remove from the oven and remove the sides from the tart pan. Cool to room temperature. To serve, cut the tart into wedges and serve with a dollop of Lemon Mascarpone Cream or Crème Fraîche.

Serves 10 to 12

LEMON MASCARPONE CREAM

Mascarpone cheese is a mildly sweet, soft, and creamy Italian cheese made from cow's milk.

**4 ounces mascarpone cheese (available
  at cheese and specialty shops)**
1 cup heavy cream

2 tablespoons sugar
Zest and juice of one lemon

Place the mascarpone cheese, cream, sugar, and lemon zest and juice in the bowl of an electric mixer. Whip on medium speed until soft peaks are formed. Keep chilled until ready to use.

MAKES APPROXIMATELY 2 1/2 CUPS

Blanched Almonds

Blanched almonds can shed their skins by being plunged briefly into boiling water. Unfortunately, blanched almonds are not as widely available as raw almonds (with skins). The good news is that blanching is something you can do easily at home, it just takes a little time.

Place the raw almonds in a bowl and pour over just enough hot water to cover the almonds. Cover and let stand for 1 minute. Drain and rinse with cold water to stop the almonds from softening. Place the almonds between two dish towels and rub back and forth to remove the skins. Most of the skins will be removed, but you will need to rub individual nuts with your hands to remove clingier skins.

JIMMY SCHMIDT

Autumn Bounty

Jimmy Schmidt selected this wonderful autumn menu with the same thoughtfulness and attention to quality that he used in building his successful restaurant empire in the Detroit metropolitan area. With his time obligations to the Rattlesnake Club and several other restaurants, along with numerous commitments to charities and community events, it is no wonder that Jimmy is not often found in front of his stove at home. But when he has the opportunity, he makes the most of the special occasions. He prepares simple meals, but with great flair. He does a lot of roasting and baking, explaining that he likes "dishes that are made slowly in the oven to allow me time with my guests as well as filling the house with wonderful fragrances that will whet their appetites." To him, the oven is perfect for entertaining since the prepared dishes can be popped in, left alone, and yet provide that wonderful just-cooked flavor.

Beginning with a simple but robust salad that stands up to a chilly fall night, the meal segues into a mature roasted chicken, which is perfectly matched with grains and seasonal vegetables. The oven continues its work with the dessert—Jimmy's version of the classic *tarte Tatin,* which is baked with the pastry on top and inverted right before serving.

Jimmy avoids preparing a seated five-course dinner at home. Instead, he chooses

MENU

*Orange, Red Onion, and Winter
Greens with Orange-Sherry Vinaigrette*

*Roasted Chicken with Ragout of
Quinoa and Autumn Vegetables*

Apple Pistachio Tart

Honey Peppercorn Ice Cream

to set up the buffet in the kitchen, so he can mingle with his guests while putting the final touches on his meal. Guests sip champagne and munch on hors d'oeuvres while meandering throughout the house, occasionally stopping back into the kitchen to refill their glasses or pick up an appetizer and catch a glimpse of their host in action.

Jimmy's introduction to food and wine began in France, when he was studying to receive an engineering degree. While going to school, he became interested in food and wine in order to eat and drink well, so he took a few cooking classes during the day and wine-tasting classes at night. Ultimately he received the Provençal Culinary Arts Diploma from Lubéron College in Avignon and the French Institute Technique du Vin Diploma from Maison du Vin in Avignon, both in 1974. At Lubéron College he met his mentor, Madeleine Kamman; after becoming close friends with her, Jimmy decided to take a break from pursuing his engineering degree and followed Madeleine back to Chez la Mère in Massachusetts.

In 1977, after becoming the executive chef of the London Chop House in Detroit, he acknowledged that the lure of the kitchen was more attractive than his slide rule and became a full-time chef and restaurateur. "I realized that I could eat and drink well every day working as a chef," he says. "I chose to make my hobby my career."

When Jimmy prepares a meal at home for his guests, he likes to use familiar ingredients that everyone will like, and then introduce a new flavor. "I like to bend their tastes, offering them something new to try, but combining it with something they are used to," says Jimmy. "I do this with the Apple Pistachio Tart. The apple is easy, everyone will like it, but I add the Honey Peppercorn Ice Cream to expand everyone's palate."

He does the same with wines, selecting a number of different wines to accompany the entire meal, rather than serving one with each course. His guests sample the variety throughout the meal, and share their preferences and observations with each other.

Jimmy explains, "I don't like to restrict my guests' tastes with the types of food I serve; otherwise I limit who I will entertain," he says. "If you've satisfied everyone's tastes, then you've hosted a good party!"

ORANGE, RED ONION, AND WINTER GREENS WITH ORANGE-SHERRY VINAIGRETTE

Any ripe sweet orange, such as navel, Valencia, or blood orange, will work in this bold salad to balance the bitterness of the endive, watercress, and radicchio.

1 cup fresh orange juice

2 tablespoons sherry vinegar

½ cup extra-virgin olive oil

¼ cup chopped scallions, green part only, cut on a diagonal

Sea salt to taste

Coarsely ground black pepper to taste

2 large Belgian endive

2 bunches watercress, washed, stems and tough leaves removed

1 small head radicchio, cut into chiffonade (see box, below)

1 small red onion, thinly sliced

4 large oranges, peeled, membrane removed (see box, page 362), and separated into segments

In a small saucepan, bring the orange juice to a simmer over medium-low heat and cook until it has reduced to ¼ cup, about 10 minutes. Remove from the heat and allow to cool to room temperature. In a small bowl, combine the reduced orange juice, vinegar, oil, and scallions. Season with salt and pepper.

Remove the larger outer leaves of the endive and arrange approximately 6 leaves, pointed ends outward, on each of 4 serving plates. Cut the remaining endive into bite-size pieces. In a large bowl, combine the endive pieces, watercress, radicchio, onion, and orange segments. Add the dressing and toss. Place equal portions of the salad mixture on the center of each plate.

SERVES 4

Chiffonade

To cut lettuce or large-leafed herbs into a chiffonade means to slice them into thin strips. Stack a few leaves of the lettuce or herb on top of one another, roll them up tightly into a cylinder, then cut the roll crosswise to make thin strips when the shreds unfurl. How thick or thin the strips are cut depends on the herb or green and how it is to be used.

Roasted Chicken with Ragout of Quinoa and Autumn Vegetables

Jimmy's roasted chicken is accompanied by quinoa, a high-protein grain, and a harmonious blend of vegetables and seasonings. Who said nutritionally sound couldn't be delicious, too? The rosemary-infused oil is a necessary component of this satisfying dish. Bottled rosemary oil may be substituted, in which case you should skip the first step of frying the rosemary leaves.

1 cup extra-virgin olive oil

¼ cup fresh rosemary leaves

1 roasting chicken, about 5 pounds

Sea salt to taste

Freshly ground pepper to taste

2 cups quinoa (available at health food stores and some supermarkets; see box, page 293)

4–4½ cups Vegetable Stock (recipe follows) or water

2 garlic cloves, finely minced

2 cups coarsely diced pumpkin or winter squash

1 cup sliced wild mushrooms, such as chanterelles or portobellos (see box, pages 36–37)

1 large red pepper, cored, seeded, and diced

1 cup fresh corn kernels or frozen kernels, thawed

½ cup finely grated Parmesan cheese

4 whole sprigs fresh rosemary, for garnish

Preheat the oven to 450° F. In a small skillet, heat the olive oil to 300–325° F. Add the rosemary leaves and cook until crisp, about 2 minutes, or until the oil stops bubbling around the rosemary. Remove the rosemary with a slotted spoon and drain on a paper towel. Set the rosemary leaves aside. Allow the oil to cool.

Thoroughly rinse the chicken inside and out under cold running water. Pat dry with paper towels. Season the cavity and skin with salt and pepper, then truss the chicken with kitchen twine to ensure even cooking. Place the chicken in a large ovenproof skillet. Rub 1 tablespoon of the rosemary-infused oil over the skin. Place the skillet on the lower oven rack with the legs toward the back of the oven. Cook until the bird starts to brown, 15 to 20 minutes. Reduce the heat to 350° F. Roast, basting every 15 to 20 minutes, until an instant-reading thermometer inserted in the thigh reads 160° F. and the juices run clear when the thigh is pricked with a fork, approximately 1½ hours more. Remove the chicken from the oven and keep in a warm place, covered lightly with a piece of foil.

Start preparing the quinoa about 20 minutes before removing the chicken from the oven.

Place the quinoa in a fine strainer and rinse under cold running water to remove any residue of the bitter husks. Allow it to drain thoroughly. Bring the stock or water to a boil in a saucepan over medium heat.

In a large saucepan, heat 2 tablespoons of the rosemary oil over medium-high heat. Add the garlic, cooking until lightly browned and tender, about 5 minutes. Add the quinoa and cook until it is heated through. Remove from the heat and carefully pour 4 cups of the boiling stock or water over the quinoa. Stir in the diced pumpkin. Return the quinoa to medium heat and bring to a simmer. Season with salt and a generous dose of pepper. Cook for about 8 minutes, stirring, until there is no more liquid left, but the quinoa is still moist, like risotto.

In a nonstick skillet, heat 1 tablespoon of the rosemary oil. Add the mushrooms, cooking until brown on all of the edges, about 4 minutes. Add the pepper and cook, stirring, until crisp-tender, about 2 minutes. Add the corn and stir to heat through. Transfer the mushrooms, pepper, and corn to the quinoa mixture with a slotted spoon and stir to combine. Set aside, covered, to keep warm.

Transfer the chicken, still covered with foil, to a carving board, pouring any juices and fat from the chicken into the skillet. Pour all the cooking fat and juices from the skillet into a glass measuring cup. If the juices are caramelized in the pan, add ½ cup of stock to the skillet to deglaze; place the pan over medium heat and scrape up any browned bits from the bottom, then add the mixture to the measuring cup. Strain off the fat.

Carve the chicken and slice the breast. Spoon an equal amount of quinoa into the center of each serving plate. Divide the chicken onto the plates, allowing the pieces to overlap the ragout. Spoon the strained juices over the chicken and sprinkle with the reserved fried rosemary leaves and Parmesan cheese. Garnish with whole sprigs of rosemary and serve.

SERVES *4*

Beverage Suggestions

For a hospitable touch, Jimmy likes to present his dining companions with a choice of more than one wine. To welcome his guests, Jimmy offers Manzanilla Fino Sherry or dry Amontillado Sherry served cool, straight up, in small wine glasses and accompanied by olives and Spicy Toasted Nuts (see box, page 292) to nibble on. With the roasted chicken, he suggests a rich white wine such as a California Chardonnay, a barrel-fermented Fumé Blanc, or a Sauvignon Blanc. If red wine is preferred, select a soft, fruity red such as Cru Beaujolais (a Morgon is nice), a Dolcetto d'Alba, or a California Pinot Noir.

VEGETABLE STOCK

2 large leeks, cleaned and diced

2 large onions, diced

1 cup chopped shallots

1 celery root, peeled and diced
  (3 stalks celery may be substituted)

12 cups water, or more as needed

3 cups dry white wine

1 bunch parsley stems (reserve leaves
  for another use)

2 bay leaves

2 tablespoons black peppercorns

In a large stockpot, combine the leeks, onions, shallots, and celery root with the water and wine. Bring to a simmer over medium heat, skimming the surface occasionally. Add the parsley stems, bay leaves, and peppercorns. Return to a simmer and cook for 4 hours, adding more water if necessary to keep the ingredients covered. Strain, let cool to room temperature, and refrigerate, tightly covered, until ready to use, up to 3 days. The stock can be frozen in tightly sealed containers, for up to 1 month.

MAKES 10 CUPS

Spicy Toasted Nuts

Little work is involved in making these nuts. They are a great opener to a hearty meal because they "satisfy an eager palate" without being too filling. Any nuts and any spices that are available will do. Spiced nuts can be purchased, but homemade is always better. One of Jimmy Schmidt's favorite combinations is 1 pound pecans mixed with 2 teaspoons cumin, 2 teaspoons chili powder, 1 tablespoon cinnamon, 1 teaspoon allspice, and ⅔ cup sugar.

Preheat the oven to 250°F. In a mixer or in a mixing bowl with a whisk, whip 2 egg whites and 2 tablespoons of cold water until foamy. Toss in 1 pound of nuts and coat well. Transfer the nut mixture to a strainer and allow the excess egg white to drain off. In a large mixing bowl, combine the dry ingredients, then add the nuts and mix until evenly coated with the spices. Transfer the nuts to a nonstick baking sheet and bake on the lower rack of the oven until dry, 20 to 30 minutes. Remove the nuts from the oven and immediately loosen from the baking sheet with a spatula. Cool to room temperature. Store in an airtight glass jar, or serve in small bowls.

Quinoa

Referred to as the "supergrain of the future" by some, quinoa (KEEN-wah) is an ancient grain from the Andes in South America. Now it is finding its way from health food stores to grocery stores all across the United States. Its recent popularity may be because it contains between 16 and 20 percent protein—higher than the 14 percent of wheat, 9.9 percent of millet, and 7.5 percent of rice. When commercially harvested (with the husks cleanly removed), quinoa tastes light and nutty with an earthy tone, and digests easily.

Quinoa is simple to prepare, quite similar to cooking rice. Add it to twice the volume of boiling salted water, then simmer until tender and all the water is absorbed, about 15 minutes. Often directions call for covering the pot, but Jimmy gets better results by very slowly simmering with the lid removed. Add garnishes, such as nuts and fresh herbs, and serve. Spices are best added to the boiling water so that they may slowly disperse through the dish.

Jimmy prefers to prepare the quinoa with a rice pilaf technique. Heat a small amount of olive oil in a saucepan. Add the dry quinoa and cook until hot. Add twice the volume of boiling salted water, with spices if preferred, cover, and place on the lower rack of an oven preheated to 350°F. for 12 to 15 minutes, until tender. Remove from the oven, stir in any garnishes, and serve.

Vegetables may also be added to the cooking quinoa. They should be cut into small dice and added at the appropriate time, depending on the type of vegetable, so that they may finish cooking about the same time as the quinoa.

Quinoa is great served warm, at room temperature, or cold. The cooled quinoa is terrific in green and vegetable salads and mixed with tender young greens. Enjoy the flavor, texture, and extra protein!

APPLE PISTACHIO TART

This familiar upside-down apple dessert is a stand-out when served with Honey Peppercorn Ice Cream, which combines sweet with hot, a flavor combination Jimmy favors. However, a good-quality store-bought vanilla ice cream, or low-fat frozen yogurt, can be substituted.

2 tablespoons (¼ stick) unsalted butter, softened

1¼ cups sugar, divided

¼ cup fresh lemon juice

½ cup water

½ cup blanched, skinned pistachios (available at health food stores and some supermarkets)

8 crisp, tart apples, such as Granny Smith, peeled, cored, and sliced ¼ inch thick

½ pound puff pastry (thawed, if frozen)

Honey Peppercorn Ice Cream (recipe follows)

Mint sprigs, for garnish (optional)

Preheat the oven to 400° F. Rub a 10-inch nonstick ovenproof frying pan (one with curved edges, like an omelet pan or an oiled cast-iron pan) with the butter. Set aside. In a medium saucepan, combine 1 cup of the sugar, the lemon juice, and the water. Bring to a simmer over high heat and cook until it becomes a light caramel, about 320° F. on a candy thermometer. Add the pistachios and stir to coat. Pour the mixture into the buttered skillet.

Arrange the apples in a single layer over the pistachio-caramel sauce in the skillet. Sprinkle the apples lightly with some of the remaining ¼ cup of sugar and continue to build layers of apples, sprinkling each layer with the sugar until all the apples are used.

Roll out the pastry on a lightly floured surface to a ⅛-inch thickness. Place it over the apples, trimming the pastry so that it extends just ½ inch beyond the apples, and tuck the pastry just along the inside rim of the pan. Bake on the lower oven rack until the pastry is golden, about 30 minutes. Remove from the oven and carefully invert onto a serving platter if baked on a nonstick pan, or if baked in a cast-iron pan, cool on a rack for 15 minutes before inverting.

To serve, cut the warm tart into slices and top with a scoop of the Honey Peppercorn Ice Cream and a mint sprig, if desired.

MAKES ONE 10-INCH TART

Table Themes

When setting the table, create a seasonal theme. Use fresh seasonal foods for the centerpiece, such as pumpkins, gourds, baby and Indian corn, sheaves of wheat, tree branches, and vibrantly colored leaves. Create a color scheme to complement the foods and the season, in this case autumn.

HONEY PEPPERCORN ICE CREAM

2 tablespoons black peppercorns
1¾ cups half-and-half
1 cup heavy cream

10 large egg yolks
⅓ cup plus 1 tablespoon brown sugar
⅔ cup honey

In a small, heavy skillet, cook the peppercorns over medium-low heat, shaking the pan occasionally to toast evenly, until they are aromatic, about 4 minutes. Remove from the pan and set aside to cool. When cool, coarsely grind the peppercorns in a pepper mill or food processor. Set aside.

In a large saucepan, combine the half-and-half and ½ cup of the cream. Bring just to a boil over medium-high heat, then remove from the heat and cool slightly. In another large saucepan, whisk together the egg yolks, brown sugar, and honey. Whisk in the scalded cream, stirring constantly. Heat the mixture over medium-low heat and cook until the custard thickens enough to coat the back of a spoon, about 10 minutes; do not boil. Remove from the heat and whisk in the remaining heavy cream. Strain into a large bowl and refrigerate until well chilled.

Process the custard in an ice cream maker according to the manufacturer's instructions, just until it has thickened. Mix in the peppercorns. Freeze in a covered container overnight, and allow the ice cream to soften slightly before serving.

MAKES 1 PINT

NANCY SILVERTON
AND MARK PEEL

Modern American Fare

Nancy Silverton and Mark Peel have played an important part in the evolution of contemporary American cuisine, first as chefs at Wolfgang Puck's internationally acclaimed Spago, and now as chef-owners of the renowned La Brea Bakery and Campanile in Los Angeles, California.

But their success has not diminished their enjoyment of easy and hearty home cooking. "I started cooking at home," says Mark. "My mom was a single mother, so I ended up cooking a lot. I especially liked holidays because I could prepare for a lot of people."

Nancy began her cooking career preparing for large groups as well. Her first formal chef experience was cooking vegetarian meals for her dormitory when she was a freshman at California State University at Sonoma. Although at the time she was studying for a liberal arts degree, her experience in the dorm kitchen made her realize that cooking was what she really wanted to do. After apprenticing at a small Northern California restaurant, she attended the Cordon Bleu School in London.

Mark, on the other hand, was hired to peel vegetables at Ma Maison under the direction of then chef Wolfgang

MENU

Fish Soup

*Pasta al Ceppo with
Wild Mushrooms and Duck Confit*

Chess Tartlets

Puck while studying hotel management at California Polytechnic College at Pomona. As he moved up the ladder and became more successful at Ma Maison, he was sent to France to expand and perfect his culinary skills as apprentice at La Tour d'Argent, in Paris, and Moulin de Mougins, near Cannes.

Their varied experiences coincided when Nancy and Mark met at the fashionable Michael's Restaurant in Santa Monica, California. He was sous-chef and she was pas-

try chef. Nancy stayed there for three years, fell in love with baking, and went on to complete a series of pastry courses at the École Lenôtre in Plaiser, France. In 1985, the two married and spent six months rejuvenating Maxwell's Plum in New York, and then moved back to Los Angeles and worked for Wolfgang Puck at Spago for three and a half years, Mark as head chef and Nancy as pastry chef. In January 1989, La Brea Bakery was opened, followed by Campanile in June 1990.

These days when they cook at home, it is an opportunity for a "shared experience with friends," Mark says. Because cooking at home is a little more limited—without the equipment and walk-in freezers or great bread ovens at the restaurant—Mark and Nancy like to serve dishes that are a "meal in and of themselves." The Fish Soup and the pasta in this menu are both examples, which Mark says should be served in big steaming bowls so people can serve themselves from the center of the table.

They also have started to order take-out more often and combine it with one dish made at home for a complete meal. "It's what all of our friends are doing as well. It's convenient, the food's good, and it's a boost to the neighborhood restaurants," Mark says.

Nancy rarely makes desserts at home because the type she prefers to make are too complicated and time-consuming. But when they have guests over, she does make these Chess Tartlets—a variation on the traditional American pie—because the recipe is simple and because she and Mark and their kids love it. "The pears and cream really send it over the top."

FISH SOUP

The name sounds so simple, but this soup is nothing less than sublime with its lush-tasting tomato-based broth, rosemary roasted potatoes, and, of course, ample amounts of seafood. In addition to a spoon, you will need a fork to extract the luscious lobster meat and mussels from their shells.

This soup adapts well to different fish and cooking methods. Make seafood substitutions based on your preference. The seafood can be poached in the soup stock or grilled or sautéed before adding to the soup (see variations). Also, the recipe can be doubled, if desired.

4 small new potatoes, scrubbed but not peeled

4 tablespoons extra-virgin olive oil

1 teaspoon chopped fresh rosemary leaves

Salt and freshly ground pepper to taste

2 medium tomatoes, cored and chopped

1 tablespoon minced garlic

4 cups fish stock

1 1¼-pound lobster, freshly killed (see box, page 233)

6 ounces (8 to 12, depending on size) mussels or clams, scrubbed, and in the shell

6 ounces calamari, cleaned and cut crosswise into thin slices

2 teaspoons chopped mixed fresh herbs, such as parsley, basil, thyme, or marjoram

Zest of 1 small lemon

½ pound sea bass fillet, cut into 4 pieces

8 medium shrimp (about ½ pound), peeled and deveined, tails left intact

4 tablespoons Rouille (recipe follows)

Preheat the oven to 400° F. Cut the potatoes into quarters and toss in a small bowl with 2 tablespoons of the olive oil, the rosemary, and salt and pepper. Place on a baking sheet and bake for about 20 to 30 minutes, until brown and tender. Set aside to cool.

Set aside a large bowl of ice water. In a 4-quart saucepan, heat the remaining olive oil over medium heat. Add the tomatoes and garlic and cook just to soften, about 2 minutes. Pour in the fish stock and bring to a boil over medium-high heat. Add the lobster and cook to rare, about 4 minutes. Using a large slotted spoon or a pair of tongs, transfer the lobster to a bowl of ice water to stop the cooking process. When cool enough to handle, remove the tail and claws. Cut the tail in half lengthwise, leaving the shell attached, and crack the claws enough to easily extract the meat, but do not remove the shell. Refrigerate the lobster pieces until needed.

Season the stock lightly with salt and pepper and return to a simmer over medium heat. Add the mussels or clams, cover, and simmer until the shells open, 3 to 4 minutes. Transfer the clams or mussels to a plate using a slotted spoon. Add the calamari, herbs, and lemon zest to the stock. Cook for 1 minute. Remove the calamari to the plate with a slotted spoon. (The stock can be removed from the heat at this point. Return the stock to a simmer over medium heat when ready to continue.)

Just before serving, return the lobster to the simmering stock over medium heat. Add the sea bass and shrimp and cook for 3 minutes. Then add the potatoes, mussels or clams, and calamari. Cook just to heat through before serving. Correct the seasoning to taste.

To serve, ladle the soup into 4 large soup bowls, distributing the seafood evenly, and top each serving with a dollop of Rouille. Serve immediately.

SERVES 4

VARIATIONS: For more flavor, grill or sauté the fish and shrimp before adding to the soup. To grill, brush the seafood lightly with olive oil, season lightly with salt and pepper, and grill to medium-rare, 3 to 5 minutes in all, depending on the heat of the grill. Use a mesh grill cover so the shrimp will not fall into the fire.

To sauté, heat 2 teaspoons extra-virgin olive oil in a large skillet over medium heat. Add the sea bass and cook for 2 minutes on each side, until medium-rare. Remove the fish from the pan and add the shrimp, cooking for 2 to 3 minutes until pink and opaque throughout. Then add the cooked bass and shrimp to the soup with the other seafood just before serving to heat through.

ROUILLE

Rouille (rü-é) is a French mayonnaiselike condiment made from moistened bread blended with herbs, garlic, and oil. It can be prepared a day in advance and kept covered in the refrigerator. Remove from the refrigerator and allow to return to room temperature, then whisk until smooth. It can also be used as a dip for crudités.

1 small sourdough roll	2 teaspoons fresh lemon juice
1 tablespoon Champagne vinegar (available at specialty stores; white wine vinegar may be substituted)	2 tablespoons plus 1 teaspoon fish stock (when using for fish soup) or chicken stock (for crudités dip)
2 garlic cloves, crushed	1 large egg yolk (see box, page 57)
¼ teaspoon salt, plus more to taste	1 cup vegetable oil
Pinch of saffron	½ cup extra-virgin olive oil

Remove the soft inside of the roll and discard the crust. Moisten the bread with the vinegar in a small bowl. Using the back of a spoon or a mortar and pestle, mash the bread, garlic, and salt to a paste. Mash in the saffron, lemon juice, stock, and egg yolk, blending in each ingredient separately. Transfer the mixture to a medium bowl. Pouring small amounts at a time, whisk in the vegetable oil, then the olive oil to make a smooth, mayonnaiselike mixture. The oils can also be added to the mixture in a food processor through the feed tube with the motor running. Correct the seasoning with salt. Cover and refrigerate until needed.

MAKES ABOUT 1½ CUPS

PASTA AL CEPPO WITH WILD MUSHROOMS AND DUCK CONFIT

Pasta al ceppo is a tube pasta shaped like a cinnamon stick, but any thin tubular pasta, such as penne or ziti, can be used. The dried mushrooms are optional, but they do add a rich woodsiness to the sauce. All of the components of this dish can be prepared one or two hours before serving and then reheated.

4 tablespoons extra-virgin olive oil, or more as needed

¾ pound domestic button mushrooms, cleaned and sliced

Salt and freshly ground pepper to taste

½ pound mixed wild mushrooms (such as shiitake and chanterelle), cleaned and sliced (see box, pages 36–37)

½ pound (1 cup packed) shredded duck confit (see Note)

¼ pound (2 medium) leeks, white part only, washed and sliced thinly crosswise

¼ cup thinly sliced shallots

½ cup port wine

1 cup duck stock (see Note; chicken stock may be substituted)

Pinch of finely chopped fresh rosemary

Pinch of finely chopped fresh thyme

1 tablespoon chopped dried porcini mushrooms (optional)

¾ pound pasta al ceppo or other dried tubular pasta

2 tablespoons balsamic vinegar (see box, page 64)

To prepare the mushrooms, heat 1 tablespoon of the olive oil over medium-high heat in a large skillet. Add the button mushrooms and sauté until lightly brown on both sides, about 4 minutes. Season with salt and pepper. Transfer to a large bowl with a slotted spoon. Add the wild mushrooms, adding more oil to the pan if needed, season with salt and pepper, and cook until lightly browned on both sides, about 4 minutes. Gently toss with the button mushrooms. Fold in the confit and set aside.

To prepare the sauce, clean the skillet and heat 1 tablespoon of the olive oil over medium-low heat. Add the leeks and shallots and cook until just softened, 2 to 4 minutes; do not let brown. Add the port to deglaze the pan. Raise the heat to medium-high and cook until the sauce has reduced by half, about 10 minutes. Add the stock, rosemary, thyme, and porcini, if using, and continue to cook until the sauce thickens slightly, about 10 minutes. Season with salt and pepper and set aside.

While the sauce is cooking, cook the pasta in a large pot of salted boiling water over high heat until *al dente,* following package instructions. Drain in a colander, rinse with cold water, and let drain completely. In a large skillet or wok, heat the remaining 2 tablespoons of olive oil over medium heat. Cook the pasta in batches, sautéing until lightly brown and crisp, 3 to 4 minutes. Using a slotted spoon, remove the pasta to a clean serving bowl. Continue with the remaining pasta, adding as little oil as necessary.

Just before serving, combine the sauce and the mushroom mixture in a large saucepan over low heat. Add the pasta and stir to heat through. Sprinkle in the balsamic vinegar to add sweetness and sharpness. Correct the seasoning with salt and pepper. Divide the pasta evenly among 4 plates and top with even amounts of the mushrooms and sauce. Serve immediately.

SERVES *4*

N O T E : If duck confit (see box, page 239) and duck stock are unavailable at your specialty food shop, try D'Artagnan, a mail-order source for duck products, 399–419 St. Paul Ave., Jersey City, New Jersey 07306; phone 1-800-DARTAGN or (201) 792-0748.

CHESS TARTLETS

Chess pie, a Southern tradition, is a favorite of homemakers because it requires only the simplest of ingredients for both the crust and the filling. Here, Nancy and Mark dress it up with baked pears and warm cream accompanying these individual chess pie tartlets.

It is best to use medium-firm, ripe pears that will maintain their shape when cooked, such as Bosc pears.

DOUGH

½ cup (1 stick) unsalted butter, softened

3 ounces cream cheese, softened

1 cup all-purpose flour

FILLING

1 cup (2 sticks) unsalted butter, softened

2 cups sugar

8 large egg yolks

4 teaspoons vanilla extract

1 tablespoon apple cider vinegar

2 tablespoons all-purpose flour

1 tablespoon cornmeal

1 cup water

GARNISH

1 firm, ripe pear, such as Bosc

½ vanilla bean

2 tablespoons (¼ stick) unsalted butter

½ cup heavy cream

With an electric mixer cream the butter in a mixing bowl until smooth and fluffy. Add the cream cheese and mix until incorporated. Add the flour and mix until blended. Wrap the dough in plastic wrap and chill for 30 minutes.

Preheat the oven to 350° F. Lightly butter four 4-inch tartlet shells with removable bottoms.

While the dough is chilling, make the filling. Cream the butter and sugar together in a large bowl with an electric mixer until fluffy. Add the egg yolks, vanilla, vinegar, flour, and cornmeal and mix with a wooden spoon until almost incorporated; do not overmix. Then add the water and stir just until blended. The filling should resemble watery ricotta cheese. Set aside until ready to use.

Roll out the dough on a lightly floured surface to a ¼-inch thickness and cut out two 6-inch circles, using a plate as a guide. Gather up the remaining dough, reroll it to a ¼-inch thickness and cut out two more 6-inch circles. Line each tartlet shell with a dough circle, leaving an overhang of 1 inch all around. Ladle the filling into each lined shell, filling them three-quarters full. Roughly fold over the dough to partially cover the filling, and bake for 20 to 25 minutes, until the dough is golden brown and the top is crispy. Place on a wire rack to cool. Raise the oven temperature to 400° F. while preparing the garnish.

Peel and cut the pear lengthwise into quarters, leaving the stem intact. Remove the core and seeds. Cut the vanilla bean in half lengthwise and scrape the seeds into a small ovenproof skillet with the butter. Melt the butter over medium heat, without letting it brown. Add the pear and quickly sauté for about 1 minute, stirring occasionally; do not let it brown. Transfer the skillet to the hot oven and bake until the pear is tender, 10 to 15 minutes, depending on the ripeness of the pear.

Just before serving, heat the cream in a small saucepan over medium-high heat to just below a simmer. Remove the sides from each tart pan, place each tartlet on a dessert plate, and slide the bottom of the pan out from underneath. Pour enough warm cream around the tartlets to cover the plates and garnish each with one section of the pear. Serve immediately so a skin does not form on the cream.

SERVES 4

Pears

How often does one bite into a pear, only to be disappointed by its grainy and mushy texture, or underripe crunch? Both the beauty of and the problem with pears is that they ripen after they have been picked. Picking underripe pears prevents them from bruising or turning rotten before they get to the market. However, ripe pears may be hard to find in the store the day you need them. Furthermore, different varieties take different amounts of time to ripen to melt-in-your mouth texture, making it difficult to capture a pear at its peak. Tree-ripened pears are mealy and good for neither cooking nor eating. The best strategy is to buy pears unripened and leave them in a bowl on the counter, checking them daily until they give a little when pressed and the stem moves easily.

There are more than five thousand pear varieties ranging from ambrosial and sweet to tart or spicy. Anjou, Bartlett, and Bosc pears are all good for cooking as well as eating as they hold their shape nicely. However, for Chess Pie Tartlets, where the pears are not cooked for a long time, Nancy and Mark strongly recommend using the Bosc variety. Unfortunately, only a dozen or so varieties are regularly available in this country. Among them are:

ANJOU, a sweet medium-firm winter pear, plump and egg-shaped with a light green skin. It can take up to two weeks to ripen and it is the best pear for cooking.

BARTLETT, a sweet, "musky"-flavored late summer–fall pear with a yellow-green skin with hues of red.

BOSC, a golden brown "pear-shaped" pear available from autumn through the spring, with a sweet-tart flavor and firm, dry flesh that holds its shape when cooked.

COMICE, a large pear with a delectably sweet, fruity, winey, buttery, and tender flesh, and maybe the best eating pear of all—but not ideal for baking. Look for this pale green to yellow pear with touches of red in the fall.

SECKEL, a tiny, russet pear available in the late summer–fall, with a spicy-sweet essence and crisp, slightly gritty texture. It is better for baking than eating.

SUSAN SPICER

A Garden-Inspired Menu

Susan Spicer has distinct memories of the first dish she ever prepared: a rolled-up pancake filled with grape jelly, created when she was ten years old for her six brothers and sisters while they watched cartoons. With her father in the navy, most of her childhood was spent living on bases in Holland, Florida, and Rhode Island. Her mother, who was born in Copenhagen, Denmark, and grew up in South America, did most of the cooking, preparing lots of Indonesian recipes (which she learned to make in Holland). These childhood experiences, and later her own extensive traveling, contribute to the eclectic tastes and flavor combinations with which Susan is constantly experimenting.

The family moved to New Orleans in 1960, when Susan was seven years old. After high school, Susan sent away for a brochure from the Culinary Institute of America, but then traveled around working as a secretary and cocktail waitress until she moved back to New Orleans several years later, where she got into the printing business. Susan began cooking "for fun" with a good friend who started her own catering company, and she started taking cooking classes. "I learned how to braise and sauté there—technique, not recipes, was the focus of the classes."

MENU

Linguine with Garden Vegetables and Herbs

Grilled Pork Loin with Lime Pickle

Herbed Couscous

Glazed Carrots and Turnips

Alice's Rice Pudding

After some valuable apprenticeships, she returned to New Orleans to become the executive chef at Savoir Faire, a small bistro in the St. Charles Hotel. But in 1985, the urge to travel hit again and she toured California and Europe extensively for a year before opening the Bistro at Maison de

Ville in New Orleans, where she was the chef for four years. In the spring of 1990, Susan opened Bayona in a beautiful two hundred-year-old Creole cottage in the French Quarter.

"Relaxing in my garden at home and cooking for a few friends is a great way to spend a Sunday," says Susan. "I like to grow easy things and fortunately my neighbor Rocco grows beautiful garlic and shares it with me. I also have nasturtiums, which are beautiful, multicolored edible flowers with peppery leaves that grow well in bad soil and smell divine. Dinner at my house is super casual—just me and some friends. We fire up the grill and everyone lends a hand." The tranquil atmosphere is enhanced no doubt by the garden with its flowers on the fruit trees that surround her home.

The eggplant, red bell peppers, tomatoes, basil, arugula, and nasturtium flowers that grow in Susan's garden are brought in to be added to pasta, which she always has in her pantry. "Arugula comes up early in New Orleans but also bolts quickly owing to the heat—I never get enough of it." Condiments such as pickles and relishes are her preferences over sauces for home food. She prepares them ahead of time, but reminds us that "the home cook can always buy things at the store and embellish or personalize them with a little extra effort." Lime pickle accompanies the grilled pork loin and blends hot, salty, sour, and tart flavors. The sweet earthy flavors of the glazed carrots and turnips and the simplicity of the couscous are the perfect balance for the brighter tastes of the main course. Susan's mother is the proud creator of the Danish-influenced dessert—Alice's Rice Pudding. "The nutty taste of the almonds and the tartness of the berries is an addicting flavor combination." Susan prefers a red Zinfandel, particularly the 1990 Ridge Lytton Springs Zinfandel, to be served throughout the meal, but she also recommends a Gewürztraminer or beer.

Linguine with Garden Vegetables and Herbs

This dish is so versatile, as the herbs and spices will complement just about any veggies you have on hand or in your garden. If you are drinking wine, Susan says, "a splash or two in the pan will not hurt" the sautéing vegetables.

4 tablespoons extra-virgin olive oil

2 Japanese eggplants (see box, page 310), or 1 small regular eggplant, diced (peeled or unpeeled, as you like)

1 red bell pepper, stemmed, seeded, and diced

2 tomatoes, peeled (see box, page 311), seeded, and diced

2 teaspoons chopped garlic

2 tablespoons chopped fresh basil

1 handful arugula (more or less to taste), washed, dried, and stems trimmed

Salt and freshly ground pepper to taste

Dried red pepper flakes to taste

½ pound linguine

½ cup crumbled feta cheese

Nasturtium blossoms, for garnish (optional; see Note)

Bring a large pot of water to a boil over high heat for the pasta. In a large skillet (preferably nonstick) over medium heat, heat 2 tablespoons of the olive oil and add the eggplants, tossing frequently until browned, about 5 minutes. Add 1 more tablespoon of oil, then add the pepper and cook for 2 minutes. Add the diced tomatoes and garlic and stir. Cook until the eggplant is tender, about 5 more minutes. This process of sautéing the vegetables should take only 10 to 15 minutes total. When the vegetables are finished cooking, toss in the basil and arugula, and season with salt and pepper and red pepper flakes.

Cook the pasta according to package instructions until *al dente,* drain, and toss in a large, warm bowl with the remaining 1 tablespoon of oil and a little salt and pepper. Toss the vegetables with the pasta and divide among 4 plates. Top each serving with the feta cheese and nasturtium petals, if desired.

SERVES 4

NOTE: Nasturtium blossoms, which come in vibrant shades of orange, red, yellow, and reddish brown, are great mixed in with salad greens and used as a garnish for savory dishes and desserts. Pesticide-free nasturtium blossoms are edible.

GRILLED PORK LOIN WITH LIME PICKLE

This dish is a perfect example of how Susan whips together an intriguing dish in a short amount of time using homemade condiments from her pantry. A hot, tangy, and spicy relish called a lime pickle enlivens the pork dish. Susan shares her home recipe with us, but lime pickle is also available in jars at selected markets.

2 tablespoons peanut oil

2 tablespoons *ketjap manis* (available at specialty and Asian markets, see Note)

1 teaspoon *sambal oelek* (Indonesian chili paste, available at specialty and Asian markets)

½ teaspoon minced garlic

½ teaspoon minced fresh ginger

1 pound boneless pork loin, or two 8-ounce pork tenderloins

Lime Pickle (recipe follows, or buy Patak brand, available at Asian markets or specialty food stores)

Preheat the grill or broiler. Whisk together the oil, *ketjap manis, sambal oelek,* garlic, and ginger. Turn the pork in the marinade and set aside for 30 minutes at room temperature. (When marinating the pork for longer than 30 minutes, do so in the refrigerator.)

Broil or grill the pork until it is slightly crusty but still juicy on the inside, about 5 minutes per side for the tenderloins and 7 to 8 minutes per side for a whole loin. The meat should be opaque throughout, but not dry. Cut into 4 portions and place on 4 plates with the Lime Pickle.

SERVES *4*

NOTE: *Ketjap manis* is a sweet, slightly syrupy Indonesian soy sauce available in most Asian markets. If you are unable to find any *ketjap manis,* improvise by whisking together 2 teaspoons molasses or brown sugar and 2 tablespoons soy sauce.

Japanese Eggplants

Japanese eggplants are smaller and slimmer than regular eggplants, and are easy to grow in a backyard garden. Their flavor is sweeter than larger Western or Italian eggplants, and they do not require any salting to leech out the bitterness (see box, page 336).

LIME PICKLE

This recipe makes more than enough for this dish. Store the extra, refrigerated, in an airtight jar for up to eight weeks and serve it with any type of curry dish, along with a fruity chutney for balance.

1 cup preserved limes (see Note)

¼ cup Creole mustard (grainy mustard with horseradish)

1 tablespoon *sambal oelek* (Indonesian chili paste, available at specialty and Asian markets)

2 tablespoons fresh lime juice

½ cup peanut oil

2–3 tablespoons water

Rinse the salt well from the preserved limes, pat dry, and chop roughly. Place in a food processor and pulse. Add the mustard, *sambal oelek,* and lime juice. Pulse again. With the motor running, slowly add the peanut oil. Add the water gradually until the mixture is completely emulsified into a chunky paste. Store, covered, in the refrigerator until ready to use.

MAKES ABOUT 1½ CUPS

NOTE: Preserved limes are similar to Moroccan salted lemons. They can be minced and added to various condiments (such as Susan's Lime Pickle), sauces, salsas, and salads.

To preserve limes at home, quarter several limes lengthwise (you will need three or four for the Lime Pickle recipe, but you should make more while you are at it to use in other dishes) and layer with kosher salt and fresh lime juice in an airtight jar. Cover and leave at room temperature for seven to ten days, shaking once a day. The limes are ready when the rind feels soft and juicy. Refrigerate until ready to use. Normally the pulp is scooped out and only the rind is used, but for the Lime Pickle recipe, use the whole thing.

Peeling Tomatoes

To peel a tomato, make a very shallow X just through the skin on the bottom. Drop the tomato into boiling water for 15 seconds, then remove with a slotted spoon to a bowl of ice water to stop the cooking process. When cool enough to handle, core the tomato, peel off the skin, and proceed as directed.

Herbed Couscous

Couscous, a miniature semolina pasta, is a Moroccan staple; it can be served with meat or vegetable stews for a main dish, used in salads, sweetened and served with dried fruits for desserts, or topped with warm milk for breakfast.

Couscous has worked its way into American cooking, mostly in salads and as a side dish, as it is served here. Select a mixture of favorite fresh herbs to liven it up.

1 cup couscous

1 cup boiling water, or more as needed

2 tablespoons extra-virgin olive oil

3 scallions, thinly sliced

4 tablespoons mixed fresh herbs, such as mint, parsley, cilantro, and basil

Juice of 1 lemon

Salt and freshly ground pepper to taste

Place the couscous in a large bowl. Pour the boiling water over the couscous, stir once, and cover the bowl. Set aside for 5 to 10 minutes, until all the water is absorbed and the couscous is soft and fluffy. Add a little more boiling water if the couscous is too dry. Stir again, breaking up any lumps. Stir in the olive oil, scallions, herbs, and lemon juice. Season with salt and pepper. Serve warm, at room temperature, or chilled.

Serves 4

Glazed Carrots and Turnips

All the work in making this dish is in the peeling and chopping, which can be done in advance.

2 carrots, peeled and diced

2 turnips, peeled and diced

¼ cup water

1 tablespoon unsalted butter

½ teaspoon ground cumin

2 teaspoons molasses

Salt and freshly ground pepper to taste

Place the carrots, turnips, water, butter, cumin, molasses, and salt and pepper in a medium saucepan. Bring to a boil over high heat, cover, reduce the heat to medium-low, and simmer for 5 to 10 minutes, until the vegetables are tender and glossy, and the water is absorbed.

Serves 4

ALICE'S RICE PUDDING

This recipe is from Susan's Danish mother and it often appears on the family table during the holidays. Rice flavored with almonds and sherry is combined with whipped cream and topped with a cherry–red wine sauce. It is light and fresh tasting, unlike a baked, custard-type rice pudding.

You will need to start preparing this dessert several hours (and up to one day) in advance in order to chill the cooked rice before folding in the cream.

⅜ cup white or basmati rice

2 cups milk

¼ cup sliced almonds

¼ cup sugar

¼ teaspoon almond extract

3 tablespoons sherry

1 cup heavy cream, chilled

2 ounces dried, tart cherries

¼ cup Pinot Noir wine

¼ cup water

1 tablespoon sugar or currant jelly

Preheat the oven to 350° F. In a small saucepan, cook the rice and milk together over medium heat for 30 to 40 minutes, uncovered, stirring occasionally, until the rice is tender and the milk is absorbed. While the rice is cooking, toast the sliced almonds on a baking sheet in the oven for about 5 minutes, until lightly browned, shaking the almonds occasionally to toast evenly. Watch carefully so the almonds do not burn.

When the rice is cooked, stir in the sugar, almond extract, toasted almonds, and sherry. Transfer to a large bowl, cover, and chill. (This can be prepared up to one day in advance.) When the rice mixture is cold, whip the cream in a large bowl to stiff, but not dry, peaks and fold into the rice. Refrigerate for up to 3 hours until ready to serve.

Place the cherries in a small saucepan with the Pinot Noir, water, and sugar or currant jelly. Bring to a boil over medium-high heat, reduce the heat to medium-low, and simmer until the cherries are tender and the juice is syrupy, about 10 minutes. The cherries can be served warm, at room temperature, or cold.

To serve, spoon equal amounts of the rice pudding into 4 balloon wine glasses and spoon equal amounts of the cherry–red wine sauce over each serving.

SERVES 4 GENEROUSLY

ALLEN SUSSER

An Afternoon at the Beach

Growing up in Brooklyn in a kosher home, Allen Susser had dinner with his family every night. The preparation of the meal involved the whole family, including his grandmother and his aunt. Allen says, "cooking and eating together is healthy for the family—I probably missed dinner at home no more than three days a year." When he was ten years old, Allen joined the Boy Scouts and discovered the joy of cooking for the masses: "I had everything I needed—food, knives, and fire."

After spending several summers cooking hot dogs and hamburgers at Rockaway Playland, a local amusement park, and loving it, Allen decided to expand his culinary horizons and attended New York City Technical College's Restaurant and Management School. Later, he attended Florida International University in Miami and received a degree in hospitality.

But of all Allen's learning experiences he describes his time spent working in Paris at the Bristol Hotel in 1976 with the greatest enthusiasm. "To see the life of food in Paris is amazing. I was working a split shift, and in the afternoons, I'd watch the Parisians shop at the local markets." He was particularly impressed with the street vendors and how specialized they were. He remembers: "There

MENU

Invisible Gin Cocktail

◆

Shrimp Escabeche with Lime Mojo

◆

*Watermelon and Sweet Onion Salad with
Lemongrass, Cinnamon, and Cilantro*

◆

Tamarind and Chili Barbecued Lamb Chops

◆

Mango Cobbler

was food everywhere—you'd see the rabbit guy, the fish guy, the bread guy. . . ." Dining in both the top-notch restaurants of Paris as well as the corner bistros, Allen absorbed it all. Working in Paris and later at Le Cirque back in New York, Allen learned about flavor, color, texture, and balance. And when he returned to Florida, he learned to fully respect his environment—the land, the seas, and the sun—and adjusted his cooking techniques accordingly.

Drawn to Miami to take advantage of the abundant natural resources, Allen literally tested the waters at the Turnberry Isle Resort. "When people come to Florida, they expect seafood. There is water all around you and there is a real energy to it." Allen cooked whatever game fish happened to be caught that day—fish like cobia, wahoo, parrot fish, and pompano. In addition to fresh fish, Miami offers a great variety of tropical fruits like guava, mango, star fruit, and soursop, and Allen uses all of them. Thanks to his passion for food and his openness to other cultures, Allen continues to develop his "New World Cuisine" at Chef Allen's, his restaurant, which takes full advantage of the freshest foods available and has influences of the Caribbean, South America, and Latin America.

The varied foods and textures in this menu reflect Allen's eclectic cuisine. For example, he combines fresh shrimp from the Florida waters with tropical and Latin seasonings in his Shrimp Escabeche. This dish can be prepared up to two days in advance, allowing the flavors to develop each day and making the day of the picnic a breeze. In the Watermelon and Sweet Onion Salad,  Allen mixes yellow and red watermelon for a visually stimulating dish since, he claims, "people eat with their eyes as well as their mouths." The Sussers particularly enjoy grilling on the beach. The Tamarind and Chili Barbecued Lamb Chops cook up quickly on the grill, and they are a special favorite of Deanna, Allen's daughter. Allen rounds out this meal with one of his favorite desserts, a fresh, summery Mango Cobbler. "So many refreshing and pronounced flavors of the tropics are present in this menu," he says, and it sets the stage for the perfect Sunday afternoon at the beach, relaxing by the ocean, with his wife and daughter.

INVISIBLE GIN COCKTAIL

This is called "invisible" because you can sip this drink without ever knowing there is gin in it. Teetotalers beware!

24 ice cubes

3 cups dry gin

4½ cups fresh grapefruit juice

2 tablespoons fresh lemon juice

6 dashes Angostura bitters

6 tablespoons apricot brandy

6 fresh mint sprigs, for garnish

Put the ice cubes in a shaker. Add the gin, grapefruit juice, lemon juice, bitters, and apricot brandy. Stir. Pour into 6 highball glasses, distributing the liquid and ice evenly, and garnish with fresh mint.

SERVES 6

SHRIMP ESCABECHE WITH LIME MOJO

An escabeche (es-keh-behsh) is a Spanish method of seasoning fish or seafood with a spicy marinade, such as a mojo (see box, page 319), after it has been cooked. The marinade also preserves the food.

This dish can be served hot off the stove, chilled as escabeche is traditionally, or at room temperature as Allen prefers. Whichever way it is eaten, it is deliciously tangy.

2 tablespoons extra-virgin olive oil

12 large shrimp, peeled and deveined

1 teaspoon sea salt

Pinch of ground allspice

½ teaspoon cayenne pepper

½ cup sliced yellow onion

3 tablespoons fresh lime juice

3 large garlic cloves

4 tablespoons fresh orange juice

2 tablespoons chopped scallion

2 tablespoons chopped fresh cilantro

Orange slices, for garnish (optional)

In a large skillet, heat 1 tablespoon of the olive oil over medium-high heat. Add the shrimp and sauté for 1 minute. Season with the sea salt, allspice, and cayenne. Add the onion and continue to cook for another minute, or until the shrimp are pink and opaque throughout. Stir in 1 tablespoon of the lime juice and remove from the heat. Set aside and prepare the *mojo* in the meantime.

In a small saucepan, warm the remaining tablespoon of olive oil over low heat. Add the garlic and let steep for 5 minutes. Add the remaining 2 tablespoons of lime juice, the orange juice, scallion, and cilantro. Remove from the heat and pour the *mojo* over the shrimp. Serve this dish hot, at room temperature, or chilled. Place 2 shrimp on each plate and garnish with fresh orange slices, if desired.

SERVES 6

WATERMELON AND SWEET ONION SALAD WITH LEMONGRASS, CINNAMON, AND CILANTRO

The dazzling summer salad engages all of the senses, with tantalizing flavors and colors. Be sure to use watermelons that are heavy, unblemished, and have a brightly colored flesh, not dry or grainy. Whole watermelons should be kept in the refrigerator or, if too large, stored in a cool, dry place for no more than a week. Store cut watermelon, tightly wrapped, in the refrigerator and eat within one or two days. Watermelons are in season from May to September, and sweet onions are available from May through June.

2 cups cubed yellow watermelon

2 cups cubed red watermelon

1 large Vidalia or other sweet onion, thinly sliced

1 tablespoon grated fresh ginger

2 tablespoons honey

¼ cup rice vinegar

⅓ cup Oriental sesame oil

2 tablespoons chopped fresh lemongrass (available at Asian markets and specialty stores)

½ teaspoon ground cinnamon

3 tablespoons chopped fresh cilantro

½ teaspoon chopped and seeded fresh Thai chili pepper, or other spicy red chili pepper

1 tablespoon salt

Combine the watermelon and onion in a medium bowl. In a small bowl, whisk together the ginger, honey, vinegar, oil, lemongrass, cinnamon, and cilantro. Season with the Thai chili and salt. Pour the vinaigrette over the watermelon and onion and toss.

SERVES 6

Mojo

Allen Susser encourages cooks to be adventurous with tropical fruits and vegetables. One way to experiment is by blending different citrus juices with garlic, olive oil, and herbs to make your own *mojo,* which is basically a fruit and oil marinade. Allen usually makes his with sour oranges, but a combination of lime and orange juice can be substituted. In addition to the Shrimp Escabeche, the *mojo* can be used as a dip for lobster or steamed clams. Add a little cumin and fresh oregano for extra pizzazz.

TAMARIND AND CHILI BARBECUED LAMB CHOPS

Sweet, sour, and spicy! One bite of these lamb chops and you will understand what Allen's New World Cuisine is all about. He combines the tropical tamarind with mango, jalapeño, and other seasonings for an unusual and complex flavor. The seed pod of the tamarind tree contains a sour pulp, which is used as a tart flavoring. For this dish, it is easiest to buy the jarred pulp.

3 tablespoons tamarind pulp (available in Asian, Indian, and specialty food markets; see Note)

1 large mango, peeled, pitted, and chopped

1 medium onion, diced

1 teaspoon chopped garlic

1 teaspoon grated fresh ginger

¼ teaspoon ground allspice

½ cup dry red wine

1 cup fresh orange juice

4 tablespoons molasses

1 small jalapeño pepper, seeded and chopped (see box, page 176)

2 tablespoons red wine vinegar

12 lamb chops, about 3 ounces each

1 teaspoon salt

½ teaspoon freshly ground pepper

Combine the tamarind, mango, onion, garlic, ginger, allspice, wine, orange juice, molasses, and jalapeño in a saucepan. Bring the mixture to a boil over medium-high heat, reduce the heat to medium-low, and simmer uncovered for 30 minutes. Stir in the vinegar and cook for 5 more minutes. Strain through a fine sieve into a bowl, pressing the solids against the mesh to extract the most liquid and flavor, and set aside. Discard the solids.

Preheat the grill or broiler to high heat. Season the lamb chops with salt and pepper. Grill the lamb chops; when they become charred on the underside, flip them over and char the other side. If you are using a broiler, place the broiler tray as close to the heat as possible and char on each side. Brush the lamb on both sides with the tamarind sauce. Reduce the heat or move the chops to the outer edges of the grill where the heat is less intense, or, if broiling, lower the broiler tray. Continue to barbecue the lamb chops for another 5 to 8 minutes, turning them halfway through the cooking time, until they are cooked as desired.

SERVES 6

NOTE: If tamarind pulp is unavailable, substitute a mixture of 2 parts molasses and 1 part lime juice.

MANGO COBBLER

Fresh mangoes need no enhancements and are completely delicious eaten on their own, but cobbler made with this fruit never tasted better. So resist the temptation to nibble on the fresh mango and try this dessert!

4 large ripe mangoes, peeled, pitted, and sliced

1 teaspoon grated fresh ginger

1 teaspoon ground cinnamon

½ cup fresh orange juice

1 cup all-purpose flour

1 tablespoon sugar

¼ teaspoon salt

1½ teaspoons baking powder

3 tablespoons unsalted butter, softened

½ cup milk

Preheat the oven to 350°F. In an 8-inch round ovenproof ceramic dish, combine the mangoes, ginger, cinnamon, and orange juice. In a medium bowl, mix the flour, sugar, salt, and baking powder. Add the butter and cut in until the mixture becomes a sandy consistency. Mix in the milk just until smooth. Dollop this topping on the mango mixture, covering most of the top. Bake for 25 minutes or until the top is golden brown.

SERVES 6

Buying, Storing, and Cutting Mango

Mangoes are a tropical fruit with a succulent neon yellow or orange flesh that is both sweet and tart. Most agree that this exotic fruit is best when eaten alone, but mangoes are an exciting addition to salads, salsas, and desserts. This round, oval, or kidney-shaped fruit with green skin is available at most supermarkets from May to September. Mangoes are usually firm and underripe when sold, but they will ripen in three to four days at room temperature in a paper bag. As the fruit ripens, the skin develops hues of gold or red and fragrant tropical scent, while the flesh gives a little when gently squeezed. Ripe mangoes should be kept in a plastic bag and refrigerated, if not eaten immediately.

In the center of the mango is a flat, oval-shaped pit that extends its length and makes it difficult to cut. The best cutting method is to first make an incision in the midsection of the fruit to find out which way the pit lies. Then cut the unpeeled mango lengthwise on either side of the pit. Slice each half (without cutting the skin) into cubes of the appropriate size. Then, cut the cubes along the peel.

TOMMY TANG

Dinner with Aisha and Chyna

Tommy Tang's story began in Bangkok in 1948, when he was born the eldest son in a family of ten children. His father operated a small sidewalk cafe and was well known in the community for pickling fruits and vegetables. When he was eleven years old, Tommy dropped out of school to find a job and contribute to his family's income. He worked as a welder in an icebox factory, as a construction worker, and as a tennis teacher, boxer, busboy, and drummer, all the while maintaining his childhood dream of moving to the United States and becoming a music producer. Surrounded by Americans while working at various hotel jobs in Thailand, Tommy acquired basic English skills and made the decision to move to the United States.

Arriving in California, Tommy earned a degree in auto mechanics and got a job in that field to make ends meet. Shortly thereafter, Tommy moved to Los Angeles, still determined to make it as a producer. While he was managing several rock-and-roll bands, friends asked Tommy for help revamping a little-known Thai restaurant. With no formal training or restaurant experience, Tommy redesigned the menu, redecorated the restaurant, and trained the kitchen staff. In months the clientele broadened to include Americans and Asians alike, and business at the Chandara restaurant was booming.

MENU

Thai Crab Cakes with
Santa Fe Chili–Yogurt Dipping Sauce

◆

Tomato Fettuccine with
Holy Basil Sauce

◆

Neon Fruit

Tommy and his cooking soon attracted a loyal following of celebrities to the restaurant—most of them in the music and film industry. His most-valued "regular," however, was Sandi, a young woman from Pittsburgh who was in search of the perfect Thai meal. Tommy wooed Sandi with a custom-made, heart-shaped order of his famous Thai Toast. As a tribute to the woman who has since become his wife and business partner, the popular appetizer has been served in the shape of a heart ever since. In September 1982, the couple opened Tommy Tang's Modern Thai Cuisine and Sushi on Melrose Avenue in West Hollywood. The success of the restaurant and growing popularity of Thai food, inspired Tommy to package his seasonings and sauces to help people re-create Thai food at home. His products are sold in specialty stores nationwide.

No special occasion is needed for Tommy to make dinner at home for Sandi and his little girls, Aisha and Chyna. "When time permits I choose a healthy dish, one in which I can use the helping hands of my daughters. This entire menu was inspired by them, as are many of the ideas for my restaurants." Crab cakes really caught the imagination of the girls. "Maybe it was the word *cake*," says Tommy, "or perhaps it was the tiny bits the girls helped form into patties." Whatever the reason, the girls love these seared bites with Santa Fe Chili–Yogurt Dipping Sauce that Tommy offers as a special at his restaurants. Tommy has also found that pasta is always a winner with the kids, so he tosses together a tomato fettuccine dish. Tommy lets the girls choose the types of berries for the Neon Fruit, and wield the squeeze bottles to squirt their own designs on the plate, making this dessert at least as fun to make as it is to eat.

Tommy tells us that Aisha's favorite food (aside from modern Thai, of course) has been sushi since she was two years old. He explains, "It is important to help teach them an appreciation of food as well as the art of cooking." Tommy would not dream of preparing "kiddie foods" for his girls, and, in fact, serves versions of these dishes in his newest restaurant, Tommy Tang's, in Pasadena. "I hope they will grow up to be big girls who can cook and have a wonderful sense of and respect for all kinds of cuisine."

THAI CRAB CAKES WITH SANTA FE CHILI–YOGURT DIPPING SAUCE

Tommy suggests serving these with a cool Thai brew, such as Amarit beer or Singha ale. The crab mixture can be made up to one day in advance.

Sriracha chili peppers are grown in northern Thailand, and the sauce is available at Asian markets, or Tommy Tang's brand is sold at specialty shops and in selected supermarkets.

¼ pound fresh medium shrimp

¼ pound fresh crab meat, preferably Dungeness or blue crab, picked over

¼ cup finely diced fresh mushrooms

¼ cup finely diced yellow onion

2 tablespoons minced scallion

2 tablespoons finely diced red bell pepper

2 tablespoons chopped bamboo shoots

1 tablespoon finely chopped fresh cilantro

1 large egg white

1 tablespoon sriracha chili sauce or Tabasco sauce

2 teaspoons All-Purpose Seasoning (recipe follows) or Tommy Tang's Salt-Free Seasoning (available at specialty stores and some supermarkets)

1 tablespoon fish sauce (available at Asian and specialty food markets)

1 tablespoon fresh lemon juice

3 tablespoons extra-virgin olive oil or vegetable oil

½ cup dried bread crumbs

Santa Fe Chili–Yogurt Dipping Sauce (recipe follows)

Shredded carrots, cilantro sprigs, black sesame seeds, for garnish (optional)

Place the shrimp in a food processor and process until finely minced. In a large mixing bowl, thoroughly combine the crab meat, shrimp, mushrooms, onion, scallion, red bell pepper, bamboo shoots, cilantro, egg white, chili sauce, seasoning, fish sauce, lemon juice, and 1 tablespoon of the olive oil. Separate the mixture into 8 portions. Using your hands, shape each portion into a ball and gently flatten into a ½-inch-thick disc. Dredge each crab cake in the bread crumbs to coat well.

Heat the remaining 2 tablespoons of oil in a large nonstick skillet over medium heat. Cook the crab cakes, in batches if necessary to avoid overcrowding, until dark brown on both sides, 6 minutes per side. Garnish with shredded carrots, cilantro sprigs, and black sesame seeds, if desired. Serve warm or at room temperature with the dipping sauce.

SERVES 4

Fish Sauce

In most Southeast Asian cooking, especially Thai and Vietnamese, fish sauce is used in place of salt or soy sauce, enhancing and rounding out the flavors of various dishes. It has a strong and somewhat unpleasant odor, but its taste is much more mellow than its scent. Try it instead of soy sauce the next time you make a stir-fry.

Fish sauce is produced by marinating anchovies in salt in wooden casks, resulting in a pungent liquid. Like the cream that rises to the top, the best fish sauce collects at the top of the barrel; this is pure fish sauce. The farther down the barrel, the more watered down the sauce is. For that reason, fish sauce ranges in price and quality.

Buy only Thai fish sauce, as it is preferable to other Southeast Asian varieties for its guaranteed quality. Also be sure to buy only smaller bottles marked Grade A. Tommy points out that the cheap, larger bottles of fish sauce (under $4 for 24 ounces) available in Asian markets, though labeled Grade A, often have been watered down. Go for the more expensive brand, as in this case price is definitely a reliable indicator of quality.

ALL-PURPOSE SEASONING

2 teaspoons minced garlic   1 teaspoon ground black pepper
1 teaspoon ground white pepper   1 teaspoon cayenne pepper

Combine all the ingredients in a small bowl. Store at room temperature, tightly covered, for up to 1 day.

MAKES ABOUT 1 1/2 TABLESPOONS

Santa Fe Chili–Yogurt Dipping Sauce

¾ cup plain low-fat yogurt

1 teaspoon ground Santa Fe chili pepper (available at Latin and specialty markets; cayenne pepper may be substituted)

1 tablespoon finely chopped fresh cilantro

Thoroughly mix the yogurt, chili pepper, and cilantro in a small mixing bowl, using a wire whisk. Store, covered, in the refrigerator until ready to use.

Makes ¾ cup

Tomato Fettuccine with Holy Basil Sauce

Tommy fuses Italian and Thai cuisines to create a complexly flavored and satisfying pasta dish. Tomato fettuccine is tossed in a fresh tomato purée infused with Thai seasonings such as serrano peppers, fish sauce, sweet black bean sauce, and Thai holy basil. Substitute plain pasta if tomato pasta is hard to find.

3 large tomatoes, peeled and seeded (see box, page 311) or 1 cup canned tomato purée

2 tablespoons plus ½ teaspoon chopped garlic

1 pound tomato fettuccine

½ cup extra-virgin olive oil

1½ cups diced onions

1 tablespoon chopped fresh seeded serrano pepper (see box, page 176)

½ cup diced tomato

2 tablespoons fish sauce (available at Asian and specialty markets)

2 tablespoons sweet black bean sauce (available at Asian and specialty markets)

1 teaspoon freshly ground pepper

1 cup chicken or vegetable stock

1 cup chopped holy basil (see box, page 328) or sweet basil

4 sprigs basil, for garnish

If you are using fresh tomatoes, purée the peeled tomatoes in a food processor or blender. Transfer the purée to a small saucepan with the ½ teaspoon of garlic over high heat and bring to a boil. Reduce the heat to low and simmer for 15 minutes. Remove from the heat and set aside until ready to use.

Bring a large pot of salted water to a boil over high heat. Add the fettuccine and cook until *al dente*. Drain.

Heat the olive oil in a large skillet over high heat. Add the remaining 2 tablespoons of garlic and stir until lightly browned. Add the onions, chili pepper, diced tomato, fish sauce, black bean sauce, and ground pepper and stir for 2 minutes. Add the tomato purée, stock, and holy basil. Bring the mixture to a boil and stir for 3 minutes. Add the cooked pasta and toss until well coated. Transfer the pasta to a large serving platter and garnish with the basil sprigs.

SERVES 4

Holy Basil

Holy basil is grown in some Asian countries, including India and Thailand. This is a different basil from Thai basil (see Tom Douglas's section, page 79). It is said that wealthy Thai students educated in India stole this basil, which was sacrificed to the gods by some Indians, to prepare their favorite Thai dishes while away from home. When Indian students inquired what this earthy and almost flowerlike herb was, the Thai students revealed that it was "holy basil." It has a darker leaf and a slightly more spicy and sharp flavor than sweet basil, but the latter may be substituted if necessary.

NEON FRUIT

Fresh mixed berries and melon drizzled with fresh fruit purée make a healthful and delicious dessert that is also very appealing to children. The fruit purée can be made one to three days in advance and kept in the refrigerator. Even better, purée the ripest of summer fruits and freeze for the winter months when berries and tropical fruits are hard to come by. Use whatever fruits look the best.

About 2 pints diced mixed fresh fruit (such as raspberries, strawberries, mango, papaya, or kiwi), washed or peeled

Sugar to taste (optional)

3 cups diced mixed fresh fruit (any berries, melon, mango, papaya, orange, grapefruit), washed or peeled

Shortbread cookies (optional)

Purée the 2 pints of fruit in a blender. Strain through a fine sieve to remove the seeds. Sugar may be added, depending on the sweetness of the berries. Pour the sauce into a clean squeeze bottle.

To serve, squirt the sauce on each plate to create a freehand design: just allow the sauce to flow by painting the plate with back and forth motions of the wrist. Artfully arrange equal amounts of the diced fruit mixture on the plate and, if desired, serve shortbread cookies on the side.

SERVES 4 GENEROUSLY

ELIZABETH TERRY

A Casual Al Fresco Lunch

Elizabeth Terry is the quintessential home cook. She had virtually no knowledge of or interest in cooking until she married at age twenty-four, when her husband gave her two cookbooks. Naive in the kitchen yet fearless, Elizabeth dove right in, beginning with the very first recipe in *The Gourmet Cooking School Cookbook* by Dione Lucas. She recalls the dish: "Filets de Sole Joinville—salmon, sole, and shrimp with three sauces. The recipe was five pages long, and it turned out great." Elizabeth cooked everything else in the book and kept on cooking, sharpening her skills at home. Today, with no formal training, she is recognized as a leader of "New Southern Cuisine."

In 1981, she opened her restaurant, Elizabeth on 37th, in the elegant surroundings of a turn-of-the-century mansion in Savannah, Georgia. "When we decided to move to Savannah, we looked at every funky, weird building until, there it was, this old white elephant." Elizabeth runs the back of the house and her husband, Michael, the front, also taking on the role of wine steward. The Terrys live with their two children on the second floor, above the restaurant. There

MENU

Mint Juleps

*Grilled Eggplant and
Herbed Goat Cheese Sandwiches*

Potato-Pepper Bread

*Tomato, Cucumber, and Onion Salad with
Garlic-Sesame Dressing*

Fettuccine with Zucchini, Peanuts, and Basil

Scottish Trifle

Elizabeth can usually be found cooking for her family in a separate kitchen, which she describes as "simple, but fully equipped with everything I need."

Fresh herbs such as Italian parsley, mint, chives, and basil bring her Grilled Eggplant and Herbed Goat Cheese Sandwiches to life. "Herbs wake up the palate, so I use them liberally." Elizabeth rises early when it is still relatively cool and works in the garden. "I do a bit of weeding or watering or tie up a drooping branch of pineapple sage. This inspires me to take some herbs inside for dinner."

She and her youngest daughter, Celeste, love preparing and eating homemade bread. "Before we opened the restaurant, I made bread all the time because the smell of baking bread is so romantic." Early in their marriage, when Elizabeth and Michael were living in Cambridge, they would often bake several loaves of bread together, run around the neighborhood ringing door bells, and drop off loaves to special friends and neighbors. The Terrys continued this tradition when they moved to Atlanta several years later, making friends quickly.

Whenever she can find the time, Elizabeth likes to entertain at her family's beach house. She mostly enjoys cooking creative sandwiches and pastas for Celeste and her friends on a Sunday afternoon. "When Alexis, our elder daughter, was home from college, we worked up this menu together for Celeste and her friends—simple preparation, high flavors, Italian overtones and casual presentation."

Elizabeth reminds us that sometimes we get caught up in the preparation of a meal and forget the social aspect of cooking. Asked who has inspired her, she replies, "I watched Julia Child faithfully and she always reinforced my approach to cooking, which is that cooking is fun, and that sharing food is important."

MINT JULEPS

Elizabeth tells us how Southerners love "sippin' drinks" like the Mint Julep: "They are potent, but you only drink one and they are so refreshing in the summer." A Mint Julep is the perfect drink to launch this summer supper. For an intensely minty punch, Elizabeth combines the mint and bourbon the night before.

12 4-inch mint sprigs
1½ cups Wild Turkey bourbon
6 tablespoons simple syrup (see box, below)

Finely crushed ice to fill 6 cocktail glasses or julep cups

Coarsely chop 6 sprigs of mint and place in a 16-ounce (or larger) glass container with a lid. Add the bourbon, shake well, and refrigerate for 12 hours or overnight to allow the flavors to combine.

Chill 6 cocktail glasses. Just before serving, add the syrup to the mint and bourbon and stir well. Pack the chilled glasses with the ice. Strain the bourbon mixture and divide among the glasses. Adorn with a mint sprig and serve.

SERVES 6

Simple Syrup

Simple syrup is the best "secret" ingredient for the bar. It eliminates the sugar granules in drinks to which you would add sugar directly, and provides a more concentrated flavor. It will keep in the refrigerator for weeks. It is also great for making fruit sorbets.

TO MAKE simple syrup, combine 2 cups sugar with 1 cup water in a medium saucepan and bring to a boil over high heat. Reduce the heat to medium-low, and simmer for 5 minutes. Cool and refrigerate in a tightly sealed container.

GRILLED EGGPLANT AND HERBED GOAT CHEESE SANDWICHES

Elizabeth loves to make these sandwiches with her homemade Potato-Pepper Bread. You can, however, substitute a store-bought bread or even focaccia, for more immediate gratification. The sandwiches are served open-faced and slightly warmed.

6 ounces goat cheese, such as Montrachet, crumbled

⅓ cup plus ¼ cup extra-virgin olive oil

¼ cup minced fresh basil

2 tablespoons minced fresh Italian parsley

2 tablespoons minced fresh mint

2 tablespoons minced fresh chives

2 tablespoons minced, good-quality Greek olives

2 medium eggplants, very bright purple and very firm (see box, page 336)

¼ cup water

1 loaf Potato–Pepper Bread (recipe follows), cut into 12 thick slices

1 tablespoon kosher salt, or to taste

1 teaspoon freshly ground pepper, or to taste

Combine the goat cheese, ⅓ cup olive oil, basil, parsley, mint, chives, and olives in the bowl of a food processor and pulse a few times until the mixture is well combined. Place in a small bowl, cover, and set aside until ready to use.

Preheat the grill or broiler. Peel the eggplants and slice them crosswise into twelve ¼-inch-thick rounds. Whisk the remaining ¼ cup olive oil and the water together in a small bowl and brush on both sides of the eggplant. Grill or broil the eggplant until golden on each side and tender, 1 to 2 minutes per side. Transfer the eggplant to a plate and keep warm. Add the bread to the grill, or place under the broiler. Place an equal amount of the herbed goat cheese mixture on top and grill or broil until the bread is lightly toasted. Transfer 2 pieces of the bread to each of 6 plates and top with 2 eggplant slices. Sprinkle with salt and pepper.

MAKES 12 OPEN-FACE SANDWICHES; SERVES 6

> ## Keeping Yeast Alive
>
> Elizabeth says she has found, without exception, that bread fails when the warm water is actually hot, which kills the yeast instead of activating it. The warm water called for in bread making should be neither hot nor cold to the touch—lukewarm, really. She admits, "This might just be a misunderstanding in the South, where we often say, 'My, it's warm today' when the thermometer hovers at 100 degrees and an egg would fry on the sidewalk."

POTATO-PEPPER BREAD

This dense and flavorful bread is great for sandwiches or eating on its own with soups and salads.

2 cups water

½ cup peeled and finely diced Idaho
   potatoes

1 tablespoon extra-virgin olive oil

1 teaspoon sugar

1 teaspoon salt

2 teaspoons freshly ground pepper

1½ teaspoons active dry yeast

½ cup whole wheat flour

2½–3 cups unbleached all-purpose or
   bread flour

In a medium saucepan, bring the water to a boil over medium-high heat, then add the potatoes, reduce the heat to medium-low, and simmer for 15 minutes, until very tender. Remove the pan from the heat and transfer 1½ cups of the potato water and all the potatoes to a large bowl or the bowl of an electric mixer (adding additional water, if there is not enough potato water). When the potatoes and water are cool, stir in the oil, sugar, salt, pepper, yeast, and whole wheat flour. Set aside in a warm spot, loosely covered with plastic wrap, for 30 minutes to proof.

Stir in 2½ cups of the all-purpose flour and knead in an electric mixer with a dough hook, or by hand on a lightly floured surface, for about 10 minutes, until soft and elastic. The potatoes will mash into the bread, but do not worry if a few potato bits do not get blended in; they add nice texture to the bread. Add more flour (up to ½ cup) if the dough is too sticky.

Shape the dough into a ball and place in a large oiled bowl, cover loosely with plastic wrap, and allow to rise for 1½ hours, or until doubled in bulk.

Preheat the oven to 350° F. Punch the dough down and place in a 1½- to 2-quart loaf pan, such as a 9 × 5 × 3-inch pan, loosely cover with plastic wrap, and allow to rise for 1 hour. Bake for 40 minutes. Remove the bread from the pan to a wire rack to cool completely, then slice.

MAKES 1 LOAF; SERVES 6

To Salt or Not to Salt Eggplant

Many chefs salt the eggplant to remove the bitter flavor that is present in those that are past their prime. (Actually, even perfectly ripe eggplants impart a slight bitterness, but it grows stronger with age.)

To avoid the hassle of salting but still avoid any hint of bitterness, Elizabeth chooses smaller eggplants that are very firm, with smooth, taut, unblemished skin. Soft eggplants with wrinkled skins are a sign of age and guaranteed bitter flavor. Eggplant is quite perishable, so use it within a day or two of buying and store in a cool, dry place.

If you think you might have a bitter eggplant, proceed with the salting process. Cut the eggplant as needed and place in a colander, sprinkle with salt (preferably coarse salt), toss, and let sit for 20 minutes. Then, rinse briefly and dry thoroughly with paper towels.

TOMATO, CUCUMBER, AND ONION SALAD WITH GARLIC-SESAME DRESSING

People really seem to love the taste of sesame, and this zingy dressing is just delicious. Try this salad with other menus; it goes well with everything from chicken and fish to steak.

¼ cup light sesame oil

1 teaspoon freshly ground pepper

½ teaspoon sugar

1 teaspoon salt

1 tablespoon sherry vinegar

2 tablespoons minced garlic

1 cup minced scallions

5 cups 1-inch diced, ripe tomatoes

1½ cups seeded, diced cucumber

¼ cup chopped fresh basil

1 cup watercress, washed and large
   stems discarded

Whisk together the oil, pepper, sugar, salt, vinegar, and garlic in a small bowl. Stir in the scallions and set aside for 15 to 60 minutes to allow the flavors to combine. Just before serving, toss the tomatoes, cucumber, basil, and watercress with the dressing in a large serving bowl.

SERVES 6

FETTUCCINE WITH ZUCCHINI, PEANUTS, AND BASIL

Fans of sesame noodles will like this delicious pasta concoction. It is dressed with just the right balance of peanut, soy, lemon, and garlic flavors. Serve it at room temperature for a side dish or lunch entrée.

1 tablespoon peanut butter

2 tablespoons soy sauce

2 tablespoons mayonnaise

2 tablespoons fresh lemon juice

1 teaspoon freshly ground pepper

1 pound fettuccine

2 tablespoons peanut oil

1 tablespoon chopped garlic

2 cups chopped zucchini

¼ cup toasted peanuts

¼ cup chopped fresh basil

In a small bowl, whisk together the peanut butter, soy sauce, mayonnaise, lemon juice, and pepper. Set aside. Bring a large saucepan of water to boil over medium-high heat, add the pasta, and cook according to package directions until *al dente*. Drain the pasta and toss, while still warm, with the peanut-soy dressing. Set aside to cool.

In a large skillet over medium heat, heat the oil. Add the garlic and zucchini and sauté until the zucchini is crisp-tender, about 4 minutes. Pour this over the pasta. Just before serving, add the peanuts and basil. Serve at room temperature.

SERVES 6

Whipping Hints

One of the keys to successfully beating egg whites is to bring the eggs to room temperature before beating them. A quick way to warm egg whites is to place them in a bowl over warm water for about 2 minutes. Cream of tartar and the acid in lemon juice act as stabilizers so the whipped egg whites hold their shape.

Conversely, for whipped cream, both the bowl and the cream should be chilled before whipping. Be careful not to overwhip the cream; even a few extra strokes can allow the cream to separate and start to turn to butter. If the cream begins to look even slightly grainy, stop whisking.

SCOTTISH TRIFLE

Elizabeth's daughter brought this recipe home from Scotland. Orange whipped cream is blended with crisp meringue cookies and fresh raspberries. Do not be fooled by its "lightness"; it is not a low-fat dessert, but it is worth every bite!

The meringue must cool completely before being incorporated into the whipped cream, but you can also make it up to a week ahead.

1½ cups heavy cream

⅓ cup sugar

2 tablespoons Triple Sec or fresh
    orange juice

1 cup sour cream

Crisp Meringue Puffs (recipe follows)

1½ pints fresh raspberries or other
    berries, washed and picked over

In a large chilled bowl, whip the heavy cream with an electric mixer or a balloon whisk until soft peaks begin to form. Add the sugar and Triple Sec or orange juice and whip until firm. Fold in the sour cream. Refrigerate for up to 6 hours before serving.

Just before serving, gently fold the meringue puffs and berries into the cream. Divide the mixture among 6 stemmed goblets and serve.

SERVES 6

CRISP MERINGUE PUFFS

3 large egg whites, at room
    temperature

½ teaspoon cream of tartar

¼ teaspoon fresh lemon juice

½ cup sugar

Preheat the oven to 225°F. Beat the egg whites (preferably with the whisk attachment of an electric mixer) until foamy. Add the cream of tartar and lemon juice, and beat until soft peaks form. With the mixer still running, add the sugar, 2 tablespoons at a time, beating until glossy. This will take about another 3 minutes.

On a greased baking sheet, spoon 24 heaping tablespoons of meringue. Bake for 1 hour, until the meringue is dry and crisp. Remove from the baking sheet and cool on wire racks. Store in an airtight container until ready to use (up to 1 week), as the meringues will become soft if the air is moist.

MAKES 24 PUFFS

BARBARA TROPP

A One-Dish Affair

I confess to favoring one-dish suppers," says Barbara Tropp, chef and owner of the groundbreaking China Moon Cafe, a Chinese bistro located in downtown San Francisco. "It's such a relief from the endless dishes at the restaurant! With a simple something to greet the guests and an equally simple note of sweetness to end, I can concentrate all my attention on the main dish and my friends."

True to her scheme of things, Barbara begins this menu with Golden Caviar on Croutons to greet her guests and ends the dinner with a light Grape Ice Cream, because living in the grape-growing country makes it a natural choice for a grape-lover. But her main focus is the Baked Salmon on a Bed of Wok-Seared Vegetables. The combination of fresh vegetables and salmon, enhanced with ginger and white wine and served with rice, is a deliciously filling and healthful meal. "Aside from the KISS rule (Keep It Simple, Stupid), I stay true to *yin* and *yang,* the ancient Chinese scheme of complementary opposites: To wit, if the main course is a bit of a do, everything else must be stupidly simple. If one thing requires last-minute attention, all else must be done in advance. If I'm working with something costly—sashimi-grade fish, caviar, wild mushrooms—I use other things that are simple and cheap—pasta, greens, veggies," says Barbara.

MENU

Golden Caviar on Croutons

—

*Baked Ivory Salmon
on a Bed of Wok-Seared Vegetables
with Perfect Steamed Rice*

—

Grape Ice Cream

"The idea is that nothing and no one drowns from overkill."

A "China scholar turned Chinese cook," Barbara was educated in Chinese language, poetry, and art history at Columbia, Yale, and Princeton universities and at the University of Taiwan in Taipei. She lived for two years in Taiwan with traditional Chinese families, and it was during this time that she really learned to love food. She decided to move to San Francisco, abandoning her thesis on Tang dynasty poetry, and wrote instead a book about Chinese cooking and culture.

In 1986, she opened China Moon Cafe in an old coffee shop owned by Chinese since the 1930s, and she spent every waking moment working to make it a success. "I never cooked for family or friends—not once—during the first three or four years of China Moon's life," says Barbara. "I had no family, living solo, and my very large, far-flung circle of friends became even more out of reach, given my schedule and crazed obsessiveness. The restaurant swallowed me alive, and I went home only to sleep."

She later fell in love, got married, and began having late-night dinners for two at the apartment she'd previously only slept in. Then she and her husband purchased a home on orchard land in the Napa Valley. "We've been living here on weekends for a few years now, and much to my shock, I sometimes cook for friends," she says.

It's also a comforting change for her to be so relaxed at home, as opposed to at her restaurant, where she must have everything in absolutely perfect order. "It's enough if the friends and wine are great and the food is merely good. With that attitude, the food is often excellent, and it's only me who is surprised."

GOLDEN CAVIAR ON CROUTONS

Asked to give an accurate index of the amount of caviar to buy, Barbara says, "I'm hopeless! My atti-tude is to buy as much as you can afford!" Golden caviar is her particular favorite for a country dinner with friends. She serves it without adornment, on croutons, accompanied by very dry Champagne.

Start the croutons the day before your dinner. There will be more than enough for appetizers for four, but they keep nicely, if sealed airtight, and make great between-meal munchies.

1 day-old French baguette   **¼ cup corn, peanut, or canola oil**
1 large garlic clove, smashed (optional)   **¼ cup or more golden caviar**

Cut the baguette on the diagonal into ¼-inch-thick slices, using a serrated bread knife. Put the slices in an airtight container and leave at room temperature overnight. (This allows the bread to firm up and it will absorb less oil.) At the same time, combine the garlic, if using, and oil in a small bowl. Set aside for 2 to 24 hours to infuse.

Preheat the oven to 350° F. Arrange the oven rack in the middle position. Put the bread slices side by side on a baking sheet. Brush the tops very lightly with the oil. (Leftover oil can be used for stir-frying.) Bake the croutons until lightly golden, 8 to 10 minutes, turning the baking sheet halfway around after 4 to 5 minutes for even coloring. Let the croutons cool on the baking sheet.

To serve, spoon the caviar on top of the croutons. Be pure; avoid lemon and other frills.

SERVES 4

On Choosing Caviar

Barbara Tropp says, "I'm one of those people who like only top-quality caviar. Dyed, frozen, or pasteurized fish eggs are not for me. Like a bad date, they ruin a meal."

Look for impeccably fresh caviar. Buy it in a place where the turnover is regular and the standards are high. Eat it within two weeks of purchase, and store it in the coldest part of the refrigerator. If the finest caviar is beyond your reach, select the best fresh, natural type you can afford. Russian, Iranian, and American fresh caviar are usually excellent. Chinese is chancy; the quality is too variable. So-called golden caviar, harvested from American whitefish, is very tasty and the bead is small and delicate. It is available in high-volume gourmet specialty shops. Barbara likes it because "it isn't flashy. It makes its point in an understated way."

Baked Ivory Salmon on a Bed of Wok-Seared Vegetables with Perfect Steamed Rice

Ivory salmon is Barbara's favorite species. If it is unavailable, use any fresh salmon or other fresh fish that takes well to baking. For thinner fish fillets, shorten the marinating and cooking times accordingly. Barbara likes to prepare this dish up to the baking stage hours in advance of dinner.

Barbara enjoys this dish with a Robert Mondavi Reserve Chardonnay. A French white Burgundy or California Fumé Blanc would also pair nicely.

⅓ cup corn, peanut, or canola oil

2 teaspoons finely minced garlic

2 teaspoons finely minced fresh ginger

2 teaspoons grated fresh orange peel

¼–½ teaspoon hot red pepper flakes

8 small new potatoes, scrubbed

1 yellow onion, halved lengthwise, then cut crosswise into slices

1 carrot, cut into very thin rounds

1 small fennel bulb, halved and sliced crosswise into paper-thin arcs

1 small red bell pepper, cut into thin strips

1 small yellow bell pepper, cut into thin strips

¼ cup dry white wine

1 small head napa cabbage, halved and cut crosswise into 1-inch bands (see box, page 106)

Kosher salt to taste

Freshly ground pepper to taste

4 6–8-ounce pieces skinless and boneless fresh salmon (fillets or steaks)

4 teaspoons soy sauce

2 teaspoons Japanese sesame oil

4 teaspoons dry white wine

2 quarter-size pieces fresh ginger, smashed

2 scallions, cut into 1-inch nuggets and smashed

2 teaspoons Chinese fermented black beans, coarsely chopped (do not rinse; available at Asian or specialty markets)

8 cups Perfect Steamed Rice (recipe follows)

Small fronds of fresh fennel, or green and white scallion rings, for garnish

In a small saucepan, heat the oil, garlic, ginger, orange peel, and red pepper flakes over low heat until the mixture begins to foam. Let foam 1 minute, then remove from the heat and set aside. Slice the potatoes into thin rounds. Bring a medium saucepan of water to a boil over medium-high heat, add the potatoes, and simmer for 3 minutes, until barely tender. Drain in a colander, rush under cold water to stop the cooking, then set aside to drain completely.

Heat a wok or large, heavy skillet over high heat until a bead of water evaporates on contact. Add 2 tablespoons of the flavored oil, swirl to glaze the pan, then reduce the heat to medium–high. Add the onion and toss until pale gold at the edges, 1 to 2 minutes, adjusting the heat so it sizzles without scorching. Add the carrot and toss until hot, about 30 seconds. Add the fennel and toss 1 minute more. Drizzle in a bit more oil down the side of the pan as needed to prevent sticking. Add the bell pepper strips and toss 1 minute to heat through. Add the wine in a "necklace" around the pan, pouring it around the sides in a circular motion. Raise the heat to bring the wine to a simmer, then add the cabbage and toss to mix. Lower the heat to medium–low, cover the pan, and cook until the cabbage is just wilted, about 1 minute. Turn off the heat. The vegetables should be only half-cooked.

Season the vegetables generously with the salt and pepper. Season fairly heavily, as the seasoning will mute upon reheating. Spread the vegetables and any pan juices in a large ovenproof casserole that will hold the fish in a single layer.

Once the vegetables have cooled a bit, arrange the potatoes on top; choose 4 equidistant spots on which you will bake the fish and arrange a bed of potato slices as a platform for each piece by making concentric circles of overlapping rounds about the size of each fillet or steak. Sprinkle the potatoes with more salt and pepper. (The finished vegetable bed can be sealed with plastic wrap and left at room temperature for several hours.)

Up to several hours in advance of baking, marinate the fish. Combine the soy sauce, sesame oil, and wine along with ginger, scallions, and black beans in a shallow dish large enough to hold the fish. Add the fish and toss gently to coat. Set aside for 10 to 12 minutes, turning the fish once midway to redistribute the seasonings. (If using thinner fillets of other fish, cut the marinating time in half.) Drain and reserve the marinade, and set the fish aside until ready to bake.

Preheat the oven to 375° F. and arrange the oven rack in the middle position. About 15 minutes before serving, put a piece of fish on top of each potato platform. Drizzle the reserved marinade on top. Slide the dish into the oven and bake until a knife cut into the thickest portion of the fish shows that it is cooked the way you like it. Medium-rare salmon will take 7 to 8 minutes to cook.

To serve, divide the steamed rice among 4 heated plates. With a large spatula, lift each portion of fish on top of its vegetable bed, and place alongside the rice. Divide the pan juices among the plates, spooning them on top of the fish and rice. Garnish the plates with the fennel fronds or scallions, then serve promptly.

SERVES 4

PERFECT STEAMED RICE

A rice cooker is a friendly thing. It does the work while your back is turned. If you do not have one, follow the directions below, using a heavy pot with a tight-fitting lid.

Whatever the tool, first rinse the rice the traditional Chinese way, as described in box below.

2½ cups short- or medium-grain white rice   **2¾ cups cold water**

Wash the rice repeatedly until the rinse water is clear, following the directions alongside. Drain the rice well, and put it in a 4- to 6-quart heavy pot with a tight-fitting lid. Add the cold water. Bring to a rapid boil over high heat, stirring once or twice. When the starchy bubbles climb nearly to the rim, in about 30 seconds, reduce the heat to low and cover the pot. (If using an electric stove, move the pot to a second burner pre-set to low.)

Simmer the rice over low heat undisturbed for 15 minutes. Then transfer the pot to a cool burner and let it sit undisturbed for 20 minutes more. Do not lift the lid. At the end of the resting time, uncover the pot and gently fluff the rice with a wooden rice paddle or spoon. If your main course is not yet ready, let the pot remain undisturbed for up to 30 minutes before uncovering it and fluffing the rice.

MAKES 8 CUPS; SERVES 4

About Rice

"We don't know how to choose or cook rice in America, and it's a shame," Barbara says. "For the most part, we buy the stuff in boxes, which is flawed to begin with, and then we ruin any chance of decent rice by boiling it." Here's some advice from Barbara:

Before you cook it, use the centuries-old Chinese and Japanese method of rinsing the rice: Put it in a large bowl, cover generously with cold water, then stir slowly in one direction with your hand for a minute or so while the water turns cloudy. Tilt the bowl to drain the rice, add more cold water, and repeat the process four or five times more until the water turns clear. The result is fabulous: a discernibly fresher and better-tasting rice.

To cook rice, the simplest and surest method is a rice cooker. They are cheap and foolproof. Stovetop cooking is also easy; the key is a heavy pot with a tight-fitting lid, and enough willpower to let the pot sit undisturbed. Fork-fluffers and lid-lifters will be frustrated, but the results warrant the restraint.

Ginger Juice

To extract the juice from fresh ginger, grate or finely mince three times as much ginger as you need juice. Then squeeze the ginger in your fist, over a small bowl, to extract the juice.

GRAPE ICE CREAM

"When you live in a grape-growing region, it's easy to become fascinated with the flavors of different grapes," Barbara tells us. "They are as intriguing to the tongue as wine, which is not surprising!"

This is a delicate ice cream, totally dependent on the quality of the grape. Small or large, red or green does not matter; all that is needed is a bursting-with-flavor grape with a good-tasting skin. "I favor seedless organic grapes with thin skins for this recipe; it saves the trouble of seeding and straining, and they taste better," Barbara explains.

Grape ice cream is a fleeting beauty. Freeze it shortly after blending and eat it within a day. For a nice presentation, rim the bowl with small clusters of grapes or slices of sweet melon.

½ cup plus 1–2 tablespoons sugar

Zest of a well-scrubbed tangerine, orange, or lemon (see box, page 269)

¾ pound stemmed, seedless grapes with thin, tasty skins, washed

2 cups half-and-half

1½–2 teaspoons fresh ginger juice (see box, above), or fresh lemon or lime juice

Put ½ cup of the sugar in the work bowl of a food processor fitted with a sharp steel knife. Add a bit of zest directly to the sugar, more or less as desired—make sure the zest does not have any of the bitter white pith, just the colored skin of the fruit. Process for 30 seconds to infuse the sugar with the peel. Add the grapes and process until puréed.

Scrape the mixture into a large, noncorrosive bowl. Stir in the half-and-half. Taste, then add sugar if needed until the mixture tastes a touch too sweet. If too sweet at room temperature, it will taste perfect frozen. Add the ginger (or lemon or lime) juice by half-teaspoonfuls until the flavor peaks.

Freeze in an ice cream maker according to manufacturer's instructions. Store with a piece of plastic wrap pressed directly on the surface. Remove from the freezer 10 to 15 minutes before serving.

MAKES 1 QUART

TOM VALENTI

Bold Summer Flavors

W hen I'm cooking at home, I can relax!" Tom explains, "Cooking professionally is usually a high-visibility thing. You hope your 'guests' appreciate it, but they are paying for your efforts. At home, there is simply less
pressure and I thoroughly enjoy it." When cooking for friends, Tom's approach is
much the same as his approach at the restaurant: "always organize your ingredients and
equipment."

Tom's interest in cooking surfaced in his high school days, when he found himself
tinkering in the kitchen while his parents were working or traveling. He remembers,
"Mom would stuff the fridge with lots of food, my friends would come over, and I
would cook for them. I realized how much I enjoyed that form of expression and,
well, one thing led to another." Tom has cooked his way through some of New York's
best restaurants, including Gotham Bar and Grill, where he says that Alfred Portale was
a great inspiration, Le Perigord Park,
Café Greco, and, most recently, Alison
on Dominick, where his career took
off. In March 1994, Tom moved to
Cascabel in the SoHo district of
Manhattan, concentrating on American
cooking with Italian and French overtones. He says, "The atmosphere of the
restaurant is fun, not too serious, and a

MENU

Herbed Vegetable Tart

❧

Swordfish Wrapped in Bacon

❧

Stewed Green Lentils

❧

Individual Berry Tarts

place where the local neighborhood folks tend to spill in."

"What I particularly like about this meal is that it can be quickly finished up at the last minute." He prepares the lentils earlier that day, though they can be stored for up to two days. The swordfish can be cut and wrapped with bacon, browned, then set aside and simply popped into the oven just before you are ready to serve the meal, which Tom accompanies with "lots of beer." "I love the flavor that the bacon imparts to the fish." The fusion of these flavors goes back to Tom's early days when he spent a lot of time at his grandmother's side. He remembers, "she would take onions and garlic, stew them in bacon fat and add oil-packed canned tuna, then throw in some overripe tomatoes, finish it with hot pepper, and spoon the sauce over spaghetti."

Born and raised in upstate New York, Tom has powerful memories of his grandparents' beautiful garden, barrels of wine in the basement, and fresh herbs hanging from the rafters to dry. His grandfather would take the screen door off the hinges, lie it down between two sawhorses, and dry tomatoes in the sun. "These images stayed with me as I grew up, and all the freshness and big flavors have had a great impact on my cooking today."

Living in the countryside also taught Tom about cooking with the seasons. For this summertime meal's dessert, Tom prepares fruit tartlets with ripe berries. "This is a great recipe because everything maintains its integrity." The fruit gets just warmed through but still has a firm texture, and the crust on the tart, best done the same day, stays crisp.

Tom's philosophy of entertaining is simple: "A chef's workday is long and time off is always precious, so spending time with who you are cooking for can certainly be as important as, or more important than, what you are cooking."

HERBED VEGETABLE TART

Garden-fresh produce is seasoned with garlic and herb-infused olive oil and baked slowly to allow the vegetables to soak up the seasonings and release their juices. Tom likes to garnish the tart with fresh basil and goat cheese.

This uncomplicated dish must be started well in advance, as it bakes for three hours and then should rest for thirty minutes before eating. In this menu it is served as a first course, leaving leftovers for brunch or lunch the next day.

A tart pan with a removable bottom is needed to bake this crustless tart because it allows some of the juices to escape, resulting in a firm, free-standing tart. The uncooked tart stands up to 1 inch above the rim of the pan, but it will shrink when baked.

1 cup plus 1 teaspoon extra-virgin olive oil

6 garlic cloves, smashed

1 bay leaf

2 bunches fresh thyme

Salt and freshly ground pepper to taste

1 tablespoon unsalted butter

4 onions, sliced as thinly as possible

1½ large eggplants, very thinly sliced

3 zucchini, thinly sliced

6 ripe medium tomatoes, cored and thinly sliced

¼ cup chopped fresh basil (optional)

¼ cup crumbled goat cheese (optional), such as Coach Farms or Bucheron

Preheat the oven to 275°F. Combine 1 cup of the olive oil, the garlic, bay leaf, thyme, and salt and pepper in a saucepan over low heat and simmer for 10 minutes. Remove from the heat. (For even more flavor, you can do this the day before and transfer to a covered jar).

Heat the remaining 1 teaspoon olive oil and melt the butter in a large skillet over medium-low heat. Add the onions, and gently cook for 25 minutes until very soft and browned. Line a 9- or 10-inch removable-bottom tart pan with the caramelized onions. Layer the eggplant over the onions, brushing each layer with the infused olive oil and seasoning with salt and pepper. Once all of the eggplant has been used, layer all of the zucchini and then the tomatoes in the same fashion, brushing each layer with the oil and seasoning lightly with salt and pepper.

Place the tart on a baking sheet with a rim, as the tart will give off quite a bit of liquid as it bakes, and bake for 3 hours. Allow the tart to cool for 30 minutes on a rack before cutting. Cut into wedges, and top each piece with the chopped fresh basil and crumbled goat cheese, if desired. Serve warm, at room temperature or cold.

SERVES 6 GENEROUSLY

SWORDFISH WRAPPED IN BACON

Usually, swordfish is cut crosswise into steaks. For this recipe, ask your fishmonger to cut the fish loin lengthwise into cylindrical pieces. The "log shape" cut makes it easier for wrapping the bacon.

Double-smoked bacon gives the swordfish just the right flavor and eliminates the need for any other seasonings, except perhaps some salt and pepper. Any smoked bacon will work, but Tom recommends using slab bacon from a butcher, and not presliced packaged bacon.

**4 pounds center-cut boneless sword-
fish, cut into 6 logs roughly 5 inches
long and 1½ inches square**

**Salt and freshly ground pepper to taste
½ pound slab double-smoked bacon,
thinly sliced (30 to 36 slices)**

Preheat the oven to 400°F. Season the swordfish logs lightly with salt and pepper. Place 5 or 6 slices of bacon on parchment paper lengthwise, side by side and slightly overlapping. Place one swordfish log perpendicular to the bacon slices at the end farthest from you, and roll the fish toward you, making sure that the bacon adheres to the fish. Roll tightly. Repeat with the other pieces of bacon and swordfish.

Heat a dry, nonstick skillet over medium-high heat and place 1 or 2 pieces of bacon-wrapped fish in the pan, making sure to place the side where the bacon ends onto the pan, so the heat will seal the bacon together. Brown on all 4 sides for about 30 seconds per side. Transfer the browned fish to a sheet pan, and brown the remaining fish, 1 or 2 pieces at a time. Once all the fish has been browned, bake on the sheet pan for 7 to 8 minutes, or until done. To check for doneness, simply slice a small piece of fish off the end. The fish should be slightly pink and cooked evenly throughout. Serve immediately.

SERVES 6

STEWED GREEN LENTILS

"Lentils are a wonderful complement to pork," says Tom, and recommends French green Puy lentils (see box, page 239) for their superior flavor and texture.

If you would prefer to cook the lentils in advance, pour the cooked lentils onto a sheet pan in a thin layer and place in the refrigerator to cool. Then transfer to a covered container and refrigerate until ready to use. Reheat the lentils in a saucepan with a little water added over low heat.

12 ounces green lentils, rinsed and
   picked over
1 small carrot, peeled and diced
1 small yellow onion, diced
2–3 garlic cloves, minced
1 tablespoon fresh thyme, or
   1 teaspoon dried

1 bay leaf, preferably fresh
3 tablespoons extra-virgin olive oil
Salt and freshly ground black pepper
   to taste
2–3 cups chicken stock

In a medium, heavy saucepan, combine the lentils, carrot, onion, garlic, thyme, bay leaf, olive oil, and salt and pepper. Add enough stock to just cover the lentils. Cook over medium heat, adding small amounts of the stock and stirring occasionally until the lentils are tender and most of the liquid has been absorbed, 20 to 25 minutes. Remove the bay leaf, season with salt and pepper, and serve hot.

SERVES 6

Garlic Tips

Garlic is almost always peeled before using, unless it is baked. To remove the cloves from the bulb you often need to peel your way through several layers of papery encasement. Here's a quick trick around that: place the bulb, root side up, on a flat surface. Use the heel of your palm to press on the bulb until the cloves become detached.

Removing the peel can also be frustrating, so use this helpful trick: place the widest spot of a large chef's knife flat side down on top of the clove; with your fist, pound down on top of the knife to split the clove, separating the peel from the clove. This same method of pounding the clove results in a "smashed" garlic, which Tom uses to infuse the olive oil for the Herbed Vegetable Tart.

INDIVIDUAL BERRY TARTS

Any combination of berries, such as raspberries, blackberries, strawberries, or blueberries, is elevated to a gorgeous and luscious dessert when encased between a rich, sweet pastry shell and a sabayon spiked with Grand Marnier. The tarts are baked just enough to brown the top and slightly warm the sauce.

Sabayon (also known as zabaglione by the Italians, from whom it originated) is a sweet egg-based sauce, often flavored with wine or liqueur. It has a light and frothy consistency and is usually served warm over fruit. If you are running short on time, forgo the pastry and simply fill the tartlet pans or a gratin dish with the fruit, top with the sabayon, and bake until golden.

PASTRY

1 cup plus 2 tablespoons all-purpose
   flour
1 cup plus 2 tablespoons cake flour
⅛ teaspoon baking powder
¼ teaspoon salt
⅔ cup unsalted butter, softened
⅔ cup granulated sugar
½ teaspoon vanilla extract
1 large egg
1 tablespoon milk

SABAYON

½ cup heavy cream
4 large egg yolks
½ cup sugar
Pinch of salt
½ cup fresh orange juice
¼ cup Grand Marnier or other orange-
   flavored liqueur

Confectioners' sugar, for dusting
2 pints fresh ripe berries, washed,
   stemmed, and picked over
Mint sprigs, for garnish

To make the pastry, combine the flours, baking powder, and salt in a bowl and set aside. In the bowl of an electric mixer, combine the butter and sugar on medium speed until pale in color. Add the vanilla and egg and continue beating until incorporated. Scrape down the sides of the bowl. With the machine on low speed, slowly add the dry ingredients until fully incorporated. Add the milk and mix just until absorbed. Shape into a ball, wrap in plastic wrap, and chill for at least 30 minutes.

Preheat the oven to 325°F. Cut the dough into 6 equal pieces and, on a lightly floured surface, roll each out to a 5-inch circle of ¼-inch thickness. Line six 4-inch tartlet shells with removable bottoms with the dough circles. Cover the dough with parchment paper or foil and fill the pans with uncooked rice or beans or pie weights to keep the dough from shrinking from the edges. Bake for 15 minutes. Remove the rice, beans, or weights and paper or foil and prick the bottom of each tart in a few places with a fork. Return the shells to the oven for about 7 more minutes, until the bottoms are slightly golden in color. Transfer to a wire rack to cool, but leave the oven on. (Alternatively, the tartlet shells can be made up to a day in advance and kept well wrapped.)

Shortly before serving, prepare the sabayon. Whip the cream in the bowl of an electric mixer on high speed until soft peaks form, and refrigerate, covered. Whisk together the yolks, sugar, and salt in the top part of a double boiler, or in a stainless-steel mixing bowl that will fit over a saucepan. Whisk in the orange juice and Grand Marnier. Place the double boiler over medium heat, or place the metal bowl over a saucepan of simmering water, and whisk vigorously until the mixture has tripled in volume, about 5 minutes. Remove from the heat and mix with an electric mixer on high speed until cool. Fold in the chilled whipped cream.

To assemble the tarts, sprinkle confectioners' sugar into each shell. Line the tarts with the berries, reserving a few of the prettiest for garnish. Divide the sabayon evenly among the tarts, smoothing out the tops. Place the tarts on a baking sheet in the oven for about 5 minutes, until the tops are slightly golden brown. Remove from the oven. Dust the tops with confectioners' sugar and garnish with a sprig of mint and the extra berries.

Serves 6

The Art of the Whisk

Even with the invention of the electric mixer, the whisk has not lost its value among kitchen utensils. While the mixer can do what the whisk can do, and usually quicker, easier, and with satisfactory results, a whisk and a steady wrist will usually do a superior job. It is important, however, to use the proper type of whisk.

There are two basic shapes for whisks, although they come in myriad sizes. An egg whisk is balloon shaped, with rounded, supple wires and a wide base. These are used for aerating mixtures such as eggs (especially egg whites) and whipping cream.

Whisks that have long, straight, stiff wires and a narrow base are known as sauce whisks. This type of whisk is used to remove lumps from mixtures such as gravy or custard, or to emulsify mixtures such as salad dressings and homemade mayonnaise.

To make a perfectly foamy sabayon sauce without allowing the eggs to scramble requires some skill and the right equipment. Use a balloon (egg) whisk to make the sabayon, and concentrate on whisking the mixture vigorously and steadily. If the eggs cook and the mixture has lumps, salvage it by straining the egg mixture through a fine sieve before folding in the whipped cream.

ALICE WATERS

Fresh from the Market

lice Waters begins every home-cooked meal with a trip to the local farmers'
market, where she determines the evening's fare based on the best-looking
fruits, vegetables, cheeses, fish, and meats. She prepares meals that are "unbe-
lievably uncomplicated," so that the menu allows her to sit down at the table with her
guests. "Every time I've been unhappy is at a meal when I've tried to be too ambitious.
At home you don't have the assistance that you do at the restaurant. I've learned to
really pare down to the bare bones." Her rule is to make only one hot dish and to serve
something cold or room temperature as the first course; to make the process even easier, the last course is always something that can be prepared well ahead of time. "I
always have a salad," she says. "Sometimes I make it the first course, and other times I
serve it afterward."

Alice selected this three-course menu because of its simplicity and because it can all
be made in advance, with the duck legs
kept warm in the oven until serving
time. "I never used to like foods that
were braised," she says, "but now I have
new feelings about it. If you have good
ingredients and they're cooked properly,
this cooking method really brings out
the flavors." She likes the savory taste of
the duck and the fact that the legs are

MENU

*Blood Orange, Beet, Dandelion Green, and
Walnut Salad*

—

*Duck Legs Braised in Red Wine with
Orange Zest and Garlic*

—

Pear and Muscat Raisin Tarte Tatin

inexpensive. As an appetizer she offers something as basic as olives and slices of prosciutto, and she might end the meal with store-bought *biscotti* and roasted almonds. "And I always make sure to serve good bread and great wine, making any meal very special."

An influential figure in the culinary world, Alice has inspired a generation of chefs who have helped shape both the present and the future of American cooking. It was a trip to France that clarified her desire to become a chef and restaurateur. After receiving a degree in French cultural studies from the University of California at Berkeley in the late 1960s, Alice completed a teacher-training program at the Montessori school in London. She then traveled around France and fell in love with the food. She returned to Berkeley with the confidence and wish to own her own restaurant.

She opened Chez Panisse in 1971, after cooking for her friends in her home became too much work and her desire to own her own restaurant had evolved into an achievable dream. "I wanted a place where my friends and I could come and eat. A place that served real food, cooked in the way I would cook it at home or might have tasted it in Europe." The restaurant is named after a character in Marcel Pagnol's *Fanny*—and Fanny is the name she chose for her daughter.

More than twenty years later, Alice keeps to her same philosophy of cooking with organically grown fresh foods. And she still shares many meals with those same close friends, either at her home or at theirs. "Cooking at home is about getting together," says Alice. "One of our favorite things to do is to share in the cooking by preparing pot-luck. I'll make a dish and take it over to a friend's home, or they'll bring something over to my house. Sometimes we'll even select a menu together and divide up the recipes to prepare." Wherever the dinner takes place, Alice knows that the most important part of the meal is sharing the food experience.

BLOOD ORANGE, BEET, DANDELION GREEN, AND WALNUT SALAD

This is a winter salad with a lot of flavors. Dandelion greens have a spicy bite to them. If they are hard to find, you may substitute arugula, but, as Alice says, the resulting salad tastes completely different.

¾ pound (approximately 8) medium beets, preferably 2 or 3 different kinds, washed

¾ cup water

4 shallots, minced

4 tablespoons red wine vinegar

4 tablespoons balsamic vinegar

3 blood oranges

¾ cup extra-virgin olive oil

Salt and freshly ground pepper to taste

½ pound young dandelion greens, carefully washed and dried (store in refrigerator until ready to use)

⅓ cup walnuts, toasted (see box, page 117) and roughly chopped

Preheat the oven to 350° F. Trim the tops and roots from the beets. Place in a baking pan in a single layer with the water and bake until soft, approximately 45 minutes. When cooked, remove the beets from the oven and let them cool. Peel the beets and slice into thin wedges.

While the beets are baking, combine the shallots with the red wine and balsamic vinegars in a small bowl to marinate for about 30 minutes.

Completely remove the membrane from the oranges (see box, page 362). Cut the oranges crosswise into ¼-inch-thick slices. When working with the oranges, try to catch any of the juices that escape and incorporate them into the vinaigrette. Whisk the olive oil and salt and pepper into the vinegar mixture.

In a mixing bowl, toss the dandelion greens with enough vinaigrette to coat lightly and place on a platter or salad bowl. Then toss the beets and orange slices together with additional vinaigrette and salt and pepper, and place on the dandelion greens. Sprinkle the walnuts all over.

SERVES 8

Duck

Chances are you will not find fresh duck in the stores, unless you live in duck-cultivating country from spring to early winter. Domestic ducks are generally of the mallard or muscovy species, weighing in at a mere 3 to 6 pounds, as they are generally no more than 4 months old and often less than 8 weeks.

Duck meat is moist, delicate, and tasty. It is more fatty than chicken or turkey but is a good source of iron and protein.

When buying duck, be sure to buy only Grade A. Look for plump meat and moist, pliable skin on a fresh duck. Be sure frozen duck is well packaged; thaw it completely in the refrigerator before using, about 1 to 1½ days.

DUCK LEGS BRAISED IN RED WINE WITH ORANGE ZEST AND GARLIC

Braising is a simple way of cooking meat by simmering it in any seasoned liquid. This slow cooking method allows the flavor of the duck to blend with the seasonal vegetables, herbs, spices, and the stock, resulting in a succulent main course. Your kitchen will smell incredible, too!

16 duck legs

Salt and freshly ground pepper to taste

3 yellow onions, thinly sliced

8 cups duck or chicken stock

Zest of ¼ orange

1 bay leaf

2 sprigs fresh thyme, or ¼ teaspoon dried

2 garlic cloves, thinly sliced

1 cup dry red wine

Trim the excess fat from the duck legs and render it by cooking it in a skillet over low heat until liquid. Allow it to cool slightly, then strain it and discard any solids. Transfer the rendered fat to a jar, cover, and refrigerate until ready to use.

Season the legs with salt and pepper and allow them to rest at room temperature for 1 hour. Preheat the oven to 450° F.

In a skillet, melt 1 tablespoon of the rendered fat over low heat. Add a couple of duck legs at a time and brown on all sides, about 1 or 2 minutes per batch. Add more fat as you cook each batch. After browning all of the legs, remove from the pan with tongs. Add the onions and soften and brown them slightly over medium-low heat for 3 to 4 minutes. Deglaze the pan by pouring ¼ cup of the stock into the pan and scraping up any browned bits from the bottom.

Transfer the onions and pan drippings to a baking dish large enough to fit the legs in a cozy single layer (use 2 dishes if necessary). Add the orange zest, bay leaf, thyme, garlic, and red wine. Arrange the legs, skin side down, in one layer in the pan. Heat the remaining stock just until warm on the stove and pour enough over the legs to nearly cover them. Tightly seal the baking dish with foil and bake for 20 to 30 minutes, until the stock starts to simmer gently. Reduce the oven temperature to 350° F. and continue to cook, covered, for another 45 minutes. Turn the legs over, skin side up, and cook uncovered for 15 more minutes, allowing them to brown until their skin is crisp and golden and the meat is done. To check for doneness, use a small knife to cut through the meat. If it offers no resistance and separates gently from the bone, it is done.

Remove the legs from the baking dish, set aside, and strain the braising juice through a sieve into a tall, narrow container. Skim off the fat that rises to the top. Just before serving, reheat the duck and braising juice in a large covered skillet over medium-low heat, simmering it gently for about 5 minutes. Place the duck legs on a serving platter with some of the juice drizzled on top and serve family style at the table.

SERVES 8

Blood Oranges

Succulent blood oranges are grown in Italy and Israel, but are also widely available in California, and they can be purchased in other states as well from December through April. These winter fruits have a sweet-tart flavor and their blood-red color enlivens many dishes. Of course, blood oranges can be eaten on their own, but Alice suggests making the most of this colorful, flavorful fruit. Try blood oranges in other salads such as those made with arugula, mesclun (see box, page 90), or watercress.

Preparing Oranges

TO CUT the orange in order to remove the pith and the membrane, use a sharp medium-size chef's knife. Slice the two ends of the orange off, just to the point of exposing the pulp of the fruit and flattening the ends. Then stand the orange up, with one of the cut ends on the cutting board. Cutting in strips from top to bottom, place the knife between the pith and the pulp and begin to cut downward, following the contour of the fruit so that you only remove the pith and membrane, and not the pulp. Repeat until the orange is completely peeled. Gently peel off any remaining pith.

TO SECTION an orange, first remove the pith and the outer membrane. Using a pairing knife, cut each segment on both sides of the membrane that separates each segment. Gently loosen each segment from the center of the orange.

PEAR AND MUSCAT RAISIN TARTE TATIN

Alice offers us a lovely variation of the traditional French tarte Tatin, *a caramelized apple upside-down tart, using ripe pears and sweet golden Muscat raisins. She serves it warm from the oven with fresh whipped cream or crème fraîche. It also may be served with vanilla ice cream.*

If not serving the tart immediately, leave it in the pan for 15 minutes or so and then invert and serve, or remove it from the pan up to 30 minutes before serving and reheat in a 350°F. oven.

2 tablespoons (¼ stick) unsalted butter

½ cup sugar

1 cup Muscat raisins

5 or 6 medium (2½–3 pounds) ripe Bosc pears (see box, page 305), cut in half, cored, and seeded

1 tablespoon Cognac, Armagnac, or brandy (optional)

1 frozen puff pastry sheet (half of a 17¼-ounce package), thawed

Whipped cream or Crème Fraîche (see box, page 237) (optional)

Fill a large bowl with ice and water. Melt the butter in a heavy 9-inch skillet (preferably cast-iron) over medium heat. Add the sugar, stirring constantly until the sugar dissolves and turns a golden brown, about 5 minutes. Remove the skillet from the heat before the sugar becomes too dark, as it will continue to cook from the heat of the pan. Place the bottom of the skillet in the bowl of ice water to stop the cooking process. Cool until the caramel is firm. (The recipe can be prepared to this point up to 8 hours in advance.)

Preheat the oven to 400°F. Place the raisins in a small bowl and cover with hot water. Let stand for 5 minutes. Meanwhile, in a large bowl toss the pears with the brandy, if using. Arrange the pears, rounded side down, around the edge of the skillet, slightly overlapping. Continue adding pears in concentric circles until the skillet is tightly packed with pears. Drain the raisins and sprinkle them over the pears, tucking them in between the pears.

Trim the pastry to an 11-inch circle, rolling out the dough on a lightly floured surface, if necessary. Set the pastry on top of the fruit and tuck it down between the sides of the pan and the pears. Using a toothpick or fork, pierce several small holes in the crust so steam can escape during cooking. Bake until the dough is golden and the pears are tender, about 30 minutes. Remove the tart from the oven and let stand for 5 minutes. Set a serving plate upside down on top of the pan. Using potholders, lift the two together, tightly holding the plate to the pan, and quickly flip the pan over away from you so the juices do not spatter. Lift the pan off. If any fruit has stuck to the pan, simply rearrange it on the tart. Serve warm with whipped cream or Crème Fraîche, if desired.

SERVES 8

SYLVIA WOODS

Southern Comfort Food

"Soul food is what made me and soul food is going to see me through," says Sylvia Woods, who has been operating Sylvia's, the landmark restaurant in Harlem, for more than thirty-two years. "Soul food comes from the days of slavery, when blacks didn't have much *but* their soul," she explains. "We took all the food that was left over or rejected and made the very best out of it—soul food is pure emotion." Catering to a diverse crowd of locals, celebrities, and tourists from around the world, Sylvia is surrounded by her family, including her husband, Herbert, her four children, grandchildren, and several relatives, many of whom work at the restaurant (otherwise known to them as their "home away from home"). In fact, if it were not for the commercial kitchen and 250 seats, you would literally feel "at home" at Sylvia's.

Born in Hemingway, South Carolina, in 1926, Sylvia never dreamed she would own her own restaurant, but she hoped for an easier life than the rural one she was born into. "I never liked farm work. I saw how hard my family worked and I knew I had to do better for myself and the children that I wanted." Sylvia moved to New York City when she was twenty years old and eventually "got up the nerve" to apply for a waitressing job. She lied about having experience at

MENU

Vinegar-Roasted Turkey with Barbecue Sauce

❧

*Fried Sweet Potatoes with Raisins
and Marshmallows*

❧

Collard Greens with Bacon

❧

Southern-Style Corn Bread with Fresh Corn

a small luncheonette called Johnsons. Her prospective employer was not fooled but was impressed with her determination and hired her. To Sylvia, waitressing meant that "you brought home money every day"; in her case, $38 a week. Eight years later, with a loan from her mother, Sylvia and her hus-  band bought the luncheonette from her employer, expanded the menu to include a wide variety of Southern down-home food, and renamed it Sylvia's. "I consider myself a good home cook who happens to own a restaurant and has a knack for business."

At least twice a year, the entire family goes south, back to Hemingway, back to Sylvia's roots. The farmhouse where she grew up is still there and is opened by relatives who live nearby to celebrate the holidays. For breakfast, the family enjoys fried fish, hominy grits, okra, stewed tomatoes, and biscuits. The menu Sylvia prepares here is reminiscent of a family dinner reunion. Dinner is served informally, of course, but requires two settings around the dining room table: the first at three o'clock and a sec- ond at five o'clock for the late arrivals. "This is what you call togetherness," says Sylvia as everyone starts snacking in the kitchen, "pinching and pulling" at the roasted turkey prepared with Sylvia's famous barbecue sauce. Her son, Van, describes the sauce as a "perfectly balanced" blend of sweet, sour, and tangy flavors. Before it was available bottled in selected supermarkets and specialty stores, customers would buy a cup of the sauce right from the restaurant to take home. Platters of Collard Greens with Bacon; Fried Sweet Potatoes with Raisins and Marshmallows; and Southern-Style Corn Bread with Fresh Corn complete this traditional Southern meal. Homemade apple pies, cakes, and peach cobbler arrive with the relatives for dessert.

But first, before anyone so much as lifts a fork, a lovely tradition takes place. Sylvia's children begin, one at a time, with a prayer or special sentiment for their parents, fol- lowed by the grandchildren, who do the same. Finally, Sylvia and Herbert say a prayer to bless the meal and the family, signaling that the meal is about to begin. "No matter how much they snacked before dinner, one bite of the food makes them hungry all over again," says Sylvia.

Vinegar-Roasted Turkey with Barbecue Sauce

For a tangy turkey, Sylvia's special recipe calls for vinegar (and lots of it) in the roasting pan. For even more flavor, she often seasons the turkey with the spices the day before.

1 12- to 14-pound turkey	1 tablespoon poultry seasoning
2 tablespoons salt	2 quarts vinegar
2 tablespoons freshly ground pepper	½ cup (1 stick) unsalted butter
1 tablespoon chopped garlic (optional)	1 quart Sylvia's Famous Barbecue
2 tablespoons paprika	Sauce (available in some specialty
3 tablespoons hot red pepper flakes	stores), or your favorite recipe

Preheat the oven to 350°F. Place the turkey on a flat surface, breast down. Split the turkey through the back, cutting with a sharp knife or poultry shears, and crack the breast open so the turkey will lie flat. Place it in a large roasting pan, skin side up. Combine the salt, pepper, garlic, if using, paprika, red pepper flakes, and poultry seasoning in a cup or small bowl and massage them thoroughly into the turkey. (For more flavor, store the seasoned turkey, covered, in the refrigerator up to 1 day before roasting.) Add 2 quarts of vinegar to the roasting pan. Melt the butter in a saucepan over medium-low heat and massage into the turkey, on all sides.

Transfer the seasoned turkey to the oven and bake for about 2 hours, basting every 15 to 20 minutes (see Note). Remove any vinegar left in the pan and baste the turkey with the barbecue sauce, then pierce the meat in several places to allow the sauce to permeate. Continue to bake for another 25 to 40 minutes, or until done, basting periodically. Remove from the oven and let stand for 15 to 30 minutes before serving.

For a nice presentation, slice one half of the turkey, removing the wing first, and place on a platter with the other half, uncarved and skin side up.

SERVES 8 TO 10

NOTE: Sylvia's a "real" Southern cook, never using a recipe or relying on standard cooking times because "every oven works differently and every bird is different." Her advice is to keep a watchful eye on the bird and test for doneness with a fork each time you baste during the last hour of cooking. When cooked, clear juices will run from the thigh when pricked with a fork and the meat will easily separate from the bone. Having said all that, here are some general guidelines: A split turkey roasting in a 350°F. oven should cook for about 12 minutes per pound (a 13-pound bird will need about 2 hours and 40 minutes total).

FRIED SWEET POTATOES WITH RAISINS AND MARSHMALLOWS

Sylvia's family prefers these rich potatoes with the skins on, but you can remove the skins if you choose. You can also sprinkle on raisins and marshmallows, although some may feel this is gilding the lily.

4–5 pounds medium sweet potatoes, scrubbed and unpeeled (see box, opposite)

½ cup (1 stick) unsalted butter

1½ cups sugar mixed with 3 tablespoons cinnamon

½ cup raisins (optional)

1 cup mini marshmallows (optional)

Preheat the oven to 350°F. Slice the potatoes into ½-inch-thick pieces. In a very large skillet, heat 2 tablespoons of the butter over low heat. Add a single layer of potatoes and fry for 4 to 5 minutes on each side, until golden brown. Cook the potatoes in batches so they will brown evenly. Add more butter, up to 4 tablespoons, as needed. Transfer the fried potatoes to a large bowl and stir in the cinnamon-sugar mixture and raisins (if desired) until the potatoes are well coated. Transfer the mixture to a 13 × 9 × 2-inch baking dish. Cut the remaining butter into small pieces and distribute over the potatoes. If desired, sprinkle the marshmallows on top. Cover the pan loosely with foil so the marshmallows will not stick and bake for 15 minutes. If topped with marshmallows, remove the foil and bake for another 5 minutes to brown.

SERVES 8 TO 10

COLLARD GREENS WITH BACON

Sylvia says that any flavorful meat, such as smoked turkey or ham hocks, will season the greens.

4–5 pounds collard greens, washed thoroughly

½ pound bacon slab, thinly sliced

1 cup rendered bacon fat and lard or unsalted butter, melted (1–2 sticks)

1 tablespoon sugar

1 tablespoon salt

1 tablespoon hot red pepper flakes

Cut the stems of the greens from just below the leaf and discard. "Chomp" the collard greens across the center vein into ½-inch pieces. Set aside. In a large skillet over medium-high heat, fry the bacon until crisp. Using a slotted spoon, transfer the bacon pieces to a 5-quart stockpot. Transfer the rendered bacon fat to a glass measuring cup and add enough melted butter or lard

Sweet Potato or Yam?

If you are looking for sweet potatoes in the supermarket but only find yams, chances are they are, in fact, sweet potatoes. In the United States, and particularly in the South, the sweet potato is often erroneously referred to as a yam. A true yam grows in the tropics. While some varieties (there are more than 150!) may resemble the sweet potato, yams are tubers and sweet potatoes are root vegetables—two different plant species.

The sweet potato's flavor is enhanced by sugar, molasses, and spices like cinnamon and nutmeg. Sweet potatoes are full of vitamins A and C, fiber, potassium, and calcium, making them one of the most nutritionally sound vegetables.

to make 1 cup. Add the fat to the stockpot, along with the sugar, salt, and red pepper flakes. Place the collard greens on top and add 2 cups of water. Cover and cook over medium-high heat, stirring occasionally for 30 minutes, or until the collard greens are just tender. Add water as needed to keep the collard greens from burning. Transfer the greens with a slotted spoon to a serving dish. Discard the bacon.

SERVES 8 TO 10

SOUTHERN-STYLE CORN BREAD WITH FRESH CORN

Sylvia has been serving up this moist, sweet corn bread for years.

2 cups yellow cornmeal
2 cups all-purpose flour
1 cup sugar
2 tablespoons baking powder
1 tablespoon salt

2½ cups milk
1½ cups vegetable or corn oil
5 large eggs
1½ cups fresh corn kernels (2 to 3 ears), cooked

Preheat the oven to 350°F. Grease a 13 × 9 × 2-inch baking pan. In a large bowl, combine the cornmeal, flour, sugar, baking powder, and salt. In another large bowl, beat the milk, oil, and eggs together until well blended. Add the milk mixture to the dry ingredients and mix by hand, just until completely blended. Fold in the corn kernels, if using. Pour the batter into the baking pan and bake for 30 to 40 minutes, until golden brown.

SERVES 8 TO 10

ROY YAMAGUCHI

Cooking from the Heart

I t seems that I have always loved to cook, whether it was fried Portuguese sausage and eggs for breakfast or a full-on Thanksgiving dinner in home economics class." Well known for his contribution to contemporary Hawaiian regional cuisine, Roy Yamaguchi is most proud of his original cooking style, which he calls "Euro-Asian." It is a style that reflects his personal style, training, and a lifetime of experience, which began in Japan where he was born in 1956.

Roy attributes his earliest appreciation of food to his father, a career military man born and raised on Maui, and to his Okinawan-born mother. Brought up in this bilingual environment in Tokyo until the age of seventeen, Roy could not help but absorb much of the Japanese culture. The Hawaiian influence began with Roy's grandfather, who owned a tavern in the 1940s in Wailuku, Maui. Roy still vividly recalls visits back

to Maui to see his grandparents, and his first food memories of the Pacific. "My father would drive for hours and hours just to get fresh fish, crabs, and octopus from the piers. From trips to Okinawa, my mom would haul back live spiny lobsters."

Roy knew, even before graduating from high school in 1974, that he wanted to learn the classical tradition of cuisine. He graduated from the Culinary Institute of

MENU

Pork and Egg Drop Miso Soup with Green Onion and Tofu

◆

Teriyaki Chicken

◆

Maui Onion Salsa with Tomatoes and Hawaiian Chili-Pepper Water

◆

Coffee Gelatin

America in Hyde Park, New York, in 1976 and then headed west for Los Angeles, where he began his series of apprenticeships at L'Escoffier, L'Ermitage, and Michael's. In 1984, after a few years as executive chef at Le Serene and then at Le Gourmet in the Sheraton Plaza La Reina, he opened a restaurant of his own in Los Angeles called 385 North. After four years of presenting his unique food to an ever-growing number of fans, Roy sold the restaurant and headed across the Pacific to Honolulu to renew his acquaintance with island life, opening Roy's Restaurant. Next came Roy's Kahana Bar & Grill and Roy's Nicolina on Maui; Roy's Poipu Bar & Grill on Kauai; Roy's Tokyo, to delve into his international aspirations; and Roy's Restaurant Guam, in the Guam Hilton.

Roy's personal approach is present in his home cooking. He maintains that the only real difference for him between cooking at home and at the restaurant is that he has to clean up after himself at home. The dishes he selected for this menu are versions of his favorites while growing up in Japan. "The miso soup was always prepared in a large

pot, and was stored in the refrigerator to keep fresh. Our breakfasts more often than not began with miso soup; and when I have it even today, I can still taste 'Tokyo.'" The Teriyaki Chicken he enjoys preparing for his kids because they like its sweetness, but also because teriyaki was part of almost every meal while Roy was growing up. "I'll never let it go. Our family's teriyaki marinade was kept in a heavy, brown ceramic pot, which my father simply replenished after using the marinade for barbecuing. Since I never saw the container completely empty, I would guess that the marinade's base was never less than ten years old; and it became more flavorful as the barbecue drippings made their way in." Roy continues this tradition with his own ceramic pot of teriyaki. He serves this main course with rice, which he believes is a necessary component of just about any meal.

Roy selected this menu because the flavors and ingredients remind him of his family and his heritage, which are the influence behind so much of his cooking style. "I've always believed that cooking begins from the heart. All your technical training and experience follow—and if it keeps coming from the heart, it flows."

PORK AND EGG DROP MISO SOUP WITH GREEN ONION AND TOFU

This healthful soup is very simple to make and well worth the requisite slicing and chopping. All the ingredients can be found at Asian markets, and most have substitutes that are available at many supermarkets. But do not be too quick to use the substitutes; if there is an Asian market nearby, take the time to make the real thing.

1 tablespoon Oriental sesame oil

3 ounces boneless pork, julienne

½ teaspoon grated fresh ginger

½ teaspoon minced garlic

4½ cups water

2 ounces canned bamboo shoots, sliced

¼ cup red miso (see box, page 374)

1 large egg, beaten

4 ounces soft tofu, diced

⅛ teaspoon *hichimi* (Japanese red pepper mix; hot red pepper flakes can be substituted)

½ teaspoon *rayu* (a spicy sesame oil; ½ teaspoon Oriental sesame oil and 2 drops hot chili oil may be substituted)

1 scallion, finely chopped

4 ounces *konyaku* (a Japanese paste, see Note; optional)

In a 2-quart stockpot, heat the sesame oil over medium-high heat. Add the pork, ginger, and garlic and sauté for about 1 minute, until the pork is opaque. Add the water and bamboo shoots and cook until the liquid starts to boil. Put the miso in a small, fine sieve and lower it into the broth, using a spoon to press the miso against the sieve to help it dissolve. Reduce the heat to medium-low and simmer. Place the sieve over the simmering broth and slowly pour the egg through the sieve. Remove the sieve and add the tofu, *hichimi, rayu,* scallion, and *konyaku,* if desired. Continue to simmer until the tofu is heated through, 1 to 2 minutes. Serve immediately.

SERVES *4*

NOTE: Sometimes known as alimentary paste, *konyaku* is a paste that actually has very little flavor. It is made from a plant called devil's tongue, which is in the same family as the yam, and comes in grayish cakes with a gelatinous texture. It is very low in calories and is said to help keep the digestive tract clean. It will keep wrapped in plastic in the refrigerator for a week.

Miso

Miso is a Japanese condiment made of fermented cooked soy beans. It is available in three basic categories: barley, soybean, and rice, all of which are either red or white in color. Several factors affect the color, taste, and texture, such as aging time and salt content. Red miso tends to be saltier, and is the type Roy prefers. If a sweeter-tasting soup is preferred, substitute white miso, which has a mellower flavor. All miso pastes have a hefty amount of protein and are very nutritious. Miso should be kept refrigerated in a tightly sealed container. It is often used in sauces, dressings, and marinades, as well as soups.

TERIYAKI CHICKEN

Forget bottled teriyaki sauce! It is too easy to make a homemade version, and all the ingredients may already be in your kitchen. This marinade is versatile, working well with fish, meat, poultry, and even stir-fried vegetables. It will last indefinitely, stored tightly covered in the refrigerator. Roy serves his teriyaki with short-grain white rice and the Maui Onion Salsa (recipe follows).

Keep in mind that owing to its high sugar content, teriyaki marinade is best for quick cooking methods such as grilling or broiling. Sugar becomes bitter when cooked at length, as in baking or sautéing.

1 cup soy sauce	1 cup sugar
1 tablespoon chopped garlic	4 boneless chicken breasts, with skin
1 tablespoon minced fresh ginger	3 cups short- or medium-grain cooked
1 or 2 scallions, chopped	rice (see box, page 346)

In a medium bowl, combine the soy sauce, garlic, ginger, scallions, and sugar. Pour the marinade into a shallow dish large enough to hold the chicken breasts in a single layer and add the chicken. Set aside in the refrigerator to marinate for about 1 hour, turning the chicken halfway through the marinating time. Light the grill or preheat the broiler. Cook the chicken over medium-high heat if grilling, or under the broiler, for 3 to 4 minutes on each side, until it is opaque throughout.

SERVES 4

VARIATION: Try salmon or steak in place of the chicken. Prepare it the same way, and cook until the desired doneness is reached.

MAUI ONION SALSA WITH TOMATOES AND HAWAIIAN CHILI-PEPPER WATER

This crunchy hot and sweet salsa is so good, Roy says it can be eaten on its own, like a salad. It makes a lively side dish for the Teriyaki Chicken.

Maui onions are sweet even when raw, as are Vidalia and Walla Walla, which can be substituted. Roy likes to use Kula tomatoes, which are sweet and tasty. These are grown in the town of Kula on Maui, and you probably will not find them on the Mainland, so try to find the sweetest, ripest tomatoes available. Japanese cucumbers are small, seedless, and much crunchier than regular ones, which makes them perfect for this salsa. Look for them at gourmet food stores.

1 Maui onion (or Vidalia or Walla Walla), sliced very thin

1 large, ripe tomato, coarsely diced

1 avocado, coarsely diced

2 Japanese cucumbers, coarsely diced, or 1 English cucumber or large regular cucumber, seeded

½ cup Japanese spice sprouts (available at Asian markets; optional)

1 cup *ogo* (fresh seaweed; optional)

1 tablespoon soy sauce

4 tablespoons Hawaiian Chili-Pepper Water (recipe follows)

Combine all the ingredients in a medium bowl and refrigerate, covered, until ready to use, for up to 1 week (though it is best eaten that day).

SERVES *4*

HAWAIIAN CHILI-PEPPER WATER

½ cup water

½ teaspoon finely minced garlic

½ teaspoon finely minced fresh ginger

½ teaspoon salt

3–4 Hawaiian red chili peppers, or
Thai red chili or serrano peppers
(see box, page 176)

1½ teaspoons rice vinegar

In a small saucepan over medium-high heat, simmer the water with the garlic, ginger, and salt for about 10 minutes. In a food processor or blender, finely chop the peppers and add them to the flavored water, a little at a time to adjust the hotness to taste. Add the vinegar and set aside until ready to use.

MAKES ABOUT ½ CUP

COFFEE GELATIN

This dessert is a grown-up version of a childhood favorite. Roy ends many of his menus with it, serving it plain; however, it can also be topped with whipped cream.

4½ packages unflavored gelatin

10 tablespoons water

2¼ cups freshly brewed coffee

1 14-ounce can sweetened condensed
milk

In a large bowl, combine the gelatin and the water; let sit for 2 to 3 minutes to soften. Bring the coffee to a simmer over medium heat and pour over the gelatin and water mixture. Stir until the gelatin is dissolved. Stir in the condensed milk until well blended, then pour into an 8-inch square pan and chill, covered with plastic wrap, in the refrigerator until firm, about 2 hours. Slice in diamond shapes and serve.

SERVES 4 TO 6

Regional Listing of Chefs

SOUTHWEST

Noel Cunningham	Denver, Colo.	*Ciao, Baby, 240 Union, Strings*
Vincent Guerithault	Phoenix, Ariz.	*Vincent Guerithault on Camelback*
Mark Miller	Santa Fe, N.Mex.	*Coyote Cafe*
	Las Vegas, Nev.	*Coyote Cafe*
	Washington, D.C.	*Red Sage*
Stephan Pyles	Dallas, Tex.	*Star Canyon*

CALIFORNIA

John Ash	Hopland	*Fetzer Valley Oaks Food & Wine Center*
David and Anne Gingrass	San Francisco	*Postrio*
Joyce Goldstein	San Francisco	*Square One*
Madeleine Kamman	St. Helena	*Beringer Vineyards*
Mary Sue Milliken	Santa Monica	*Border Grill*
Bradley Ogden	San Francisco	*Lark Creek Inn, One Market*
Michel Richard	San Francisco	*Bistro M*
	Los Angeles	*Citrus*
	Santa Barbara	*Citronelle*
	Washington, D.C.	*Citronelle*
	Baltimore, Md.	*Citronelle*
	Santa Monica	*Broadway Deli*
	Philadelphia, Pa.	*Michel's*
Nancy Silverton & Mark Peel	Los Angeles	*Campanile, La Brea Bakery*
Tommy Tang	Pasadena	*Tommy Tang's*
	Los Angeles	*Tommy Tang's Modern Thai Cuisine and Sushi*
Barbara Tropp	San Francisco	*China Moon Cafe*
Alice Waters	Berkeley	*Chez Panisse*

NORTHWEST AND PACIFIC

Monique Barbeau	Seattle, Wash.	*Fullers at the Seattle Sheraton Hotel & Towers*
Tom Douglas	Seattle, Wash.	*Dahlia Lounge*
Roy Yamaguchi	Honolulu, Hawaii	*Roy's Restaurant,*
	Maui, Hawaii	*Roy's Kahana Bar & Gril, Roy's Nicolina*
	Kauai, Hawaii	*Roy's Poipu Bar & Grill*
	Tokyo	*Roy's Tokyo*
	Guam	*Roy's Restaurant Guam in the Guam Hilton*

Information About Share Our Strength

SOS MISSION

Share Our Strength works to alleviate and prevent hunger throughout the United States and the world. With the help of thousands of volunteers, SOS fights hunger through grant distribution, public education, community outreach, and direct service. Founded in 1984, SOS has become one of the nation's largest and most effective hunger-relief organizations.

SOS HISTORY

Share Our Strength was founded to mobilize the food service industry on behalf of hunger relief. The SOS network now includes chefs, restaurateurs, authors, photographers, artists, business leaders, corporate partners, concerned individuals, and a wide variety of others who share their skills to help end hunger

SOS PROGRAMS

Grants

SOS awards grants to hundreds of nonprofit hunger-relief programs, ranging from direct food assistance such as food banks or prepared and perishable food rescue programs, to long-term prevention programs such as nutrition education and advocacy. Since its founding, SOS has distributed more than $20 million in grants to innovative antihunger programs worldwide. Funds for SOS grants are raised year-round through special events and creative projects.

Public Education

Through events, special programs, and memberships, SOS works to educate the public, mobilize individuals and groups in their communities, and generate support for the fight against hunger. FRONTIER, SOS's quarterly magazine, educates and informs readers and is a useful tool for other antihunger organizations.

Direct Service

Operation Frontline, SOS's first direct service programs, works to prevent hunger by training chefs to share their knowledge of cooking, nutrition, and food budgeting with people who are at risk of hunger, including those who rely on public or private food assistance. Volunteer chefs are trained to teach six-session cooking courses at nonprofit, communit-based centers that serve low-income people in their communities. Operation Frontline is organized nationally by SOS and takes place in major U.S. cities.

SOS PROJECTS

Taste of the Nation

As the largest nationwide benefit for hunger relief, Taste of the Nation involves six thousand chefs in more than one hundred cities who host food and wine tasting benefits throughout the month of April. Taste of the Nation is sponsored nationally by American Express, coordinated by SOS, and organized locally by volunteers in the food service industry. Sponsors, donors, and volunteers enable SOS to distribute 100 percent of all event ticket proceeds to hunger-relief organizations. Taste of the Nation is the American food service industry's premier culinary benefit for hunger relief.

Writers Harvest

In hundreds of cities across the United States and Canada on one day each fall, authors give readings from their work to help raise funds for SOS grants. Local writers and volunteers in the book-selling field organize Writers Harvest events in bookstores, coffee houses, and on college campuses. Sponsors and volunteers ensure that 100 percent of ticket proceeds benefit hunger relief. Writers Harvest has helped mobilize writers, booksellers, college students, and literary enthusiasts on behalf of hunger relief.

Corporate Partnerships

SOS works with corporations to create ongoing partnerships that help generate funds and support for hunger relief. The **Charge Against Hunger** is a corporate partnership between SOS and American Express to raise $5 million in 1993 and 1994. This campaign aims to make a long-term impact on hunger and raise public awareness of the issue.

Book Projects

Including *Home Food,* Share Our Strength's first cookbook, SOS has coordinated the production of eight anthologies of work by renowned authors, chefs, and artists to raise funds for SOS programs. Authors contribute original unpublished manuscripts, and SOS works with major publishing houses to publish and distribute the anthologies to bookstores. SOS books include fiction anthologies, children's books, and collections of science and nature essays.

SOS Products

Each year, SOS offers a lively array of gifts produced with the creative contributions of chefs, artists, authors, and designers. All gifts are available through the SOS catalog. In selected produce markets across the country, SOS booths distribute hunger information, sell SOS gifts, and collect unsold produce at the end of the day for distribution to local food assistance programs

Ingredient Mail-Order Source List

ASIAN SPECIALTY FOODS

CHINESE AMERICAN TRADING CO.
91 Mulberry Street
New York, NY 10013
212/267-5224
•*Dried, canned, and bottled Asian foods such as wasabi powder, sesame oil, rice vinegar, and miso*

KATAGIRI & CO.
224 East 59th Street
New York, NY 10022
212/755-3566
•*Fresh and dried Japanese products such as miso, hichimi, rayu, konyaku, sushi-quality fish (available only at the store), Japanese spice sprouts, ogo, and fish sauce*

ORIENTAL FOOD MARKET
2801 West Howard Street
Chicago, IL 60645
312/274-2826
•*Various Asian products such as pockey sticks, bamboo shoots, lemon grass, sweet bean sauce, fish sauce, rice vinegar, sesame oil, tamarind, and cooking utensils*

EXOTIC PRODUCE AND GOURMET ITEMS

BALDUCCI'S
11-02 Queens Plaza South
Long Island City, NY
11101-4908
718/786-9690
800/822-1444
In New York: 800/247-2450
•*Gourmet foods, specializing in Italian food; they also carry items such as lemon oil, blue cornmeal, walnut oil, and lentils*

DEAN & DELUCA
560 Broadway
New York, NY 10012
212/431-1691
800/221-7714
•*Gourmet and ethnic foods of all kinds, including cajeta, chimayo chili powder, blue cornmeal, lemon oil, all types of nut oils, sweet unsalted Gorgonzola, and excellent quality chocolate*

FREIDA'S FINEST
4465 Corporate Center Drive
Los Alamitos, CA 90720-2561
714/826-6100
800/421-9477
•*Both unusual and usual fruits and vegetables such as mangos, plantains, bing cherries, tart dried cherries, fresh wild mushrooms, seasonal Maui onions, dandelion greens, hot peppers, fresh and dried chili peppers, jicama, fresh herbs (potted and cut), canned bamboo shoots, Blood oranges, and hothouse cucumbers, as well as basmati rice, several different types of polenta and other grains*

MISSION ORCHARDS
P.O Box 6497
2296 Senter Road
San Jose, CA 95150
800/333-1448
•*Many different fruits and vegetables, including Black Mission figs, Blood oranges, California artichokes, and avocados*

PHIPPS RANCH
P.O. Box 349
Pescadero, CA 94060
415/879-0787
•*Rare varieties of beans, several different kinds of lentils, including French lentils, and grains of all sorts such as polenta and basmati rice*

WEST POINT MARKET
1711 West Market Street
Akron, OH 44313
216/864-2151
•*A gourmet specialty food store carrying such items as crème fraîche, mascarpone, basmati rice, sambal oelek, and ketjap manis*

LATIN AMERICAN FOODS

EL PASO CHILI
909 Texas Avenue
El Paso, TX 79901
915/544-3434
Fax: 915/544-7552
•*Cajeta, "every" kind of chili pepper known to man, spices, salsas, and marinades*

JOSIE'S BEST
P.O. Box 87501
1130 Agua Fria Street
Santa Fe, NM 87501
505/473-3437
•*Frozen, fresh peppers, blue cornmeal, New Mexican cuisine*

SPECIAL MEATS AND FISH

CAVIARTERIA
29 East 69th Street
New York, NY 10022
212/759-7410
800/4-CAVIAR
•*Fresh caviar shipped nationwide; they also carry pâtés, foie gras, truffles, and smoked fish*

MARGIE'S NATURALLY RAISED VEAL
RFD 1, Box 436
Northwood, NH 03261
603/942-5427
•*Calf's foot and other veal parts, including veal breast*

NODINE'S SMOKEHOUSE
P.O. Box 1787
Torrington, CT 06790
800/222-2059
•*Smoked bacon and ham*

OLDE HOUSE SMOKE HOUSE
335 Brier House Road
Canterbury, NH 03820
603/783-4405
•*Oak-smoked meats and fish, hickory smoked cheeses; custom smoking available*

PINEBROOK RABBIT PROCESSING
Box 2655
Sam Allen Road
Sanford, ME 04073
207/324-3390
•*Rabbit shipped fresh throughout New England; frozen everywhere else*

FRESH SEAFOOD

LARKIN'S SEA FOOD
325 Dukeland St.
Baltimore, MD 21223
301/233-8000
(800/666-FISH
•*Fresh fish caught daily; call to order between 6 a.m. and 3 p.m.*

PURE FOOD FISH MARKET
1511 Pike Place Market
Seattle, WA 98101
206/622-5765
800/392-3474
•*Salmon (smoked and fresh), Dungeness crab, and sushi-grade tuna*

WISCONSIN FISHING CO.
P.O. Box 965
1112 McDonald Street
Green Bay, WI 54305
414/437-3582
800/236-1457
•*Salt and freshwater fish and seafood; sushi-grade tuna available on special order*

EXCELLENT QUALITY CHOCOLATE

PARADIGM CHOCOLATE
5775 S.W. Jean Road.,
Suite 106A
Lake Oswego, OR 97035
503/636-4880
800/234-0250
•*Baking chocolate, gourmet milk and dark chocolate, and white chocolate; they carry brands such as Lindt, Guittard, Blommer, and Ghirardelli*

Other Share Our Strength Books

Rosen, Michael J. *The Greatest Table.* New York: Harcourt Brace & Company, 1994. ($18.95)

———. *Home.* New York: HarperCollins, 1992. ($11.00)

Shore, William H., ed. *Mysteries of the Life and the Universe: New Essays from America's Finest Writers on Science.* New York: Harcourt Brace Jovanovich, 1992. ($24.95)

———. *The Nature of Nature: New Essays from America's Finest Writers on Nature.* Introduction by Vice President Al Gore. San Diego, Calif.: Harcourt Brace Jovanovich, 1994. ($24.95)

———. *Voices Louder Than Words: A Second Collection.* New York: Vintage, 1991. ($11.00)

———. *Writer's Harvest.* New York: Harcourt Brace & Company, 1994. ($11.95)

Index

Conversion Chart
Equivalent Imperial and Metric Measurements

American cooks use standard containers, the 8-ounce cup and a tablespoon that takes exactly 16 level fillings to fill that cup level. Measuring by cup makes it very difficult to give weight equivalents, as a cup of densely packed butter will weigh considerably more than a cup of flour. The easiest way therefore to deal with cup measurements in recipes is to take the amount by volume rather than by weight. Thus the equation reads:

1 cup = 240 ml = 8 fl. oz.   ½ cup = 120 ml = 4 fl. oz.

It is possible to buy a set of American cup measures in major stores around the world.

In the States, butter is often measured in sticks. One stick is the equivalent of 8 tablespoons. One tablespoon of butter is therefore the equivalent to ½ ounce/15 grams.

SOLID MEASURES

U.S. and Imperial Measures		Metric Measures	
ounces	pounds	grams	kilos
1		28	
2		56	
3½		100	
4	¼	112	
5		140	
6		168	
8	½	225	
9		250	¼
12	¾	340	
16	1	450	
18		500	½
20	1¼	560	
24	1½	675	
27		750	¾
28	1¾	780	
32	2	900	
36	2¼	1000	1
40	2½	1100	
48	3	1350	
54		1500	1½
64	4	1800	
72	4½	2000	2
80	5	2250	2¼
90		2500	2½
100	6	2800	2¾

LIQUID MEASURES

Fluid ounces	U.S.	Imperial	Milliliters
	1 teaspoon	1 teaspoon	5
¼	2 teaspoons	1 dessertspoon	10
½	1 tablespoon	1 tablespoon	14
1	2 tablespoons	2 tablespoons	28
2	¼ cup	4 tablespoons	56
4	½ cup		110
5		¼ pint or 1 gill	140
6	¾ cup		170
8	1 cup		225
9			250, ¼ liter
10	1¼ cups	½ pint	280
12	1½ cups		340
15		¾ pint	420
16	2 cups		450
18	2¼ cups		500, ½ liter
20	2½ cups	1 pint	560
24	3 cups		675
25		1¼ pints	700
27	3½ cups		750
30	3¾ cups	1½ pints	840
32	4 cups or 1 quart		900
35		1¾ pints	980
36	4½ cups		1000, 1 liter
40	5 cups	2 pints or 1 quart	1120
48	6 cups		1350
50		2½ pints	1400
60	7½ cups	3 pints	1680
64	8 cups or 2 quarts		1800
72	9 cups		2000, 2 liters

OVEN TEMPERATURE EQUIVALENTS

Fahrenheit	Celsius	Gas Mark	Description
225	110	¼	Cool
250	130	½	
275	140	1	Very Slow
300	150	2	
325	170	3	Slow
350	180	4	Moderate
375	190	5	
400	200	6	Moderately Hot
425	220	7	Fairly Hot
450	230	8	Hot
475	240	9	Very Hot
500	250	10	Extremely Hot

EQUIVALENTS FOR INGREDIENTS

all-purpose flour—plain flour
arugula—rocket
baking sheet—oven tray
buttermilk—ordinary milk
cheesecloth—muslin
coarse salt—kitchen salt
confectioners' sugar—icing sugar
cornstarch—cornflour

eggplant—aubergine
granulated sugar—caster sugar
half and half—12% fat milk
heavy cream—double cream
light cream—single cream
lima beans—broad beans
parchment paper—greaseproof paper
plastic wrap—cling film

scallion—spring onion
sour cherry—morello cherry
unbleached flour—strong, white flour
vanilla bean—vanilla pod
zest—rind
zucchini—courgettes or marrow